Mental Health Disorders

SOURCEBOOK

SEVENTH EDITION

Mental Health Disorders
SOURCEBOOK

SEVENTH EDITION

Basic Consumer Health Information about Healthy Brain Functioning and Mental Illnesses, Including Depression, Bipolar Disorder, Anxiety Disorders, Posttraumatic Stress Disorder, Obsessive-Compulsive Disorder, Psychotic and Personality Disorders, Eating Disorders, Impulse Control Disorders, and More

Along with Information about Medications and Treatments, Mental-Health Concerns in Specific Groups, Such as Children, Adolescents, Older Adults, Minority Populations, and People in Poverty, a Glossary of Related Terms, and Directories of Resources for Additional Help and Information

OMNIGRAPHICS

615 Griswold, Ste. 901, Detroit, MI 48226

Bibliographic Note

Because this page cannot legibly accommodate all the copyright notices, the Bibliographic Note portion of the Preface constitutes an extension of the copyright notice.

* * *

OMNIGRAPHICS

Angela L. Williams, *Managing Editor*

* * *

Library of Congress Cataloging-in-Publication Data

Names: Omnigraphics, Inc., issuing body.

Title: Mental health disorders sourcebook : basic consumer health information about healthy brain functioning and mental illnesses, including depression, bipolar disorder, anxiety disorders, posttraumatic stress disorder, obsessive-compulsive disorder, psychotic and personality disorders, eating disorders, compulsive hoarding disorder, and more; along with information about medications and treatments, mental health concerns in specific groups, such as children, adolescents, older adults, minority populations, and lgbt community, a glossary of related terms, and directories of resources for additional help and information.

Description: Seventh edition. | Detroit, MI : Omnigraphics, Inc., [2019] | "Angela L. Williams, editorial manager."

Identifiers: LCCN 2018053295| ISBN 9780780816794 (hard cover : alk. paper) | ISBN 9780780816800 (ebook)

Subjects: LCSH: Mental illness. | Psychiatry.

Classification: LCC RC454.4 .M458 2019 | DDC 616.89--dc23

LC record available at https://lccn.loc.gov/2018053295

Table of Contents

Part V: Other Populations with Distinctive Mental-Health Concerns

Part VII: Living with a Mental-Health Condition

Preface

About This Book

Mental health encompasses thoughts, actions, and feelings. Mentally healthy individuals are able to cope with life's challenges, handle stressful situations, deal with anger, maintain meaningful relationships with others, and enjoy life. Despite the benefits, maintaining a healthy mind is not always possible, and mental disorders are common. Mental illnesses are common in the United States. Nearly one in five U.S. adults suffer from mental illness, which is estimated to be 44.7 million in 2016. Mental illnesses include many different conditions that vary in degree of severity, ranging from mild to moderate to severe and estimates suggest that only half of people with mental illnesses receive treatment.

Mental Health Disorders Sourcebook, Seventh Edition discusses how the brain works, the components of mental wellness, and the processes that lead to illness. It offers information about the major types of mental illness and their treatments, including affective disorders, anxiety disorders, psychotic disorders, personality disorders, and disorders that impact behavior, including impulse control disorders, addictions, and eating disorders. A special section looks at pediatric issues in mental health and another examines the distinctive concerns of other specific populations. Information is also included about the relationship between mental health and chronic illnesses, such as cancer, epilepsy, heart disease, pain, and sleep disorders. The book concludes with a glossary of mental-health terms, a list of crisis hotlines, and a directory of mental-health organizations.

How to Use This Book

This book is divided into parts and chapters. Parts focus on broad areas of interest. Chapters are devoted to single topics within a part.

Part One: The Brain and Mental Health explains the components of healthy brain functioning and the processes that can go awry leading to mental illness. It also discusses lifestyle and other factors that can help reinforce mental wellness.

Part Two: Mental Illnesses begins with information about the link between suicide and mental illness and facts about suicide prevention. It goes on to describe the various classifications of mental-health disorders, including depressive and other affective disorders, anxiety disorders, psychotic disorders, personality disorders, and other disorders that impact behavior.

Part Three: Mental-Health Treatments addresses the different ways mental-health disorders are diagnosed and treated. It offers guidelines for identifying mental-health emergencies, explains the services available from different types of mental-health professionals, and discusses medications used to help control symptoms of mental illness. The part concludes with a chapter about complementary and alternative medicine for mental healthcare, which includes facts about dietary, physical, and spiritual therapies.

Part Four: Pediatric Mental-Health Concerns describes the special issues that arise when children and teens have psychiatric needs. It offers specific details about some of the most commonly occurring mental-health issues among young people, including attention deficit hyperactivity disorder, autism spectrum disorder, bipolar disorder, depression, and learning disabilities.

Part Five: Other Populations with Distinctive Mental-Health Concerns addresses concerns among men, women, older adults, and other groups for whom special considerations may impact mental wellness. These include people dealing with the psychological impact of prejudice and discrimination, trauma or disaster, cultural isolation, and poverty.

Part Six: Mental Illness Co-Occurring with Other Disorders explains the ways physical conditions can sometimes affect psychological well-being. It discusses some specific disorders commonly associated with changes in mental-health status, including cancer, diabetes, epilepsy, heart disease, and stroke. It also addresses issues related to sleep disorders and mental functioning, and it examines the complex relationship between mental health and the experience of pain.

Part Seven: Additional Help and Information provides a glossary of mental-health terms, a list of toll-free helplines and hotlines for people in crisis, and a directory of mental-health organizations.

Bibliographic Note

This volume contains documents and excerpts from publications issued by the following U.S. government agencies: Centers for Disease Control and Prevention (CDC); Early Childhood Learning and Knowledge Center (ECLKC); *Go4Life*; National Cancer Institute (NCI); National Center for Biotechnology Information (NCBI); National Center for Complementary and Integrative Health (NCCIH); National Heart, Lung, and Blood Institute (NHLBI); National Institute of Diabetes and Digestive and Kidney Diseases (NIDDK); National Institute of Mental Health (NIMH); National Institute on Minority Health and Health Disparities (NIMHD); National Institute of Neurological Disorders and Stroke (NINDS); National Institute on Aging (NIA); National Institute on Drug Abuse (NIDA); National Institutes of Health (NIH); *NIH News in Health*; Office of Disease Prevention and Health Promotion (ODPHP); Office of Minority Health (OMH); Office of the Assistant Secretary for Preparedness and Response (ASPR); Office of the Surgeon General (OSG); Office on Women's Health (OWH); Substance Abuse and Mental Health Services Administration (SAMHSA); U.S. Department of Health and Human Services (HHS); and U.S. Department of Veterans Affairs (VA).

It may also contain original material produced by Omnigraphics and reviewed by medical documents.

About the Health Reference Series

The *Health Reference Series* is designed to provide basic medical information for patients, families, caregivers, and the general public. Each volume takes a particular topic and provides comprehensive coverage. This is especially important for people who may be dealing with a newly diagnosed disease or a chronic disorder in themselves or in a family member. People looking for preventive guidance, information about disease warning signs, medical statistics, and risk factors for health problems will also find answers to their questions in the *Health Reference Series*. The *Series*, however, is not intended to serve as a tool for diagnosing illness, in prescribing treatments, or as a substitute for the physician/patient relationship. All people concerned about medical symptoms or the possibility of disease are encouraged to seek professional care from an appropriate healthcare provider.

A Note about Spelling and Style

Health Reference Series editors use *Stedman's Medical Dictionary* as an authority for questions related to the spelling of medical terms and the *Chicago Manual of Style* for questions related to grammatical structures, punctuation, and other editorial concerns. Consistent adherence is not always possible, however, because the individual volumes within the *Series* include many documents from a wide variety of different producers, and the editor's primary goal is to present material from each source as accurately as is possible. This sometimes means that information in different chapters or sections may follow other guidelines and alternate spelling authorities. For example, occasionally a copyright holder may require that eponymous terms be shown in possessive forms (Crohn's disease vs. Crohn disease) or that British spelling norms be retained (leukaemia vs. leukemia).

Medical Review

Omnigraphics contracts with a team of qualified, senior medical professionals who serve as medical consultants for the *Health Reference Series*. As necessary, medical consultants review reprinted and originally written material for currency and accuracy. Citations including the phrase "Reviewed (month, year)" indicate material reviewed by this team. Medical consultation services are provided to the *Health Reference Series* editors by:

Dr. Vijayalakshmi, MBBS, DGO, MD
Dr. Senthil Selvan, MBBS, DCH, MD
Dr. K. Sivanandham, MBBS, DCH, MS (Research), PhD

Our Advisory Board

We would like to thank the following board members for providing initial guidance on the development of this series:

- Dr. Lynda Baker, Associate Professor of Library and Information Science, Wayne State University, Detroit, MI

- Nancy Bulgarelli, William Beaumont Hospital Library, Royal Oak, MI

- Karen Imarisio, Bloomfield Township Public Library, Bloomfield Township, MI

- Karen Morgan, Mardigian Library, University of Michigan-Dearborn, Dearborn, MI

- Rosemary Orlando, St. Clair Shores Public Library, St. Clair Shores, MI

Health Reference Series *Update Policy*

The inaugural book in the *Health Reference Series* was the first edition of *Cancer Sourcebook* published in 1989. Since then, the *Series* has been enthusiastically received by librarians and in the medical community. In order to maintain the standard of providing high-quality health information for the layperson the editorial staff at Omnigraphics felt it was necessary to implement a policy of updating volumes when warranted.

Medical researchers have been making tremendous strides, and it is the purpose of the *Health Reference Series* to stay current with the most recent advances. Each decision to update a volume is made on an individual basis. Some of the considerations include how much new information is available and the feedback we receive from people who use the books. If there is a topic you would like to see added to the update list, or an area of medical concern you feel has not been adequately addressed, please write to:

Managing Editor
Health Reference Series
Omnigraphics
615 Griswold, Ste. 901
Detroit, MI 48226

Part One

The Brain and Mental Health

Chapter 1

Mental Health Begins with Healthy Brain Functions

Chapter Contents

Section 1.1

Brain Basics

This section includes text excerpted from "Brain Basics:
Know Your Brain," National Institute of Neurological
Disorders and Stroke (NINDS), October 28, 2018.

The brain is the most complex part of the human body. This three-pound organ is the seat of intelligence, interpreter of the senses, initiator of body movement, and controller of behavior. Lying in its bony shell and washed by protective fluid, the brain is the source of all the qualities that define our humanity. The brain is the crown jewel of the human body.

For centuries, scientists and philosophers have been fascinated by the brain, but until recently they viewed the brain as nearly incomprehensible. Now, however, the brain is beginning to relinquish its secrets. Scientists have learned more about the brain in the last ten years than in all previous centuries because of the accelerating pace of research in neurological and behavioral science and the development of new research techniques. As a result, Congress named the 1990s the "Decade of the Brain."

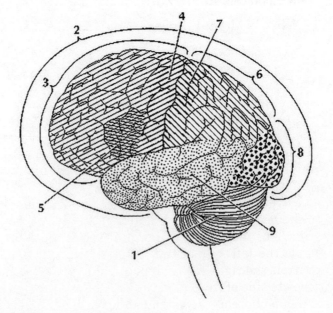

Figure 1.1. *Structure of the Brain*

4

This section is a basic introduction to the human brain. It may help you understand how the healthy brain works, how to keep it healthy, and what happens when the brain is diseased or dysfunctional.

The Architecture of the Brain

The brain is like a committee of experts. All the parts of the brain work together, but each part has its own special properties. The brain can be divided into three basic units: the forebrain, the midbrain, and the hindbrain.

The hindbrain includes the upper part of the spinal cord, the brain stem, and a wrinkled ball of tissue called the **cerebellum (1).** The hindbrain controls the body's vital functions such as respiration and heart rate. The cerebellum coordinates movement and is involved in learned rote movements. When you play the piano or hit a tennis ball you are activating the cerebellum. The uppermost part of the brainstem is the midbrain, which controls some reflex actions and is part of the circuit involved in the control of eye movements and other voluntary movements. The forebrain is the largest and most highly developed part of the human brain: it consists primarily of the **cerebrum (2)** and the structures hidden beneath it.

When people see pictures of the brain it is usually the cerebrum that they notice. The cerebrum sits at the topmost part of the brain and is the source of intellectual activities. It holds your memories, allows you to plan, enables you to imagine and think. It allows you to recognize friends, read books, and play games.

The cerebrum is split into two halves (hemispheres) by a deep fissure. Despite the split, the two cerebral hemispheres communicate with each other through a thick tract of nerve fibers that lies at the base of this fissure. Although the two hemispheres seem to be mirror images of each other, they are different. For instance, the ability to form words seems to lie primarily in the left hemisphere, while the right hemisphere seems to control many abstract reasoning skills.

For some as-yet-unknown reason, nearly all of the signals from the brain to the body and vice-versa crossover on their way to and from the brain. This means that the right cerebral hemisphere primarily controls the left side of the body and the left hemisphere primarily controls the right side. When one side of the brain is damaged, the opposite side of the body is affected. For example, a stroke in the right hemisphere of the brain can leave the left arm and leg paralyzed.

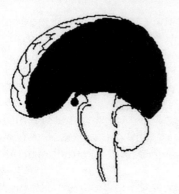

Figure 1.2. *Forebrain*

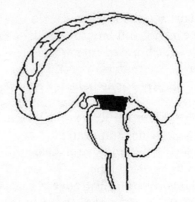

Figure 1.3. *Midbrain*

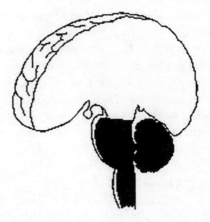

Figure 1.4. *Hindbrain*

The Geography of Thought

Each cerebral hemisphere can be divided into sections, or lobes, each of which specializes in different functions. To understand each lobe and its specialty we will take a tour of the cerebral hemispheres, starting with the two **frontal lobes (3),** which lie directly behind the forehead. When you plan a schedule, imagine the future, or use reasoned arguments, these two lobes do much of the work. One of the ways the frontal lobes seem to do these things is by acting as short-term storage sites, allowing one idea to be kept in mind while other ideas are considered. In the rearmost portion of each frontal lobe is a

motor area (4), which helps control voluntary movement. A nearby place on the left frontal lobe called **Broca's area (5)** allows thoughts to be transformed into words.

When you enjoy a good meal—the taste, aroma, and texture of the food—two sections behind the frontal lobes called the **parietal lobes (6)** are at work. The forward parts of these lobes, just behind the motor areas, are the primary **sensory areas (7)**. These areas receive information about temperature, taste, touch, and movement from the rest of the body. Reading and arithmetic are also functions in the repertoire of each parietal lobe.

As you look at the content and images on this sections, two areas at the back of the brain are at work. These lobes, called the **occipital lobes (8)**, process images from the eyes and link that information with images stored in memory. Damage to the occipital lobes can cause blindness.

The last lobes on our tour of the cerebral hemispheres are the **temporal lobes (9)**, which lie in front of the visual areas and nest under the parietal and frontal lobes. Whether you appreciate symphonies or rock music, your brain responds through the activity of these lobes. At the top of each temporal lobe is an area responsible for receiving information from the ears. The underside of each temporal lobe plays a crucial role in forming and retrieving memories, including those associated with music. Other parts of this lobe seem to integrate memories and sensations of taste, sound, sight, and touch.

The Cerebral Cortex

Coating the surface of the cerebrum and the cerebellum is a vital layer of tissue the thickness of a stack of two or three dimes. It is called the cortex, from the Latin word for bark. Most of the actual information processing in the brain takes place in the cerebral cortex. When people talk about "gray matter" in the brain they are talking about this thin rind. The cortex is gray because nerves in this area lack the insulation that makes most other parts of the brain appear to be white. The folds in the brain add to its surface area, and therefore, increase the amount of gray matter and the quantity of information that can be processed.

The Inner Brain

Deep within the brain, hidden from view, lies structures that are the gatekeepers between the spinal cord and the cerebral hemispheres.

These structures not only determine our emotional state they also modify our perceptions and responses depending on that state and allow us to initiate movements that you make without thinking about them. Like the lobes in the cerebral hemispheres, the structures described below come in pairs: each is duplicated in the opposite half of the brain.

The **hypothalamus (10)**, about the size of a pearl, directs a multitude of important functions. It wakes you up in the morning and gets the adrenaline flowing during a test or job interview. The hypothalamus is also an important emotional center, controlling the molecules that make you feel exhilarated, angry, or unhappy. Near the hypothalamus lies the **thalamus (11)**, a major clearinghouse for information going to and from the spinal cord and the cerebrum.

An arching tract of nerve cells leads from the hypothalamus and the thalamus to the **hippocampus (12)**. This tiny nub acts as a memory indexer—sending memories out to the appropriate part of the cerebral hemisphere for long-term storage and retrieving them when necessary. The basal ganglia (not shown) are clusters of nerve cells surrounding the thalamus. They are responsible for initiating and integrating movements. Parkinson disease (PD), which results in tremors, rigidity, and a stiff, shuffling walk, is a disease of nerve cells that lead into the basal ganglia.

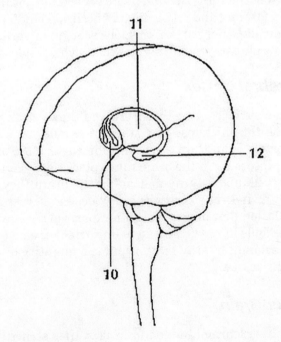

Figure 1.5. *The Inner Brain*

Making Connections

The brain and the rest of the nervous system are composed of many different types of cells, but the primary functional unit is a cell called the neuron. All sensations, movements, thoughts, memories, and feelings are the result of signals that pass through neurons. Neurons consist of three parts. The **cell body (13)** contains the nucleus, where most of the molecules that the neuron needs to survive and function are manufactured. **Dendrites (14)** extend out from the cell body like the branches of a tree and receive messages from other nerve cells. Signals then pass from the dendrites through the cell body and may travel away from the cell body down an **axon (15)** to another neuron, a muscle cell, or cells in some other organ. The neuron is usually surrounded by many support cells. Some types of cells wrap around the axon to form an insulating **sheath (16)**. This sheath can include a fatty molecule called myelin, which provides insulation for the axon and helps nerve signals travel faster and farther. Axons may be very short, such as those that carry signals from one cell in the cortex to another cell less than a hair's width away. Or axons may be very long, such as those that carry messages from the brain all the way down the spinal cord.

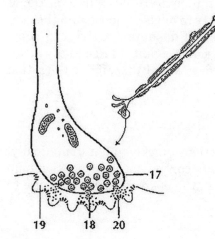

Figure 1.6. *Cell Body*

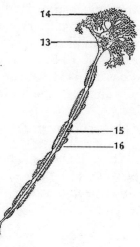

Figure 1.7. *Axons*

Scientists have learned a great deal about neurons by studying the synapse—the place where a signal passes from the neuron to another cell. When the signal reaches the end of the axon it stimulates the release of tiny **sacs (17)**. These sacs release chemicals are known as **neurotransmitters (18)** into the **synapse (19)**. The neurotransmitters cross the synapse and attach to **receptors (20)** on the neighboring cell. These receptors can change the properties of the receiving cell. If the receiving cell is also a neuron, the signal can continue the transmission to the next cell.

Some Key Neurotransmitters at Work

Acetylcholine is called an excitatory neurotransmitter because it generally makes cells more excitable. It governs muscle contractions and causes glands to secrete hormones. Alzheimer disease (AD), which initially affects memory formation, is associated with a shortage of acetylcholine.

GABA (gamma-aminobutyric acid) is called an inhibitory neurotransmitter because it tends to make cells less excitable. It helps control muscle activity and is an important part of the visual system. Drugs that increase GABA levels in the brain are used to treat epileptic seizures and tremors in patients with Huntington disease (HD).

Serotonin is a neurotransmitter that constricts blood vessels and brings on sleep. It is also involved in temperature regulation. Dopamine is an inhibitory neurotransmitter involved in mood and the control of complex movements. The loss of dopamine activity in some portions of the brain leads to the muscular rigidity of PD. Many medications used to treat behavioral disorders work by modifying the action of dopamine in the brain.

Neurological Disorders

When the brain is healthy it functions quickly and automatically. But when problems occur, the results can be devastating. Some 50 million people in this country—one in five—suffer from damage to the nervous system.

Section 1.2

What Is Mental Health?

This section includes text excerpted from "What Is Mental Health?" MentalHealth.gov, U.S. Department of Health and Human Services (HHS), August 29, 2017.

Mental health includes our emotional, psychological, and social well-being. It affects how we think, feel, and act. It also helps determine how we handle stress, relate to others, and make choices. Mental health is important at every stage of life, from childhood and adolescence through adulthood.

Over the course of your life, if you experience mental-health problems, your thinking, mood, and behavior could be affected. Many factors contribute to mental-health problems, including:

- Biological factors, such as genes or brain chemistry

- Life experiences, such as trauma or abuse

- The family history of mental-health problems

Mental-health problems are common but help is available. People with mental-health problems can get better and many recover completely.

Early Warning Signs

Not sure if you or someone you know is living with mental-health problems? Experiencing one or more of the following feelings or behaviors can be an early warning sign of a problem:

- Eating or sleeping too much or too little

- Pulling away from people and usual activities

- Having low or no energy

- Feeling numb or like nothing matters

- Having unexplained aches and pains

- Feeling helpless or hopeless

- Smoking, drinking, or using drugs more than usual

- Feeling unusually confused, forgetful, on edge, angry, upset, worried, or scared

- Yelling or fighting with family and friends
- Experiencing severe mood swings that cause problems in relationships
- Having persistent thoughts and memories you can't get out of your head
- Hearing voices or believing things that are not true
- Thinking of harming yourself or others
- Inability to perform daily tasks like taking care of your kids or getting to work or school

Mental Health and Wellness

Positive mental health allows people to:

- Realize their full potential
- Cope with the stresses of life
- Work productively
- Make meaningful contributions to their communities

Ways to maintain positive mental health include:

- Getting professional help if you need it
- Connecting with others
- Staying positive
- Getting physically active
- Helping others
- Getting enough sleep
- Developing coping skills

Section 1.3

What Is Mental Illness?

This section includes text excerpted from "Mental Illness," National Institute of Mental Health (NIMH), November 2017.

Mental illnesses are common in the United States. Nearly one in five U.S. adults lives with a mental illness (44.7 million in 2016). Mental illnesses include many different conditions that vary in degree of severity, ranging from mild to moderate to severe. Two broad categories can be used to describe these conditions: any mental illness (AMI) and serious mental illness (SMI). AMI encompasses all recognized mental illnesses. SMI is a smaller and more severe subset of AMI.

The data presented in this section are from the 2016 National Survey on Drug Use and Health (NSDUH) by the Substance Abuse and Mental Health Services Administration (SAMHSA). For inclusion in NSDUH prevalence estimates, mental illnesses include those that are diagnosable currently or within the past year; of sufficient duration to meet diagnostic criteria specified within the 4th edition of the *Diagnostic and Statistical Manual of Mental Disorders* (DSM-IV); and, exclude developmental and substance-use disorders (SUD).

Categories of Mental Illness
Any Mental Illness

AMI is defined as a mental, behavioral, or emotional disorder. AMI can vary in impact, ranging from no impairment to mild, moderate, and even severe impairment (e.g., individuals with as defined below).

Serious Mental Illness

SMI is defined as a mental, behavioral, or emotional disorder resulting in serious functional impairment, which substantially interferes with or limits one or more major life activities. The burden of mental illnesses is particularly concentrated among those who experience disability due to SMI.

Prevalence of Any Mental Illness

Figure 1.8 shows the of AMI among U.S. adults in 2016.

- In 2016, there were an estimated 44.7 million adults aged 18 or older in the United States with AMI. This number represented (18.3%) of all U.S. adults.

- The prevalence of AMI was higher among women (21.7%) than men (14.5%).

- Young adults aged 18 to 25 years had the highest prevalence of AMI (22.1%) compared to adults aged 26 to 49 years (21.1%) and aged 50 and older (14.5%).

- The prevalence of AMI was highest among the adults reporting two or more races (26.5%), followed by the American Indian/ Alaska Native group (22.8%). The prevalence of AMI was lowest among the Asian group (12.1%).

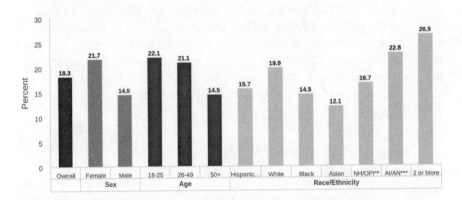

Figure 1.8. *Prevalence of Any Mental Illness among U.S. Adults in 2016*

Mental-Health Treatment—Any Mental Illness

Figure 1.9 presents data on mental-health treatment received within the past year by U.S. adults aged 18 or older with any mental illness (AMI). NSDUH defines mental-health treatment as having received inpatient treatment/counseling or outpatient treatment/ counseling, or having used prescription medication for problems with emotions, nerves, or mental health.

- In 2016, among the 44.7 million adults with AMI, 19.2 million (43.1%) received mental-health treatment in the past year.

- More women with AMI (48.8%) received mental-health treatment than men with AMI (33.9%).

- The percentage of young adults aged 18 to 25 years with AMI who received mental-health treatment (35.1%) was lower than adults with AMI aged 26 to 49 years (43.1%) and aged 50 and older (46.8%).

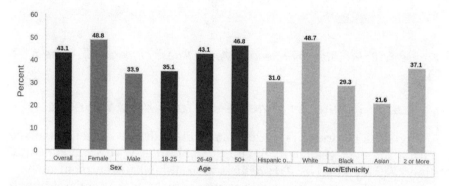

Figure 1.9. *Mental Health Treatment Received in 2016 among U.S. Adults with Any Mental Illness*

Prevalence of Serious Mental Illness

Figure 1.10 shows the past year prevalence of SMI among U.S. adults.

- In 2016, there were an estimated 10.4 million adults aged 18 or older in the United States with SMI. This number represented (4.2%) of all U.S. adults.

- The prevalence of SMI was higher among women (5.3%) than men (3.0%).

- Young adults aged 18 to 25 years had the highest prevalence of SMI (5.9%) compared to adults aged 26 to 49 years (5.3%) and aged 50 and older (2.7%).

- The prevalence of SMI was highest among the adults reporting two or more races (7.5%), followed by the American Indian/ Alaska Native group (AI/AN) (4.9%). The prevalence of SMI was lowest among the Asian group (1.6%).

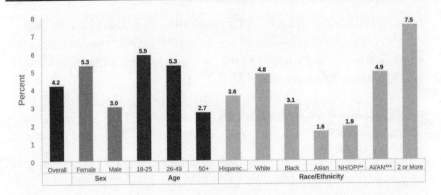

Figure 1.10. *Prevalence of Serious Mental Illness among U.S. Adults in 2016*

Mental-Health Treatment—Serious Mental Illness

Figure 1.11 presents data on mental-health treatment received within the past year by U.S. adults 18 or older with serious mental illness (SMI). The NSDUH defines mental-health treatment as having received inpatient treatment/counseling or outpatient treatment/counseling or having used prescription medication for problems with emotions, nerves, or mental health.

- In 2016, among the 10.4 million adults with SMI, 6.7 million (64.8%) received mental-health treatment in the past year.

- More women with SMI (68.8%) received mental-health treatment than men with AMI (57.4%).

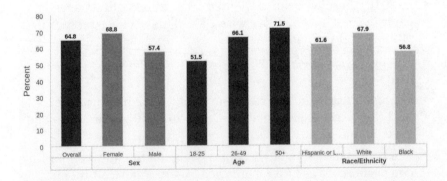

Figure 1.11. *Mental-Health Treatment Received in 2016 among U.S. Adults with Serious Mental Illness*

- The percentage of young adults aged 18 to 25 years with AMI who received mental-health treatment (51.5%) was lower than adults with AMI aged 26 to 49 years (66.1%) and aged 50 and older (71.5%).

Prevalence of Any Mental Disorder among Adolescents

Based on diagnostic interview data from National Comorbidity Survey Adolescent Supplement (NCS-A), Figure 1.12 shows lifetime prevalence of any mental disorder among U.S. adolescents aged 13 to 18.

- An estimated (49.5%) of adolescents had any mental disorder.

- Of adolescents with any mental disorder, an estimated (22.2%) had severe impairment. *Diagnostic and Statistical Manual of Mental Disorders* (DSM)-IV criteria were used to determine impairment.

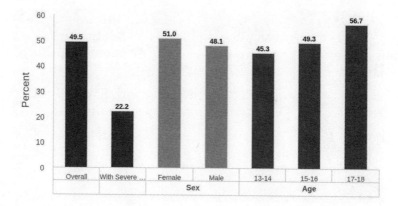

Figure 1.12. *Lifetime Prevalence of Any Mental Disorder among Adolescents (2001–2004)*

Chapter 2

The Components of Mental Health

Chapter Contents

Section 2.1

Myths about Mental Health

This section includes text excerpted from "Mental Health Myths and Facts," MentalHealth.gov, U.S. Department of Health and Human Services (HHS), August 29, 2017.

Mental-Health Problems Affect Everyone

Myth: Mental-health problems don't affect me.

Fact: Mental-health problems are actually very common. In 2014, about:

- 1 in 5 American adults experienced a mental-health issue

- 1 in 10 young people experienced a period of major depression

- 1 in 25 Americans lived with a serious mental illness, such as schizophrenia, bipolar disorder, or major depression

Suicide is the tenth leading cause of death in the United States. It accounts for the loss of more than 41,000 American lives each year, more than double the number of lives lost to homicide.

Myth: Children don't experience mental-health problems.

Fact: Even very young children may show early warning signs of mental-health concerns. These mental-health problems are often clinically diagnosable and can be a product of the interaction of biological, psychological, and social factors.

Half of all mental-health disorders show first signs before a person turns 14 years old, and three-quarters of mental-health disorders begin before age 24.

Unfortunately, less than 20 percent of children and adolescents with diagnosable mental-health problems receive the treatment they need. Early mental-health support can help a child before problems interfere with other developmental needs.

Myth: People with mental-health problems are violent and unpredictable.

Fact: The vast majority of people with mental-health problems are no more likely to be violent than anyone else. Most people with mental illness are not violent and only three percent to five percent of violent acts can be attributed to individuals living with a serious mental illness. In fact, people with severe mental illnesses are over ten times more likely to be victims of violent crime than the general population. You probably know someone with a mental-health problem and don't even realize it, because many people with mental-health problems are highly active and productive members of our communities.

Myth: People with mental health needs, even those who are managing their mental illness, cannot tolerate the stress of holding down a job.

Fact: People with mental-health problems are just as productive as other employees. Employers who hire people with mental-health problems report good attendance and punctuality as well as motivation, good work, and job tenure on par with or greater than other employees.

When employees with mental-health problems receive effective treatment, it can result in:

- Lower total medical costs
- Increased productivity
- Lower absenteeism
- Decreased disability costs

Myth: Personality weakness or character flaws cause mental-health problems. People with mental-health problems can snap out of it if they try hard enough.

Fact: Mental-health problems have nothing to do with being lazy or weak and many people need help to get better. Many factors contribute to mental-health problems, including:

- Biological factors, such as genes, physical illness, injury, or brain chemistry
- Life experiences, such as trauma or a history of abuse
- The family history of mental-health problems

People with mental-health problems can get better and many recover completely.

Helping Individuals with Mental-Health Problems

Myth: There is no hope for people with mental-health problems. Once a friend or a family member develops mental-health problems, she or he will never recover.

Fact: Studies show that people with mental-health problems get better and many recover completely. Recovery refers to the process in which people are able to live, work, learn, and participate fully in their communities. There are more treatments, services, and community support systems than ever before, and they work.

Myth: Therapy and self-help are a waste of time. Why bother when you can just take a pill?

Fact: Treatment for mental-health problems varies depending on the individual and could include medication, therapy, or both. Many individuals work with a support system during the healing and recovery process.

Myth: I can't do anything for a person with a mental-health problem.

Fact: Friends and loved ones can make a big difference. Only 44 percent of adults with diagnosable mental-health problems and less than 20 percent of children and adolescents receive needed treatment. Friends and family can be important influences to help someone get the treatment and services they need by:

- Reaching out and letting them know you are available to help

- Helping them access mental-health services

- Learning and sharing the facts about mental health, especially if you hear something that isn't true

- Treating them with respect, just as you would anyone else

- Refusing to define them by their diagnosis or using labels such as "crazy"

Myth: Prevention doesn't work. It is impossible to prevent mental illnesses.

Fact: Prevention of mental, emotional, and behavioral disorders focuses on addressing known risk factors such as exposure to trauma that can affect the chances that children, youth, and young adults will develop mental-health problems. Promoting the social-emotional well-being of children and youth leads to:

- Higher overall productivity

- Better educational outcomes

- Lower crime rates
- Stronger economies
- Lower healthcare costs
- Improved quality of life (QOL)
- Increased lifespan
- Improved family life

Section 2.2

Good Mental Health

This section includes text excerpted from "Good Mental Health at Every Age," Office on Women's Health (OWH), U.S. Department of Health and Human Services (HHS), August 28, 2018.

Each stage of your life can create different challenges to good mental health. The events that worry you as a 20-year-old probably won't be the same as what causes you stress when you're 50. Eating right, staying physically active, getting enough sleep, and having healthy relationships will help support good physical and mental health throughout life. If you're worried about your mental health, talk to someone right away.

What You Need to Know about Mental Health in Your Teens and Twenties

Researchers think that most mental-health conditions begin early in life, usually, by 25 years old. Mental-health conditions are common in young people, but some conditions are more serious or last longer than others. A survey showed that one in four young women 18 to 25 said they had a mental-health condition in the past year. One in about every 12 young women has a serious mental-health condition that impacts daily activities such as working or going to school.

In your early twenties, you may be dealing with stressful life situations such as finding a job or finishing college, moving out of a family home, and becoming financially independent. This can be a stressful time for anyone. It can be more difficult to handle these life changes if you have a mental-health condition. Also, if you have lived with a mental-health condition for most of your life, it can be difficult to know that you have a health problem that can be treated.

What you can do:

- Protect your mental health by knowing the signs of a mental-health condition.

- Get help. If you feel hopeless or your thoughts or actions feel out of control, get help. You could have a mental-health condition that can be treated with medicine or counseling.

- Talk to a mental-health professional. Treatment works, and the earlier you get treatment, the better it works.

- Start building healthy habits now.

What You Need to Know about Mental Health in Your Thirties and Forties

In your thirties and forties, you may be building a career, raising a family, or juggling many different responsibilities all at the same time. These changes can be exhausting and stressful and make it difficult to maintain good mental health. A woman's menstrual cycle or pregnancy can also affect her mental well-being, from mood swings during her period or pregnancy to problems getting pregnant.

Perimenopause, the transition to menopause, often begins in a woman's late forties. Perimenopause can cause sudden hormonal ups and downs that can affect a woman's physical and mental health.

What men and women in their thirties and forties can do:

- **Don't forget about your own health.** During your annual health checkup, often called a "wellness visit," talk to your doctor or nurse about your mental health and well-being.

- **Follow your doctor's advice.** If you've already been diagnosed with a mental-health condition, follow your doctor's advice about any medicines and steps you can take at home to feel better.

- **Develop healthy habits.** Eating right, exercising, getting enough sleep, and staying connected with others can make it easier to deal with many of the stresses of your thirties and forties. Having healthy habits can make it easier to find the energy to get help for mental-health conditions.

What You Need to Know about Mental Health in Your Fifties and Sixties

A woman in her early fifties will probably experience menopause, which can affect her mental health or stress levels. If you are in a romantic relationship, you may find that expectations and roles have changed over the years. By your sixties, you may be facing retirement or dealing with a chronic illness. You may also find yourself suddenly in an emptier house if you have children who have moved out, or you might be a caretaker for an elderly parent. Such major life changes can have emotional and even physical effects.

What you can do:

- **Treat menopause symptoms.** Talk to your doctor about relief for menopause symptoms if they are uncomfortable or add stress to your life. Changing hormone levels during menopause and perimenopause can also affect your emotions.

- **Prioritize your own health.** If you are a caregiver, try to be aware of your own stress levels and physical needs. You can also find help through a local support group, hospital services, or other community resources.

- **Stay active.** If you are retired, keep your mind and body active. Retirement is an opportunity to spend time doing things you never had time for, such as learning a new skill or hobby, volunteering, or seeing friends and family more often. But being without a regular job and coworkers you see every day can also feel lonely.

- **Try something new.** If you have "empty nest syndrome"—a phrase parents often use for the feelings of sadness or loneliness they experience when their children move out of the house—try something new. Volunteer, join a club, play a sport, or make a list of places to visit or things you've always wanted to do.

- **Stay in touch.** Reach out to someone if you're having trouble coping with the physical or emotional effects of aging. Lean on friends or loved ones, or make time to talk to a mental-health professional. You are not alone.

What You Need to Know about Mental Health after Age Seventy

Your seventies and beyond can be a time of enjoying retirement, starting new hobbies, and seeing friends and family more often. It can also be the time when many people are diagnosed with serious health problems, such as heart disease or cancer. Sometimes, you're dealing with the death of a loved one. People in their seventies and beyond may also face tough financial situations due to medical bills or running out of retirement savings.

Older adults who have serious physical conditions are more likely to develop depression. About one in eight older adults said they had a mental-health condition in the past year. Adults over 65 also may have more trouble sleeping, which can make mental-health conditions worse.

Although these challenges can be stressful and upsetting, there are tools you can use to help achieve good mental health in your seventies and beyond.

What you can do:

- **Maintain strong relationships.** Older adults can be more isolated from their friends, family, and community. Having a strong social network of close family and friends can help your mental and even physical health.

- **Give something back.** Research shows that volunteering your time and talents to benefit others can help you feel more connected and lower your stress levels.

- **Eat well.** Older people need just as many nutrients as younger people but may need fewer calories for energy. Find out how many calories you need each day based on your age, height, weight, and activity level. Talk to your doctor about whether you might need to take supplements.

- **Be active.** Physical activity can help your bones, heart, and mood. Ask your doctor about what activities are right for you. Most adults need to get at least two hours and 30 minutes a week of moderate aerobic physical activity or one hour and 15 minutes of vigorous aerobic activity, or some combination of the two. Talk to your doctor before starting a new exercise program. Most adults also need two days of strengthening activities to keep bones and muscles healthy.

- **Use the resources in your community.** As you get older, it can be difficult to face a loss of independence like driving or living in your own home. Learn about the free and low-cost resources in your community that can allow you to maintain independence in older age.

Section 2.3

Good Emotional Health

This section includes text excerpted from "Positive Emotions and Your Health," *NIH News in Health*, National Institutes of Health (NIH), August 2015. Reviewed December 2018.

Do you tend to look on the sunny side, or do you see a future filled with dark, stormy skies? A growing body of research suggests that having a positive outlook can benefit your physical health. The National Institutes of Health (NIH) funded scientists are working to better understand the links between your attitude and your body. They're finding some evidence that emotional wellness can be improved by developing certain skills.

Having a positive outlook doesn't mean you never feel negative emotions, such as sadness or anger, says Dr. Barbara L. Fredrickson, a psychologist, and expert on emotional wellness at the University of North Carolina—Chapel Hill. "All emotions—whether positive or negative—are adaptive in the right circumstances. The key seems to be finding a balance between the two," she says.

"Positive emotions expand our awareness and open us up to new ideas, so we can grow and add to our toolkit for survival," Fredrickson explains. "But people need negative emotions to move through difficult situations and respond to them appropriately in the short term. Negative emotions can get us into trouble, though, if they're based on too much rumination about the past or excessive worry about the future, and they're not really related to what's happening in the here and now."

People who are emotionally well, experts say, have fewer negative emotions and are able to bounce back from difficulties faster. This quality is called resilience. Another sign of emotional wellness is being able to hold onto positive emotions longer and appreciate the good times. Developing a sense of meaning and purpose in life—and

27

focusing on what's important to you—also contributes to emotional wellness.

Research has found a link between an upbeat mental state and improved health, including lower blood pressure, reduced risk for heart disease, healthier weight, better blood sugar levels, and longer life. But many studies can't determine whether positive emotions lead to better health, if being healthy causes positive emotions, or if other factors are involved.

"While earlier research suggests an association between positive emotions and health, it doesn't reveal the underlying mechanisms," says Dr. Richard J. Davidson, a neuroscientist at the University of Wisconsin—Madison. "To understand the mechanisms, I think it will be crucial to understanding the underlying brain circuits."

By using brain imaging, Davidson and others have found that positive emotions can trigger "reward" pathways located deep within the brain, including in an area known as the ventral striatum.

"Individuals who are able to savor positive emotions have lasting activation in the ventral striatum," Davidson says. "The longer the activation lasts, the greater her or his feelings of well-being." Continued activation of this part of the brain has been linked to healthful changes in the body, including lower levels of a stress hormone.

Negative emotions, in contrast, can activate a brain region known as the amygdala, which plays a role in fear and anxiety. "We've shown that there are big differences among people in how rapidly or slowly the amygdala recovers following a threat," Davidson says. "Those who recover more slowly may be more at risk for a variety of health conditions compared to those who recover more quickly."

Among those who appear more resilient and better able to hold on to positive emotions are people who've practiced various forms of meditation. In fact, growing evidence suggests that several techniques—including meditation, cognitive therapy (a type of psychotherapy), and self-reflection (thinking about the things you find important)—can help people develop the skills needed to make positive, healthful changes.

"Research points to the importance of certain kinds of training that can alter brain circuits in a way that will promote positive responses," Davidson says. "It's led us to conclude that well-being can be considered as a life skill. If you practice, you can actually get better at it."

In one study, Davidson and his colleagues found changes in reward-related brain circuits after people had two weeks of training in a simple form of meditation that focuses on compassion and kindness. These changes, in turn, were linked to an increase in positive social behaviors, such as increased generosity.

Fredrickson and her colleagues are also studying meditation. They found that after six weeks of training in compassion and kindness meditation, people reported increased positive emotions and social connectedness compared to an untrained group. The meditation group also had improved functioning in a nerve that helps to control heart rate. "The results suggest that taking time to learn the skills to self-generate positive emotions can help us become healthier, more social, more resilient versions of ourselves," Fredrickson says.

Dr. Emily Falk, a neuroscientist at the University of Pennsylvania, is taking a different approach. Falk is exploring how self-affirmation—that is, thinking about what's most important to you—can affect your brain and lead to positive, healthful behaviors. Her team found that when people are asked to think about things that they find meaningful, a brain region that recognizes personally relevant information becomes activated. This brain activity can change how people respond to health advice.

"In general, if you tell people that they sit too much and they need to change their behavior, they can become defensive. They'll come up with reasons why the message doesn't apply to them," Falk says. But if people reflect on the things they value before the health message, the brain's reward pathways are activated.

This type of self-affirmation, Falk's research shows, can help physically inactive "couch potatoes" get more active. In a study, inactive adults received typical health advice about the importance of moving more and sitting less. But before the advice, about half of the participants were asked to think about things that they value most.

The "self-affirmation" group became more physically active during the month-long study period that followed compared to the group that hadn't engaged in self-affirmation. "The study shows one way that we can open the brain to positive change and help people achieve their goals," Falk says.

Being open to positive change is key to emotional wellness. "Sometimes people think that emotions just happen, kind of like the weather," Fredrickson says. "But research suggests that we can have some control over which emotions we experience." As mounting research suggests, having a positive mindset might help to improve your physical health as well.

Enhance Your Emotional Wellness

To develop a more positive mindset:

- **Remember your good deeds.** Give yourself credit for the good things you do for others each day.

- **Forgive yourself.** Everyone makes mistakes. Learn from what went wrong, but don't dwell on it.

- **Spend more time with your friends.** Surround yourself with positive, healthy people.

- **Explore your beliefs about the meaning and purpose of life.** Think about how to guide your life by the principles that are important to you.

- **Develop healthy physical habits.** Healthy eating, physical activity, and regular sleep can improve your physical and mental health.

Section 2.4

Mental and Emotional Well-Being

This section includes text excerpted from "Mental and Emotional Well-Being," Office of the Surgeon General (OSG), June 18, 2011. Reviewed December 2018.

Mental and emotional well-being is essential to overall health. Positive mental health allows people to realize their full potential, cope with the stresses of life, work productively, and make meaningful contributions to their communities. Early childhood experiences have lasting, measurable consequences later in life; therefore, fostering emotional well-being from the earliest stages of life helps build a foundation for overall health and well-being. Anxiety, mood (e.g., depression), and impulse control disorders are associated with a higher probability of risky behaviors (e.g., tobacco, alcohol, and other drug use; risky sexual behavior), intimate partner and family violence, many other chronic and acute conditions (e.g., obesity, diabetes, cardiovascular disease (CVD), human immunodeficiency virus (HIV), sexually transmitted infections (STIs)), and premature death.

Recommendations for national prevention strategy:

- Promote positive early childhood development, including positive parenting and violence-free homes.

- Facilitate social connectedness and community engagement across the lifespan.

- Provide individuals and families with the support necessary to maintain positive mental well-being.

- Promote early identification of mental health needs and access to quality services.

Role of State, Tribal, Local, and Territorial Governments

The state, tribal, local, and territorial governments can:

- Enhance data collection systems to better identify and address mental and emotional health needs

- Include safe shared spaces for people to interact (e.g., parks, community centers) in community development plans which can foster healthy relationships and positive mental health among community residents

- Ensure that those in need, especially potentially vulnerable groups, are identified and referred to mental-health services

- Pilot and evaluate models of integrated mental and physical health in primary care, with particular attention to underserved populations and areas, such as rural communities

Role of Businesses and Employers

Businesses and employers can:

- Implement organizational changes to reduce employee stress (e.g., develop clearly defined roles and responsibilities) and provide reasonable accommodations (e.g., flexible work schedules, assistive technology, adapted work stations)

- Ensure that mental-health services are included as a benefit on health plans and encourage employees to use these services as needed

- Provide education, outreach, and training to address mental-health parity in employment-based health insurance coverage and group health plans

Role of Healthcare Systems, Insurers, and Clinicians

The healthcare systems, insurers, and clinicians can:

- Educate parents on normal child development and conduct early childhood interventions to enhance mental and emotional well-being and provide support (e.g., home visits for pregnant women and new parents)

- Screen for mental health needs among children and adults, especially those with disabilities and chronic conditions, and refer people to treatment and community resources as needed

- Develop integrated care programs to address mental health, substance abuse, and other needs within primary care settings

- Enhance communication and data sharing (with patient consent) with social services networks to identify and treat those in need of mental-health services

Role of Learning Centers, Schools, Colleges, and Universities

The early learning centers, schools, colleges, and universities can:

- Implement programs and policies to prevent abuse, bullying, violence, and social exclusion, build social connectedness, and promote positive mental and emotional health

- Implement programs to identify risks and early indicators of mental, emotional, and behavioral problems among youth and ensure that youth with such problems are referred to appropriate services

- Ensure students have access to comprehensive health services, including mental health and counseling services

Role of Community, Nonprofit, and Faith-Based Organizations

The community, nonprofit, and faith-based organizations can:

- Provide space and organized activities (e.g., opportunities for volunteering) that encourage social participation and inclusion for all people, including older people and persons with disabilities

- Support child and youth development programs (e.g., peer mentoring programs, volunteering programs) and promote inclusion of youth with mental, emotional, and behavioral problems
- Train key community members (e.g., adults who work with the elderly, youth, and armed services personnel) to identify the signs of depression and suicide and refer people to resources
- Expand access to mental-health services (e.g., patient navigation and support groups) and enhance linkages between mental health, substance abuse, disability, and other social services

Role of Individuals and Families

The individuals and families can:

- Build strong, positive relationships with family and friends
- Become more involved in their community (e.g., mentor or tutor youth, join a faith or spiritual community)
- Encourage children and adolescents to participate in extracurricular and out-of-school activities
- Work to make sure children feel comfortable talking about problems such as bullying and seek appropriate assistance as needed

Chapter 3

Lifestyles and Mental Health

Chapter Contents

Section 3.1

Eating Well and Mental Health

This section contains text excerpted from the following sources:
Text beginning with the heading "Importance of Good Nutrition" is
excerpted from "Importance of Good Nutrition," U.S. Department of
Health and Human Services (HHS), January 26, 2017; Text under
the heading "How Does What You Eat and Drink Affect Your Mental
Health?" is excerpted from "Steps to Support Good Mental Health,"
Office on Women's Health (OWH), U.S. Department of Health and
Human Services (HHS), August 28, 2018.

Importance of Good Nutrition

Your food choices each day affect your health—how you feel today,
tomorrow, and in the future.

Good nutrition is an important part of leading a healthy lifestyle.
Combined with physical activity, your diet can help you to reach and
maintain a healthy weight, reduce your risk of chronic diseases (like
heart disease and cancer), and promote your overall health.

The Impact of Nutrition on Your Health

Unhealthy eating habits have contributed to the obesity epidemic in
the United States: about one-third of U.S. adults (33.8%) are obese and
approximately 17 percent (or 12.5 million) of children and adolescents
aged 2 to 19 years are obese. Even for people at a healthy weight, a
poor diet is associated with major health risks that can cause illness
and even death. These include heart disease, hypertension (high blood
pressure), type 2 diabetes, osteoporosis, and certain types of cancer. By
making smart food choices, you can help protect yourself from these
health problems.

The risk factors for adult chronic diseases, like hypertension and
type 2 diabetes, are increasingly seen in younger ages, often a result
of unhealthy eating habits and increased weight gain. Dietary habits
established in childhood often carry into adulthood, so teaching children how to eat healthy at a young age will help them stay healthy
throughout their life.

The link between good nutrition and healthy weight, reduced
chronic disease risk, and overall health is too important to ignore.
By taking steps to eat healthy, you'll be on your way to getting the
nutrients your body needs to stay healthy, active, and strong. As with

physical activity, making small changes in your diet can go a long way, and it's easier than you think!

How Does What You Eat and Drink Affect Your Mental Health?

The foods you eat and what you drink can have a direct effect on your energy levels and mood. Researchers think that eating healthier foods can have a positive effect on your mood.

- Getting the right balance of nutrients, including enough fiber and water, can help your mood stay stable. Sugary, processed foods increase your blood sugar and then make you feel tired and irritable when your blood sugar levels drop.

- Some vitamins and minerals may help with the symptoms of depression. Experts are researching how a lack of some nutrients is linked to depression in new mothers. These include selenium, omega-3 fatty acids, folate, vitamin B_{12}, calcium, iron, and zinc.

- Drinking too much alcohol can lead to mental and physical health problems.

- Drinks with caffeine can make it harder for you to sleep, which can make some mental-health conditions worse. Also, drinking caffeine regularly and then suddenly stopping can cause caffeine withdrawal, which can make you irritable and give you headaches. Don't have drinks with caffeine within five hours of going to sleep.

Eating nutritious foods may not cure a mental-health condition, but eating healthy is a good way to start feeling better. Ask your doctor or nurse for more information about the right foods to eat to help keep your mind and body healthy.

Section 3.2

Sleep and Mental Health

This section contains text excerpted from the following sources: Text
in this section begins with excerpts from "Sleep and Your Health,"
Office on Women's Health (OWH), U.S. Department of Health and
Human Services (HHS), August 28, 2018; Text beginning with
the heading "The Basics" is excerpted from "Get Enough Sleep,"
Office of Disease Prevention and Health Promotion (ODPHP), U.S.
Department of Health and Human Services (HHS), July 18, 2018.

Sleep affects your mental and physical health. Getting good sleep
helps boost your mind and mood and can help prevent health problems. Your mind and body are healthier when you sleep well. Your
body needs time every day to rest and heal. Some sleep disorders, such
as insomnia, sleep apnea, and restless leg syndrome (RLS), make it
harder to fall asleep or stay asleep. This can lead to daytime sleepiness
and make it more difficult to stay in good mental health.

Having a sleep problem can also trigger a mental-health condition
or make current mental-health conditions worse. Also, mental-health
conditions or treatments can sometimes cause sleep problems.

The Basics

It's important to get enough sleep. Sleep helps keep your mind and
body healthy.

How Much Sleep Do Adult Need?

Most adults need seven to eight hours of good quality sleep on a
regular schedule each night. Make changes to your routine if you can't
find enough time to sleep. Getting enough sleep isn't only about total
hours of sleep. It's also important to get good quality sleep on a regular
schedule so you feel rested when you wake up.

If you often have trouble sleeping—or if you often still feel tired
after sleeping—talk with your doctor.

How Much Sleep Do Children Need?

Kids need even more sleep than adults.

- Teens need 8 to 10 hours of sleep each night
- School-aged children need 9 to 12 hours of sleep each night

- Preschoolers need to sleep between 10 and 13 hours a day (including naps)
- Toddlers need to sleep between 11 and 14 hours a day (including naps)
- Babies need to sleep between 12 and 16 hours a day (including naps)

Why Is Getting Enough Sleep Important?

Getting enough sleep has many benefits. It can help you:

- Get sick less often
- Stay at a healthy weight
- Lower your risk for serious health problems, like diabetes and heart disease
- Reduce stress and improve your mood
- Think more clearly and do better in school and at work
- Get along better with people
- Make good decisions and avoid injuries—for example, sleepy drivers cause thousands of car accidents every year

Does It Matter When You Sleep?

Yes. Your body sets your "biological clock" according to the pattern of daylight where you live. This helps you naturally get sleepy at night and stay alert during the day. If you have to work at night and sleep during the day, you may have trouble getting enough sleep. It can also be hard to sleep when you travel to a different time zone.

Why Can't You Fall Asleep?

Many things can make it harder for you to sleep, including:

- Stress or anxiety
- Pain
- Certain health conditions, like heartburn or asthma
- Some medicines
- Caffeine (usually from coffee, tea, and soda)

- Alcohol and other drugs

- Untreated sleep disorders, like sleep apnea or insomnia

If you are having trouble sleeping, try making changes to your routine to get the sleep you need. You may want to:

- Change what you do during the day—for example, get your physical activity in the morning instead of at night

- Create a comfortable sleep environment—and make sure your bedroom is dark and quiet

- Set a bedtime routine—and go to bed at the same time every night

How Can You Tell If You Have a Sleep Disorder?

Sleep disorders can cause many different problems. Keep in mind that it's normal to have trouble sleeping every now and then. People with sleep disorders generally experience these problems on a regular basis.

Common signs of sleep disorders include:

- Trouble falling or staying asleep

- Still feeling tired after a good night's sleep

- Sleepiness during the day that makes it difficult to do everyday activities, like driving a car or concentrating at work

- Frequent loud snoring

- Pauses in breathing or gasping while sleeping

- Itchy feelings in your legs or arms at night that feel better when you move or massage the area

- Trouble moving your arms and legs when you wake up

If you have any of these signs, talk to a doctor or nurse. You may need to be tested or treated for a sleep disorder.

Take Action!

Making small changes to your daily routine can help you get the sleep you need.

Change what you do during the day.

- Try to spend some time outdoors every day.

- Plan your physical activity for earlier in the day, not right before you go to bed.

- Stay away from caffeine (including coffee, tea, and soda) late in the day.

- If you have trouble sleeping at night, limit daytime naps to 20 minutes or less.

- If you drink alcohol, drink only in moderation. This means no more than one drink a day for women and no more than two drinks a day for men. Alcohol can keep you from sleeping well.

- Don't eat a big meal close to bedtime.

- Quit smoking. The nicotine in cigarettes can make it harder for you to sleep.

Create a good sleep environment.

- Make sure your bedroom is dark. If there are street lights near your window, try putting up light-blocking curtains.

- Keep your bedroom quiet.

- Consider keeping electronic devices—such as TVs, computers, and smartphones—out of the bedroom.

Set a bedtime routine.

- Go to bed at the same time every night.

- Get the same amount of sleep each night.

- Avoid eating, talking on the phone, or reading in bed.

- Avoid using computers or smartphones, watching TV, or playing video games at bedtime.

If you are still awake after staying in bed for more than 20 minutes, get up. Do something relaxing, like reading or meditating, until you feel sleepy.

If you are concerned about your sleep, see a doctor.

Talk with a doctor or nurse if you have any of the following signs of a sleep disorder:

- Frequent, loud snoring

- Pauses in breathing during sleep

- Trouble waking up in the morning

- Pain or itchy feelings in your legs or arms at night that feel better when you move or massage the area

- Trouble staying awake during the day

Even if you aren't aware of problems like these, talk with a doctor if you feel like you often have trouble sleeping.

Section 3.3

Physical Activity and Mental Health

This section contains text excerpted from the following sources:
Text in this section begins with excerpts from "Physical Activity Guidelines Advisory Committee Report—Part G. Section 8: Mental Health," Office of Disease Prevention and Health Promotion (ODPHP), U.S. Department of Health and Human Services (HHS), November 21, 2018; Text under the heading "The Impact of Physical Activity on Your Health" is excerpted from "Importance of Physical Activity," U.S. Department of Health and Human Services (HHS), January 26, 2017; Text under the heading "What Being Active Does for Your Mental Health" is excerpted from "Why Physical Activity Is Important," girlshealth.gov, Office on Women's Health (OWH), March 27, 2015. Reviewed December 2018.

Poor mental health, including diseases of the central nervous system (CNS), reduces the quality of life and adds a burden on public health. People with anxiety or depression disorders are more likely to have chronic physical conditions, and depression and dementia were among the ten leading risk factors of disability—adjusted life expectancy in high-income nations worldwide during 2001. They are projected to rank first and third by the year 2030. In the United States, dementia and other CNS disorders are a leading cause of death, and mental disorders are estimated to account for more than 40 percent of years lost to disability.

The Impact of Physical Activity on Your Health

Regular physical activity can produce long-term health benefits. It can help:

- Prevent chronic diseases such as heart disease, cancer, and stroke (the three leading health-related causes of death)
- Control weight
- Make your muscles stronger
- Reduce fat
- Promote strong bone, muscle, and joint development
- Condition heart and lungs
- Build overall strength and endurance
- Improve sleep
- Decrease potential of becoming depressed
- Increase your energy and self-esteem
- Relieve stress
- Increase your chances of living longer

When you are not physically active, you are more at risk for:

- High blood pressure
- High blood cholesterol
- Stroke
- Type 2 diabetes
- Heart disease
- Cancer

What Being Active Does for Your Mental Health

Did you know being physically active can affect how good you feel? It also can affect how well you do your tasks, and even how pleasant you are to be around. That's partly because physical activity gets your brain to make "feel-good" chemicals called endorphins. Regular physical activity may help you by:

- Reducing stress
- Improving sleep
- Boosting your energy
- Reducing symptoms of anxiety and depression

- Increasing your self-esteem

- Making you feel proud for taking good care of yourself

- Improving how well you do at school

Section 3.4

Keeping Mentally Fit as You Age

This section contains text excerpted from the following
sources: Text under the heading "Emotional Benefits of Exercise" is
excerpted from "Feel Down? Get Up! Emotional Benefits of Exercise,"
Go4Life, National Institutes of Health (NIH), August 19, 2018;
Text under the heading "Exercises and Physical Activities That Can
Help You" is excerpted from "Real Life Benefits of Exercise
and Physical Activity," *Go4Life*, National Institutes of
Health (NIH), August 19, 2018.

Emotional Benefits of Exercise

Research has shown that the benefits of exercise go beyond just
physical well-being. Exercise helps support emotional and mental
health. So, next time you're feeling down, anxious, or stressed, try to
get up and start moving!

Physical activity can help:

- Reduce feelings of depression and stress, while improving your
  mood and overall emotional well-being

- Increase your energy level

- Improve sleep

- Empower you to feel more in control

In addition, exercise and physical activity may possibly improve
or maintain some aspects of cognitive function, such as your ability
to shift quickly between tasks, plan an activity, and ignore irrelevant
information.

Exercise ideas to help you lift your mood:

- **Walking, bicycling, or dancing.** Endurance activities increase your breathing, get your heart pumping, and also boost chemicals in your body that may improve mood.

- **Yoga.** A mind and body practice with origins in ancient Indian philosophy. The various styles of yoga typically combine physical postures, breathing techniques, and meditation or relaxation.

- **Tai chi.** A "moving meditation" that involves shifting the body slowly, gently, and precisely, while breathing deeply.

- **Activities you enjoy.** Whether it's gardening, playing tennis, kicking around a soccer ball with your grandchildren, or something else, choose an activity you want to do, not have to do.

Exercises and Physical Activities That Can Help You

Exercise and physical activity aren't just good for your mind and body, it can help you stay active and mobile as you age! Regularly including all four types of exercise will give you a wide range of real-life benefits.

Endurance activities help you:

- Keep up with your grandchildren during a trip to the park

- Dance to your favorite songs at the next family wedding

- Rake the yard and bag up the leaves

Strength training will make it easier to:

- Lift your carry-on bag into the overhead bin of the airplane

- Carry groceries in from the car

- Pick up bags of mulch

Balance exercises help you:

- Turn around quickly when you're on a walk and hear a bicycle bell behind you

- Walk along a cobblestone path without losing your balance

- Stand on tiptoe to reach something on a top shelf

Flexibility exercises make it easier to:

- Bend down to tie your shoes
- Look over your shoulder as you're backing out of the driveway
- Stretch to clean hard-to-reach areas of the house

Chapter 4

Developing and Reinforcing Mental Wellness

Chapter Contents

Section 4.1

Becoming More Resilient

This section includes text excerpted from "Individual
Resilience," Office of the Assistant Secretary for Preparedness
and Response (ASPR), U.S. Department of Health and Human
Services (HHS), January 29, 2018.

What Is Individual Resilience?

Individual resilience involves behaviors, thoughts, and actions that
promote personal well-being and mental health. People can develop
the ability to withstand, adapt to, and recover from stress and adversity—and maintain or return to a state of mental health well-being—by
using effective coping strategies. This is called individual resilience.

A disaster can impair resilience due to stress, traumatic exposure,
distressing psychological reactions, and disrupted social networks.
Feelings of grief, sadness, and a range of other emotions are common
after traumatic events. Resilient individuals, however, are able to
work through the emotions and effects of stress and painful events
and rebuild their lives.

What Contributes to Individual Resilience?

People develop resilience by learning better skills and strategies for
managing stress and better ways of thinking about life's challenges.
To be resilient one must tap into personal strengths and the support
of family, friends, neighbors, and/or faith communities.

What Are the Characteristics That Support Individual Resilience?

Age, gender, health, biology, education level, cultural beliefs and
traditions, and economic resources can play important roles in psychological resilience. The following characteristics also contribute to
individual resilience:

- **Social support and close relationships with family and
  friends.** People who have close social support and strong
  connections with family and friends are able to get help during
  tough times and also enjoy their relationships during everyday
  life.

- **The ability to manage strong feelings and impulses.** People who are able to manage strong emotions are less likely to get overwhelmed, frustrated, or aggressive. People who are able to manage feelings can still feel sadness or loss, but they are also able to find healthy ways to cope and heal.

- **Good problem-solving skills.** People problem-solve daily. Thinking, planning, and solving problems in an organized way are important skills. Problem-solving skills contribute to feelings of independence and self-competence.

- **Feeling in control.** After the chaos of a disaster, it can be useful to engage in activities that help people regain a sense of control. This will help support the healing and recovery process.

- **Asking for help and seeking resources.** Resourceful people will get needed help more quickly if they know how to ask questions, are creative in their thinking about situations, are good problem-solvers and communicators, and have a good social network to reach out to.

- **Seeing yourself as resilient.** After a disaster many people may feel helpless and powerless, especially when there has been vast damage to the community. Being able to see yourself as resilient, rather than as helpless or as a victim, can help build psychological resilience.

- **Coping with stress in healthy ways.** People get feelings of pleasure and self-worth from doing things well. Strategies that use positive and meaningful ways to cope are better than those which can be harmful such as drinking too much or smoking.

- **Helping others and finding positive meaning in life.** Positive emotions like gratitude, joy, kindness, love, and contentment can come from helping others. Acts of generosity can add meaning and purpose to your life, even in the face of tragedy.

Resilient Individuals and Their Abilities

Resilient individuals are able to:

- Care for themselves and others day-to-day and during emergency situations

- Actively support their neighborhoods, workplaces, and communities to recover after disaster

- Be confident and hopeful about overcoming present and future difficulties

- Get needed resources more effectively and quickly

- Be physically and mentally healthier and have overall lower recovery expenses and service needs

- Miss fewer days of work

- Maintain stable family and social connections

- Re-establish routines more quickly, which helps children and adults alike

Ways to Strengthen Resilience

You can build your resilience by taking care of your health, managing stress, and being an active participant in the life of your community. For example, try to:

- Develop coping skills and practice stress-management activities, such as yoga, exercise, and meditation

- Eat healthy and exercise

- Get plenty of sleep

- Maintain social connections to people and groups that are meaningful for you

- Volunteer in your community

- Get training in first aid, cardiopulmonary resuscitation (CPR), community emergency response team (CERT), and psychological first aid

- Create evacuation and family reunification plans

- Make a disaster kit and stock supplies to shelter in place for up to three days

- Find things that bring you pleasure and enjoyment such as reading a book or watching a movie, writing in a journal, or engaging in an art activity

Does Individual Resilience Help Build Community Resilience?

Yes! Individual resilience is important to community resilience in that healthy people make for a healthier community. Healthy communities are better able to manage and recover from disasters and other emergencies.

Section 4.2

Stress and How to Handle It

This section contains text excerpted from the following sources: Text in this section begins with excerpts from "5 Things You Should Know about Stress," National Institute of Mental Health (NIMH), 2016; Text beginning with the heading "The Basics" is excerpted from "Manage Stress," Office of Disease Prevention and Health Promotion (ODPHP), U.S. Department of Health and Human Services (HHS), September 26, 2018.

Stress is how the brain and body respond to any demand. Every type of demand or stressor—such as exercise, work, school, major life changes, or traumatic events—can be stressful.

Stress can affect your health. It is important to pay attention to how you deal with minor and major stress events so that you know when to seek help. Stress is how the brain and body respond to any demand. Every type of demand or stressor—such as exercise, work, school, major life changes, or traumatic events—can be stressful.

Stress can affect your health. It is important to pay attention to how you deal with minor and major stress events so that you know when to seek help.

The Basics
What Are the Signs of Stress?

When people are under stress, they may feel:

- Worried

- Angry

- Irritable

- Depressed

- Unable to focus

51

Stress also affects your body. Physical signs of stress include:

- Headaches
- Back pain
- Problems sleeping
- Upset stomach
- Weight gain or loss
- Tense muscles
- Frequent or more serious colds

Stress is different for everyone.

What Causes Stress

Change is often a cause of stress. Even positive changes, like having a baby or getting a job promotion, can be stressful. Stress can be short term or long term.
Common causes of short-term stress include:

- Needing to do a lot in a short amount of time
- Experiencing many small problems in the same day, like a traffic jam or running late
- Getting lost
- Having an argument

Common causes of long-term stress include:

- Problems at work or at home
- Money problems
- Caring for someone with a serious illness
- Chronic (ongoing) illness
- Death of a loved one

What Are the Benefits of Managing Stress?

Over time, chronic stress can lead to health problems. Managing stress can help you:

- Sleep better

- Control your weight
- Get sick less often
- Feel better faster when you do get sick
- Have less neck and back pain
- Be in a better mood
- Get along better with family and friends

Take Action!

You can't always avoid stress, but you can take steps to deal with your stress in a positive way. Follow these nine tips for preventing and managing stress.

Being prepared and feeling in control of your situation might help lower your stress.

Tip 1. Plan your time. Think ahead about how you are going to use your time. Write a to-do list and figure out what's most important—then do that thing first. Be realistic about how long each task will take.

Tip 2. Prepare yourself. Prepare ahead of time for stressful events like a job interview or a hard conversation with a loved one.

- Stay positive.
- Picture what the room will look like and what you will say.
- Have a backup plan.

Tip 3. Relax with deep breathing or meditation. Deep breathing and meditation are two ways to relax your muscles and clear your mind.

- Find out how easy it is to use deep breathing to relax.
- Try meditating for a few minutes today.

Tip 4. Relax your muscles. Stress causes tension in your muscles. Try stretching or taking a hot shower to help you relax. Check out these stretches you can do.

Tip 5. Get active. Regular physical activity can help prevent and manage stress. It can also help relax your muscles and improve your mood.

- Aim for 2 hours and 30 minutes a week of physical activity. Try going for a bike ride or taking a walk.

- Be sure to exercise for at least 10 minutes at a time.

- Do strengthening activities—like crunches or lifting weights—at least 2 days a week.

- Find out more about getting active.

Tip 6. Eat healthy. Give your body plenty of energy by eating healthy—including vegetables, fruits, and lean sources of protein.

Tip 7. Drink alcohol only in moderation. Avoid using alcohol or other drugs to manage stress. If you choose to drink, drink only in moderation. This means no more than one drink a day for women and no more than two drinks a day for men.

Tip 8. Talk to friends and family. Tell your friends and family if you are feeling stressed. They may be able to help.

Tip 9. Get help if you need it. Stress is a normal part of life. But if your stress doesn't go away or keeps getting worse, you may need help. Over time, stress can lead to serious problems like depression or anxiety.

- If you are feeling down or hopeless, talk to a doctor about depression.

- If you are feeling anxious, find out how to get help for anxiety.

- If you have lived through an unsafe event, find out about treatment for PTSD (posttraumatic stress disorder).

A mental-health professional (like a psychologist or social worker) can help treat these conditions with talk therapy (called psychotherapy) or medicine.

Lots of people need help dealing with stress—it's nothing to be ashamed of!

Section 4.3

Controlling Anger

This section includes text excerpted from "Anger Management," Mental Illness Research, Education and Clinical Centers (MIRECC), U.S. Department of Veterans Affairs (VA), July 2013. Reviewed December 2018.

What Is Anger?

Anger is a complex and confusing emotion that you may experience in response to specific stressors. It is a feeling, an emotion, and is quite different than aggression, which is an action and intended to cause harm to others. Anger is created by how you think about external events that are occurring; therefore, you can have control over your anger.

Consider figure 4.1 below and the following example:

As you are driving home from work one late afternoon, you get cut off by a person in another car (external event). You begin to think, "What a jerk!" (internal event/thought). You become frustrated and angry (emotion). Finally, you begin to yell out your window at the person, plan revenge, and speed up to try to catch them (behavior).

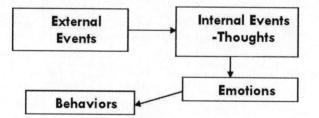

Figure 4.1. *What Makes a Person Angry*

What Are the Functions of Anger?

Anger may have both positive and negative effects on you. When you learn how to appropriately express your anger, it can lead to beneficial consequences.

Some examples of positive functions include:

- Anger can serve as a signal to you that you are becoming frustrated or annoyed.

- It can be an energizer and may help you to deal with conflict and solve problems.

- Anger can prompt us to communicate with others to resolve a conflict.

- It may create a sense of control and allow us to be more assertive.

Some examples of positive functions include:

- Being in a state of anger may cause increased heart rate, blood pressure, and tension headaches (among other negative physical effects).

- Excess anger may disrupt thoughts and make it difficult to think clearly.

- It may help us to avoid other feelings such as sadness, anxiety, or embarrassment.

- Anger can lead to aggression (like in the example above!)

- It may cause problems in relationships, if it builds up.

What Causes Anger

Anger is an internal response to things in your environment that happen (external factors), based on how you experience and think about those things. It is important to remember that while you may have no control over the external factors, you do have control over how you think about and interpret them. The following are examples of external and internal factors, which may cause you to become angry.

- **Frustrations.** When you try to do something and you are prevented, blocked or disappointed.

- **Tension.** When you are feeling "strung out" and your stress level is high, you may be quicker to anger.

- **Ill humor.** When you take things too seriously and are unable to "roll with the punches"; when you become moody or crabby and are more inclined to become angry easily.

- **Withdrawal avoidance.** When you actively avoid conflict and walk away without resolving an issue, you tend to internalize the feelings and become angry.

How Can You Control Your Anger?

Controlling your anger means learning how to manage the frequency and duration of your anger. Anger that happens often and lasts a long time can be a heavy burden. The continuous increased emotional state can drain your energy and affect you physically. Learning anger management will help you to become aware of your triggers to anger and will teach you more productive ways to respond to the feeling. It also provides you with skills to learn how to control those internal factors which you have control over. There are several strategies you can use to help you gain control over your anger.

They include:

- Relaxation techniques

- Quick stress relievers

- Time-out

- Humor

- Thought stopping

- Conflict negotiation

- Problem solving

- Challenging negative thinking

- Choosing assertiveness versus aggression

Section 4.4

Coping with a Break Up

This section contains text excerpted from the following sources: Text in this section begins with excerpts from "Relationships," girlshealth. gov, Office on Women's Health (OWH), November 2, 2015. Reviewed December 2018; Text beginning with the heading "Break Ups" is excerpted from "Breaking Up," girlshealth.gov, Office on Women's Health (OWH), November 3, 2015. Reviewed December 2018.

Relationships can make us feel fantastic! But a fight with a close friend can really hurt. It's also upsetting when the people closest to you, like your family, don't seem to get you. Plus, relationships can be very confusing, especially when they change as you get older.

Break Ups

Break ups can be so hard! However, you can get through them.

- How do you get over a break up?
- How do you break up with someone?

How Do You Get Over a Break Up?

You may feel awful after a break up. In fact, scientists say breaking up may have the same effects in a person's brain as getting off a drug like cocaine! But time really does help heal wounds. Sometimes, people blame themselves too much for a break up. Just because this relationship didn't work out doesn't mean there's something wrong with you. It just means this wasn't a good fit. Try to remember what's great about you. Keep doing things you love. This might include hanging out with friends or writing in a journal. Learn ways to cope when you're feeling sad. Give yourself a break. If the relationship is over, try to move on. Don't check your ex's social media accounts or find excuses to be in touch a lot.

How Do You Break Up with Someone?

Here are some tips to help make a break up easier—and kinder.

- **Remember your rights.** You deserve to have the kind of relationship you want. It's OK to break up if this one isn't working for you.

- **Remember the other's person's feelings.** Say what's true for you, but gently. Avoid blaming, complaining, or yelling. If you're feeling angry, try to calm down before talking.

- **Plan ahead.** Think about what to say so you're not on the spot. You might practice with a trusted adult.

- **Face the person.** Breaking up online or by text may seem easier, but think about how that must feel. Plus, when a person can't see your face or hear your voice, there's a greater chance of misunderstandings.

- **Leave others out.** Don't spread nasty gossip or blab on social media. Meanness likely will lower other people's respect for you—and your respect for yourself!

- **Think back.** Was there anything good about this relationship? Tell your partner what worked.

- **Think ahead.** What can you learn from this about the kind of relationship you'd like to have in the future?

Section 4.5

Coping with Grief

This section includes text excerpted from "Coping with Grief," *NIH News in Health*, National Institutes of Health (NIH), October 15, 2017.

Losing someone you love can change your world. You miss the person who has died and want them back. You may feel sad, alone, or even angry. You might have trouble concentrating or sleeping. If you were a busy caregiver, you might feel lost when you're suddenly faced with lots of unscheduled time. These feelings are normal. There's no right or wrong way to mourn. Scientists have been studying how we process grief and are learning more about healthy ways to cope with loss.

The death of a loved one can affect how you feel, how you act, and what you think. Together, these reactions are called grief. It's a natural response to loss. Grieving doesn't mean that you have to feel certain emotions. People can grieve in very different ways.

Cultural beliefs and traditions can influence how someone expresses grief and mourns. For example, in some cultures, grief is expressed quietly and privately. In others, it can be loud and out in the open. Culture also shapes how long family members are expected to grieve.

"People often believe they should feel a certain way," says Dr. Wendy Lichtenthal, a psychologist at Memorial Sloan-Kettering Cancer Center. "But such 'shoulds' can lead to feeling badly about feeling badly. It's hugely important to give yourself permission to grieve and allow yourself to feel whatever you are feeling. People can be quite hard on themselves and critical of what they are feeling. Be compassionate and kind to yourself."

Adapting to Loss

Experts say you should let yourself grieve in your own way and time. People have unique ways of expressing emotions. For example, some might express their feelings by doing things rather than talking about them. They may feel better going on a walk or swimming, or by doing something creative like writing or painting. For others, it may be more helpful to talk with family and friends about the person who's gone, or with a counselor.

"Though people don't often associate them with grief, laughing and smiling are also healthy responses to loss and can be protective," explains Dr. George Bonanno, who studies how people cope with loss and trauma at Columbia University. He has found that people who express flexibility in their emotions often cope well with loss and are healthier over time.

"It's not about whether you should express or suppress emotion, but that you can do this when the situation calls for it," he says. For instance, a person with emotional flexibility can show positive feelings, like joy, when sharing a happy memory of the person they lost and then switch to expressing sadness or anger when recalling more negative memories, like an argument with that person.

Grief is a process of letting go and learning to accept and live with loss. The amount of time it takes to do this varies with each person. "Usually people experience a strong acute grief reaction when someone dies and at the same time they begin the gradual process of adapting to the loss," explains psychiatrist Dr. M. Katherine Shear at Columbia University. "To adapt to a loss, a person needs to accept its finality and understand what it means to them. They also have to find a way to re-envision their life with possibilities for happiness and for honoring their enduring connection to the person who died."

Researchers like Lichtenthal have found that finding meaning in life after loss can help you adapt. Connecting to those things that are most important, including the relationship with the person who died, can help you co-exist with the pain of grief.

Types of Grief

About ten percent of bereaved people experience complicated grief, a condition that makes it harder for some people to adapt to the loss of a loved one. People with this prolonged, intense grief tend to get caught up in certain kinds of thinking, says Shear, who studies complicated grief. They may think the death did not have to happen or, happen in the way that it did. They also might judge their grief—questioning if it's too little or too much—and focus on avoiding reminders of the loss.

"It can be very discouraging to experience complicated grief, but it's important not to be judgmental about your grief and not to let other people judge you," Shear explains.

Shear and her research team created and tested a specialized therapy for complicated grief in three National Institutes of Health (NIH)-funded studies. The therapy aimed to help people identify the thoughts, feelings, and actions that can get in the way of adapting to loss. They also focused on strengthening one's natural process of adapting to loss. The studies showed that 70 percent of people taking part in the therapy reported improved symptoms. In comparison, only 30 percent of people who received the standard treatment for depression had improved symptoms.

You may begin to feel the loss of your loved one even before their death. This is called anticipatory grief. It's common among people who are long-term caregivers. You might feel sad about the changes you are going through and the losses you are going to have. Some studies have found that when patients, doctors, and family members directly address the prospect of death before the loss happens, it helps survivors cope after the death.

Life beyond Loss

NIH-funded scientists continue to study different aspects of the grieving process. They hope their findings will suggest new ways to help people cope with the loss of a loved one.

Although the death of a loved one can feel overwhelming, many people make it through the grieving process with the support of family and friends. Take care of yourself, accept offers of help from those around you, and be sure to get counseling if you need it.

"We believe grief is a form of love and it needs to find a place in your life after you lose someone close," Shear says. "If you are having trouble moving forward in your own life, you may need professional help. Please don't lose hope. We have some good ways to help you."

Tips to Cope with Loss

- **Take care of yourself.** Try to exercise regularly, eat healthy food, and get enough sleep. Avoid habits that can put your health at risk, like drinking too much alcohol or smoking.

- **Talk with caring friends.** Let others know if you need to talk.

- **Try not to make any major changes right away.** It's a good idea to wait for a while before making big decisions, like moving or changing jobs.

- **Join a grief support group in person or online.** It might help to talk with others who are also grieving. Check with your local hospice, hospitals, religious communities, and government agencies to find a group in your area.

- **Consider professional support.** Sometimes talking to a counselor about your grief can help.

- **Talk to your doctor.** Be sure to let your healthcare provider know if you're having trouble with everyday activities, like getting dressed, sleeping, or fixing meals.

- **Be patient with yourself.** Mourning takes time. It's common to feel a mix of emotions for a while.

Section 4.6

Pets Are Good for Mental Health

This section includes text excerpted from "The Power of Pets," *NIH News in Health*, National Institutes of Health (NIH), February 2018.

Nothing compares to the joy of coming home to a loyal companion. The unconditional love of a pet can do more than keep you company. Pets may also decrease stress, improve heart health, and even help children with their emotional and social skills.

An estimated 68 percent of U.S. households have a pet. But who benefits from an animal? And which type of pet brings health benefits?

Over the past ten years, National Institutes of Health (NIH) has partnered with the Mars Corporation's Waltham Centre for Pet Nutrition to answer questions like these by funding research studies.

Scientists are looking at what the potential physical and mental-health benefits are for different animals—from fish to guinea pigs to dogs and cats.

Possible Health Effects

Research on human–animal interactions is still relatively new. Some studies have shown positive health effects, but the results have been mixed.

Interacting with animals has been shown to decrease levels of cortisol (a stress-related hormone) and lower blood pressure. Other studies have found that animals can reduce loneliness, increase feelings of social support, and boost your mood.

The NIH/Mars Partnership is funding a range of studies focused on the relationships we have with animals. For example, researchers are looking into how animals might influence child development. They're studying animal interactions with kids who have autism, attention deficit hyperactivity disorder (ADHD), and other conditions.

"There's not one answer about how a pet can help somebody with a specific condition," explains Dr. Layla Esposito, who oversees NIH's Human–Animal Interaction (HAI) Research Program. "Is your goal to increase physical activity? Then you might benefit from owning a dog. You have to walk a dog several times a day and you're going to increase physical activity. If your goal is reducing stress, sometimes watching fish swim can result in a feeling of calmness. So there's no one type fits all."

NIH is funding large-scale surveys to find out the range of pets people live with and how their relationships with their pets relate to health. "We're trying to tap into the subjective quality of the relationship with the animal—that part of the bond that people feel with animals—and how that translates into some of the health benefits," explains Dr. James Griffin, a child development expert at NIH.

Health Risks from Your Pet

Kids, pregnant women, and people with weakened immune systems are at greater risk for getting sick from animals. Take these steps to reduce your risk:

- Wash your hands thoroughly after contact with animals.

- Keep your pet clean and healthy, and keep vaccinations up to date.

- Supervise children when they're interacting with animals.

- Prevent kids from kissing their pets or putting their hands or other objects in their mouths after touching animals.

- Avoid changing litter boxes during pregnancy. Problems with pregnancy may occur from exposure to toxoplasmosis, a parasitic disease spread through the feces of infected cats.

Animals Helping People

Animals can serve as a source of comfort and support. Therapy dogs are especially good at this. They're sometimes brought into hospitals or nursing homes to help reduce patients' stress and anxiety.

"Dogs are very present. If someone is struggling with something, they know how to sit there and be loving," says Dr. Ann Berger, a physician and researcher at the NIH Clinical Center in Bethesda, Maryland. "Their attention is focused on the person all the time."

Berger works with people who have cancer and terminal illnesses. She teaches them about mindfulness to help decrease stress and manage pain.

"The foundations of mindfulness include attention, intention, compassion, and awareness," Berger says. "All of those things are things that animals bring to the table. People kind of have to learn it. Animals do this innately."

Researchers are studying the safety of bringing animals into hospital settings because animals may expose people to more germs. A current study is looking at the safety of bringing dogs to visit children with cancer, Esposito says. Scientists will be testing the children's hands to see if there are dangerous levels of germs transferred from the dog after the visit.

Dogs may also aid in the classroom. One study found that dogs can help children with ADHD focus their attention. Researchers enrolled two groups of children diagnosed with ADHD into 12-week group therapy sessions. The first group of kids read to a therapy dog once a week for 30 minutes. The second group read to puppets that looked like dogs.

Kids who read to the real animals showed better social skills and more sharing, cooperation, and volunteering. They also had fewer behavioral problems.

Another study found that children with autism spectrum disorder (ASD) were calmer while playing with guinea pigs in the classroom. When the children spent ten minutes in a supervised group playtime with guinea pigs, their anxiety levels dropped. The children also had better social interactions and were more engaged with their peers. The researchers suggest that the animals offered unconditional acceptance, making them a calm comfort to the children.

"Animals can become a way of building a bridge for those social interactions," Griffin says. He adds that researchers are trying to better understand these effects and who they might help.

Animals may help you in other unexpected ways. A study showed that caring for fish helped teens with diabetes better manage their disease. Researchers had a group of teens with type 1 diabetes care for a pet fish twice a day by feeding and checking water levels. The caretaking routine also included changing the tank water each week. This was paired with the children reviewing their blood glucose (blood sugar) logs with parents.

Researchers tracked how consistently these teens checked their blood glucose. Compared with teens who weren't given a fish to care for, fish-keeping teens were more disciplined about checking their own blood glucose levels, which is essential for maintaining their health.

While pets may bring a wide range of health benefits, an animal may not work for everyone. Studies suggest that early exposure to pets may help protect young children from developing allergies and asthma. But for people who are allergic to certain animals, having pets in the home can do more harm than good.

Helping Each Other

Pets also bring new responsibilities. Knowing how to care for and feed an animal is part of owning a pet. NIH/Mars funds studies looking into the effects of human-animal interactions for both the pet and the person.

Remember that animals can feel stressed and fatigued, too. It's important for kids to be able to recognize signs of stress in their pet and know when not to approach. Animal bites can cause serious harm.

"Dog bite prevention is certainly an issue parents need to consider, especially for young children who don't always know the boundaries of what's appropriate to do with a dog," Esposito explains.

Researchers continue to explore the many health effects of having a pet. "We're trying to find out what's working, what's not working, and what's safe—for both the humans and the animals," Esposito says.

Chapter 5

Mental Health at Work

The Cost Burden of Mental Illness to Employers

Mental and behavioral health problems are prevalent among adults, with mood and substance-use disorders (SUDs) having peak incidence occurring around 20 to 30 years of age. Successful public health efforts tend to intervene in environments where at-risk populations spend the most time. Given that about 63 percent of Americans participate in the labor force, the workplace represents an often neglected setting for focused prevention efforts. By addressing mental health at the workplace, psychological disorders can be better identified and addressed, and negative sequelae of mental illness can be mitigated. Offering such services as employee assistance programs (EAPs), child care and eldercare support services, and financial counseling are important benefits available to some, but not all, employees. Few can argue that more can be done to promote health and well-being at work.

Employers and employees spent on average $18,142 for family health insurance coverage in 2016 compared to $11,480 in 2006, a 58 percent increase that far outpaced the general rate of inflation. Mental disorders top the list of the most burdensome and costly illnesses in the United States at over $200 billion a year, well exceeding the cost burden of heart disease, stroke, cancer, and obesity.

This chapter includes text excerpted from "Mental Health in the Workplace: A Call to Action Proceedings from the Mental Health in the Workplace: Public Health Summit," National Center for Biotechnology Information (NCBI), April 9, 2018.

Approximately one-third of the mental-health cost burden is related to productivity losses including unemployment, disability, and lower work performance. For example, in one study workers with severe depressive episodes were significantly less productive than those with mild or moderate depressive episodes, and a significant proportion of those with moderate (57%) or severe (40%) depression did not use any treatment. In another study, it was found that a minority of workers with major depressive disorder (i.e., 20%) received treatment that would be considered minimally adequate while those with severe depression were more likely to receive adequate treatment.

Cataloging health issues into either physical or mental health may be misleading and may partially account for the inadequacy of treatment received. There is growing evidence that mental illnesses are often obscured by physical ailments whereas the reverse is also true. Consequently, poor mental health can lead to the development of physical health conditions and poor physical health can lead to the development of adverse mental-health outcomes. Psychological problems are commonly comorbid conditions associated with costly physical health problems such as cardiovascular disease (CVD), diabetes, musculoskeletal disorders (MSDs), and respiratory disorders.

Data from large-scale insurance claims analyses reveal that costs for treating patients with comorbid mental health and SUDs can be two to three times as high as those for patients without the comorbid conditions. For example, there is a high prevalence of depression for patients with asthma (45%) and diabetes (27%). Depressed persons are twice as likely to develop coronary artery disease (CAD) or stroke and more than four times as likely to die within six months from a heart attack. A study revealed a strong linkage between depression and obesity, where those with depression had a 58 percent greater risk of developing obesity that nondepressed individuals, and people with obesity had a 55 percent increased risk of being depressed than nonobese individuals. An added concern is that people with depression also exhibit poor adherence with medication or other prescribed treatments.

The underlying problem is apparent to those who provide care. When presenting to a physician, patients generally complain about their physical health problems. They may or may not bring up mental or emotional pain because of time constraints on the part of either the patient or physician, unwillingness to directly face emotional health problems, and the stigma associated with care seeking behaviors related to mental health. Thus, cases of mental illness may be masked, and therefore, missed by physical health ailments in primary care settings. That, in turn, undercounts the substantial financial toll mental-health problems pose to employers.

In sum, when people suffer from mental illnesses, other dimensions of health are similarly affected, which, in turn, increase healthcare spending and diminish individuals' ability to gain or regain meaningful employment or perform at their optimal level while at work.

The Health and Productivity Burden of Mental Illness

Individuals with untreated mental illnesses who go to work do so with an illness that impairs them physically, mentally, and emotionally. Statistics related to mental health in general, and in the workplace specifically, are compelling. Data from a range of studies show that between 30 to 50 percent of all adults in the United States experience mental illness at some point in their lives. Additionally, 20.2 million (8.4% of adults) have a SUD and 7.9 million have both mental illness and SUDs. By 2030, the global societal impact is expected to rise to $6 trillion.

Among employed adults, anxiety, depression, and SUDs are the most common mental-health problems. Unfortunately, about 50 to 60 percent of adults with mental illness do not receive the mental-health services they need, 28 to 31 and those who do receive care often suffer for years, typically a decade or more, before receiving treatment, during which time additional problems may arise, including physical, social and other emotional impairments.

In addition to the direct costs associated with mental illnesses, there are many indirect costs. These include increased rates of short-term disability, safety incidents, absenteeism and presenteeism (working while sick), underperformance and unrealized output, stress imposed on team members, overtime and overstaffing to cover sick-day absences, and hiring costs related to recruitment and retention.

Productivity losses due to mental-health problems have been quantified in several studies. For example, research shows that there are more workers absent from work because of stress and anxiety than because of physical illness or injury. Further, more days of work loss and work impairment are caused by mental illness than other chronic conditions such as diabetes, asthma, and arthritis. Employees with depression report their productivity at 70 percent of their peak performance, and approximately 32 incremental workdays are lost to presenteeism for individuals with major depressive disorders.

While mental-health problems exert a toll on all workers, they may especially affect knowledge workers whose mental acuity and creativity are key job requirements. These workers face multiple personal and business challenges that include long hours and 24/7 availability even across the globe; speed to market pressures underscored by rapid technology advances; and balancing work and family obligations often encumbered by long commutes or feelings of isolation associated with telecommuting.

As for disability losses, depression is the leading cause of disability among U.S. adults ages 15 to 44. Approximately 80 percent of persons with depression report some level of functional impairment because of their depression and 27 percent report serious difficulties in their work and home life.

Addressing Risk Factors for Mental Illness

In two studies conducted in partnership with the Health Enhancement Research Organization (HERO), it was found that employees scoring at "high risk" for depression also had the highest levels of medical expenditures during the three years following their initial health risk assessments (HRAs), even after controlling for nine other risk factors such as smoking, obesity, high blood pressure, high cholesterol, and high blood glucose. Other studies have demonstrated a clear relationship between self-reported psychosocial risk factors, such as depression, stress, and anxiety, and future detrimental effects on worker productivity measured in terms of absenteeism, presenteeism, workers' compensation claims, and short-term disability. There is also evidence that physical and psychosocial risk factors are associated; meaning that people with mental-health problems are more likely to have poor lifestyle behaviors such as smoking, poor diet, physical inactivity, low rates of preventive screenings, and poor safety habits.

The spillover effect on business performance is palpable. The Integrated Benefits Institute (IBI) studied ways employees' health may undermine their productivity. The researchers found that while physical health symptoms primarily affect absence, mental-health problems tended to affect performance, and unsupportive work cultures exacerbated the effects of both. Harmful work cultures were characterized by unsafe working conditions, low respect and trust, lack of variety in tasks performed, high workloads and lack of control in decision making. Those working in unsupportive work cultures experienced higher absence rates and lower job performance.

Recommendations

Mental and behavioral health are important public health issues, affecting between a third and one half of all Americans sometime in their life. Since most of life is spent in working years, the workplace is an ideal setting for public health-informed initiatives that promote mental and behavioral health and prevent illness. For businesses, improvement of employee mental health can save substantial resources by decreasing presenteeism, increasing productivity, and encouraging retention while decreasing healthcare costs. Mental health and well-being at the workplace are attainable if employers follow best- and promising-practices, but there is a critical need for a centralized, concerted effort to build the evidence base, maintain information on best practices, and effectively disseminate and implement policies and practices that connects academic, government, business, and health professional institutions. For example, integrated policy approaches are needed to support better mental-health promotion in the workplace, which entails providing key players, including employers, with clear guidelines on their responsibilities, tools and training opportunities for identifying and addressing mental-health issues in a timely fashion, and financial incentives for doing the right thing by integrating healthcare delivery and employment services to better serve workers.

Chapter 6

The Stigma of Mental Illness

Attitudes toward Mental Illness and Stigma

People's beliefs and attitudes toward mental illness set the stage for how they interact with, provide opportunities for, and help support a person with mental illness. People's beliefs and attitudes toward mental illness also frame how they experience and express their own emotional problems and psychological distress and whether they disclose these symptoms and seek care. About one in four U.S. adults (26.2%) age 18 and older, in any given year, has a mental disorder (e.g., mood disorder, anxiety disorder, impulse control disorder (ICD), or substance-abuse disorder (SUD)), meaning that mental disorders are common and can affect anyone. Many adults with common chronic conditions such as arthritis, cancer, diabetes, heart disease, and epilepsy experience concurrent depression and anxiety—further complicating self-management of these disorders and adversely affecting the quality of life (QOL). Attitudes and beliefs about mental illness are shaped by personal knowledge about mental illness, knowing and interacting with someone living with mental illness, cultural stereotypes about mental illness, media stories, and familiarity with institutional practices and past restrictions (e.g., health insurance restrictions, employment restrictions, and adoption restrictions). When such attitudes and beliefs are expressed positively, they can

This chapter includes text excerpted from "Attitudes toward Mental Illness," Centers for Disease Control and Prevention (CDC), 2012. Reviewed December 2018.

result in supportive and inclusive behaviors (e.g., willingness to date a person with a mental illness or to hire a person with mental illness). When such attitudes and beliefs are expressed negatively, they may result in avoidance, exclusion from daily activities, and, in the worst case, exploitation and discrimination. Stigma has been described as "a cluster of negative attitudes and beliefs that motivate the general public to fear, reject, avoid, and discriminate against people with mental illnesses." When stigma leads to social exclusion or discrimination ("experienced" stigma), it results in unequal access to resources that all people need to function well: educational opportunities, employment, a supportive community, including friends and family, and access to quality healthcare. These types of disparities in education, employment, and access to care can have cumulative long-term negative consequences. For example, a young adult with an untreated mental illness who is unable to graduate from high school is less likely to find a good paying job that can support her or his basic needs, including access to healthcare. These disadvantages can cause a person to experience more negative outcomes. Being unemployed, living at or below the poverty line, being socially isolated, and living with other social disadvantages can further deflate self-esteem, compounding mental illness symptoms, and add to the burden of stigma. Sometimes stigma is simply "felt" in the absence of being discriminated against and results from internalizing perceived negative attitudes associated with a characteristic (e.g., age), a disorder (e.g., human immunodeficiency virus (HIV)/acquired immunodeficiency syndrome (AIDS)), a behavior (e.g., smoking), or another factor (e.g., place of birth).

Whether stigma is experienced as social exclusion or discrimination or felt as a pervasive and underlying sense of being different from others, it can be debilitating for people and poses a challenge for public health prevention efforts. Different opinions exist regarding the implications of different labels associated with describing mental illness (e.g., brain disease) and felt or experienced stigma. However, the prevailing view of health-related stigma is that it refers to perceived, enacted, or anticipated avoidance or social exclusion, and not to an individual blemish or mark. Different methods exist for measuring health-related stigma, and challenges and limitations associated with distinguishing between felt versus experienced stigma in attitudinal research have been described.

Consequences of Negative Attitudes toward Mental Illness and Stigma

Only about 20 percent of adults with a diagnosable mental disorder or with a self-reported mental-health condition saw a mental-health provider in the previous year. Embarrassment associated with accessing mental-health services is one of the many barriers that cause people to hide their symptoms and to prevent them from getting necessary treatment for their mental illness symptoms. Stigma poses a barrier for public health primary prevention efforts designed to minimize the onset of mental illness, as well as with secondary prevention efforts aimed at promoting early treatment to prevent worsening of symptoms over time. Stigma can also interfere with the self-management of mental disorders (tertiary prevention). Untreated symptoms can have grave consequences for people living with mental illness and negatively impact families affected by these disorders. For example, most people with serious and persistent mental illness (mental disorders that interfere with some area of social functioning) are unemployed and live below the poverty line, and many face major barriers to obtaining decent, affordable housing. These individuals may need a number of additional social supports (e.g., job training, peer-support networks) to live successfully in the community, but such supports may not be available. Other individuals with depression and anxiety might avoid disclosing their symptoms and instead adopt unhealthy behaviors to help them cope with their distress (e.g., smoking, excessive alcohol use, binge-eating). These behaviors can increase their risk of developing chronic diseases, worsening their overall health over time. Studies have found an increased risk of death at younger ages for people with mental illness. State-level factors such as unemployment levels and access to mental-health services and the presence or absence of other state resources may affect public attitudes and merit study.

Chapter 7

Mental Health Statistics

Fast Facts on Mental Health
Mental Illness and Adults

- In 2015, there were an estimated 43.4 million adults—about 1 in 5 Americans aged 18 or older—with a mental illness within the previous year.

- In 2015, there were an estimated 9.8 million adults—about 1 in 25 Americans aged 18 or older—with serious mental illness. "Serious mental illness" is defined as individuals experiencing within the past year a mental illness or disorder with a serious functional impairment that substantially interferes with or limits one or more major life activities.

Mental Illness and Children and Teens

- Just over 20 percent—or 1 in 5—children, have had a seriously debilitating mental disorder.

- Half of all chronic mental illness begins by age 14 and three-quarters begin by age 24.

This chapter includes text excerpted from "Learn about Mental Health," Centers for Disease Control and Prevention (CDC), January 26, 2018.

Treatment

- A number of visits to physician offices with mental disorders as the primary diagnosis: 5.9 million.

- In 2015, 75 percent of children aged 4 to 17 received treatment for their mental disorders within a year.

Impact of Mental Illness

- Suicide, which is often associated with symptoms of mental illness, is the tenth leading cause of death in the United States and the second leading cause of death among people aged 15 to 34.

- Serious mental illness costs in the United States amount to $193.2 billion in lost earnings per year.

- Mood disorders, including major depression, dysthymic disorder, and bipolar disorder, are the third most common cause of hospitalization in the United States. for both youth and adults aged 18 to 44.

- Individuals living with serious mental illness face an increased risk of physical health problems, such as heart disease, diabetes, and human immunodeficiency virus (HIV), the virus that causes acquired immunodeficiency syndrome (AIDS).

- U.S. adults living with serious mental illness die on average 25 years earlier than others, largely due to treatable medical conditions.

Mental-Health Promotion and Prevention

Preventing mental illness and promoting good mental health involves actions to create living conditions and environments that support mental health and allow people to adopt and maintain healthy lifestyles. These include a range of actions to increase the chances of more people experiencing better mental health, such as:

- Early childhood interventions (for e.g., home visits for pregnant women and programs that help young children build social and emotional skills)

- Social support for elderly persons

- Programs targeted to people affected by disasters or other traumatic events

- Mental health interventions at work (for e.g., stress prevention programs)
- Violence prevention strategies (for e.g., reducing violence in the community and the home)
- Campaigns to change the culture of mental health so that all of those in need receive the care and support they deserve

Part Two

Mental Illnesses

Chapter 8

Types of Mental Illnesses

People can experience different types of mental illnesses or disorders, and they can often occur at the same time. Mental illnesses can occur over a short period of time or be episodic. This means that the mental illness comes and goes with discrete beginnings and ends. Mental illness can also be ongoing or long-lasting.

There are more than 200 classified types of mental illness. Some of the main types of mental illness and disorders are listed below; however, this list is not exhaustive.

Anxiety Disorders

People with anxiety disorders respond to certain objects or situations with fear and dread or terror. Anxiety disorders include generalized anxiety disorder, social anxiety, panic disorders, and phobias.

Attention Deficit Hyperactivity Disorder

Attention deficit hyperactivity disorder (ADHD) is one of the most common childhood mental disorders. It can continue through adolescence and adulthood. People diagnosed with ADHD may have trouble paying attention, controlling impulsive behaviors (may act without thinking about what the result will be), or be overly active.

This chapter includes text excerpted from "Learn about Mental Health," Centers for Disease Control and Prevention (CDC), January 26, 2018.

Disruptive Behavioral Disorders

Behavioral disorders involve a pattern of disruptive behaviors in children that last for at least six months and cause problems in school, at home, and in social situations. Behavioral symptoms can also continue into adulthood.

Depression and Other Mood Disorders

While bad moods are common and usually pass in a short period, people suffering from mood disorders live with more constant and severe symptoms. People living with this mental illness find that their mood impacts both mental and psychological well-being nearly every day, and often for much of the day.

It is estimated that one in ten adults suffer from some type of mood disorder, with the most common conditions being depression and bipolar disorder. With proper diagnosis and treatment, most of those living with mood disorders lead healthy, normal, and productive lives. If left untreated, this illness can affect role functioning, quality of life, and lead to long-lasting physical health problems such as diabetes and heart disease.

Eating Disorders

Eating disorders involve obsessive and sometimes distressing thoughts and behaviors, including:

- Reduction of food intake

- Overeating

- Feelings of depression or distress

- Concern about weight and body shape, a poor self-image

Common types of eating disorders include anorexia, bulimia, and binge eating.

Personality Disorders

People with personality disorders have extreme and inflexible personality traits that cause problems in work, school, or social relationships. Personality disorders include antisocial personality disorder and borderline personality disorder.

Posttraumatic Stress Disorder

A person can get posttraumatic stress disorder (PTSD) after living through or seeing a traumatic event, such as war, a hurricane, physical abuse, or a serious accident. PTSD can make someone feel stressed and afraid after the danger is over. People with PTSD may experience symptoms such as reliving the event over and over, sleep problems, become very upset if something causes memories of the event, constantly looking for possible threats, and changes in emotions such as irritability, outbursts, helplessness, or feelings of numbness.

Schizophrenia Spectrum and Other Psychotic Disorders

People with psychotic disorders hear, see, and believe things that aren't real or true. They may also show signs of disorganized thinking, confused speech, and muddled or abnormal motor behavior. An example of a psychotic disorder is schizophrenia. People with schizophrenia may also have low motivation and blunted emotions.

Substance-Use Disorders

Substance-use disorders (SUDs) occur when frequent or repeated use of alcohol and/or drugs causes significant impairment, such as health problems, disability, and failure to meet major responsibilities at work, school, or home. Substance-use problems can be fatal to the user or others. Examples include drunk driving fatalities and drug overdoses.

Mental illnesses and SUDs often occur together. Sometimes one disorder can be a contributing factor to or can make the other worse. Sometimes they simply occur at the same time.

Chapter 9

Suicide and Mental Illness

Chapter Contents

Section 9.1

Facts about Suicide

This section includes text excerpted from "Suicide Prevention,"
Centers for Disease Control and Prevention (CDC), June 6, 2018.

Suicide, death caused by self-directed injurious behavior with an
intent to die as a result of the behavior, is a serious public health
problem that can have lasting harmful effects on individuals, families,
and communities. Its causes are complex and determined by multiple
factors.

Risk Factors for Suicide

A combination of individual, relationship, community, and societal
factors contribute to the risk of suicide. Risk factors are those characteristics associated with suicide—they might not be direct causes.
Some of them are listed below.

- Family history of suicide
- Family history of child maltreatment
- Previous suicide attempt(s)
- History of mental-disorders, particularly clinical depression
- History of alcohol and substance abuse
- Feelings of hopelessness
- Impulsive or aggressive tendencies
- Cultural and religious beliefs (e.g., belief that suicide is noble
  resolution of a personal dilemma)
- Local epidemics of suicide
- Isolation, a feeling of being cut off from other people
- Barriers to accessing mental-health treatment
- Loss (relational, social, work, or financial)
- Physical illness
- Easy access to lethal methods
- Unwillingness to seek help because of the stigma attached to
  mental health and substance-abuse disorders (SUDs) or to
  suicidal thoughts

Protective Factors for Suicide

Protective factors buffer individuals from suicidal thoughts and behavior. To date, protective factors have not been studied as extensively or rigorously as risk factors. Identifying and understanding protective factors are, however, equally as important as researching risk factors. Some of the protective factors are listed below.

- Effective clinical care for mental, physical, and SUDs
- Easy access to a variety of clinical interventions and support for help-seeking
- Family and community support (connectedness)
- Support from ongoing medical and mental-healthcare relationships
- Skills in problem-solving, conflict resolution, and nonviolent ways of handling disputes
- Cultural and religious beliefs that discourage suicide and support instincts for self-preservation

Suicide: Consequences

Suicide and suicide attempts take an enormous toll on society.

- Suicide is the tenth leading cause of death among Americans.
- Nearly 45,000 people died by suicide in 2016.
- An estimated 1.3 million people made a suicide attempt in the past year.
- Almost 10 million adults reported having serious thoughts about suicide in the past year.
- Suicide and self-harm injuries cost society about $70 billion a year in combined medical and work loss costs.

Survivors

- A survivor of suicide is a family member or friend of a person who died by suicide.
- Surviving the loss of a loved one to suicide is a risk factor for suicide.
- Surviving family members and close friends are deeply impacted by each suicide and experience a range of complex

grief reactions, including, guilt, anger, abandonment, denial, helplessness, and shock.

- No exact figure exists, but it is estimated that between 6 and 32 survivors exist for each suicide, depending on the definition used.

- According to another estimate, approximately 7 percent of the U.S. population knew someone who died by suicide during the past 12 months.

Section 9.2

Suicide Rising across the United States

This section includes text excerpted from "Suicide Rates Rising across the U.S.," Centers for Disease Control and Prevention (CDC), June 7, 2018.

Suicide rates have been rising in nearly every state, according to the latest Vital Signs report by the Centers for Disease Control and Prevention (CDC). In 2016, nearly 45,000 Americans age 10 or older died by suicide. Suicide is the tenth leading cause of death and is one of just three leading causes that are on the rise.

Suicide is rarely caused by a single factor. Although suicide prevention efforts largely focus on identifying and providing treatment for people with mental-health conditions, there are many additional opportunities for prevention.

"Suicide is a leading cause of death for Americans—and it's a tragedy for families and communities across the country," said CDC Principal Deputy Director Anne Schuchat, M.D. "From individuals and communities to employers and healthcare professionals, everyone can play a role in efforts to help save lives and reverse this troubling rise in suicide."

Many Factors Contribute to Suicide

CDC researchers examined state-level trends in suicide rates from 1999 to 2016. In addition, they used 2015 data from the CDC National

Violent Death Reporting System (NVDRS), which covered 27 states, to look at the circumstances of suicide among people with and without known mental-health conditions.

Researchers found that more than half of people who died by suicide did not have a known diagnosed mental-health condition at the time of death. Relationship problems or loss; substance misuse; physical-health problems; and job, money, legal, or housing stress often contributed to the risk for suicide. Firearms were the most common method of suicide used by those with and without a known diagnosed mental-health condition.

State Suicide Rates Vary Widely

The most recent overall suicide rates (2014 to 2016) varied four-fold; from 6.9 per 100,000 residents per year in Washington, D.C. to 29.2 per 100,000 residents in Montana.

Across the study period, rates increased in nearly all states. Percentage increases in suicide rates ranged from just under six percent in Delaware to over 57 percent in North Dakota. Twenty-five states had suicide rate increases of more than 30 percent.

Wide Range of Prevention Activities Needed

The report recommends that states take a comprehensive public-health approach to suicide prevention and address the range of factors contributing to suicide. This requires coordination and cooperation from every sector of society: government, public-health, healthcare, employers, education, media, and community organizations.

To help states with this important work, in 2017 the CDC released a technical package on suicide prevention that describes strategies and approaches based on the best available evidence. This can help inform states and communities as they make decisions about prevention activities and priorities.

Everyone can help prevent suicide:

- Learn the warning signs of suicide in order to identify and appropriately respond to people at risk.

- Reduce access to lethal means—such as medications and firearms—among people at risk of suicide.

- Contact the National Suicide Prevention Lifeline (NSPL) for help at 800-273-8255.

The media can avoid increasing risk when reporting on suicide by:

- Providing information on suicide warning signs and suicide prevention resources; and

- Sharing stories of hope and healing.

Section 9.3

Questions about Suicide Risk

This section includes text excerpted from "Suicide in America: Frequently Asked Questions," National Institute of Mental Health (NIMH), February 9, 2018.

Suicide is a major public-health problem and a leading cause of death in the United States. The effects of suicide go beyond the person who acts to take her or his life: it can have a lasting effect on family, friends, and communities.

Who Is at Risk for Suicide?

Suicide does not discriminate. People of all genders, ages, and ethnicities can be at risk.

The main risk factors for suicide are:

- A prior suicide attempt

- Depression and other mental-health disorders

- Substance-abuse disorder (SUD)

- Family history of a mental health or SUD

- Family history of suicide

- Family violence, including physical or sexual abuse

- Having guns or other firearms in the home

- Being in prison or jail

- Being exposed to others' suicidal behavior, such as a family member, peer, or media figure

- Medical illness

- Being between the ages of 15 and 24 years of age or over 60

Even among people who have risk factors for suicide, most do not attempt suicide. It remains difficult to predict who will act on suicidal thoughts.

What Are the Warning Signs of Suicide?

The behaviors listed below may be signs that someone is thinking about suicide.

- Talking about wanting to die or wanting to kill themselves

- Talking about feeling empty, hopeless, or having no reason to live

- Planning or looking for a way to kill themselves, such as searching online, stockpiling pills, or newly acquiring potentially lethal items (e.g., firearms or ropes)

- Talking about great guilt or shame

- Talking about feeling trapped or feeling that there are no solutions

- Feeling unbearable pain, both physical or emotional

- Talking about being a burden to others

- Using alcohol or drugs more often

- Acting anxious or agitated

- Withdrawing from family and friends

- Changing eating and/or sleeping habits

- Showing rage or talking about seeking revenge

- Taking risks that could lead to death, such as reckless driving

- Talking or thinking about death often

- Displaying extreme mood swings, suddenly changing from very sad to very calm or happy

- Giving away important possessions

- Saying goodbye to friends and family

- Putting affairs in order, making a will

Do People Threaten Suicide to Get Attention?

Suicidal thoughts or actions are a sign of extreme distress and a warning that someone needs help. Any warning sign or symptom of suicide should not be ignored. All talk of suicide should be taken seriously and requires attention. Threatening to die by suicide is not a normal response to stress and should not be taken lightly.

If You Ask Someone about Suicide, Does It Put the Idea into Their Head?

Asking someone about suicide is not harmful. There is a common myth that asking someone about suicide can put the idea into their head. This is not true. Several studies examining this concern have demonstrated that asking people about suicidal thoughts and behavior does not induce or increase such thoughts and experiences. In fact, asking someone directly, "Are you thinking of killing yourself," can be the best way to identify someone at risk for suicide.

What Should You Do If You Are in Crisis or Someone You Know Is Considering Suicide?

If you or someone you know has warning signs or symptoms of suicide, particularly if there is a change in behavior or new behavior, get help as soon as possible.

Often, family and friends are the first to recognize the warning signs of suicide and can take the first step toward helping an at-risk individual find treatment with someone who specializes in diagnosing and treating mental-health conditions. If someone is telling you that they are going to kill themselves, do not leave them alone. Do not promise anyone that you will keep their suicidal thoughts a secret. Make sure to tell a trusted friend or family member, or, if you are a student, an adult with whom you feel comfortable. You can also contact the resources provided later in this section.

What If Someone Is Posting Suicidal Messages on Social Media?

Knowing how to get help for a friend posting suicidal messages on social media can save a life. Many social media sites have a process to report suicidal content and get help for the person posting the message. In addition, many of the social media sites use their analytic capabilities to identify and help report suicidal posts. Each offers different options on how to respond if you see concerning posts about suicide. For example:

- Facebook's suicide prevention webpage can be found at www. facebook.com (use the search term "suicide" or "suicide prevention").

- Instagram uses automated tools in the app to provide resources, which can also be found online at help.instagram.com (use the search term, "suicide," self-injury," or "suicide prevention").

- Snapchat's support provides guidance at support.snapchat.com (use the search term, "suicide" or "suicide prevention").

- Tumblr counseling and prevention resources webpage can be found at tumblr.zendesk.com (use the search term "counseling" or "prevention," then click on "Counseling and prevention resources").

- Twitter's best practices in dealing with self-harm and suicide at support.twitter.com (use the search term "suicide," "self-harm," or "suicide prevention").

- YouTube's safety center webpage can be found at support.google. com/youtube (use the search term "suicide and self-injury").

If you see messages or live streaming suicidal behavior on social media, call 911 or contact the toll-free National Suicide Prevention Lifeline (NSPL) at 800-273-8255, or text the crisis text line (text HOME to 741741) available 24 hours a day, 7 days a week. Deaf and hard-of-hearing individuals can contact the Lifeline via TTY at 800-799-4889. All calls are confidential. This service is available to every-one. People—even strangers—have saved lives by being vigilant.

Section 9.4

Suicide Prevention

This section contains text excerpted from the following
sources: Text in this section begins with excerpts from "Preventing
Suicide," Centers for Disease Control and Prevention (CDC),
September 10, 2018; Text under the heading "Five Action
Steps for Helping Someone in Emotional Pain" is excerpted
from "Suicide Prevention," National Institute of Mental
Health (NIMH), March 2017.

Suicide can be prevented. September tenth is World Suicide Prevention Day (WSPD), and the entire month is dedicated to suicide prevention awareness in the United States. Help prevent suicide in your community by knowing the warning signs and where to get help.

Suicide is a serious public-health problem that affects people of all ages.

- Suicide is the tenth leading cause of death for Americans overall and the second leading cause of death among young people ages 10 to 34.

- Suicide rates increased more than 30 percent in half of U.S. states since 1999.

- In 2016, nearly 45,000 lives were lost to suicide across the United States.

Deaths from suicide are only part of the problem.

- More than 1.3 million adults self-reported a suicide attempt.

- Almost 10 million adults self-reported serious thoughts of suicide.

Everyone Can Know the Warning Signs and Get Help

Suicide has warning signs, such as expressing hopelessness, threatening to hurt oneself, or talking about wanting to die; increasing alcohol and drug use; and withdrawing from friends and family.

If you or someone you know is having thoughts of suicide, contact the National Suicide Prevention Lifeline (NSPL) at 800-273-8255 or visit the National Suicide Prevention Lifeline.

Five Action Steps for Helping Someone in Emotional Pain

Step 1. Ask. "Are you thinking about killing yourself?" It's not an easy question, but studies show that asking at-risk individuals if they are suicidal does not increase suicides or suicidal thoughts.

Step 2. Keep them safe. Reducing a suicidal person's access to highly lethal items or places is an important part of suicide prevention. While this is not always easy, asking if the at-risk person has a plan and removing or disabling the lethal means can make a difference.

Step 3. Be there. Listen carefully and learn what the individual is thinking and feeling. Findings suggest acknowledging and talking about suicide may in fact reduce rather than increase suicidal thoughts.

Step 4. Help them connect. Save the National Suicide Prevention Lifeline's (NSPL) number in your phone so it's there when you need it: 800-273-8255. You can also help make a connection with a trusted individual such as a family member, friend, spiritual advisor, or mental-health professional.

Step 5. Stay connected. Staying in touch after a crisis or after being discharged from care can make a difference. Studies have shown the number of suicide deaths goes down when someone follows up with the at-risk person.

Section 9.5

Treatments and Therapies

This section includes text excerpted from "Suicide Prevention,"
National Institute of Mental Health (NIMH), March 2017.

Research has shown that there are multiple risk factors for suicide and that these factors may vary with age, gender, physical and mental well-being, and with individual experiences. Treatments and therapies for people with suicidal thoughts or actions will vary as well.

Psychotherapies

Multiple types of psychosocial interventions have been found to be beneficial for individuals who have attempted suicide. These types of interventions may prevent someone from making another attempt. Psychotherapy, or "talk therapy," is one type of psychosocial intervention and can effectively reduce suicide risk.

One type of psychotherapy is called cognitive behavioral therapy (CBT). CBT can help people learn new ways of dealing with stressful experiences through training. CBT helps individuals recognize their own thought patterns and consider alternative actions when thoughts of suicide arise.

Another type of psychotherapy, called dialectical behavior therapy (DBT), has been shown to reduce the rate of suicide among people with borderline personality disorder, a serious mental illness characterized by unstable moods, relationships, self-image, and behavior. A therapist trained in DBT helps a person recognize when her or his feelings or actions are disruptive or unhealthy, and teaches the skills needed to deal better with upsetting situations.

National Institute of Mental Health's (NIMH) Find Help for Mental Illnesses page (www.nimh.nih.gov/health/find-help/index.shtml) can help you locate a mental-health provider in your area.

Medication

Some individuals at risk for suicide might benefit from medication. Doctors and patients can work together to find the best medication or medication combination, as well as the right dose.

Clozapine is an antipsychotic medication used primarily to treat individuals with schizophrenia. However, it is the only medication with a specific U.S. Food and Drug Administration (FDA) indication for reducing the risk of recurrent suicidal behavior in patients with schizophrenia or schizoaffective disorder who are at risk for ongoing suicidal behavior. Because many individuals at risk for suicide often have psychiatric and substance-use problems, individuals might benefit from medication along with psychosocial intervention.

If you are prescribed a medication, be sure you:

- Talk with your doctor or a pharmacist to make sure you understand the risks and benefits of the medications you're taking

- Do not stop taking a medication without talking to your doctor first. Suddenly stopping a medication may lead to "rebound," or a worsening of symptoms. Other uncomfortable or potentially dangerous withdrawal effects also are possible.

- Report any concerns about side effects to your doctor right away. You may need a change in the dose or a different medication.

- Report serious side effects to the FDA MedWatch Adverse Event Reporting program online or by phone at 800-332-1088. You or your doctor may send a report.

Other medications have been used to treat suicidal thoughts and behaviors, but more research is needed to show the benefit of these options. For basic information about these medications, you can visit the NIMH Mental Health Medications webpage (www.nimh.nih.gov/health/topics/mental-health-medications/index.shtml). For the most up-to-date information on medications, side effects, and warnings, visit the FDA website (www.fda.gov).

Chapter 10

Depressive Disorders

Chapter Contents

Section 10.1

Depression

This section includes text excerpted from "Depression Basics," National Institute of Mental Health (NIMH), December 2016.

Do you feel sad, empty, and hopeless most of the day, nearly every day? Have you lost interest or pleasure in your hobbies or being with friends and family? Are you having trouble sleeping, eating, and functioning? If you have felt this way for at least two weeks, you may have depression, a serious but treatable mood disorder.

What Is Depression?

Everyone feels sad or low sometimes, but these feelings usually pass with a little time. Depression—also called "clinical depression" or a "depressive disorder"—is a mood disorder that causes distressing symptoms that affect how you feel, think, and handle daily activities such as sleeping, eating, or working. A diagnosis of depression requires symptoms to be present most of the day, nearly every day for at least two weeks.

What Are the Different Types of Depression?

Two of the most common forms of depression are:

- **Major depression**—having symptoms of depression most of the day, nearly every day, for at least two weeks that interfere with your ability to work, sleep, study, eat, and enjoy life. An episode can occur only once in a person's lifetime, but A person more often has several episodes.

- **Persistent depressive disorder (PDD) (Dysthymia)**— having symptoms of depression that last for at least two years. A person diagnosed with this form of depression may have episodes of major depression along with periods of less severe symptoms.

Some forms of depression are slightly different, or they may develop under unique circumstances, such as:

- **Perinatal depression.** Women with perinatal depression experience full-blown major depression during pregnancy or after delivery (postpartum depression).

- **Seasonal affective disorder (SAD).** SAD is a type of depression that comes and goes with the seasons, typically starting in the late fall and early winter and going away during the spring and summer.

- **Psychotic depression.** This type of depression occurs when a person has severe depression plus some form of psychosis, such as having disturbing false, and fixed beliefs (delusions) or hearing or seeing upsetting things that others cannot hear or see (hallucinations).

Other examples of depressive disorders include disruptive mood dysregulation disorder (diagnosed in children and adolescents) and premenstrual dysphoric disorder. Depression can also be one phase of bipolar disorder (formerly called manic-depression). But a person with bipolar disorder also experiences extreme high—euphoric or irritable—moods called "mania" or a less severe form called "hypomania."

What Causes Depression

Scientists at the National Institute of Mental Health (NIMH) and across the country are studying the causes of depression. Research suggests that a combination of genetic, biological, environmental, and psychological factors play a role in depression.

Depression can occur along with other serious illnesses, such as diabetes, cancer, heart disease, and Parkinson disease (PD). Depression can make these conditions worse and vice versa. Sometimes medications taken for these illnesses may cause side effects that contribute to depression symptoms.

What Are the Signs and Symptoms of Depression?

Sadness is only one small part of depression and some people with depression may not feel sadness at all. Different people have different symptoms. Some symptoms of depression include:

- Persistent sad, anxious, or "empty" mood

- Feelings of hopelessness or pessimism

- Feelings of guilt, worthlessness, or helplessness

- Loss of interest or pleasure in hobbies or activities

- Decreased energy, fatigue, or being "slowed down"

- Difficulty concentrating, remembering, or making decisions
- Difficulty sleeping, early-morning awakening, or oversleeping
- Appetite and/or weight changes
- Thoughts of death or suicide or suicide attempts
- Restlessness or irritability
- Aches or pains, headaches, cramps, or digestive problems without a clear physical cause and/or that do not ease even with treatment

Does Depression Look the Same in Everyone?

No. Depression affects different people in different ways. For example:

Women have depression more often than men. Biological, life cycle, and hormonal factors that are unique to women may be linked to their higher depression rate. Women with depression typically have symptoms of sadness, worthlessness, and guilt.

Men with depression are more likely to be very tired, irritable, and sometimes angry. They may lose interest in work or activities they once enjoyed, have sleep problems, and behave recklessly, including the misuse of drugs or alcohol. Many men do not recognize their depression and fail to seek help.

Older adults with depression may have less obvious symptoms, or they may be less likely to admit to feelings of sadness or grief. They are also more likely to have medical conditions, such as heart disease, which may cause or contribute to depression.

Younger children with depression may pretend to be sick, refuse to go to school, cling to a parent, or worry that a parent may die.

Older children and teens with depression may get into trouble at school, sulk, and be irritable. Teens with depression may have symptoms of other disorders, such as anxiety, eating disorders, or substance abuse.

How Is Depression Treated?

The first step in getting the right treatment is to visit a health-care provider or mental-health professional, such as a psychiatrist or psychologist. Your healthcare provider can do an exam, interview, and lab tests to rule out other health conditions that may have the same symptoms as depression. Once diagnosed, depression can be treated with medications, psychotherapy, or a combination of the two. If these treatments do not reduce symptoms, brain stimulation therapy may be another treatment option to explore.

Medications

Medications called antidepressants can work well to treat depression. They can take two to four weeks to work. Antidepressants can have side effects, but many side effects may lessen over time. Talk to your healthcare provider about any side effects that you have. Do not stop taking your antidepressant without first talking to your healthcare provider.

Please Note. *Although antidepressants can be effective for many people, they may present serious risks to some, especially children, teens, and young adults. Antidepressants may cause some people, especially those who become agitated when they first start taking the medication and before it begins to work, to have suicidal thoughts or make suicide attempts. Anyone taking antidepressants should be monitored closely, especially when they first start taking them. For most people, though, the risks of untreated depression far outweigh those of antidepressant medications when they are used under a doctor's careful supervision. Information about medications changes frequently.*

Psychotherapy

Psychotherapy helps by teaching new ways of thinking and behaving, and changing habits that may be contributing to depression. Therapy can help you understand and work through difficult relationships or situations that may be causing your depression or making it worse.

Brain Stimulation Therapies

Electroconvulsive therapy (ECT) and other brain stimulation therapies may be an option for people with severe depression who do not respond to antidepressant medications. ECT is the best-studied brain stimulation therapy and has the longest history of use. Other stimulation therapies discussed here are newer, and in some cases still experimental methods.

How Can You Help Yourself If You Are Depressed?

As you continue treatment, you may start to feel better gradually. Remember that if you are taking an antidepressant, it may take two to four weeks to start working. Try to do things that you used to enjoy. Go easy on yourself. Other things that may help include:

- Trying to be active and exercise

- Breaking up large tasks into small ones, setting priorities, and doing what you can as you can

- Spending time with other people and confiding in a trusted friend or relative

- Postponing important life decisions until you feel better. Discuss decisions with others who know you well.

- Avoiding self-medication with alcohol or with drugs not prescribed for you

How Can You Help a Loved One Who Is Depressed?

If you know someone who has depression, first help her or him see a healthcare provider or mental-health professional. You can also:

- Offer support, understanding, patience, and encouragement.

- Never ignore comments about suicide, and report them to your loved one's healthcare provider or therapist.

- Invite her or him out for walks, outings, and other activities.

- Help her or him adhere to the treatment plan, such as setting reminders to take prescribed medications.

- Help her or him by ensuring that transportation is available for therapy appointments.

- Remind her or him that, with time and treatment, the depression will lift.

Where Can You Go for Help?

If you are unsure where to go for help, ask your health provider or check out the NIMH Help for Mental Illnesses website (www.nimh.nih. gov/findhelp). Another federal health agency, the Substance Abuse and Mental Health Services Administration (SAMHSA), maintains an online behavioral-health treatment services locator (findtreatment.samhsa.gov).

You can also check online for mental-health professionals; contact your community health center, local mental-health association, or insurance plan to find a mental-health professional. Hospital doctors can help in an emergency.

If you or someone you know is in crisis, get help quickly.

- Call your or your loved one's mental-health professional.

- Call 911 for emergency services.

- Go to the nearest hospital emergency room.

- Call the toll-free, 24-hour hotline of the National Suicide Prevention Lifeline (NSPL) at 800-273-8255; TTY: 800-799-4889.

Section 10.2

Persistent Depressive Disorder

This section includes text excerpted from "Persistent Depressive Disorder (Dysthymic Disorder)," National Institute of Mental Health (NIMH), November 2017.

Persistent depressive disorder (formerly dysthymic disorder) is characterized by chronic low-level depression that is not as severe but may be longer lasting than, major depressive disorder. A diagnosis of persistent depressive disorder requires having experienced a combination of depressive symptoms for two years or more.

Prevalence of Persistent Depressive Disorder among Adults

The diagnostic interview data from National Comorbidity Survey Replication (NCS-R), shows the prevalence of persistent depressive disorder among U.S. adults aged 18 or older. An estimated 1.5 percent of U.S. adults had persistent depressive disorder in the past year. It also reveals that the prevalence of persistent depressive disorder among adults was higher for females (1.9%) than for males (1.0%). An estimated 1.3 percent of U.S. adults experience persistent depressive disorder at some time in their lives.

Persistent Depressive Disorder with Impairment among Adults

Of adults with persistent depressive disorder, the degree of impairment ranged from mild to severe. Impairment was determined by scores on the Sheehan Disability Scale. An estimated 49.7 percent of people with persistent depressive disorder had serious impairment, 32.1 percent had moderate impairment, and 18.2 percent had mild impairment.

Section 10.3

Seasonal Affective Disorder

This section includes text excerpted from "Seasonal Affective Disorder," National Institute of Mental Health (NIMH), March 2016.

Seasonal affective disorder (SAD) is a type of depression that comes and goes with the seasons, typically starting in the late fall and early winter and going away during the spring and summer. Depressive episodes linked to the summer can occur but are much less common than winter episodes of SAD.

Signs and Symptoms of Seasonal Affective Disorder

SAD is not considered as a separate disorder. It is a type of depression displaying a recurring seasonal pattern. To be diagnosed with SAD, people must meet full criteria for major depression coinciding with specific seasons (appearing in the winter or summer months) for at least two years. Seasonal depressions must be much more frequent than any nonseasonal depressions.

Symptoms of Major Depression

The symptoms of major depression include:

• Feeling depressed most of the day, nearly every day

- Feeling hopeless or worthless
- Having low energy
- Losing interest in activities you once enjoyed
- Having problems with sleep
- Experiencing changes in your appetite or weight
- Feeling sluggish or agitated
- Having difficulty concentrating
- Having frequent thoughts of death or suicide

Symptoms of the winter pattern of SAD include:

- Having low energy
- Hypersomnia
- Overeating
- Weight gain
- Craving for carbohydrates
- Social withdrawal (feel like "hibernating")

Symptoms of the less frequently occurring summer SAD include:

- Poor appetite with associated weight loss
- Insomnia
- Agitation
- Restlessness
- Anxiety
- Episodes of violent behavior

Risk Factors of Seasonal Affective Disorder

Attributes that may increase your risk of SAD include:

- **Being female.** SAD is diagnosed four times more often in women than men.
- **Living far from the equator.** SAD is more frequent in people who live far north or south of the equator. For example, one percent of those who live in Florida and nine percent of those who live in New England or Alaska suffer from SAD.

- **Family history.** People with a family history of other types of depression are more likely to develop SAD than people who do not have a family history of depression.

- **Having depression or bipolar disorder.** The symptoms of depression may worsen with the seasons if you have one of these conditions (but SAD is diagnosed only if seasonal depressions are the most common).

- **Younger age.** Younger adults have a higher risk of SAD than older adults. SAD has been reported even in children and teens.

The causes of SAD are unknown, but research has found some biological clues:

- People with SAD may have trouble regulating one of the key neurotransmitters involved in mood, serotonin. One study found that people with SAD have five percent more serotonin transporter protein in winter months than summer months. Higher serotonin transporter protein leaves less serotonin available at the synapse because the function of the transporter is to recycle neurotransmitter back into the presynaptic neuron.

- People with SAD may overproduce the hormone melatonin. Darkness increases production of melatonin, which regulates sleep. As winter days become shorter, melatonin production increases, leaving people with SAD to feel sleepier and more lethargic, often with delayed circadian rhythms.

- People with SAD also may produce less Vitamin D. Vitamin D is believed to play a role in serotonin activity. Vitamin D insufficiency may be associated with clinically significant depression symptoms.

Treatments and Therapies for Seasonal Affective Disorder

There are four major types of treatment for SAD:

- Medication
- Light therapy
- Psychotherapy
- Vitamin D

These may be used alone or in combination.

Medication

Selective serotonin reuptake inhibitors (SSRIs) are used to treat SAD. The U.S. Food and Drug Administration (FDA) has also approved the use of bupropion, another type of antidepressant, for treating SAD.

As with other medications, there are side effects to SSRIs. Talk to your doctor about the possible risks of using this medication for your condition. You may need to try several different antidepressant medications before finding the one that improves your symptoms without causing problematic side effects. Check the FDA's website for the latest information on warnings, patient medication guides, or newly approved medications.

Light Therapy

Light therapy has been a mainstay of treatment for SAD since the 1980s. The idea behind light therapy is to replace the diminished sunshine of the fall and winter months using daily exposure to bright, artificial light. Symptoms of SAD may be relieved by sitting in front of a light box first thing in the morning, on a daily basis from the early fall until spring. Most typically, light boxes filter out the ultraviolet rays and require 20 to 60 minutes of exposure to 10,000 lux of cool-white fluorescent light, an amount that is about 20 times greater than ordinary indoor lighting.

Psychotherapy

Cognitive-behavioral therapy (CBT) is a type of psychotherapy that is effective for SAD. Traditional CBT has been adapted for use with SAD (CBT-SAD). CBT-SAD relies on basic techniques of CBT such as identifying negative thoughts and replacing them with more positive thoughts along with a technique called behavioral activation. Behavioral activation seeks to help the person identify activities that are engaging and pleasurable, whether indoors or outdoors, to improve coping with winter.

Vitamin D

At present, vitamin D supplementation by itself is not regarded as an effective SAD treatment. The reason behind its use is that low blood levels of vitamin D were found in people with SAD. The low levels are usually due to insufficient dietary intake or insufficient exposure to sunshine. However, the evidence for its use has been mixed. While some studies suggest vitamin D supplementation may be as effective as light therapy, others found vitamin D had no effect.

Chapter 11

Bipolar Disorder

Bipolar disorder, also known as manic-depressive illness, is a brain disorder that causes unusual shifts in mood, energy, activity levels, and the ability to carry out day-to-day tasks.

There are four basic types of bipolar disorder; all of them involve clear changes in mood, energy, and activity levels. These moods range from periods of extremely "up," elated, and energized behavior (known as manic episodes) to very sad, "down," or hopeless periods (known as depressive episodes). Less severe manic periods are known as hypomanic episodes.

1. **Bipolar I disorder** is defined by manic episodes that last at least seven days, or by manic symptoms that are so severe that the person needs immediate hospital care. Usually, depressive episodes occur as well, typically lasting at least two weeks. Episodes of depression with mixed features (having depression and manic symptoms at the same time) are also possible.

2. **Bipolar II disorder** is defined by a pattern of depressive episodes and hypomanic episodes, but not the full-blown manic episodes described above.

3. **Cyclothymic disorder (also called cyclothymia)** is defined by numerous periods of hypomanic symptoms as well as

This chapter includes text excerpted from "Bipolar Disorder," National Institute of Mental Health (NIMH), April 2016.

numerous periods of depressive symptoms lasting for at least two years (one year in children and adolescents). However, the symptoms do not meet the diagnostic requirements for a hypomanic episode and a depressive episode.

4. **Other specified and unspecified bipolar and related disorders** is defined by bipolar disorder symptoms that do not match the three categories listed above.

Signs and Symptoms of Bipolar Disorder

People with bipolar disorder experience periods of unusually intense emotion, changes in sleep patterns and activity levels, and unusual behaviors. These distinct periods are called "mood episodes." Mood episodes are drastically different from the moods and behaviors that are typical for the person. Extreme changes in energy, activity, and sleep go along with mood episodes.

Table 11.1. Bipolar Disorder Symptoms

People having a manic episode may:	People having a depressive episode may:
Feel very "up," "high," or elated	Feel very sad, down, empty, or hopeless
Have a lot of energy	Have very little energy
Have increased activity levels	Have decreased activity levels
Feel "jumpy" or "wired"	Have trouble sleeping, they may sleep too little or too much
Have trouble sleeping	Feel like they can't enjoy anything
Become more active than usual	Feel worried and empty
Talk really fast about a lot of different things	Have trouble concentrating
Be agitated, irritable, or "touchy"	Forget things a lot
Feel like their thoughts are going very fast	Eat too much or too little
Think they can do a lot of things at once	Feel tired or "slowed down"
Do risky things, like spend a lot of money or have reckless sex	Think about death or suicide

Sometimes a mood episode includes symptoms of both manic and depressive symptoms. This is called an episode with mixed features.

People experiencing an episode with mixed features may feel very sad, empty, or hopeless, while at the same time feeling extremely energized.

Bipolar disorder can be present even when mood swings are less extreme. For example, some people with bipolar disorder experience hypomania, a less severe form of mania. During a hypomanic episode, an individual may feel very good, be highly productive, and function well. The person may not feel that anything is wrong, but family and friends may recognize the mood swings and/or changes in activity levels as a possible bipolar disorder. Without proper treatment, people with hypomania may develop severe mania or depression.

Diagnosis of Bipolar Disorder

Proper diagnosis and treatment help people with bipolar disorder lead healthy and productive lives. Talking with a doctor or other licensed mental-health professional is the first step for anyone who thinks she or he may have bipolar disorder. The doctor can complete a physical exam to rule out other conditions. If the problems are not caused by other illnesses, the doctor may conduct a mental-health evaluation or provide a referral to a trained mental-health professional, such as a psychiatrist, who is experienced in diagnosing and treating bipolar disorder.

Bipolar Disorder and Other Illnesses

Some bipolar disorder symptoms are similar to other illnesses, which can make it hard for a doctor to make a diagnosis. In addition, many people have bipolar disorder along with another illness, such as anxiety disorder, substance abuse, or an eating disorder. People with bipolar disorder are also at higher risk for thyroid disease, migraine headaches, heart disease, diabetes, obesity, and other physical illnesses.

Psychosis. Sometimes, a person with severe episodes of mania or depression also has psychotic symptoms, such as hallucinations or delusions. The psychotic symptoms tend to match a person's extreme mood. For example:

- Someone having psychotic symptoms during a manic episode may believe she is famous, has a lot of money, or has special powers

- Someone having psychotic symptoms during a depressive episode may believe he is ruined and penniless, or that he has committed a crime

As a result, people with bipolar disorder who also have psychotic symptoms are sometimes misdiagnosed with schizophrenia.

Anxiety and attention deficit hyperactivity disorder (ADHD). Anxiety disorders and ADHD are often diagnosed among people with bipolar disorder.

Substance abuse. People with bipolar disorder may also misuse alcohol or drugs, have relationship problems, or perform poorly in school or at work. Family, friends, and people experiencing symptoms may not recognize these problems as signs of a major mental illness such as bipolar disorder.

Risk Factors for Bipolar Disorder

Scientists are studying the possible causes of bipolar disorder. Most agree that there is no single cause. Instead, it is likely that many factors contribute to the illness or increase risk.

Brain structure and functioning. Some studies show how the brains of people with bipolar disorder may differ from the brains of healthy people or people with other mental disorders. Learning more about these differences, along with new information from genetic studies, helps scientists better understand bipolar disorder and predict which types of treatment will work most effectively.

Genetics. Some research suggests that people with certain genes are more likely to develop bipolar disorder than others. But genes are not the only risk factor for bipolar disorder. Studies of identical twins have shown that even if one twin develops bipolar disorder, the other twin does not always develop the disorder, despite the fact that identical twins share all of the same genes.

Family history. Bipolar disorder tends to run in families. Children with a parent or sibling who has bipolar disorder are much more likely to develop the illness, compared with children who do not have a family history of the disorder. However, it is important to note that most people with a family history of bipolar disorder will not develop the illness.

Treatments and Therapies for Bipolar Disorder

Treatment helps many people—even those with the most severe forms of bipolar disorder—gain better control of their mood swings and other bipolar symptoms. An effective treatment plan usually includes a combination of medication and psychotherapy (also called "talk therapy"). Bipolar disorder is a lifelong illness. Episodes of mania and depression typically come back over time. Between episodes, many people with bipolar disorder are free of mood changes, but some people may have lingering symptoms. Long-term, continuous treatment helps to control these symptoms.

Medications for Bipolar Disorder

Different types of medications can help control symptoms of bipolar disorder. An individual may need to try several different medications before finding ones that work best.

Medications generally used to treat bipolar disorder include:

- Mood stabilizers

- Atypical antipsychotics

- Antidepressants

Anyone taking a medication should:

- Talk with a doctor or a pharmacist to understand the risks and benefits of the medication

- Report any concerns about side effects to a doctor right away. The doctor may need to change the dose or try a different medication.

- Avoid stopping a medication without talking to a doctor first. Suddenly stopping a medication may lead to "rebound" or worsening of bipolar disorder symptoms. Other uncomfortable or potentially dangerous withdrawal effects are also possible.

Psychotherapy

When done in combination with medication, psychotherapy (also called "talk therapy") can be an effective treatment for bipolar disorder. It can provide support, education, and guidance to people with bipolar disorder and their families. Some psychotherapy treatments used to treat bipolar disorder include:

- Cognitive-behavioral therapy (CBT)
- Family-focused therapy (FFT)
- Interpersonal and social rhythm therapy (SRT)
- Psychoeducation

Other Treatment Options

Electroconvulsive therapy (ECT). ECT can provide relief for people with a severe bipolar disorder who have not been able to recover with other treatments. Sometimes ECT is used for bipolar symptoms when other medical conditions, including pregnancy, make taking medications too risky. ECT may cause some short-term side effects, including confusion, disorientation, and memory loss. People with bipolar disorder should discuss possible benefits and risks of ECT with a qualified health professional.

Sleep medications. People with bipolar disorder who have trouble sleeping usually find that treatment is helpful. However, if sleeplessness does not improve, a doctor may suggest a change in medications. If the problem continues, the doctor may prescribe sedatives or other sleep medications.

Keeping a life chart. Even with proper treatment, mood changes can occur. Treatment is more effective when a client and doctor work closely together and talk openly about concerns and choices. Keeping a life chart that records daily mood symptoms, treatments, sleep patterns, and life events can help clients and doctors track and treat bipolar disorder most effectively.

Chapter 12

Anxiety Disorders

Chapter Contents

Section 12.1

Understanding Anxiety Disorders

This section includes text excerpted from "Understanding
Anxiety Disorders," *NIH News in Health*, National
Institutes of Health (NIH), March 2016.

Many of us worry from time to time. We fret over finances, feel
anxious about job interviews, or get nervous about social gatherings.
These feelings can be normal or even helpful. They may give us a boost
of energy or help us focus. But for people with anxiety disorders, they
can be overwhelming.

Anxiety disorders affect nearly one in five American adults each
year. People with these disorders have feelings of fear and uncertainty
that interfere with everyday activities and last for six months or more.
Anxiety disorders can also raise your risk for other medical problems
such as heart disease, diabetes, substance abuse, and depression.

The good news is that most anxiety disorders get better with therapy. The course of treatment depends on the type of anxiety disorder.
Medications, psychotherapy ("talk therapy"), or a combination of both
can usually relieve troubling symptoms.

"Anxiety disorders are one of the most treatable mental-health
problems we see," says Dr. Daniel Pine, a National Institutes of Health
(NIH) neuroscientist and psychiatrist. "Still, for reasons we don't fully
understand, most people who have these problems don't get the treatments that could really help them."

One of the most common types of anxiety disorder is social anxiety disorder (SAD), or social phobia. It affects both women and men
equally—a total of about 15 million U.S. adults. Without treatment,
social phobia can last for years or even a lifetime. People with social
phobia may worry for days or weeks before a social event. They're often
embarrassed, self-conscious, and afraid of being judged. They find it
hard to talk to others. They may blush, sweat, tremble, or feel sick to
their stomachs when around other people.

Other common types of anxiety disorders include generalized anxiety disorder (GAD), which affects nearly seven million American
adults, and panic disorder, which affects about six million. Both are
twice as common in women as in men.

People with GAD worry endlessly over everyday issues—such as
health, money, or family problems—even if they realize there's little
cause for concern. They startle easily, can't relax, and can't concentrate.

They find it hard to fall asleep or stay asleep. They may get headaches, muscle aches, or unexplained pains. Symptoms often get worse during times of stress.

People with panic disorder have sudden, repeated bouts of fear—called panic attacks—that last several minutes or more. During a panic attack, they may feel that they can't breathe or that they're having a heart attack. They may fear loss of control or feel a sense of unreality. Not everyone who has panic attacks will develop panic disorder. But if the attacks recur without warning, creating fear of having another attack at any time, then it's likely panic disorder.

Anxiety disorders tend to run in families. But researchers aren't certain why some family members develop these conditions while others don't. No specific genes have been found to actually cause an anxiety disorder. "Many different factors—including genes, stress, and the environment—have small effects that add up in complex ways to affect a person's risk for these disorders," Pine says.

"Many kids with anxiety disorders will outgrow their conditions. But most anxiety problems we see in adults started during their childhood," Pine adds.

"Anxiety disorders are among the most common psychiatric disorders in children, with an estimated one in three suffering anxiety at some point during childhood or adolescence," says Dr. Susan Whitfield-Gabrieli, a brain imaging expert at the Massachusetts Institute of Technology (MIT). "About half of diagnosable mental-health disorders start by age 14, so there's a lot of interest in uncovering the factors that might influence the brain by those early teen years."

Whitfield-Gabrieli is launching a National Institutes of Health (NIH)-funded study to create detailed magnetic resonance imaging (MRI) images of the brains of more than 200 teens, ages 14 to 15, with and without anxiety or depression. The scientists will then assess what brain structures and activities might be linked to these conditions. The study is part of NIH's Human Connectome Project, in which research teams across the country are studying the complex brain connections that affect health and disease.

Whitfield-Gabrieli and colleagues have shown that analysis of brain connections might help predict which adults with social phobia will likely respond to cognitive-behavioral therapy (CBT). CBT is a type of talk therapy known to be effective for people with anxiety disorders. It helps them change their thinking patterns and how they react to anxiety-provoking situations. But it doesn't work for everyone.

Of 38 adults with social phobia, those who responded best after three months of CBT had similar patterns of brain connections. This brain analysis led to major improvement, compared to a clinician's assessment alone, in predicting treatment response. Larger studies will be needed to confirm the benefits of the approach.

"Ultimately, we hope that brain imaging will help us predict clinical outcomes and actually tailor the treatment to each individual—to know whether they'll respond best to psychotherapy or to certain medications," Whitfield-Gabrieli says.

Other researchers are focusing on our emotions and our ability to adjust them. "We want to understand not only how emotions can help us but also how they can create difficulties if they're of the wrong intensity or the wrong type for a particular situation," says Dr. James Gross, a clinical psychologist at Stanford University.

We all use different strategies to adjust our emotions, often without thinking about it. If something makes you angry, you may try to tamp down your emotion to avoid making a scene. If something annoys you, you might try to ignore it, modify it, or entirely avoid it.

But these strategies can turn harmful over time. For instance, people with social phobia might decide to avoid attending a professional conference so they can keep their anxiety in check. That makes them lose opportunities at work and miss chances to meet people and make friends.

Gross and others are examining the differences between how people with and without anxiety disorders regulate their emotions. "We're finding that CBT is helpful in part because it teaches people to more effectively use emotion regulation strategies," Gross says. "They then become more competent in their ability to use these strategies in their everyday lives."

"It's important to be aware that many different kinds of treatments are available, and people with anxiety disorders tend to have very good responses to those treatments," Pine adds. The best way to start is often by talking with your physician. If you're a parent, talk with your child's pediatrician. "These health professionals are generally prepared to help identify such problems and help patients get the appropriate care they need," Pine says.

If feelings of anxiety seem overwhelming or interfere with everyday activities:

- See your family doctor or nurse practitioner.

- The next step may be talking to a mental-health professional. Consider finding someone trained in CBT who is also open to using medication if needed. You may need to try several medicines before finding the right one.

- Consider joining a self-help or support group to share problems and achievements with others.

- Stress-management techniques and mindfulness meditation may help relieve anxiety symptoms.

Section 12.2

Compulsive Hoarding

This section contains text excerpted from the following sources: Text in this section begins with excerpts from "Treatment of Compulsive Hoarding," ClinicalTrials.gov, National Institutes of Health (NIH), June 20, 2013. Reviewed December 2018; Text under the heading "Distinct Brain Activity in Hoarders" is excerpted from "Distinct Brain Activity in Hoarders," National Institutes of Health (NIH), August 20, 2012. Reviewed December 2018.

Compulsive hoarding is a form of obsessive-compulsive disorder (OCD) that is characterized by excessive acquisition of possessions, difficulty discarding possessions, and excessive clutter. This condition is resistant to both pharmacological and psychotherapeutic interventions that are effective in treating other symptoms of OCD.

Distinct Brain Activity in Hoarders

Certain brain regions under-activate in people with hoarding disorder when dealing with others' possessions but over-activate when deciding whether to keep or discard their own things. Findings give insight into the biology of hoarding and may guide future treatment strategies.

People with hoarding disorder have trouble making decisions about when to throw things away. Possessions can pile up and result in debilitating clutter. In the past, hoarding disorder was considered a type of obsessive-compulsive disorder (OCD). Many experts, however, now consider it a unique diagnosis.

Previous studies of brain function in hoarders implicated regions associated with decision-making, attachment, reward processing, impulse control, and emotional regulation. But the patient populations and research methods varied between the studies, making it difficult to draw clear conclusions.

In a study, a research team led by Dr. David Tolin of Hartford Hospital and Yale University used functional magnetic resonance imaging (MRI) to investigate the neural basis for hoarding disorder. They compared the brains of patients with hoarding disorder to patients with OCD and healthy controls as they decided whether to keep or discard possessions. The study was funded by the National Institutes of Health's (NIH) National Institute of Mental Health (NIMH).

The researchers analyzed brain images of 43 hoarders, 31 people with OCD and 33 healthy controls. Participants were given six seconds to make a decision about whether to keep or discard junk mail that either belonged to them or to someone else. Participants later watched as the items they chose to discard were placed in a paper shredder. They were then asked to rate their emotions and describe how they felt during the decision-making tasks. The results appeared in the August 2012 issue of the *Archives of General Psychiatry*.

The hoarders chose to keep more mail that belonged to them than those in the OCD or healthy control groups. Hoarders also took longer to make decisions and reported greater anxiety, indecisiveness, and sadness than the other groups.

The imaging analysis revealed that hoarders differ from both healthy controls and patients with OCD in two specific brain regions: the anterior cingulate cortex and insula. Scientists believe that these areas are part of a brain network involved in processing emotion. Both regions were more active in hoarders when they were making decisions about mail that belonged to them, but less active when making decisions about mail that didn't belong to them.

These results suggest that hoarders' decisions about possessions are hampered by abnormal activity in brain regions used to identify the emotional significance of things. "They lose the ability to make relative judgments, so the decision becomes absolutely overwhelming and aversive to them," Tolin says.

The scientists believe that these brain abnormalities are specific to hoarding and separate the disorder from OCD. In addition to further exploring the unique traits of hoarders, the researchers are now using this information to help assess potential treatments.

Section 12.3

Generalized Anxiety Disorder

This section includes text excerpted from "Generalized Anxiety Disorder: When Worry Gets out of Control," National Institute of Mental Health (NIMH), August 2016.

What Is Generalized Anxiety Disorder?

Occasional anxiety is a normal part of life. You might worry about things like health, money, or family problems. But people with generalized anxiety disorder (GAD) feel extremely worried or feel nervous about these and other things—even when there is little or no reason to worry about them. People with GAD find it difficult to control their anxiety and stay focused on daily tasks.

The good news is that GAD is treatable. Call your doctor to talk about your symptoms so that you can feel better.

What Are the Signs and Symptoms of Generalized Anxiety Disorder?

GAD develops slowly. It often starts during the teen years or young adulthood. People with GAD may:

- Worry very much about everyday things

- Have trouble controlling their worries or feelings of nervousness

- Know that they worry much more than they should

- Feel restless and have trouble relaxing

- Have a hard time concentrating

- Be easily startled

- Have trouble falling asleep or staying asleep

- Feel easily tired or tired all the time

- Have headaches, muscle aches, stomach aches, or unexplained pains

- Have a hard time swallowing

- Tremble or twitch

- Be irritable or feel "on edge"

- Sweat a lot, feel light-headed or out of breath
- Have to go to the bathroom a lot

Children and teens with GAD often worry excessively about:

- Their performance, such as in school or in sports
- Catastrophes, such as earthquakes or war

Adults with GAD are often highly nervous about everyday circumstances, such as:

- Job security or performance
- Health
- Finances
- The health and well-being of their children
- Being late
- Completing household chores and other responsibilities

Both children and adults with GAD may experience physical symptoms that make it hard to function and that interfere with daily life.

Symptoms may get better or worse at different times, and they are often worse during times of stress, such as with a physical illness, during exams at school, or during a family or relationship conflict.

What Causes Generalized Anxiety Disorder

GAD sometimes runs in families, but no one knows for sure why some family members have it while others don't. Researchers have found that several parts of the brain, as well as biological processes, play a key role in fear and anxiety. By learning more about how the brain and body function in people with anxiety disorders, researchers may be able to create better treatments. Researchers are also looking for ways in which stress and environmental factors play a role.

How Is Generalized Anxiety Disorder Treated?

First, talk to your doctor about your symptoms. Your doctor should do an exam and ask you about your health history to make sure that an unrelated physical problem is not causing your symptoms. Your doctor may refer to you a mental-health specialist, such as a psychiatrist or psychologist.

GAD is generally treated with psychotherapy, medication, or both. Talk with your doctor about the best treatment for you.

Psychotherapy

A type of psychotherapy called cognitive behavioral therapy (CBT) is especially useful for treating GAD. CBT teaches a person different ways of thinking, behaving, and reacting to situations that help her or him feel less anxious and worried.

Medication

Doctors may also prescribe medication to help treat GAD. Your doctor will work with you to find the best the and dose for you. Different types of medication can be effective in GAD:

- Selective serotonin reuptake inhibitors (SSRIs)
- Serotonin-norepinephrine reuptake inhibitors (SNRIs)
- Other serotonergic medication
- Benzodiazepines

Doctors commonly use SSRIs and SNRIs to treat depression, but they are also helpful for the symptoms of GAD. They may take several weeks to start working. These medications may also cause side effects, such as headaches, nausea, or difficulty sleeping. These side effects are usually not severe for most people, especially if the dose starts off low and is increased slowly over time. Talk to your doctor about any side effects that you have.

Buspirone is another serotonergic medication that can be helpful in GAD. Buspirone needs to be taken continuously for several weeks for it to be fully effective.

Benzodiazepines, which are sedative medications, can also be used to manage severe forms of GAD. These medications are powerfully effective in rapidly decreasing anxiety, but they can cause tolerance and dependence if you use them continuously. Therefore, your doctor will only prescribe them for brief periods of time if you need them.

Don't give up on treatment too quickly. Both psychotherapy and medication can take some time to work. A healthy lifestyle can also help combat anxiety. Make sure to get enough sleep and exercise, eat a healthy diet, and turn to family and friends who you trust for support.

Section 12.4

Obsessive-Compulsive Disorder

This section includes text excerpted from "Obsessive-Compulsive Disorder," National Institute of Mental Health (NIMH), January 2016.

Obsessive-compulsive disorder (OCD) is a common, chronic, and long-lasting disorder in which a person has uncontrollable, reoccurring thoughts (obsessions) and behaviors (compulsions) that she or he feels the urge to repeat over and over.

Signs and Symptoms of Obsessive-Compulsive Disorder

People with OCD may have symptoms of obsessions, compulsions, or both. These symptoms can interfere with all aspects of life, such as work, school, and personal relationships.

Obsessions are repeated thoughts, urges, or mental images that cause anxiety. Common symptoms include:

- Fear of germs or contamination
- Unwanted forbidden or taboo thoughts involving sex, religion, and harm
- Aggressive thoughts toward others or self
- Having things symmetrical or in a perfect order

Compulsions are repetitive behaviors that a person with OCD feels the urge to do in response to an obsessive thought. Common compulsions include:

- Excessive cleaning and/or handwashing
- Ordering and arranging things in a particular, precise way
- Repeatedly checking on things, such as repeatedly checking to see if the door is locked or that the oven is off
- Compulsive counting

Not all rituals or habits are compulsions. Everyone double checks things sometimes. But a person with OCD generally:

- Can't control her or his thoughts or behaviors, even when those thoughts or behaviors are recognized as excessive

- Spends at least one hour a day on these thoughts or behaviors

- Doesn't get pleasure when performing the behaviors or rituals, but may feel brief relief from the anxiety the thoughts cause

- Experiences significant problems in their daily life due to these thoughts or behaviors

- Some individuals with OCD also have a tic disorder. Motor tics are sudden, brief, repetitive movements, such as eye blinking and other eye movements, facial grimacing, shoulder shrugging, and head or shoulder jerking. Common vocal tics include repetitive throat-clearing, sniffing, or grunting sounds.

Symptoms may come and go, ease over time, or worsen. People with OCD may try to help themselves by avoiding situations that trigger their obsessions, or they may use alcohol or drugs to calm themselves. Although most adults with OCD recognize that what they are doing doesn't make sense, some adults and most children may not realize that their behavior is out of the ordinary. Parents or teachers typically recognize OCD symptoms in children.

If you think you have OCD, talk to your doctor about your symptoms. If left untreated, OCD can interfere in all aspects of life.

Risk Factors of Obsessive-Compulsive Disorder

OCD is a common disorder that affects adults, adolescents, and children all over the world. Most people are diagnosed by about age 19, typically with an earlier age of onset in boys than in girls, but onset after age 35 does happen.

The causes of OCD are unknown, but risk factors include:

Genetics

Twin and family studies have shown that people with first-degree relatives (such as a parent, sibling, or child) who have OCD are at a higher risk for developing OCD themselves. The risk is higher if the first-degree relative developed OCD as a child or teen. Ongoing research continues to explore the connection between genetics and OCD and may help improve OCD diagnosis and treatment.

Brain Structure and Functioning

Imaging studies have shown differences in the frontal cortex and subcortical structures of the brain in patients with OCD. There appears to be a connection between the OCD symptoms and abnormalities in certain areas of the brain, but that connection is not clear. Understanding the causes will help determine specific, personalized treatments to treat OCD.

Environment

People who have experienced abuse (physical or sexual) in childhood or other trauma are at an increased risk for developing OCD.

In some cases, children may develop OCD or OCD symptoms following a streptococcal infection—this is called Pediatric Autoimmune Neuropsychiatric Disorders Associated with Streptococcal Infections (PANDAS).

Treatments and Therapies for Obsessive-Compulsive Disorder

OCD is typically treated with medication, psychotherapy or a combination of the two. Although most patients with OCD respond to treatment, some patients continue to experience symptoms.

Sometimes people with OCD also have other mental disorders, such as anxiety, depression, and body dysmorphic disorder (BDD), a disorder in which someone mistakenly believes that a part of their body is abnormal. It is important to consider these other disorders when making decisions about treatment.

Medication

Serotonin reuptake inhibitors (SRIs) and selective serotonin reuptake inhibitors (SSRIs) are used to help reduce OCD symptoms. Examples of medications that have been proven effective in both adults and children with OCD include clomipramine, which is a member of an older class of "tricyclic" antidepressants, and several newer "SSRIs," including:

- Fluoxetine

- Fluvoxamine

- Sertraline

SRIs often require higher daily doses in the treatment of OCD than of depression and may take 8 to 12 weeks to start working, but some patients experience more rapid improvement.

If symptoms do not improve with these types of medications, research shows that some patients may respond well to an anti-psychotic medication (such as risperidone). Although research shows that an antipsychotic medication may be helpful in managing symptoms for people who have both OCD and a tic disorder, research on the effectiveness of antipsychotics to treat OCD is mixed.

If you are prescribed a medication, be sure you:

- Talk with your doctor or a pharmacist to make sure you understand the risks and benefits of the medications you're taking.

- Do not stop taking a medication without talking to your doctor first. Suddenly stopping a medication may lead to "rebound" or worsening of OCD symptoms. Other uncomfortable or potentially dangerous withdrawal effects are also possible.

- Report any concerns about side effects to your doctor right away. You may need a change in the dose or a different medication.

- Report serious side effects to the U.S. Food and Drug Administration (FDA) MedWatch Adverse Event Reporting program online at www.fda.gov/Safety/MedWatch or by phone at 800-332-1088. You or your doctor may send a report.

Other medications have been used to treat OCD, but more research is needed to show the benefit of these options.

Psychotherapy

Psychotherapy can be an effective treatment for adults and children with OCD. Research shows that certain types of psychotherapy, including cognitive-behavior therapy (CBT) and other related therapies (e.g., habit reversal training) can be as effective as medication for many individuals. Research also shows that a type of CBT called Exposure and Response Prevention (EX/RP) is effective in reducing compulsive behaviors in OCD, even in people who did not respond well to SRI medication. For many patients, EX/RP is the add-on treatment of choice when SRIs or SSRIs medication does not effectively treat OCD symptoms.

Other Treatment Options

NIMH is supporting research into treatment approaches for people whose OCD does not respond well to the usual therapies. These approaches include combination and add-on (augmentation) treatments, as well as novel techniques such as deep brain stimulation (DBS).

Finding Treatment

For general information on mental health and to locate treatment services in your area, call the Substance Abuse and Mental Health Services Administration (SAMHSA) Treatment Referral Helpline at 800-662-4357. SAMHSA also has a Behavioral Health Treatment Locator on its website that can be searched by location.

Section 12.5

Panic Disorder

This section includes text excerpted from "Panic Disorder:
When Fear Overwhelms," National Institute of Mental
Health (NIMH), 2016.

Do you sometimes have sudden attacks of anxiety and overwhelming fear that last for several minutes? Maybe your heart pounds, you sweat, and you feel like you can't breathe or think. Do these attacks occur at unpredictable times with no obvious trigger, causing you to worry about the possibility of having another one at any time?

If so, you may have a type of anxiety disorder called panic disorder. Left untreated, panic disorder can lower your quality of life because it may lead to other fears and mental-health disorders, problems at work or school, and social isolation.

What Is It like to Have Panic Disorder?

"One day, without any warning or reason, a feeling of terrible anxiety came crashing down on me. I felt like I couldn't get enough air, no matter how hard I breathed. My heart was pounding out of my chest, and I thought I might die. I was sweating and felt dizzy. I felt like I had no control over these feelings and like I was drowning and couldn't think straight.

"After what seemed like an eternity, my breathing slowed and I eventually let go of the fear and my racing thoughts, but I was totally drained and exhausted. These attacks started to occur every couple of weeks, and I thought I was losing my mind. My friend saw how I was struggling and told me to call my doctor for help."

What Is Panic Disorder?

People with panic disorder have sudden and repeated attacks of fear that last for several minutes or longer. These are called panic attacks. Panic attacks are characterized by a fear of disaster or of losing control even when there is no real danger. A person may also have a strong physical reaction during a panic attack. It may feel like having a heart attack. Panic attacks can occur at any time, and many people with panic disorder worry about and dread the possibility of having another attack.

A person with panic disorder may become discouraged and feel ashamed because she or he cannot carry out normal routines like going to school or work, going to the grocery store, or driving.

Panic disorder often begins in the late teens or early adulthood. More women than men have panic disorder. But not everyone who experiences panic attacks will develop panic disorder.

What Causes Panic Disorder

Panic disorder sometimes runs in families, but no one knows for sure why some family members have it while others don't. Researchers have found that several parts of the brain, as well as biological processes, play a key role in fear and anxiety. Some researchers think that people with panic disorder misinterpret harmless bodily sensations as threats. By learning more about how the brain and body functions in people with panic disorder, scientists may be able to create better treatments. Researchers are also looking for ways in which stress and environmental factors may play a role.

What Are the Signs and Symptoms of Panic Disorder?

People with panic disorder may have:

- Sudden and repeated panic attacks of overwhelming anxiety and fear

- A feeling of being out of control, or a fear of death or impending doom during a panic attack

- Physical symptoms during a panic attack, such as a pounding or racing heart, sweating, chills, trembling, breathing problems, weakness or dizziness, tingly or numb hands, chest pain, stomach pain, and nausea

- An intense worry about when the next panic attack will happen

- A fear or avoidance of places where panic attacks have occurred in the past

How Is Panic Disorder Treated?

First, talk to your doctor about your symptoms. Your doctor should do an exam and ask you about your health history to make sure that an unrelated physical problem is not causing your symptoms. Your doctor may refer to you a mental-health specialist, such as a psychiatrist or psychologist.

Panic disorder is generally treated with psychotherapy, medication, or both. Talk with your doctor about the best treatment for you.

Psychotherapy. A type of psychotherapy called cognitive behavioral therapy (CBT) is especially useful as a first-line treatment for panic disorder. CBT teaches you different ways of thinking, behaving, and reacting to the feelings that come on with a panic attack. The attacks can begin to disappear once you learn to react differently to the physical sensations of anxiety and fear that occur during panic attacks.

Medication. Doctors also may prescribe different types of medications to help treat panic disorder:

- Selective serotonin reuptake inhibitors (SSRIs)

- Serotonin-norepinephrine reuptake inhibitors (SNRIs)

- Beta-blockers

- Benzodiazepines

SSRIs and SNRIs are commonly used to treat depression, but they are also helpful for the symptoms of panic disorder. They may take several weeks to start working. These medications may also cause side-effects, such as headaches, nausea, or difficulty sleeping. These side effects are usually not severe for most people, especially if the dose starts off low and is increased slowly over time. Talk to your doctor about any side effects that you have.

Another type of medication called beta-blockers can help control some of the physical symptoms of panic disorder, such as rapid heart rate. Although doctors do not commonly prescribe beta-blockers for panic disorder, they may be helpful in certain situations that precede a panic attack.

Benzodiazepines, which are sedative medications, are powerfully effective in rapidly decreasing panic attack symptoms, but they can cause tolerance and dependence if you use them continuously. Therefore, your doctor will only prescribe them for brief periods of time if you need them.

Your doctor will work with you to find the best medication and dose for you.

Don't give up on treatment too quickly. Both psychotherapy and medication can take some time to work. A healthy lifestyle can also help combat panic disorder. Make sure to get enough sleep and exercise, eat a healthy diet, and turn to family and friends who you trust for support.

Section 12.6

Social Anxiety Disorder

This section includes text excerpted from "Social Anxiety Disorder: More Than Just Shyness," National Institute of Mental Health (NIMH), December 21, 2016.

Are you extremely afraid of being judged by others?

Are you very self-conscious in everyday social situations?

Do you avoid meeting new people?

If you have been feeling this way for at least six months and these feelings make it hard for you to do everyday tasks—such as talking to people at work or school—you may have a social anxiety disorder (SAD).

SAD (also called social phobia) is a mental-health condition. It is an intense, persistent fear of being watched and judged by others. This fear can affect work, school, and your other day-to-day activities. It can even make it hard to make and keep friends. But SAD doesn't have to stop you from reaching your potential. Treatment can help you overcome your symptoms.

What Is It like Having Social Anxiety Disorder?

"In school, I was always afraid of being called on, even when I knew the answers. I didn't want people to think I was stupid or boring. My heart would pound and I would feel dizzy and sick. When I got a job, I hated to meet with my boss or talk in a meeting. I couldn't attend my best friend's wedding reception because I was afraid of having to meet new people. I tried to calm myself by drinking several glasses of wine before an event and then I started drinking every day to try to face what I had to do."

"I finally talked to my doctor because I was tired of feeling this way and I was worried that I would lose my job. I now take medicine and meet with a counselor to talk about ways to cope with my fears. I refuse to use alcohol to escape my fears and I'm on my way to feeling better."

What Is Social Anxiety Disorder?

SAD is a common type of anxiety disorder. A person with SAD feels symptoms of anxiety or fear in certain or all social situations, such as meeting new people, dating, being on a job interview, answering a question in class, or having to talk to a cashier in a store. Doing everyday things in front of people—such as eating or drinking in front of others or using a public restroom—also causes anxiety or fear. The person is afraid that she or he will be humiliated, judged, and rejected.

The fear that people with SAD have in social situations is so strong that they feel it is beyond their ability to control. As a result, it gets in the way of going to work, attending school, or doing everyday things. People with SAD may worry about these and other things for weeks before they happen. Sometimes, they end up staying away from places or events where they think they might have to do something that will embarrass them.

Some people with the disorder do not have anxiety in social situations but have performance anxiety instead. They feel physical symptoms of anxiety in situations such as giving a speech, playing a sports game, or dancing or playing a musical instrument on stage.

SAD usually starts during youth in people who are extremely shy. SAD is not uncommon; research suggests that about seven percent of Americans are affected. Without treatment, SAD can last for many years or a lifetime and prevent a person from reaching her or his full potential.

What Are the Signs and Symptoms of Social Anxiety Disorder?

When having to perform in front of or be around others, people with SAD tend to:

- Blush, sweat, tremble, feel a rapid heart rate, or feel their "mind going blank"

- Feel nauseous or sick to their stomach

- Show a rigid body posture, make little eye contact, or speak with an overly soft voice

- Find it scary and difficult to be with other people, especially those they don't already know and have a hard time talking to them even though they wish they could

- Be very self-conscious in front of other people and feel embarrassed and awkward

- Be very afraid that other people will judge them

- Stay away from places where there are other people

What Causes Social Anxiety Disorder

SAD sometimes runs in families, but no one knows for sure why some family members have it while others don't. Researchers have found that several parts of the brain are involved in fear and anxiety. Some researchers think that misreading of others' behavior may play a role in causing or worsening social anxiety. For example, you may think that people are staring or frowning at you when they truly are not. Underdeveloped social skills are another possible contributor to social anxiety. For example, if you have underdeveloped social skills, you may feel discouraged after talking with people and may worry about doing it in the future. By learning more about fear and anxiety in the brain, scientists may be able to create better treatments. Researchers are also looking for ways in which stress and environmental factors may play a role.

How Is Social Anxiety Disorder Treated?

First, talk to your doctor or healthcare professional about your symptoms. Your doctor should do an exam and ask you about your health history to make sure that an unrelated physical problem is not causing your symptoms. Your doctor may refer you to a mental-health specialist, such as a psychiatrist, psychologist, clinical social worker, or counselor. The first step to effective treatment is to have a diagnosis made, usually by a mental-health specialist.

SAD is generally treated with psychotherapy (sometimes called "talk" therapy), medication, or both. Speak with your doctor or healthcare provider about the best treatment for you. If your healthcare provider cannot provide a referral, visit the National Institute of Mental Health (NIMH) Help for Mental Illnesses web page at www.nimh.nih.gov/findhelp for resources you may find helpful.

Psychotherapy

A type of psychotherapy called cognitive-behavioral therapy (CBT) is especially useful for treating SAD. CBT teaches you different ways of thinking, behaving, and reacting to situations that help you feel less anxious and fearful. It can also help you learn and practice social skills. CBT delivered in a group format can be especially helpful.

Support Groups

Many people with social anxiety also find support groups helpful. In a group of people who all have SAD, you can receive unbiased, honest feedback about how others in the group see you. This way, you can learn that your thoughts about judgment and rejection are not true or are distorted. You can also learn how others with SAD approach and overcome the fear of social situations.

Medication

There are three types of medications used to help treat SAD:

- Antianxiety medications
- Antidepressants
- Beta-blockers

Antianxiety medications are powerful and begin working right away to reduce anxious feelings; however, these medications are usually not taken for long periods of time. People can build up a tolerance if they are taken over a long period of time and may need higher and higher doses to get the same effect. Some people may even become dependent on them. To avoid these problems, doctors usually prescribe anti-anxiety medications for short periods, a practice that is especially helpful for older adults.

Antidepressants are mainly used to treat depression but are also helpful for the symptoms of SAD. In contrast to antianxiety medications, they may take several weeks to start working. Antidepressants may also cause side effects, such as headaches, nausea, or difficulty sleeping. These side effects are usually not severe for most people, especially if the dose starts off low and is increased slowly over time. Talk to your doctor about any side effects that you have.

Beta-blockers are medicines that can help block some of the physical symptoms of anxiety on the body, such as an increased heart rate, sweating, or tremors. Beta-blockers are commonly the medications of choice for the "performance anxiety" type of social anxiety.

Your doctor will work with you to find the best medication, dose, and duration of treatment. Many people with SAD obtain the best results with a combination of medication and CBT or other psychotherapies.

Don't give up on treatment too quickly. Both psychotherapy and medication can take some time to work. A healthy lifestyle can also help combat anxiety. Make sure to get enough sleep and exercise, eat a healthy diet, and turn to family and friends who you trust for support.

Chapter 13

Phobias and Fears

What Is a Phobia?

A phobia is a type of anxiety disorder. It is a strong, irrational fear of something that poses little or no actual danger. People with phobias try to avoid what they are afraid of. If they cannot, they may experience:

- Panic and fear
- Rapid heartbeat
- Shortness of breath
- Trembling
- A strong desire to get away

Phobias usually start in children or teens and continue into adulthood.

This chapter contains text excerpted from the following sources: Text under the heading "What Is a Phobia?" is excerpted from "Phobias," MedlinePlus, National Institutes of Health (NIH), August 9, 2016; Text under the heading "What Are Specific Phobias?" is excerpted from "Phobias," MentalHealth.gov, U.S. Department of Health and Human Services (HHS), August 22, 2017; Text beginning with the heading "Prevalence of Specific Phobia among Adults in the United States" is excerpted from "Specific Phobia," National Institute of Mental Health (NIMH), November 2017.

The causes of specific phobias are not known, but they sometimes run in families.

Treatment helps most people with phobias. Options include medicines, therapy, or both.

What Are Specific Phobias?

A specific phobia is an intense, irrational fear of something that poses little or no actual danger. There are many specific phobias.

Acrophobia is a fear of heights. You may be able to ski the world's tallest mountains but be unable to go above the fifth floor of an office building. **Agoraphobia** is a fear of public places, and **claustrophobia** is a fear of closed-in places.

If you become anxious and extremely self-conscious in everyday social situations, you could have a social phobia. Other common phobias involve tunnels, highway driving, water, flying, animals, and blood.

Prevalence of Specific Phobia among Adults in the United States

Based on diagnostic interview data from National Comorbidity Survey Replication (NCS-R), figure 13.1 shows prevalence of specific phobia among U.S. adults aged 18 or older in 2016. An estimated 9.1 percent of U.S. adults had specific phobia. The prevalence of specific phobia among adults was higher for females (12.2%) than for males (5.8%). According to this data an estimated 12.5 percent of U.S. adults experience specific phobia at some time in their lives.

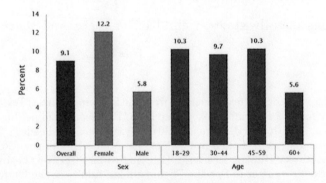

Figure 13.1. *Prevalence of Specific Phobia among U.S. Adults in 2016*

Specific Phobia with Impairment among Adults

Of adults with specific phobia, degree of impairment ranged from mild to serious. Impairment was determined by scores on the Sheehan Disability Scale. Among these adults with specific phobia, an estimated 21.9 percent had serious impairment, 30.0 percent had moderate impairment, and 48.1 percent had mild impairment.

Lifetime Prevalence of Specific Phobia among Adolescents

Based on diagnostic interview data from National Comorbidity Survey Adolescent Supplement (NCS-A), figure 13.2 shows lifetime prevalence of specific phobia among U.S. adolescents aged 13 to 18. An estimated 19.3 percent of adolescents had specific phobia, and an estimated 0.6 percent had severe impairment. The prevalence of specific phobia among adolescents was higher for females (22.1%) than for males (16.7%).

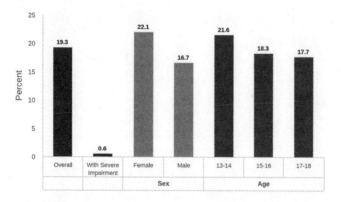

Figure 13.2. *Lifetime Prevalence of Specific Phobia among Adolescents*

Chapter 14

Posttraumatic Stress Disorder

Posttraumatic stress disorder (PTSD) is a disorder that develops in some people who have experienced a shocking, scary, or dangerous event.

It is natural to feel afraid during and after a traumatic situation. Fear triggers many split-second changes in the body to help defend against danger or to avoid it. This "fight-or-flight" response is a typical reaction meant to protect a person from harm. Nearly everyone will experience a range of reactions after trauma, yet most people recover from initial symptoms naturally. Those who continue to experience problems may be diagnosed with PTSD. People who have PTSD may feel stressed or frightened even when they are not in danger.

Signs and Symptoms of Posttraumatic Stress Disorder

Not every traumatized person develops ongoing (chronic) or even short-term (acute) PTSD. Not everyone with PTSD has been through a dangerous event. Some experiences, like the sudden, unexpected death of a loved one, can also cause PTSD. Symptoms usually begin early, within three months of the traumatic incident, but sometimes they

---

This chapter includes text excerpted from "Post-Traumatic Stress Disorder," National Institute of Mental Health (NIMH), February 9, 2016.

begin years afterward. Symptoms must last more than a month and be severe enough to interfere with relationships or work to be considered PTSD. The course of the illness varies. Some people recover within six months, while others have symptoms that last much longer. In some people, the condition becomes chronic.

A doctor who has experience helping people with mental illnesses, such as a psychiatrist or psychologist, can diagnose PTSD. To be diagnosed with PTSD, an adult must have all of the following for at least one month:

- At least one re-experiencing symptom
- At least one avoidance symptom
- At least two arousal and reactivity symptoms
- At least two cognition and mood symptoms

Re-experiencing symptoms include:

- Flashbacks—reliving the trauma over and over, including physical symptoms like a racing heart or sweating
- Bad dreams
- Frightening thoughts

Re-experiencing symptoms may cause problems in a person's everyday routine. The symptoms can start from the person's own thoughts and feelings. Words, objects, or situations that are reminders of the event can also trigger re-experiencing symptoms.

Avoidance symptoms include:

- Staying away from places, events, or objects that are reminders of the traumatic experience
- Avoiding thoughts or feelings related to the traumatic event

Things that remind a person of the traumatic event can trigger avoidance symptoms. These symptoms may cause a person to change her or his personal routine. For example, after a bad car accident, a person who usually drives may avoid driving or riding in a car.

Arousal and reactivity symptoms include:

- Being easily startled
- Feeling tense or "on edge"
- Having difficulty sleeping

- Having angry outbursts

Arousal symptoms are usually constant, instead of being triggered by things that remind one of the traumatic events. These symptoms can make a person feel stressed and angry. They may make it hard to do daily tasks, such as sleeping, eating, or concentrating.

Cognition and mood symptoms include:

- Trouble remembering the key features of the traumatic event

- Negative thoughts about oneself or the world

- Distorted feelings like guilt or blame

- Loss of interest in enjoyable activities

Cognition and mood symptoms can begin or worsen after the traumatic event but are not due to injury or substance use. These symptoms can make a person feel alienated or detached from friends or family members.

It is natural to have some of these symptoms after a dangerous event. Sometimes people have very serious symptoms that go away after a few weeks. This is called acute stress disorder, or ASD. When the symptoms last more than a month, seriously affect one's ability to function, and are not due to substance use, medical illness, or anything except the event itself, they might be PTSD. Some people with PTSD don't show any symptoms for weeks or months. PTSD is often accompanied by depression, substance abuse, or one or more of the other anxiety disorders.

Do Children React Differently Than Adults?

Children and teens can have extreme reactions to trauma, but their symptoms may not be the same as adults. In very young children (less than six years of age), these symptoms can include:

- Wetting the bed after having learned to use the toilet

- Forgetting how to or being unable to talk

- Acting out the scary event during playtime

- Being unusually clingy with a parent or other adult

Older children and teens are more likely to show symptoms similar to those seen in adults. They may also develop disruptive, disrespectful, or destructive behaviors. Older children and teens may feel guilty for not preventing injury or deaths. They may also have thoughts of revenge.

Risk Factors of Posttraumatic Stress Disorder

Anyone can develop PTSD at any age. This includes war veterans, children, and people who have been through a physical or sexual assault, abuse, accident, disaster, or any other serious events. According to the National Center for PTSD, about 7 or 8 out of every 100 people will experience PTSD at some point in their lives. Women are more likely to develop PTSD than men, and genes may make some people more likely to develop PTSD than others.

Not everyone with PTSD has been through a dangerous event. Some people develop PTSD after a friend or family member experiences danger or harm. The sudden, unexpected death of a loved one can also lead to PTSD.

Why Do Some People Develop Posttraumatic Stress Disorder and Other People Do Not?

It is important to remember that not everyone who lives through a dangerous event develops PTSD. In fact, most people will not develop the disorder. Many factors play a part in whether a person will develop PTSD. Some examples are listed below. Risk factors make a person more likely to develop PTSD. Other factors, called resilience factors, can help reduce the risk of the disorder.

Risk Factors and Resilience Factors for Posttraumatic Stress Disorder

Some factors that increase the risk for PTSD include:

- Living through dangerous events and traumas
- Getting hurt
- Seeing another person hurt, or seeing a dead body
- Childhood trauma
- Feeling horror, helplessness, or extreme fear
- Having little or no social support after the event
- Dealing with extra stress after the event, such as loss of a loved one, pain and injury, or loss of a job or home
- Having a history of mental illness or substance abuse

Some resilience factors that may reduce the risk of PTSD include:

- Seeking out support from other people, such as friends and family

- Finding a support group after a traumatic event

- Learning to feel good about one's own actions in the face of danger

- Having a positive coping strategy, or a way of getting through the bad event and learning from it

- Being able to act and respond effectively despite feeling fear

Researchers are studying the importance of these and other risk and resilience factors, including genetics and neurobiology. With more research, someday it may be possible to predict who is likely to develop PTSD and to prevent it.

Treatments and Therapies for Posttraumatic Stress Disorder

The main treatments for people with PTSD are medications, psychotherapy ("talk" therapy), or both. Everyone is different, and PTSD affects people differently so a treatment that works for one person may not work for another. It is important for anyone with PTSD to be treated by a mental-health provider who is experienced with PTSD. Some people with PTSD need to try different treatments to find what works for their symptoms.

If someone with PTSD is going through an ongoing trauma, such as being in an abusive relationship, both of the problems need to be addressed. Other ongoing problems can include panic disorder, depression, substance abuse, and feeling suicidal.

Medications

The most studied medications for treating PTSD include antidepressants, which may help control PTSD symptoms such as sadness, worry, anger, and feeling numb inside. Antidepressants and other medications may be prescribed along with psychotherapy. Other medications may be helpful for specific PTSD symptoms. For example, the U.S. Food and Drug Administration (FDA) approved research has shown that Prazosin may be helpful with sleep problems, particularly nightmares, commonly experienced by people with PTSD.

Doctors and patients can work together to find the best medication or medication combination, as well as the right dose.

Psychotherapy

Psychotherapy (sometimes called "talk therapy") involves talking with a mental-health professional to treat a mental illness. Psychotherapy can occur one-on-one or in a group. Talk therapy treatment for PTSD usually lasts 6 to 12 weeks, but it can last longer. Research shows that support from family and friends can be an important part of recovery.

Many types of psychotherapy can help people with PTSD. Some types target the symptoms of PTSD directly. Other therapies focus on social, family, or job-related problems. The doctor or therapist may combine different therapies depending on each person's needs.

Effective psychotherapies tend to emphasize a few key components, including education about symptoms, teaching skills to help identify the triggers of symptoms, and skills to manage the symptoms. One helpful form of therapy is called cognitive behavioral therapy, or CBT. CBT can include:

- **Exposure therapy.** This helps people face and control their fear. It gradually exposes them to the trauma they experienced in a safe way. It uses imagining, writing, or visiting the place where the event happened. The therapist uses these tools to help people with PTSD cope with their feelings.

- **Cognitive restructuring.** This helps people make sense of the bad memories. Sometimes people remember the event differently than how it happened. They may feel guilt or shame about something that is not their fault. The therapist helps people with PTSD look at what happened in a realistic way.

There are other types of treatment that can help as well. People with PTSD should talk about all treatment options with a therapist. Treatment should equip individuals with the skills to manage their symptoms and help them participate in activities that they enjoyed before developing PTSD.

How Talk Therapies Help People Overcome Posttraumatic Stress Disorder

Talk therapies teach people helpful ways to react to the frightening events that trigger their PTSD symptoms. Based on this general goal, different types of therapy may:

- Teach about trauma and its effects

- Use relaxation and anger-control skills

- Provide tips for better sleep, diet, and exercise habits

- Help people identify and deal with guilt, shame, and other feelings about the event

- Focus on changing how people react to their PTSD symptoms. For example, therapy helps people face reminders of the trauma.

Beyond Treatment: How Can You Help Yourself?

It may be very hard to take that first step to help yourself. It is important to realize that although it may take some time, with treatment, you can get better. If you are unsure where to go for help, ask your family doctor. You can also check the National Institute of Mental Health's (NIMH) Help for Mental Illnesses page (www.nimh.nih.gov/health/find-help/index.shtml) or search online for "mental health providers," "social services," "hotlines," or "physicians" for phone numbers and addresses. An emergency room doctor can also provide temporary help and can tell you where and how to get further help.

To help yourself while in treatment:

- Talk with your doctor about treatment options.

- Engage in mild physical activity or exercise to help reduce stress.

- Set realistic goals for yourself.

- Break up large tasks into small ones, set some priorities, and do what you can as you can.

- Try to spend time with other people, and confide in a trusted friend or relative. Tell others about things that may trigger symptoms.

- Expect your symptoms to improve gradually, not immediately.

- Identify and seek out comforting situations, places, and people.

Caring for yourself and others is especially important when large numbers of people are exposed to traumatic events (such as natural disasters, accidents, and violent acts).

Chapter 15

Psychotic Disorders

Chapter Contents

Section 15.1

Delusional Disorder

What Is Delusional Disorder?

A delusion is a mistaken impression maintained by an individual that is contradictory to reality or plausible explanation. Persons with delusional disorder (DD) have untrue beliefs that persist for more than a month's duration. Some delusions that patients experience cannot be explained, but some of them could be realistic, lead to the disorder remaining undiagnosed. Delusional disorder, previously known as paranoid disorder, is classified under psychotic illnesses. People with delusional disorder perceive things differently and misinterpret experiences.

Delusional disorder differs from other psychotic disorders with respect to how people carry on with their daily lives. People with more common psychotic disorders, such as schizophrenia, become so preoccupied with their delusions that it hampers their daily routine. Those with delusional disorder, on the other hand, function normally in society. They remain employed, perform daily tasks without hindrance, and do not act bizarrely. The incidence of delusional disorder in the general population is rare. The disorder occurs in middle to late adulthood and occurs more in women than men.

What Are the Symptoms and Subtypes of Delusional Disorder?

The dominant or only symptom of delusional disorder is delusions. While delusions are prominent in other psychotic disorders such as schizophrenia and bipolar disorder, the absence of accompanying symptoms such as hallucinations, mood swings, disorganized thinking, and cognitive deficits are used to make the diagnosis of delusional disorder. Early signs of illness may include a basic mistrust with people, unwarranted jealousy of spouse, or preoccupation with loyalty in relation to friends and relatives. The person is also overly sensitive to harmless remarks or perceived slights and tends to hold a long-standing grudge toward the subject of their delusion despite evidence to the contrary.

Some of the recognized subtypes of delusional disorder are:

- **Erotomania:** Implausible belief held by the affected person that another person is in love her or him. The person believed to be in love with the delusional person can be a famous person or a total stranger. Those suffering from this type of delusional disorder will often try to establish contact with the object of their fixation through letters, telephone calls, and surveillance is seen. This may be tantamount to stalking and may have legal implications.

- **Jealous type:** Delusional belief that her or his spouse (or sexual partner) is unfaithful. Also known as conjugal paranoia, or Othello syndrome, the affected person justifies her or his conviction on the basis of false conclusions despite the lack of objective evidence. Physical violence may or may not accompany this subtype.

- **Grandiose type:** Also called megalomania, this type is characterized by exaggerated beliefs of grandeur and self-worth as well as extreme arrogance. The affected person believes he is omnipotent, famous, and powerful and the delusions typically have a religious, fictional, or supernatural content.

- **Persecutory:** Persistent conviction that she or he is being plotted against, maligned, or harassed with intent to cause harm. The delusional person may relentlessly seek legal recourse through courts and law-enforcement agencies and may even resort to violence in retaliation for the perceived threat.

- **Somatic:** Characterized by intense preoccupation with imagined defects in physical appearance (body dysmorphic disorder) and bodily function (hypochondriasis), which focuses on imagined illnesses/disorders contrary to medical evidence. This type may also include delusional infestation (DI) in which the affected persons hold a rigid belief that they are infested with parasites or pathogens and patients may typically describe sensations of "crawling" and "biting" to substantiate their beliefs.

How Is Delusional Disorder Diagnosed?

Delusional disorder is diagnosed on the basis of a thorough psychological assessment. A physical examination and diagnostic tests, including imaging tests and blood tests, are carried out to rule out other causes. Interviews with family members and friends to understand past history and behavioral symptoms are important tools that assist in diagnosis. Nonbizarre delusions persisting for more than a month and absence of symptoms related to schizophrenia and other psychotic disorders lead to confirmation of diagnosis. The doctor will also assess if the person will likely act on delusions.

What Causes Delusional Disorder

The causes and triggers for delusional disorder are not known in medical circles. But the following factors are thought to play a role.

- **Genetics:** The disorder is seen in families that have a history of schizophrenia and delusional disorder suggesting a genetic link. The disorder might be inherited from parents to their children hereditarily.

- **Environmental or psychological:** There is evidence that suggests that the disorder may develop as a result of stress. Substance abuse such as alcoholism and drug abuse could lead to the disorder. Remaining in isolation is also a risk factor. The disorder has been identified in refugees particularly in people with low sight and hearing leading to the observation.

- **Biological:** Researchers are investigating anomalies in the brain that could be a contributing factor for the disorder. Defects in regions of the brain that control perception and thinking may be linked to the disorder.

What Is the Treatment for Delusional Disorder?

A combination of psychotherapy and medication is used to treat delusional disorder. Denial about delusions, poor insight, and refusal to seek help are deterrents to treatment. Establishing a good rapport between doctor and patient is crucial to successful treatment. Medications help in recovery to some extent. Medications commonly used for treatment include conventional antipsychotics (neuroleptics), atypical antipsychotics, tranquilizers, and antidepressants. Psychotherapy is also recommended and therapy types such as cognitive-behavior therapy (CBT), family therapy, and individual counseling help the person manage stress and the impact of delusions in daily functioning.

What Are the Complications that Arise due to Delusional Disorder?

Delusions could lead to depression because of difficulties that arise out of such thinking. Persons who act on their delusions may become violent and get into legal difficulties. If the delusions are severe, then people could become alienated from family and friends.

What Is the Outlook for Recovery?

The outlook for recovery depends on factors such as the type of delusional disorder, life circumstances, what support is available for the person, and her or his willingness to remain under treatment. Delusional disorder is a chronic condition with chances of complete recovery. Some patients experience periods that are free of incidents mixed with episodes of delusions. Most patients with delusional disorder do not seek help because of fear or embarrassment. If treatment is not sought, delusional disorder becomes a lifelong affliction.

Is Delusional Disorder Preventable?

Prevention strategies do not exist currently for delusional disorder but the effect of illness can be minimized with treatment, and the patient can lead a productive life in the company of family and friends.

References

1. "Delusional Disorder and Substance Abuse," American Addiction Centers, n.d.

2. "Treatments for Delusional Disorder," Cochrane, n.d.

3. "Delusional Disorder as a Partial Psychosis," U.S. National Library of Medicine (NLM), National Institutes of Health (NIH), 2014.

4. "Understanding Delusions," U.S. National Library of Medicine (NLM), National Institutes of Health (NIH), 2009.

5. Schulz, Charles "Delusional Disorder," Merck Manual, n.d.

6. "Mental Health and Delusional Disorder," WebMD, n.d.

Section 15.2

Factitious Disorders

Difficult to diagnose and treat, factitious disorder is a rare mental disorder in which individuals act as though they are sick when in reality they are mimicking or intentionally creating the symptoms of a disease or condition. Patients with factitious disorder may lie about symptoms, bring about symptoms by self-injury, needlessly undergo painful diagnostic procedures, and tamper with the results of the medical tests. Unlike those who lie about medical conditions for monetary gain or other compensation, the only goal of those with factitious disorder is to receive sympathy and special attention from family, friends, and the medical community. Factitious disorder is associated with preexisting mental illnesses such as depression and anxiety as well as stressful living conditions.

Factitious disorder can be subdivided into two types. The first is referred to factitious disorder imposed on self (in the past this subtype was referred to as Munchausen syndrome after the 18th-century German figure who regularly exaggerated his exploits). The person affected will themselves mimic a mental or physical illness. For example, the person will appear confused, make absurd statements, and say they are hallucinating. They may also bring about physical symptoms such as stomach pains or seizures. The second type is factitious disorder imposed on others (previously referred to as Munchausen by proxy). In this manifestation, the person will impose false physical or psychological symptoms on another person. This is usually seen with a parent falsely presenting their child as sick, often putting the child at serious risk of harm as the result of unnecessary tests or medical procedures.

What Are the Symptoms of Factitious Disorders?

The symptoms of factitious disorder are difficult to identify because the person can go to great lengths to hide their deception. Warning signs usually involve mimicking or exaggerating sickness or injury as well as:

- Episodes of lying

- Self-injury—Individuals may inject themselves with harmful bacteria, milk, or feces to bring about symptoms or physically injure themselves by cutting or burning

- Tampering with the results of diagnostic tests by such actions as manipulating medical instruments or contaminating urine samples with blood

- Using aliases in order to visit a range of medical facilities and doctors

- Persistent symptoms even after appropriate treatment

- Extensive and specialized knowledge of medical conditions, tests, and treatment procedures

- Repeated hospital stays

- Unwillingness to allow healthcare professionals to talk to their family and friends

- Unwillingness to submit to psychiatric evaluation

What Are the Causes of Factitious Disorders?

The cause of factitious disorder is unknown, but researchers have found a strong link to preexisting behavioral and psychological issues along with stressful living conditions.

There may be several possible risk factors associated with factitious disorder. Research suggests that childhood trauma in the form of physical, verbal, or emotional abuse as well as neglect can be a major factor. This can lead to a poor sense of self or a loss of identity. Loss of a loved one that leads to a persistent sense of abandonment can also be a factor as well as past experiences of hospital stays that attracted significant attention from family and others. This condition can occasionally be seen in healthcare workers.

Diagnosis of Factitious Disorders

Diagnosing factitious disorder is challenging given the amount of misinformation provided by the patient. Medical professionals first must gather as much of an accurate medical history as possible despite the exaggerations, misdirection, and potential use of aliases during treatment. They must then also rule out any possible physical or alternate mental condition (such as psychosis), which requires a thorough review of medical tests, imagery, and lab work. Interviewing the patient and observing her or his behavior is also key to diagnosing the condition. The patient may overdramatize his or symptoms, may present information that contradicts previous medical findings or the recollections of their caregivers, and may appear overeager to submit to painful or invasive tests. Medical professionals will then compare their findings to the criteria for factitious disorder as outlined in *Diagnostic and Statistical Manual of Mental Disorder,* Fifth Edition (DSM-5), published by the American Psychiatric Association (APA).

Treatment of Factitious Disorders

No standard protocols or therapies are available as of now for treatment of factitious disorders. However, it has been found that the affected person will respond better to a nonjudgmental approach. With this kind of approach, they may be more willing to be treated by a mental-health professional. Also, having a primary care physician, or other medical professional act as a gatekeeper who monitors all medical care of a patient, is the key to accomplishing the first goal of treatment, which is to end or reduce that person's misuse of the medical system.

Psychotherapy will help in coping with underlying issues including stress and depression. Medications for preexisting mental-health disorders may be used. If the disorder is found to be serious, extensive hospital stay and treatment may be required.

References

1. "An Overview of Factitious Disorders," Cleveland Clinic, March 28, 2017.

2. "Factitious Disorder," Mayo Clinic, May 31, 2017.

Section 15.3

Psychosis

This section includes text excerpted from "RAISE Questions and Answers," National Institute of Mental Health (NIMH), October 7, 2015. Reviewed December 2018.

What Is Psychosis?

The word "psychosis" is used to describe conditions that affect the mind, where there has been some loss of contact with reality. When someone becomes ill in this way it is called a psychotic episode.

During a period of psychosis, a person's thoughts and perceptions are disturbed and the individual may have difficulty understanding what is real and what is not. Symptoms of psychosis include delusions (false beliefs) and hallucinations (seeing or hearing things that others do not see or hear). Other symptoms include incoherent or nonsense speech, and behavior that is inappropriate for the situation. A person in a psychotic episode may also experience depression, anxiety, sleep problems, social withdrawal, lack of motivation and difficulty functioning overall.

What Causes Psychosis

There is not one specific cause of psychosis. Psychosis may be a symptom of a mental illness, such as schizophrenia or bipolar disorder, but there are other causes, as well. Sleep deprivation, some general medical conditions, certain prescription medications, and the abuse of alcohol or other drugs, such as marijuana, can cause psychotic symptoms. Because there are many different causes of psychosis, it is important to see a qualified healthcare professional (e.g., psychologist, psychiatrist, or trained social worker) in order to receive a thorough assessment and accurate diagnosis. A mental illness, such as schizophrenia, is typically diagnosed by excluding all of these other causes of psychosis.

How Common Is Psychosis?

Approximately three percent of the people in the United States (3 out of 100 people) will experience psychosis at some time in their lives. About 100,000 adolescents and young adults in the United States experience first episode psychosis each year.

What Is the Connection between Psychosis and Schizophrenia?

Schizophrenia is a mental illness characterized by periods of psychosis. An individual must experience psychotic symptoms for at least six months in order to be diagnosed with schizophrenia. However, a person may experience psychosis and never be diagnosed with schizophrenia, or any other mental-health condition. This is because there are many different causes of psychosis, such as sleep deprivation, general medical conditions, the use of certain prescription medications, and the abuse of alcohol or other drugs.

What Are the Early Warning Signs of Psychosis?

Typically, a person will show changes in their behavior before psychosis develops. The list below includes behavioral warning signs for psychosis.

• Worrisome drop in grades or job performance

• New trouble thinking clearly or concentrating

• Suspiciousness, paranoid ideas, or uneasiness with others

• Withdrawing socially, spending a lot more time alone than usual

• Unusual, overly intense new ideas, strange feelings or having no feelings at all

• Decline in self-care or personal hygiene

• Difficulty telling reality from fantasy

• Confused speech or trouble communicating

Anyone of these items by itself may not be significant, but someone with several of the items on the list should consult a mental-health professional. A qualified psychologist, psychiatrist, or trained social worker will be able to make a diagnosis and help develop a treatment plan. Early treatment of psychosis increases the chance of a successful recovery. If you notice these changes in behavior and they begin to intensify or do not go away, it is important to seek help.

What Does "Duration of Untreated Psychosis" Mean?

The length of time between the start of psychotic symptoms and the beginning of treatment is called the duration of untreated psychosis, or DUP. In general, research has shown that treatments for psychosis work better when they are delivered closer to the time when symptoms first appear. This was the case in the Recovery After an Initial Schizophrenia Episode (RAISE)-Early Treatment Program (ETP) study. Individuals who had a shorter DUP when they started treatment showed much greater improvement in symptoms, functioning, and quality of life than those with longer DUP. The RAISE-ETP project also found that average DUP in the United States is typically longer than what is considered acceptable by international standards. Future RAISE-related efforts are working to find ways of decreasing DUP so that individuals receive care as early as possible after symptoms appear.

Do People Recover from Psychosis?

With early diagnosis and appropriate treatment, it is possible to recover from psychosis. Many people who receive early treatment never have another psychotic episode. For other people, recovery means the ability to live a fulfilling and productive life, even if psychotic symptoms return sometimes.

What Should You Do If You Think Someone Is Having a Psychotic Episode?

If you think someone you know is experiencing psychosis, encourage the person to seek treatment as early as possible. Psychosis can be treated effectively, and early intervention increases the chance of a successful outcome. To find a qualified treatment program, contact your healthcare professional. If someone having a psychotic episode is in distress or you are concerned about their safety, consider taking them to the nearest emergency room, or calling 911.

Why Is Early Treatment Important for Treating Psychosis?

Left untreated, psychotic symptoms can lead to disruptions in school and work, strained family relations, and separation from friends. The longer the symptoms go untreated, the greater the risk of additional problems. These problems can include substance abuse, going to the emergency department, being admitted to the hospital, having legal trouble, or becoming homeless.

Studies have shown that many people experiencing first episode psychosis in the United States typically have symptoms for more than a year before receiving treatment. It is important to reduce this duration of untreated psychosis because people tend to do better when they receive effective treatment as early as possible.

What Is Coordinated Specialty Care?

Coordinated specialty care (CSC) is a recovery-oriented treatment program for people with first episode psychosis (FEP). CSC uses a team of specialists who work with the client to create a personal treatment plan. The specialists offer psychotherapy, medication management geared to individuals with FEP, case management, family education and support, and work or education support, depending on the individual's needs and preferences. The client and the team work together to make treatment decisions, involving family members as much as possible. The goal is to link the individual with a CSC team as soon as possible after psychotic symptoms begin.

CSC is a general term used to describe a certain type of treatment for FEP. There are many different programs that are considered CSC. In the United States, examples of CSC programs include (but are not limited to) Navigate, the Connection Program, OnTrackNY, the Specialized Treatment Early in Psychosis (STEP) program, and the Early Assessment and Support Alliance (EASA). RAISE is not a CSC program. RAISE is the name of a research initiative developed and funded by the National Institute of Mental Health (NIMH) to test CSC programs. Navigate and the Connection Program were the two CSC programs tested as part of the RAISE project.

What Is Shared Decision-Making and How Does It Work in Early Treatment?

Shared decision-making means individuals and their healthcare providers work together to find the best treatment options based on the individual's unique needs and preferences. Clients, treatment-team members, and (when appropriate) relatives are active participants in the process.

What Is the Role of Medication in Treatment of Psychosis?

Antipsychotic medications help reduce psychotic symptoms. Like medications for any illness, antipsychotic drugs have benefits and risks. Individuals should talk with their healthcare providers about the benefits of taking antipsychotic medication as well as potential side effects, dosage, and preferences such as taking a daily pill or a monthly injection.

What Is Supported Employment/Education and Why Is It Important?

For young adults, psychosis can hurt school attendance and academic performance or make it difficult to find or keep a job. Supported employment/education (SEE) is one way to help individuals return to work or school. A SEE specialist helps clients develop the skills they need to achieve school and work goals. In addition, the specialist can be a bridge between clients and educators or employers. SEE services are an important part of coordinated specialty care and are valued by many clients. Findings from RAISE-Implementation and Evaluation Study (IES) showed that SEE services often brought people into care and engaged them in treatment because it directly addressed their personal goals.

Section 15.4

Schizophrenia

This section includes text excerpted from "Schizophrenia,"
Substance Abuse and Mental Health Services
Administration (SAMHSA), April 6, 2018.

Schizophrenia is a mental disorder that affects how a person thinks, feels, and acts. People with the disorder may have changes in:

Thought content—themes or topics of their thinking. For example, hearing or seeing things that do not exist or fixed false beliefs that others are trying to harm them.

Thought processes—how their thinking flows and is connected. For example, their thoughts may jump from topic to topic without reaching a conclusion, or they may repetitively speak the same words or phrases.

Emotions—how they feel and show their feelings. For example, they may not be able to express emotions or may have extreme emotions.

Behavior—how they act or do things. For example, they may have problems at school or work. They may talk with others who are not present, so they seem to be talking to themselves. They may withdraw from people and not complete daily routines.

Not everyone with schizophrenia has all the symptoms. Symptoms often occur in "episodes" that may come and go. The severity of symptoms also varies. The symptoms may impact many parts of life, including school, work, and dealing with family and friends. The symptoms tend to last through life. With treatment, a person with the disorder can achieve recovery and life goals.

Signs and Symptoms of Schizophrenia

The symptoms of schizophrenia make it hard to function in daily life. A person with the disorder has some of the following symptoms for at least six months. A trained mental-health professional should evaluate the person and make the diagnosis.

Delusions

The person has strong beliefs that don't fit with the person's culture. These beliefs persist even if not true or logical. The person believes things that are not true. For example, a person may think that they are someone famous, or that music on the radio is a message for them.

Hallucinations

The person may perceive things that others do not. For example, a person may hear a voice that no one else can hear, or see things that others do not.

Disorganized Speech

The person may have trouble organizing their thoughts. Others may find conversations with the person hard to follow. For example, the person may jump from topic to topic, make up words, and be unable to express themselves.

Disorganized Behavior

The person may behave in ways that others view as bizarre or with no purpose. They have trouble holding conversations and keeping relationships. Catatonic behavior means the person does not react to what happens around them. In contrast, catatonic excitement behavior includes excessive, purposeless activity. Rarely, a catatonic person stays in a rigid or awkward posture.

Negative Symptoms

The person has problems expressing emotion or responding to what is happening. The person may not want to start or sustain activities. They may have problems feeling pleasure. For example, a person may show little or no emotion or facial expression when speaking with others.

Risk Factors for Schizophrenia

Less than one percent of people in the United States have schizophrenia. It occurs in all ethnic and cultural groups. Symptoms usually start in the early to late twenties. The age of diagnosis is usually a few years earlier for men than women. The symptoms may start quickly but usually emerge slowly. In rare cases, children are diagnosed with schizophrenia.

There is no specific known cause. Risk factors include genetics, brain structure, brain function, environmental factors, and social factors. Having one or more of these factors does not cause schizophrenia.

Genetics

Schizophrenia tends to run in families. But many people with schizophrenia do not have a family member with the disorder. Many people with one or more family members with the disorder do not develop it themselves.

Researchers think several genes combine to increase risk, and no single gene causes the disorder by itself. Genetic information cannot predict who will develop schizophrenia.

Brain Structure and Function

For some people with schizophrenia, images of parts of the brain look different from people without the disorder. As people with schizophrenia age, their brain size seems to decrease more than in other people.

Some research shows that the disorder may be due to an imbalance of neurotransmitters. Brain cells use these substances to communicate. Dopamine and glutamate are neurotransmitters linked to schizophrenia.

Problems with brain development before birth may cause problems with neurotransmitters that can lead to the disorder. The brain undergoes changes during puberty. These may trigger symptoms in people at risk.

Co-Occurring Problems

A person with schizophrenia may be at increased risk for other mental disorders such as depression, anxiety, and substance-use disorders (SUDs). Problems with using marijuana and nicotine are common in people with the disorder.

Risk for Suicide

People with schizophrenia have an increased risk of suicide. About five to six percent of people with the disorder die by suicide. About 20 percent attempt suicide. Suicide is a major health concern and is preventable.

Evidence-Based Treatments for Schizophrenia

The causes of schizophrenia are unknown, so most treatments aim to help the person deal with or stop symptoms, not cure the disorder. Treatment usually aims to reduce symptoms, improve quality of life and ability to function, and support recovery goals. Psychotherapy and medication are often combined.

Co-occurring disorders such as anxiety, insomnia, and depression often require adding psychotherapies and medications to the treatment plan.

Because people with a diagnosis of schizophrenia have a high rate of suicide, any suicidal thoughts, self-harming actions, and risk-taking behaviors should be closely monitored. Harm-reduction steps should be taken to protect the person.

The treatment plan should consider each person's needs and choices. A person should consult a healthcare professional when choosing the right treatment and consider her or his own gender, race, ethnicity, language, and culture.

Psychotherapy

Psychotherapy, sometimes called "talk therapy," involves working with a behavioral-health professional one-to-one or in a group. Based on the person's needs, more than one form of treatment may be needed.

Cognitive-behavioral therapy (CBT) for psychosis helps the person cope with hallucinations and delusions.

The person learns to identify events or situations that make symptoms worse. They learn how to avoid those events or situations. The therapy also helps people communicate better with others, develop skills for daily life, and learn problem-solving skills.

In family psychoeducation, the person with schizophrenia and their family work with a behavioral health professional. They build a support system and enhance problem-solving, communication, and coping skills. They use a problem-solving approach to deal with the person's symptoms.

Cognitive remediation therapy (CRT) helps a person with schizophrenia learn skills to manage daily life. Exercises may involve pencil and paper, a computer, or talking with a clinician. The person works to improve attention, memory, problem-solving, organization, and planning.

Psychosocial Interventions

Assertive community treatment is helpful for people with a serious mental disorder such as schizophrenia. This team-based approach usually includes a psychiatrist, nurse, social worker, occupational therapist, and peer support specialist. Teams may provide employment services, supportive housing, substance-use treatment, and other services.

Coordinated specialty care connects people with early symptoms to treatment that may prevent long-term disability. This approach combines medication, psychosocial therapies, case management, family involvement, supported education, and employment services. The National Institute of Mental Health (NIMH) tested this model in the Recovery After an Initial Schizophrenia Episode (RAISE) study. Several states have programs in place.

Supported employment, specifically **individual placement,** and support, help people with schizophrenia and other mental disorders get jobs, earn money, and work more. Working and contributing to the community is tied to better long-term outcomes.

Smoking cessation can help people with schizophrenia reduce and or quit smoking cigarettes and using other forms of tobacco. More than 40 percent of people with a serious mental disorder, including schizophrenia, use tobacco products. Tobacco use poses health risks and can harm treatment, including the effect of medications.

Medication

People with schizophrenia often receive medications to help manage their symptoms. People with schizophrenia should work with a healthcare professional experienced in treating schizophrenia to help identify the treatment options available. Together, they can identify goals and select the best-individualized treatment

Antipsychotics are the most common medications prescribed for the symptoms of schizophrenia. These include first-generation antipsychotics and second-generation medications, sometimes called "atypicals." Many have medical side effects, so the person's physical health should be closely monitored. Antipsychotics are usually taken daily. Several antipsychotics are available in a long-lasting form and can be administered once or twice a month by a trained clinician.

Behavioral Health Advance Directive

A person with schizophrenia is encouraged to create a behavioral health advance directive, stating:

- Where they wish to receive care

- What treatments they want

- Who makes legal healthcare decisions for them if they cannot do so due to their illness

Complementary Therapies and Activities for Treating Schizophrenia

Complementary therapies and activities can help people improve their overall well-being, and are meant to be used along with evidence-based treatments.

Illness management and recovery help people with schizophrenia understand their illness, learn coping skills to help manage their illness, develop goals, and make informed decisions about treatment. Some people with schizophrenia find meditation and yoga helpful in meeting their recovery goals.

Recovery and Social Support Services and Activities

Recovery is a process of change through which people improve their health and wellness, live self-directed lives, and strive to reach their full potential. This includes:

- Overcoming or managing one's condition(s) or symptoms

- Having a stable and safe place to live

- Conducting meaningful daily activities, such as a job, school, volunteerism, and family caretaking

- Having relationships and social networks that provide support, friendship, love, and hope

Recovery helps a person develop resilience, increasing the ability to cope with adversity and adapt to challenges or change.

Self-help and mutual peer support groups can provide people with the knowledge and support to make treatment decisions that work for them. Organizations and websites provide self-help information and help people find local support groups. Peer and family support services can help foster hope and promote outreach and engagement for those with behavioral-health conditions. This includes both peer-to-peer and family-to-family supports provided by a certified peer or family support specialist who can promote hope, foster recovery, and build resiliency skills.

Peer Support Services

Peer support services are delivered by peer specialists who are persons with schizophrenia and other mental illnesses. Peer specialists are trained, and in many states certified, to provide these services. Peer specialists may be paid staff or volunteers. They offer support, strength, and hope to a person struggling with mental illness.

They also help the person feel more connected to their community. Peer support services can foster hope, aid recovery, promote resiliency, and reduces healthcare costs. Family members can also provide family support services.

171

Section 15.5

Schizoaffective Disorder

This section includes text excerpted from "Facts about
Schizoaffective Disorder," Mental Illness Research, Education and
Clinical Centers (MIRECC), U.S. Department of Veterans
Affairs (VA), November 20, 2013. Reviewed December 2018.

What Is Schizoaffective Disorder?

Schizoaffective disorder is a major psychiatric disorder that is quite
similar to schizophrenia. The disorder can affect all aspects of daily
living, including work, social relationships, and self-care skills (such
as grooming and hygiene). People with schizoaffective disorder can
have a wide variety of different symptoms, including having unusual
perceptual experiences (hallucinations) or beliefs others do not share
(delusions), mood (such as marked depression), low motivation, inability to experience pleasure, and poor attention. The serious nature of
the symptoms of schizoaffective disorder sometimes requires consumers to go to the hospital to get care. The experience of schizoaffective
disorder can be described as similar to "dreaming when you are wide
awake"; that is, it can be hard for the person with the disorder to dis-
tinguish between reality and fantasy.

How Common Is Schizoaffective Disorder?

About one in every two hundred people (1/2%) develops schizoaffective disorder at some time during her or his life. Schizoaffective
disorder, along with schizophrenia, is one of the most common serious
psychiatric disorders. More hospital beds are occupied by persons
with these disorders than any other psychiatric disorder. However,
as with other types of mental illness, individuals with schizoaffective
disorder can engage in treatment and other mental-health recovery
efforts that have the potential to dramatically improve the well-being
of the individual.

How Is the Disorder Diagnosed?

Schizoaffective disorder can only be diagnosed by a clinical interview. The purpose of the interview is to determine whether the person
has experienced specific "symptoms" of the disorder, and whether these
symptoms have been present long enough to merit the diagnosis. In

addition to conducting the interview, the diagnostician must also check to make sure the person is not experiencing any physical problems that could cause symptoms similar to schizoaffective disorder, such as a brain tumor or alcohol or drug abuse.

Schizoaffective disorder cannot be diagnosed with a blood test, X-ray*, computerized axial tomography (CAT)-scan, or any other laboratory test.

* *A type of high-energy radiation. In low doses, X-rays are used to diagnose diseases by making pictures of the inside of the body.*

The Characteristic Symptoms of Schizoaffective Disorder

The diagnosis of schizoaffective disorder requires that the person experience some decline in social functioning for at least a six-month period, such as problems with school or work, social relationships, or self-care. In addition, some other symptoms must be commonly present. The symptoms of schizoaffective disorder can be divided into five broad classes: positive symptoms, negative symptoms, symptoms of mania, symptoms of depression, and other symptoms. A person with schizoaffective disorder will usually have some (but not all) of the symptoms described below.

Positive Symptoms

Positive symptoms refer to thoughts, perceptions, and behaviors that are ordinarily **absent** in persons who are not diagnosed with schizophrenia or schizoaffective disorder but are **present** in persons with schizoaffective disorder. These symptoms often vary over time in their severity and may be absent for long periods in some persons.

Hallucinations. Hallucinations are "false perceptions"; that is, hearing, seeing, feeling, or smelling things that are not actually there. The most common type of hallucinations is auditory hallucinations. Individuals sometimes report hearing voices talking to them or about them, often saying insulting things, such as calling them names. These voices are usually heard through the ears and sound like other human voices.

Delusions. Delusions are "false beliefs"; that is, a belief which the person holds, but which others do not share. Some individuals have paranoid delusions, believing that they are not safe or others want to hurt them. Delusions of reference are common, in which the individual believes that something in the environment is referring to her or him

173

when it is not (such as the television talking to the person). Delusions of control are beliefs that others can control one's actions. Individuals may hold these beliefs strongly and cannot usually be "talked out" of them.

Thinking disturbances. This problem is reflected in a difficulty in communication. The individual talks in a manner that is difficult to follow. For example, the individual may jump from one topic to the next, stop in the middle of the sentence, make up new words, or simply be difficult to understand.

Negative Symptoms

Negative symptoms are the opposite of positive symptoms. They are the **absence** of thoughts, perceptions, or behaviors that are ordinarily **present** in people who are not diagnosed with schizophrenia or schizoaffective disorder. These symptoms can often persist for a long period of time, though with effort on the individual's part they can often be improved. Many professionals think these symptoms reflect a sense of hopelessness about the future.

Blunted affect. The expressiveness of the individual's face, voice tone, and gestures is less. However, this does not mean that the person is not reacting to her or his environment or having feelings.

Apathy. The individual does not feel motivated to pursue goals and activities. The individual may feel lethargic or sleepy and have trouble following through on even simple plans. Individuals with apathy often have little sense of purpose in their lives and have few interests.

Anhedonia. The individual experiences little or no pleasure from activities that she or he used to enjoy or that others enjoy. For example, the person may not enjoy watching a sunset, going to the movies, or a close relationship with another person.

Poverty of speech or content of speech. The individual says very little, or when she or he talks, there does not seem to be much information being conveyed. Sometimes conversing with the person with schizoaffective disorder can be very difficult.

Inattention. The individual has difficulty paying attention and is easily distracted. This can interfere with activities such as work, interacting with others, and personal care skills.

Symptoms of Mania

In general, the symptoms of mania involve an excess in behavioral activity, mood states (in particular, irritability or positive feelings), and self-esteem and confidence.

Euphoric or expansive mood. The individual's mood is abnormally elevated, such as extremely happy or excited (euphoria). The person may tend to talk more and with greater enthusiasm or emphasis on certain topics (expansiveness).

Irritability. The individual is easily angered or persistently irritable, especially when others seem to interfere with her or his plans or goals, however unrealistic they maybe.

Inflated self-esteem or grandiosity. The individual is extremely self-confident and may be unrealistic about her or his abilities (grandiosity). For example, the individual may believe she or he is a brilliant artist or inventor, a wealthy person, a shrewd businessperson, or a healer when she or he has no special competence in these areas.

Decreased need for sleep. Only a few hours of sleep are needed each night (such as less than four hours) for the individual to feel rested.

Talkativeness. The individual talks excessively and may be difficult to interrupt. The individual may jump quickly from one topic to another (called flight of ideas), making it hard for others to understand.

Racing thoughts. Thoughts come so rapidly that the individual finds it hard to keep up with them or express them.

Distractibility. The individual's attention is easily drawn to irrelevant stimuli, such as the sound of a car honking outside on the street.

Increased goal-directed activity. A great deal of time is spent pursuing specific goals at work, school, or sexually. Often these behaviors put the person at risk.

Excessive involvement in pleasurable activities with high potential for negative consequences. Common problem areas include spending sprees, sexual indiscretions, increased substance abuse, or making foolish business investments.

Symptoms of Depression

Depressive symptoms reflect the opposite end of the continuum of mood from manic symptoms, with a low mood and behavioral inactivity as the major features.

Depressed mood. Mood is low most of the time, according to the person or significant others.

Diminished interest or pleasure. The individual has few interests and gets little pleasure from anything, including activities previously found enjoyable.

Change in appetite and/or weight. Loss of appetite (and weight) when not dieting, or increased appetite (and weight gain) are evident.

Change in sleep pattern. The individual may have difficulty falling asleep, staying asleep, or wake early in the morning and not be able to get back to sleep. Alternatively, the person may sleep excessively (such as over twelve hours per night), spending much of the day in bed.

Change in activity level. Decreased activity level is reflected by slowness and lethargy, both in terms of the individual's behavior and thought processes. Alternatively, the individual may feel agitated, "on edge," and restless.

Fatigue or loss of energy. The individual experiences fatigue throughout the day or there is a chronic feeling of loss of energy.

Feelings of worthlessness, hopelessness, helplessness. Individuals may feel they are worthless as people, that there is no hope for improving their lives, or that there is no point in trying to improve their unhappy situation.

Inappropriate guilt. Feelings of guilt may be present about events that the individual did not even do, such as a catastrophe, a crime, or an illness.

Recurrent thoughts about death. The individual thinks about death a great deal and may contemplate (or even attempt) suicide.

Decreased concentration or ability to make decisions. Significant decreases in the ability to concentrate make it difficult for the individual to pay attention to others or complete simple tasks. The individual may be quite indecisive about even minor things.

Other Symptoms

Individuals with schizoaffective disorder are prone to alcohol or drug abuse. Some individuals may use alcohol and drugs excessively either because of their disturbing symptoms, to experience pleasure, or when socializing with others.

How Is Schizoaffective Disorder Distinguished from Schizophrenia and Affective (Mood) Disorders?

Many persons with a diagnosis of schizoaffective disorder have had, at a prior time, diagnosis of schizophrenia or bipolar disorder. Frequently, this previous diagnosis is revised to schizoaffective disorder when it becomes clear, over time, that the person experiences symptoms of mania or depression much of the time, but on other occasions has experienced psychotic symptoms such as hallucinations or delusions even when her or his mood is stable.

What Is the Course of Schizoaffective Disorder?

The disorder usually begins in late adolescence or early adulthood, often between the ages of sixteen and thirty. The severity of symptoms usually varies over time, at times requiring hospitalization for treatment. The disorder is often life-long, although the symptoms tend to improve gradually over the person's life and many individuals who were diagnosed with the disorder when they were younger appear to have few or no symptoms from middle age on. With schizoaffective disorder, as with other major psychiatric illnesses, individuals can work to achieve their goals and live very full lives.

What Causes Schizoaffective Disorder

The cause of schizoaffective disorder is not known, although many scientists believe it is a variant of the disorder of schizophrenia. Schizoaffective disorder (and schizophrenia) may actually be several disorders. Current theories suggest that an imbalance in brain chemicals (specifically, dopamine) may be at the root of these two disorders. Vulnerability to developing schizoaffective disorder appears to be partly determined by genetic factors and partly by early environmental factors (such as subtle insults to the brain of the baby in the womb before and during birth).

How Is Schizoaffective Disorder Treated?

Many of the same methods used to treat schizophrenia are also effective for schizoaffective disorder. Antipsychotic medications are an effective treatment for schizoaffective disorder for most, but not all, persons with the disorder. These drugs are not a "cure" for the disorder, but they can reduce symptoms and prevent relapses among the majority of people with the disorder. Antidepressant medications and mood stabilizing medications (such as lithium) are occasionally used to treat affective symptoms (depressive or manic symptoms) in schizoaffective disorder. Other important treatments include social skills training, vocational rehabilitation and supported employment, peer support, and intensive case management (ICM). Family therapy helps reduce stress in the family and teaches family members how to monitor the disorder. In addition, individual supportive counseling can help the person with the disorder learn to manage the disorder more successfully and obtain emotional support in coping with the distress resulting from the disorder. Individuals with schizoaffective disorder who work actively toward mental-health recovery can positively affect the course of their illness and improve the quality of their lives. Family support for the individual's recovery efforts can lend meaningful benefits.

Chapter 16

Personality Disorders

Chapter Contents

Section 16.1

Antisocial Personality Disorder

This section includes text excerpted from "Antisocial Personality Disorder," MentalHealth.gov, U.S. Department of Health and Human Services (HHS), August 22, 2017.

What Is Antisocial Personality Disorder?

Antisocial personality disorder (ASPD) is a mental-health condition in which a person has a long-term pattern of manipulating, exploiting, or violating the rights of others. This behavior is often criminal.

What Causes Antisocial Personality Disorder

The cause of ASPD is unknown. Genetic factors and environmental factors, such as child abuse, are believed to contribute to the development of this condition. People with an antisocial or alcoholic parent are at increased risk. Far more men than women are affected. The condition is common among people who are in prison.

Fire-setting and cruelty to animals during childhood are linked to the development of antisocial personality. Some doctors believe that psychopathic personality (psychopathy) is the same disorder. Others believe that psychopathic personality is a similar but more severe disorder.

What Are the Symptoms of Antisocial Personality Disorder?

A person with ASPD may:

- Be able to act witty and charming
- Be good at flattery and manipulating other people's emotions
- Break the law repeatedly
- Disregard the safety of self and others
- Have problems with substance abuse
- Lie, steal, and fight often
- Not show guilt or remorse
- Often be angry or arrogant

Section 16.2

Borderline Personality Disorder

This section includes text excerpted from "Borderline Personality Disorder," National Institute of Mental Health (NIMH), December 2017.

Borderline personality disorder (BPD) is a mental illness marked by an ongoing pattern of varying moods, self-image, and behavior. These symptoms often result in impulsive actions and problems in relationships. People with BPD may experience intense episodes of anger, depression, and anxiety that can last from a few hours to days.

Signs and Symptoms of Borderline Personality Disorder

People with BPD may experience mood swings and display uncertainty about how they see themselves and their role in the world. As a result, their interests and values can change quickly.

People with BPD also tend to view things in extremes, such as all good or all bad. Their opinions of other people can also change quickly. An individual who is seen as a friend one day may be considered an enemy or traitor the next. These shifting feelings can lead to intense and unstable relationships.

Other signs or symptoms may include:

- Efforts to avoid real or imagined abandonment, such as rapidly initiating intimate (physical or emotional) relationships or cutting off communication with someone in anticipation of being abandoned

- A pattern of intense and unstable relationships with family, friends, and loved ones, often swinging from extreme closeness and love (idealization) to extreme dislike or anger (devaluation)

- Distorted and unstable self-image or sense of self

- Impulsive and often dangerous behaviors, such as spending sprees, unsafe sex, substance abuse, reckless driving, and binge eating. (**Please note**: If these behaviors occur primarily during a period of elevated mood or energy, they may be signs of a mood disorder—not BPD.)

- Self-harming behavior, such as cutting

- Recurring thoughts of suicidal behaviors or threats
- Intense and highly changeable moods, with each episode lasting from a few hours to a few days
- Chronic feelings of emptiness
- Inappropriate, intense anger or problems controlling anger
- Difficulty trusting, which is sometimes accompanied by irrational fear of other people's intentions
- Feelings of dissociation, such as feeling cut off from oneself, seeing oneself from outside one's body, or feelings of unreality

Not everyone with BPD experiences every symptom. Some individuals experience only a few symptoms, while others have many. Symptoms can be triggered by seemingly ordinary events. For example, people with BPD may become angry and distressed over minor separations from people to whom they feel close, such as traveling on business trips. The severity and frequency of symptoms and how long they last will vary depending on the individual and their illness.

Risk Factors of Borderline Personality Disorder

The cause of BPD is not yet clear, but research suggests that genetics, brain structure and function, and environmental, cultural, and social factors play a role, or may increase the risk for developing BPD.

- **Family history.** People who have a close family member, such as a parent or sibling, with the disorder may be at higher risk of developing BPD.
- **Brain factors.** Studies show that people with BPD can have structural and functional changes in the brain, especially in the areas that control impulses and emotional regulation. But it is not clear whether these changes are risk factors for the disorder, or caused by the disorder.
- **Environmental, cultural, and social factors.** Many people with BPD report experiencing traumatic life events, such as abuse, abandonment, or adversity during childhood. Others may have been exposed to unstable, invalidating relationships and hostile conflicts.

Although these factors may increase a person's risk, it does not mean that the person will develop BPD. Likewise, there may be people without these risk factors who will develop BPD in their lifetime.

Treatments and Therapies for Borderline Personality Disorder

BPD has historically been viewed as difficult to treat. But, with newer, evidence-based treatment, many people with the disorder experience fewer or less severe symptoms and an improved quality of life. It is important that people with BPD receive evidence-based, specialized treatment from an appropriately trained provider. Other types of treatment, or treatment provided by a doctor or therapist who is not appropriately trained, may not benefit the person.

Many factors affect the length of time it takes for symptoms to improve once treatment begins, so it is important for people with BPD and their loved ones to be patient and to receive appropriate support during treatment.

Tests and Diagnosis

A licensed mental-health professional—such as a psychiatrist, psychologist, or clinical social worker—experienced in diagnosing and treating mental disorders can diagnose BPD by:

- Completing a thorough interview, including a discussion about symptoms

- Performing a careful and thorough medical exam, which can help rule out other possible causes of symptoms

- Asking about family medical histories, including any history of mental illness

BPD often occurs with other mental illnesses. Co-occurring disorders can make it harder to diagnose and treat BPD, especially if symptoms of other illnesses overlap with the symptoms of BPD. For example, a person with BPD may be more likely to also experience symptoms of depression, bipolar disorder, anxiety disorders, substance-use disorders (SUDs), or eating disorders.

Seek and Stick with Treatment

National Institute of Mental Health (NIMH)-funded studies show that people with BPD who don't receive adequate treatment are:

- More likely to develop other chronic medical or mental illnesses

- Less likely to make healthy lifestyle choices

BPD is also associated with a significantly higher rate of self-harm and suicidal behavior than the general public. People with BPD who are thinking of harming themselves or attempting suicide need help right away.

If you or someone you know is in crisis, call the toll-free National Suicide Prevention Lifeline (NSPL) at 800-273- 8255, 24 hours a day, 7 days a week. The service is available to everyone. The deaf and hard of hearing can contact the Lifeline via TTY at 800-799-4889. All calls are free and confidential. Contact social media outlets directly if you are concerned about a friend's social media updates or dial 911 in an emergency.

The treatments described on this section are just some of the options that may be available to a person with BPD.

Psychotherapy

Psychotherapy is the first-line treatment for people with BPD. A therapist can provide one-on-one treatment between the therapist and patient, or treatment in a group setting. Therapist-led group sessions may help teach people with BPD how to interact with others and how to effectively express themselves.

It is important that people in therapy get along with and trust their therapist. The very nature of BPD can make it difficult for people with the disorder to maintain a comfortable and trusting bond with their therapist.

Two examples of psychotherapies used to treat BPD include:

- **Dialectical-behavior therapy (DBT).** This type of therapy was developed for individuals with BPD. DBT uses concepts of mindfulness and acceptance or being aware of and attentive to the current situation and emotional state. DBT also teaches skills that can help:

  - Control intense emotions

  - Reduce self-destructive behaviors

  - Improve relationships

- **Cognitive-behavioral therapy (CBT).** This type of therapy can help people with BPD identify and change core beliefs and behaviors that underlie inaccurate perceptions of themselves and others, and problems interacting with others. CBT may help reduce a range of mood and anxiety symptoms and reduce the number of suicidal or self-harming behaviors.

Medications

Because the benefits are unclear, medications are not typically used as the primary treatment for B. However, in some cases, a psychiatrist may recommend medications to treat specific symptoms such as:

- Mood swings
- Depression
- Other co-occurring mental disorders

Treatment with medications may require care from more than one medical professional. Certain medications can cause different side effects in different people. Talk to your doctor about what to expect from a particular medication.

Section 16.3

Histrionic Personality Disorder

"Histrionic Personality Disorder,"
© 2017 Omnigraphics. Reviewed December 2018.

What Is Histrionic Personality Disorder?

The term "histrionic" means "theatrical" or "dramatic." People with histrionic personality disorder have a compelling desire to be the center of attention at all times. To gain that attention, histrionics act in an extremely self-centered way. For example, they may try to dominate conversations by interrupting others, behaving dramatically and inappropriately. Or, they may dress provocatively and act seductively in inappropriate situations to gain the attention they seek. However, patients who suffer from the disorder possess a distorted image of themselves and lack a true feeling of self-worth, needing to derive their self-esteem from the approval of others.

What Causes Histrionic Personality Disorder

The definite cause of histrionic personality disorder remains unknown. However, a variety of hereditary and learned factors are believed to play a role. The disorder runs in families, which is suggestive of a genetic link, though a child could simply be repeating the behavior of a parent. Inconsistent parenting that leads to confusion in the child about acceptable behavior is another possible factor.

What Are the Symptoms of Histrionic Personality Disorder?

The following symptoms are seen in people with histrionic personality disorder:

- Feeling uncomfortable if they are not the center of attention
- Self-centeredness to the point of being rash with others
- Rapid change in emotional states
- Behaving dramatically and exhibiting exaggerated emotions and expressions
- Giving excessive importance to physical appearance
- Dressing provocatively and looking seductive
- Shifting blame to others for failure or disappointment
- Sensitivity to disapproval or criticism
- Acting rashly without thinking rationally
- Approaches relationships in a shallow and fake manner
- Dislike for routine, often starting projects and leaving them incomplete or skipping them all together
- Seeks approval and reassurance of others
- Being gullible and easily influenced by others
- Easily frustrated and seeks instant gratification

How Is Histrionic Personality Disorder Diagnosed?

Once doctors identify the symptoms, they carry out a physical examination and review the patient's complete medical history. Laboratory tests or imaging tests may also be done to rule out any possible physical causes. The patient will then be referred to a psychiatrist or psychologist who will diagnose the disorder based on a psychological evaluation. The patient's behavior, overall appearance, and psychological profile are considered during diagnosis. Patients suffering from histrionic personality disorder often also suffer from depression or anxiety, leading them to seek out professional help.

How Is Histrionic Personality Disorder Treated?

Talk therapy, otherwise known as psychotherapy, is the preferred treatment for histrionic personality disorder. The goal of talk therapy is to help patients recognize the motivations behind their thinking and behavior and to, in turn, approach the individuals around them in a positive and productive manner. However, treating patients with the disorder can be challenging since they often believe that they do not need treatment and can despise routine. In the case of depression that co-occurs with the disorder, antidepressants are prescribed, but generally not for extended durations.

What Complications Exist for Histrionic Personality Disorder?

The disorder will often affect the patient's social and romantic relationships. Patients with histrionic personality disorder are also at a higher risk of suffering from depression compared to the general population.

Can Histrionic Personality Disorder Be Prevented?

Though the disorder cannot be prevented, people who are prone to the condition can be equipped with techniques to deal with situations in a more constructive manner.

What Is the Outlook for the Histrionic Personality Disorder?

Most people with histrionic personality disorder lead productive lives and integrate with society in the long run. However, people with severe symptoms are likely to face significant problems in day-to-day life without ongoing treatment.

References

1. "Histrionic Personality Disorder," Cleveland Clinic, March 4, 2014.

2. "Histrionic Personality Disorder," Counselling Directory, 2017.

3. Berger, Fred K., MD. "Histrionic Personality Disorder," University of Iowa Stead Family Children's Hospital, November 18, 2016.

Section 16.4

Narcissistic Personality Disorder

This section includes text excerpted from "Narcissistic Personality Disorder in Clinical Health Psychology Practice: Case Studies of Comorbid Psychological Distress and Life-Limiting Illness," U.S. Department of Health and Human Services (HHS), February 20, 2018.

What Is Narcissistic Personality Disorder?

Narcissistic personality disorder (NPD) is a psychological disorder characterized by a persistent pattern of grandiosity, fantasies of unlimited power or importance, and the need for admiration or special treatment. Core cognitive, affective, interpersonal, and behavioral features include impulsivity, volatility, attention-seeking, low self-esteem, and unstable interpersonal relationships that result in a pervasive pattern of interpersonal difficulties, occupational problems, and significant psychosocial distress.

Prevalence estimates of NPD range from 0 to 6.2 percent in community samples. Of those individuals diagnosed with NPD, 50 to 75 percent are male. The *Diagnostic and Statistical Manual of Mental Disorders*, Fifth Edition (DSM-5) classifies NPD as a Cluster B ("dramatic, emotional, and erratic") personality disorder, a category that also includes antisocial, borderline, and histrionic personality disorders.

Mental-Health Comorbidities and Social Problems Associated with Narcissistic Personality Disorder

Individuals with NPD experience significant physical and mental-health comorbidities and social problems. Researchers found high

12-month prevalence rates of substance abuse (40.6%), mood (28.6%), and anxiety (40%) disorders among participants with a diagnosis of NPD. Core features of NPD that contribute to these mental-health comorbidities include a higher frequency of experiencing shame, help-lessness, self-directed anger, higher admiration of self, and impulsivity.

NPD is a significant predictor of making multiple suicide attempts, using lethal means to attempt suicide, and making suicide attempts in proximal relationship to being fired or experiencing domestic, financial, or health-related problems.

Physical Health Outcomes Associated with Narcissistic Personality Disorder

Regarding physical health outcomes, individuals with Cluster B personality disorders, including NPD, have demonstrated significantly higher mortality rates due to cardiovascular disease than those with-out personality disorders, even after controlling for relevant medical comorbidities. NPD specifically is also associated with gastrointestinal conditions.

Characteristic Features of People with Narcissistic Personality Disorder

Not unexpectedly, NPD is strongly associated with high healthcare utilization across a variety of services. Additionally, provider–patient relationships among individuals with NPD can be challenging due to interpersonal dysfunction marked by dramatic, emotional, and erratic thinking and/or behavior. From a behavioral standpoint, individuals with a Cluster B diagnosis are more likely to have:

- A criminal conviction
- Spent time in prison
- A history of interpersonal violence
- Caused pain or suffering to others
- Evidenced overall impairment in social role functioning

Section 16.5

Obsessive-Compulsive Personality Disorder

This section contains text excerpted from the following sources:
Text under the heading "What Is Obsessive-Compulsive Personality
Disorder?" is excerpted from "Obsessive Compulsive Personality
Disorder as a Predictor of Exposure and Ritual Prevention Outcome
for Obsessive Compulsive Disorder," U.S. Department of Health
and Human Services (HHS), May 10, 2011, Reviewed December
2018; Text under the heading "Characteristic Features of People
with Obsessive-Compulsive Personality Disorder?" is excerpted from
"Interpersonal Functioning in Obsessive-Compulsive Personality
Disorder," U.S. Department of Health and Human Services (HHS),
July 21, 2014. Reviewed December 2018.

What Is Obsessive-Compulsive Personality Disorder?

The fourth edition of *Diagnostic and Statistical Manual of Mental Disorders* (DSM) defines obsessive-compulsive personality disorder (OCPD) as an enduring pattern that leads to clinically significant distress or functional impairment, marked by four or more of the following: preoccupation with details; perfectionism; excessive devotion to work; inflexibility about morality and ethics; inability to discard worn-out or worthless items; reluctance to delegate tasks; miserliness; and rigidity and stubbornness. With regard to functional impairment, OCPD is associated with poor spouse and partner relationships and overall social functioning, and hostility and anger outbursts at home and work. Furthermore, depressed patients with OCPD report more frequent, chronic suicidal ideation and more frequent attempts.

Characteristic Features of People with Obsessive-Compulsive Personality Disorder?

OCPD is characterized as a chronic maladaptive pattern of excessive perfectionism, preoccupation with orderliness and detail, and need for control over one's environment that leads to significant distress or impairment. Prevalence in outpatient settings of OCPD is estimated between eight to nine percent and in the general population between two to eight percent.

Individuals with OCPD find it difficult to relax, feel obligated to plan out their activities to the minute, and find unstructured time intolerable. In addition, they are often characterized as rigid and controlling. This need for interpersonal control in OCPD can lead to hostility and occasional explosive outbursts of anger at home and work.

The core features of OCPD include perfectionism and its associations with rigidity and aggression that lead to difficulties in interactions with others. These core features of OCPD might be related to the systemizing mechanism and that these individuals are high on systemizing and low on empathizing. Researchers observe that OCPD develops out of an inborn tendency toward systemizing, which leads to more rigidity, stubbornness, and perfectionism than average. For example, if an individual with OCPD experiences a significant other as unpredictable or not following the "rules," then she or he may experience frustration, irritability, or even rage.

OCPD is its high comorbidity with obsessive-compulsive disorder (OCD). Prevalence data support a relationship between these disorders, with elevated rates of OCPD (45–47.3%) in subjects diagnosed with OCD.

Chapter 17

Eating and Body Image Disorders

Chapter Contents

Section 17.1

Eating Disorders: An Overview

This section includes text excerpted from "Eating Disorders,"
National Institute of Mental Health (NIMH), February 2016.

There is a commonly held view that eating disorders are a lifestyle choice. Eating disorders are actually serious and often fatal illnesses that cause severe disturbances to a person's eating behaviors. Obsessions with food, body weight, and shape may also signal an eating disorder. Common eating disorders include anorexia nervosa, bulimia nervosa, and binge-eating disorder (BED).

Risk Factors for Eating Disorders

Eating disorders frequently appear during the teen years or young adulthood but may also develop during childhood or later in life. These disorders affect both genders, although rates among women are higher than among men. Like women who have eating disorders, men also have a distorted sense of body image. For example, men may have muscle dysmorphia, a type of disorder marked by an extreme concern with becoming more muscular.

Researchers are finding that eating disorders are caused by a complex interaction of genetic, biological, behavioral, psychological, and social factors. Researchers are using the latest technology and science to better understand eating disorders.

One approach involves the study of human genes. Eating disorders run in families. Researchers are working to identify deoxyribonucleic acid (DNA) variations that are linked to the increased risk of developing eating disorders.

Brain imaging studies are also providing a better understanding of eating disorders. For example, researchers have found differences in patterns of brain activity in women with eating disorders in comparison with healthy women. This kind of research can help guide the development of new means of diagnosis and treatment of eating disorders.

Treatments and Therapies for Eating Disorders

Adequate nutrition, reducing excessive exercise, and stopping purging behaviors are the foundations of treatment. Treatment plans are tailored to individual needs and may include one or more of the following:

- Individual, group, and/or family psychotherapy
- Medical care and monitoring
- Nutritional counseling
- Medications

Psychotherapies

Psychotherapies such as a family-based therapy called the Maudsley approach, where parents of adolescents with anorexia nervosa assume responsibility for feeding their child, appear to be very effective in helping people gain weight and improve eating habits and moods.

To reduce or eliminate binge-eating and purging behaviors, people may undergo cognitive behavioral therapy (CBT), which is another type of psychotherapy that helps a person learn how to identify distorted or unhelpful thinking patterns and recognize and change inaccurate beliefs.

Section 17.2

Anorexia Nervosa and Bulimia Nervosa

This section includes text excerpted from "Eating Disorders,"
MentalHealth.gov, U.S. Department of Health and
Human Services (HHS), August 24, 2017.

Anorexia Nervosa

Anorexia nervosa is an eating disorder that makes people lose more weight than is considered healthy for their age and height.

Persons with this disorder may have an intense fear of weight gain, even when they are underweight. They may diet or exercise too much, or use other methods to lose weight.

Causes of Anorexia Nervosa

The exact causes of anorexia nervosa are not known. Many factors probably are involved. Genes and hormones may play a role. Social attitudes that promote very thin body types may also be involved.

Family conflicts are no longer thought to contribute to this or other eating disorders.

Risk factors for anorexia include:

• Being more worried about, or paying more attention to, weight and shape

• Having an anxiety disorder as a child

• Having a negative self-image

• Having eating problems during infancy or early childhood

• Having certain social or cultural ideas about health and beauty

• Trying to be perfect or overly focused on rules

Anorexia usually begins during the teen years or young adulthood. It is more common in females, but may also be seen in males. The disorder is seen mainly in white women who are high academic achievers and who have a goal-oriented family or personality.

Symptoms of Anorexia Nervosa

To be diagnosed with anorexia, a person must:

• Have an intense fear of gaining weight or becoming fat, even when she is underweight

• Refuse to keep weight at what is considered normal for her age and height (15% or more below the normal weight)

• Have a body image that is very distorted, be very focused on body weight or shape, and refuse to admit the seriousness of weight loss

• Have not had a period for three or more cycles (in women)

People with anorexia may severely limit the amount of food they eat, or eat and then make themselves throw up. Other behaviors include:

• Cutting food into small pieces or moving them around the plate instead of eating

- Exercising all the time, even when the weather is bad, they are hurt, or their schedule is busy
- Going to the bathroom right after meals
- Refusing to eat around other people
- Using pills to make themselves urinate (water pills or diuretics), have a bowel movement (enemas and laxatives), or decrease their appetite (diet pills)

Other symptoms of anorexia may include:
- Blotchy or yellow skin that is dry and covered with fine hair
- Confused or slow thinking, along with poor memory or judgment
- Depression
- Dry mouth
- Extreme sensitivity to cold (wearing several layers of clothing to stay warm)
- Loss of bone strength
- Wasting away of muscle and loss of body fat

Bulimia

Bulimia is an illness in which a person binges on food or has regular episodes of overeating and feels a loss of control. The person then uses different methods—such as vomiting or abusing laxatives—to prevent weight gain.

Many (but not all) people with bulimia also have anorexia nervosa.

Causes of Bulimia

Many more women than men have bulimia. The disorder is most common in adolescent girls and young women. The affected person is usually aware that her eating pattern is abnormal and may feel fear or guilt with the binge–purge episodes.

The exact cause of bulimia is unknown. Genetic, psychological, trauma, family, society, or cultural factors may play a role. Bulimia is likely due to more than one factor.

Symptoms of Bulimia

In bulimia, eating binges may occur as often as several times a day for many months.

People with bulimia often eat large amounts of high-calorie foods, usually in secret. People can feel a lack of control over their eating during these episodes.

Binges lead to self-disgust, which causes purging to prevent weight gain. Purging may include:

• Forcing yourself to vomit

• Excessive exercise

• Using laxatives, enemas, or diuretics (water pills)

Purging often brings a sense of relief.

People with bulimia are often at a normal weight, but they may see themselves as being overweight. Because the person's weight is often normal, other people may not notice this eating disorder.

Symptoms that other people can see include:

• Compulsive exercise

• Suddenly eating large amounts of food or buying large amounts of food that disappear right away

• Regularly going to the bathroom right after meals

• Throwing away packages of laxatives, diet pills, emetics (drugs that cause vomiting), or diuretics

Section 17.3

Binge Eating Disorder

This section includes text excerpted from "Binge Eating Disorder," National Institute of Diabetes and Digestive and Kidney Diseases (NIDDK), June 2016.

Definition and Facts Related to Binge Eating Disorder
What Is Binge Eating Disorder?

Binge eating is when you eat a large amount of food in a short amount of time and feel that you can't control what or how much you are eating. If you binge eat regularly—at least once a week for three months, you may have binge eating disorder (BED).

If you have BED, you may be very upset by your binge eating. You also may feel ashamed and try to hide your problem. Even your close friends and family members may not know you binge eat.

How Is Binge Eating Disorder Different from Bulimia Nervosa?

Unlike people with BED, people who have bulimia nervosa try to prevent weight gain after binge eating by vomiting, using laxatives or diuretics, fasting, or exercising too much.

How Common Is Binge Eating Disorder?

BED is the most common eating disorder in the United States. About 3.5 percent of adult women and two percent of adult men have BED. For men, BED is most common in midlife, between the ages of 45 to 59.

For women, BED most commonly starts in early adulthood, between the ages of 18 and 29. About 1.6 percent of teenagers are affected. A much larger number of adults and children have episodes of binge eating or loss-of-control eating, but the episodes do not occur frequently enough to meet the criteria for BED.

BED affects African Americans as often as whites. More research is needed on how often BED affects people in other racial and ethnic groups.

Who Is More Likely to Develop Binge Eating Disorder?

BED can occur in people of average body weight but is more common in people with obesity, particularly severe obesity. However, it is important to note that most people with obesity do not have BED.

Painful childhood experiences—such as family problems and critical comments about your shape, weight, or eating—also are associated with developing BED. BED also runs in families, and there may be a genetic component as well.

What Other Health Problems Can You Have with Binge Eating Disorder?

BED may lead to weight gain and health problems related to obesity. Overweight and obesity are associated with many health problems, including type two diabetes, heart disease, and certain types of cancer. People with BED may also have mental-health problems such as depression or anxiety. Some people with BED also have problems with their digestive system, or joint and muscle pain.

Symptoms and Causes of Binge Eating Disorder
What Are the Symptoms of Binge Eating Disorder?

If you have BED, you may

- Eat a large amount of food in a short amount of time; for example, within two hours
- Feel you lack control over your eating; for example, you cannot stop eating or control what or how much you are eating

You also may

- Eat more quickly than usual during binge episodes
- Eat until you feel uncomfortably full
- Eat large amounts of food even when you are not hungry
- Eat alone because you are embarrassed about the amount of food you eat
- Feel disgusted, depressed, or guilty after overeating

If you think that you or someone close to you may have BED, share your concerns with a healthcare provider. She or he can connect you to helpful sources of care.

What Causes Binge Eating Disorder

No one knows for sure what causes BED. Like other eating disorders, BED may result from a mix of factors related to your genes, your thoughts and feelings, and social issues. BED has been linked to depression and anxiety.

For some people, dieting in unhealthy ways—such as skipping meals, not eating enough food, or avoiding certain kinds of food—may contribute to binge eating.

Diagnosis and Treatment of Binge Eating Disorder
How Do Doctors Diagnose Binge Eating Disorder?

Most of us overeat from time to time, and some of us often feel we have eaten more than we should have. Eating a lot of food does not necessarily mean you have BED.

To determine if you have BED, you may want to talk with a specialist in eating disorders, such as a psychiatrist, psychologist, or other mental-health professional. She or he will talk with you about your symptoms and eating patterns. If a healthcare provider determines you have BED, she or he can work with you to find the best treatment options.

How Do Doctors Treat Binge Eating Disorder?

Talk to your doctor if you think you have BED. Ask her or him to refer you to a mental-health professional in your area. A specialist, such as a psychiatrist, psychologist, or other mental-health professional, may be able to help you choose the best treatment for you. Treatment may include therapy to help you change your eating habits, as well as thoughts and feelings that may lead to binge eating and other psychological symptoms. Types of therapy that have been shown to help people with BED are called psychotherapies and include cognitive-behavioral therapy (CBT), interpersonal psychotherapy, and dialectical behavior therapy. Your psychiatrist or other healthcare provider may also prescribe medication to help you with your binge eating, or to treat other medical or mental-health problems.

Should You Try to Lose Weight If You Have Binge Eating Disorder?

Losing weight may help prevent or reduce some of the health problems related to carrying excess weight. Binge eating may make it hard to lose weight and keep it off. If you have BED and are overweight, a weight-loss program that also offers treatment for eating disorders may help you lose weight. However, some people with BED do just as well in a behavioral treatment program designed only for weight loss as people who do not binge eat. Talk with your healthcare professional to help you decide whether you should try to manage your binge eating before entering a weight-management program.

Body Dysmorphic Disorder

This section includes text excerpted from "Body Dysmorphic Disorder," Office on Women's Health (OWH), U.S. Department of Health and Human Services (HHS), August 30, 2018.

We all sometimes worry about how we look, but body dysmorphic disorder (BDD) is a serious illness in which a person is overly worried about minor or imaginary physical flaws. These perceived flaws are usually not apparent to anyone else or are seen as minor. A person with BDD may feel so anxious about these physical flaws that she avoids social situations and relationships. She may also try to fix perceived flaws with cosmetic surgery.

What Is Body Dysmorphic Disorder?

BDD is a serious illness in which a person is overly worried about their appearance or about minor or imaginary physical flaws. Most of us worry about our appearance sometimes or are unhappy with some part of the way we look, but these worries don't usually affect our daily lives, such as whether we go to work or school. People with BDD check their appearance in a mirror constantly, try to cover up their perceived flaw, or worry about it for at least an hour a day, and that worry interferes with their life in some way.

Women with BDD may worry about any part of their body, such as acne or another skin problem, a scar, the size and shape of their nose, their breast size, or their body shape.

What Are the Symptoms of Body Dysmorphic Disorder?

The symptoms of BDD include:

- Being preoccupied with minor or imaginary physical flaws, which usually can't be seen by others
- Having a strong belief that you have a defect in your appearance that makes you ugly or deformed
- Having a lot of anxiety and stress about the perceived flaw and spending a lot of time focusing on it
- Frequently picking at skin

- Excessively checking your appearance in a mirror and grooming yourself

- Hiding the perceived imperfection

- Constantly comparing appearance with others to the point that it becomes your biggest focus or worry

- Constantly seeking reassurance from others about how you look and not believing them when they compliment your appearance

- Getting cosmetic surgery but not being happy with the outcome many times

Who Gets Body Dysmorphic Disorder

One in every 50 people may have BDD. The condition is more common in women and usually starts in the teen years. People with BDD often have other mental-health conditions, especially eating disorders, depression, and anxiety.

What Causes Body Dysmorphic Disorder

Researchers aren't sure exactly what causes BDD, but certain factors probably play a role:

- **Brain differences.** Physical changes in the brain's shape or how it works may play a role in causing BDD.

- **Family history.** Some studies show that BDD is more common in people whose mother, father, or siblings also have BDD or obsessive-compulsive disorder (OCD).

- **Childhood experiences.** Situations or events that happened in your childhood may make you more likely to develop BDD. For example, people who are teased about their bodies, whose families focused on the child's worth only through physical appearance, or who were abused during childhood may be more likely to develop BDD.

Who Is at Risk for Body Dysmorphic Disorder?

Certain things seem to increase the risk of developing or triggering BDD, including:

- A mother, father, or sibling with BDD or OCD

- Negative life experiences, such as being teased, bullied, or abused

- Another mental-health condition, such as depression or an anxiety disorder

How Is Body Dysmorphic Disorder Treated?

Your doctor may treat BDD with therapy and medicines.

- **Cognitive-behavioral therapy.** This type of therapy may involve putting yourself in social situations while forcing yourself not to check or cover up your "flaws." Your therapist may also ask you to change your behaviors or environment at home by removing mirrors, taking less time with your beauty routine, or not using makeup.

- **Medicines.** Certain antidepressants can help with obsessive and compulsive thoughts and behaviors.

Getting cosmetic surgery can make BDD worse. People with BDD are often not happy with the outcome of the surgery and continue to obsess over imaginary defects.

Chapter 18

Addictions

Chapter Contents

Section 18.1

Biology of Addiction

This section includes text excerpted from "Biology of Addiction," *NIH News in Health*, National Institutes of Health (NIH), October 2015. Reviewed December 2018.

Drugs and Alcohol Can Hijack Your Brain

People with addiction lose control over their actions. They crave and seek out drugs, alcohol, or other substances no matter what the cost—even at the risk of damaging friendships, hurting family, or losing jobs. What is it about addiction that makes people behave in such destructive ways? And why is it so hard to quit?

The National Institutes of Health (NIH)-funded scientists are working to learn more about the biology of addiction. They've shown that addiction is a long-lasting and complex brain disease and that current treatments can help people control their addictions. But even for those who've successfully quit, there's always a risk of the addiction returning, which is called relapse.

The biological basis of addiction helps to explain why people need much more than good intentions or willpower to break their addictions.

"A common misperception is that addiction is a choice or moral problem, and all you have to do is stop. But nothing could be further from the truth," says Dr. George Koob, director of NIH's National Institute on Alcohol Abuse and Alcoholism (NIAAA). "The brain actually changes with addiction, and it takes a good deal of work to get it back to its normal state. The more drugs or alcohol you've taken, the more disruptive it is to the brain."

Researchers have found that much of addiction's power lies in its ability to hijack and even destroy key brain regions that are meant to help us survive.

A healthy brain rewards healthy behaviors—such as exercising, eating, or bonding with loved ones. It does this by switching on brain circuits that make you feel wonderful, which then motivates you to repeat those behaviors. In contrast, when you're in danger, a healthy brain pushes your body to react quickly with fear or alarm, so you'll get out of harm's way. If you're tempted by something questionable—such as eating ice cream before dinner or buying things you can't afford—the front regions of your brain can help you decide if the consequences are worth the actions.

But when you're becoming addicted to a substance, that normal hardwiring of helpful brain processes can begin to work against you. Drugs or alcohol can hijack the pleasure/reward circuits in your brain and hook you into wanting more and more. Addiction can also send your emotional danger-sensing circuits into overdrive, making you feel anxious and stressed when you're not using the drugs or alcohol. At this stage, people often use drugs or alcohol to keep from feeling bad rather than for their pleasurable effects.

To add to that, repeated use of drugs can damage the essential decision-making center at the front of the brain. This area, known as the prefrontal cortex, is the very region that should help you recognize the harms of using addictive substances.

"Brain imaging studies of people addicted to drugs or alcohol show decreased activity in this frontal cortex," says Dr. Nora Volkow, director of NIH's National Institute on Drug Abuse (NIDA). "When the frontal cortex isn't working properly, people can't make the decision to stop taking the drug—even if they realize the price of taking that drug may be extremely high, and they might lose custody of their children or end up in jail. Nonetheless, they take it."

Scientists don't yet understand why some people become addicted while others don't. Addiction tends to run in families, and certain types of genes have been linked to different forms of addiction. But not all members of an affected family are necessarily prone to addiction. "As with heart disease or diabetes, there's no one gene that makes you vulnerable," Koob says.

Other factors can also raise your chances of addiction. "Growing up with an alcoholic; being abused as a child; being exposed to extraordinary stress—all of these social factors can contribute to the risk for alcohol addiction or drug abuse," Koob says. "And with drugs or underage drinking, the earlier you start, the greater the likelihood of having alcohol use disorder (AUD) or addiction later in life."

Teens are especially vulnerable to possible addiction because their brains are not yet fully developed—particularly the frontal regions that help with impulse control and assessing risk. Pleasure circuits in adolescent brains also operate in overdrive, making drug and alcohol use even more rewarding and enticing.

Prevention is critical to reducing the harms of addiction. "Childhood and adolescence are times when parents can get involved and teach their kids about a healthy lifestyle and activities that can protect against the use of drugs," Volkow says. "Physical activity is important, as well as getting engaged in work, science projects, art, or social networks that do not promote the use of drugs."

To treat addiction, scientists have identified several medications and behavioral therapies—especially when used in combination—that can help people stop using specific substances and prevent relapse. Unfortunately, no medications are yet available to treat addiction to stimulants such as cocaine or methamphetamine, but behavioral therapies can help.

"Treatment depends to a large extent on the severity of addiction and the individual person," Koob adds. "Some people can stop cigarette smoking and drinking alcohol on their own. More severe cases might require months or even years of treatment and follow-up, with real efforts by the individual and usually complete abstinence from the substance afterward."

The NIH-funded researchers are also evaluating experimental therapies that might enhance the effectiveness of established treatments. Mindfulness meditation and magnetic stimulation of the brain are being assessed for their ability to strengthen brain circuits that have been harmed by addiction. Scientists are also examining the potential of vaccines against nicotine, cocaine, and other drugs, which might prevent the drug from entering the brain.

"Addiction is a devastating disease, with a relatively high death rate and serious social consequences," Volkow says. "We're exploring multiple strategies so individuals will eventually have more treatment options, which will increase their chances of success to help them stop taking the drug."

Warning Signs of Addiction

Warning signs of substance abuse or addiction may include:

- Sleep difficulties

- Anxiety or depression

- Memory problems

- Mood swings (temper flare-ups, irritability, defensiveness)

- Rapid increases in the amount of medication needed

- Frequent requests for refills of certain medicines

- A person not seeming like themselves (showing a general lack of interest or being overly energetic)

- "Doctor shopping" (moving from provider to provider in an effort to get several prescriptions for the same medication)

- Use of more than one pharmacy
- False or forged prescriptions

Section 18.2

Mental Health and Substance-Use Disorders

This section includes text excerpted from "Mental Health and Substance Use Disorders," MentalHealth.gov, U.S. Department of Health and Human Services (HHS), September 26, 2017.

Mental-health problems and substance-use disorders (SUDs) sometimes occur together. This is because:

- Certain illegal drugs can cause people with an addiction to experience one or more symptoms of a mental-health problem
- Mental-health problems can sometimes lead to alcohol or drug use, as some people with a mental-health problem may misuse these substances as a form of self-medication
- Mental and SUD share some underlying causes, including changes in brain composition, genetic vulnerabilities, and early exposure to stress or trauma

More than one in four adults living with serious mental-health problems also has a substance-use problem. Substance-use problems occur more frequently with certain mental-health problems, including:

- Depression
- Anxiety disorders
- Schizophrenia
- Personality disorders

Substance-Use Disorders

SUD can refer to substance use or substance dependence. Symptoms of SUD may include:

Behavioral changes, such as:

- Drop in attendance and performance at work or school
- Frequently getting into trouble (fights, accidents, illegal activities)
- Using substances in physically hazardous situations such as while driving or operating a machine
- Engaging in secretive or suspicious behaviors
- Changes in appetite or sleep patterns
- Unexplained change in personality or attitude
- Sudden mood swings, irritability, or angry outbursts
- Periods of unusual hyperactivity, agitation, or giddiness
- Lack of motivation
- Appearing fearful, anxious, or paranoid, with no reason

Physical changes, such as:

- Bloodshot eyes and abnormally sized pupils
- Sudden weight loss or weight gain
- Deterioration of physical appearance
- Unusual smells on breath, body, or clothing
- Tremors, slurred speech, or impaired coordination

Social changes, such as:

- Sudden change in friends, favorite hangouts, and hobbies
- Legal problems related to substance use
- Unexplained need for money or financial problems
- Using substances even though it causes problems in relationships

Recovering from Mental-Health Problems and Substance Use

Someone with a mental-health problem and SUD must treat both issues. Treatment for both mental-health problems and SUD may include rehabilitation, medications, support groups, and talk therapy.

Section 18.3

Alcoholism and Mental Health

This section includes text excerpted from "Alcohol Use Disorder, Substance Use Disorder, and Addiction," Office on Women's Health (OWH), U.S. Department of Health and Human Services (HHS), August 28, 2018.

What Is Alcoholism or Alcohol Use Disorder?

Alcoholism is also called alcohol use disorder (AUD). AUD is a medical diagnosis from a doctor. AUD is a condition in which a person cannot control how much alcohol she or he drinks. The condition also causes distress or harm in your life. AUD is chronic, or lifelong, and it can get worse over time and be life-threatening. It is a condition that happens in the brain.

How Is Alcohol Use Disorder Diagnosed?

If you can answer yes to at least two of the following questions, you may have an AUD. The more questions you answer yes to, the more serious your AUD may be.

In the past 12 months, have you:

- Ended up drinking more or longer than you meant to?

- Wanted to cut down on or stop drinking or tried to but found you couldn't?

- Spent a lot of time drinking, being sick from drinking, or experiencing other side effects from drinking?

- Wanted to drink so badly you couldn't think of anything else?

- Had trouble at home, work, or school because of drinking or being sick from drinking?

- Continued to drink even though it caused problems with friends or family?

- Cut back on activities or hobbies that you liked in order to spend time drinking?

- Gotten into a dangerous situation as a direct result of your drinking (such as driving while drunk or having unsafe sex)?

- Kept drinking despite feeling that it was making you depressed or anxious?

- Had a memory blackout?

- Had to drink a lot more to get the same effect?

- Found that when you weren't drinking, you had withdrawal symptoms such as shakiness, trouble sleeping, or nausea?

If you can answer "yes" to at least two of these questions, talk to your doctor, nurse, or a mental-health professional as soon as possible. You may have an AUD.

It is possible to misuse alcohol but not have AUD, such as by occasional binge drinking. Binge drinking is also harmful to your health. AUD can also be mild, moderate, or severe.

Who Is at Risk for Alcohol Use Disorder or Substance-Use Disorder?

A woman is more likely to misuse alcohol or drugs if she experiences:

- Parents and siblings with alcohol or drug problems

- A partner who drinks too much or misuses drugs

- Needing more and more of a drug or alcohol to get the same high

- A history of depression

- A history of childhood physical or sexual abuse

How Can You Tell If You Have a Problem with Alcohol or Drugs?

Answering the following questions can help you find out whether you or someone close to you has a problem with drinking or drugs.

- Have you ever felt that you drink too much and should cut down?

- Have you ever felt bad or guilty about your drinking?

- Have you ever had a drink as soon as you woke up to steady your nerves or to get rid of a hangover?

- Have you ever used a drug for nonmedical reasons?

- Has using drugs or alcohol created problems for you at home or at work?

- Do your family or friends complain about your drug or alcohol use?

- Have you gotten in fights or broken the law because you were on drugs or drunk?

- Do you continue to use drugs or alcohol even though you know it's harmful?

One "yes" answer suggests a possible problem. If you responded yes to more than one question, it is very likely that you have a problem. Talk to a doctor, nurse, or mental-health professional as soon as possible. You may need to talk to a psychiatrist, psychologist, or substance-abuse counselor. Your doctor may also want to test your blood or urine to help design a treatment program for you.

How Is Alcohol Use Disorder Treated?

Treatment for an AUD depends on how severe it is. Talk to your doctor or nurse about how much you drink. Your doctor or nurse can help find the ways alcohol negatively affects your life and can help you make a plan to stop.

Treatment for AUD can include counseling, behavior therapy, and medicine. Some people may need to stay at a treatment center (including sleeping there). Many people also attend support groups, such as Alcoholics Anonymous (AA), to talk to others and get support from people who have had similar problems in the past.

After treatment, some people stop drinking and stay sober. Others have periods of being sober but then start drinking again and may need treatment again. You can get better with treatment and support.

Section 18.4

Comorbidity: Addiction and Other Mental Disorders

This section includes text excerpted from "Comorbidity:
Substance Use Disorders and Other Mental Illnesses," National
Institute on Drug Abuse (NIDA), August 2018.

What Is Comorbidity?

Comorbidity describes two or more disorders or illnesses occurring
in the same person. They can occur at the same time or one after the
other. Comorbidity also implies interactions between the illnesses that
can worsen the course of both.

Is Drug Addiction a Mental Illness?

Yes. Addiction changes the brain in fundamental ways, changing
a person's normal needs and desires and replacing them with new
priorities connected with seeking and using the drug. This results
in compulsive behaviors that weaken the ability to control impulses,
despite the negative consequences, and are similar to hallmarks of
other mental illnesses.

How Common Are Comorbid Substance Use-Disorders and Other Mental Illnesses?

Many people who have a substance-use disorder (SUD) also develop
other mental illnesses, just as many people who life-threatening with
mental illness are often diagnosed with a SUD. For example, about
half of people who experience a mental illness will also experience a
SUD at some point in their lives and vice versa. Few studies have been
done on comorbidity in children, but those that have been conducted
suggest that youth with SUD also have high rates of co-occurring
mental illness, such as depression and anxiety.

Why Do These Disorders Often Co-Occur?

Although SUD commonly occurs with other mental illnesses,
this does not mean that one caused the other, even if one appeared
first. In fact, establishing which came first or why can be difficult.

However, research suggests three possibilities for this common co-occurrence:

- **Common risk factors can contribute to both mental illness and SUD.** Research suggests that there are many genes that can contribute to the risk of developing both a SUD and a mental illness. For example, some people have a specific gene that can make them at an increased risk of mental illness as an adult, if they frequently used marijuana as a child. A gene can also influence how a person responds to a drug—whether or not using the drug makes them feel good. Environmental factors, such as stress or trauma, can cause genetic changes that are passed down through generations and may contribute to the development of mental illnesses or a SUD.

- **Mental illnesses can contribute to drug use and SUD.** Some mental-health conditions have been identified as risk factors for developing a SUD. For example, some research suggests that people with mental illness may use drugs or alcohol as a form of self-medication. Although some drugs may help with mental-illness symptoms, sometimes this can also make the symptoms worse. Additionally, when a person develops a mental illness, brain changes may enhance the rewarding effects of substances, predisposing the person to continue using the substance.

- **Substance use and addiction can contribute to the development of mental illness.** Substance use may change the brain in ways that make a person more likely to develop a mental illness.

How Are These Comorbid Conditions Diagnosed and Treated?

The high rate of comorbidity between SUD and other mental illnesses calls for a comprehensive approach that identifies and evaluates both. Accordingly, anyone seeking help for either substance use, misuse, or addiction or another mental disorder should be evaluated for both and treated accordingly.

Several behavioral therapies have shown promise for treating comorbid conditions. These approaches can be tailored to patients according to age, the specific drug misused, and other factors. They can be used alone or in combinations with medications. Some effective behavioral therapies for treating comorbid conditions include:

- **Cognitive-behavioral therapy (CBT)** helps to change harmful beliefs and behaviors.

- **Dialectical-behavioral therapy (DBT)** was designed specifically to reduce self-harm behaviors including suicide attempts, thoughts, or urges; cutting; and drug use.

- **Assertive community treatment (ACT)** emphasizes outreach to the community and an individualized approach to treatment.

- **Therapeutic communities (TCs)** are a common form of long-term residential treatment that focuses on the "resocialization" of the person.

- **Contingency management (CM)** gives vouchers or rewards to people who practice healthy behaviors.

Effective medications exist for treating opioid, alcohol, and nicotine addiction and for alleviating the symptoms of many other mental disorders, yet most have not been well studied in comorbid populations. Some medications may benefit multiple problems. For example, bupropion is approved for treating both depression (Wellbutrin®) and nicotine dependence (Zyban®). More research is needed, however, to better understand how these medications work, particularly when combined in patients with comorbidities.

Chapter 19

Control Disorders

Chapter Contents

Section 19.1

Impulse Control Disorders

What Are Impulse Control Disorders?

Impulse control disorders (ICDs) are a group of disorders in which a person is unable to resist the impulse to do something negative even though it has harmful consequences. Research indicated that of those American diagnosed with a mental-health disorder, 10 percent of them suffer from ICD.

People with ICD experience a regular, overwhelming desire to engage in a negative behavior and progressive lack of control. Performing the negative behavior will provide them with a sense of relief or pleasure.

ICDs are seen more in males than in females and they generally coexist with an underlying mental-health disorder like substance abuse. It can be challenging to identify individuals with ICD as they may not seek help.

The medical community classifies the following disorders under ICDs:

- **Intermittent explosive disorder (IED)**—This disorder is characterized by uncontrolled fits of extreme anger and violence. People with this disorder usually allow their negative behavior to grow out of control, and, in the long run, their actions result in legal or financial issues, disrupt interpersonal relationships, and potentially result in problems at work or school.

- **Kleptomania**—Kleptomania is characterized by an irresistible compulsion to steal. Those who suffer from the disorder do not steal because they desire an object or seek financial gain. Their only motivation is to satisfy their desire to steal. Following an episode, the person will feel intense guilt and shame.

- **Pyromania**—Pyromaniacs have irresistible urges to set fires. Again, the person does this out of mental compulsion with no other intention.

- **Conduct disorder**—A disorder that involves an individual displaying repetitive and persistent behaviors that violate social norms and the rights of others.

Other disorders include:

- **Exhibitionism**—Compulsive need to expose one's genitals to an unsuspecting stranger.

- **Pathological gambling**—Uncontrollable addiction to gambling.

- **Trichotillomania**—Individuals with this disorder compulsively twist and pull their hair, often resulting in bald spots.

What Are the Causes of Impulse Control Disorders?

The exact cause of ICD is unknown; however, medical professionals generally agree that a combination of various factors, including biological, environmental, psychological, and even cultural or societal factors, may play a role in causing this disorder. Research has also indicated that these disorders may be caused by a neurotransmitter imbalance in the brain as well as hormonal imbalances, such as elevated testosterone levels, that can result in aggressive behaviors.

Other risk factors, including stressful living conditions, childhood trauma or neglect, and mitigating environmental factors, may also influence the disorder's onset. Medical disorders such as seizures may cause trauma to the brain, resulting in ICD.

Preexisting mental-health disorders such as substance abuse can alter the brain's chemistry and thereby increase the risk of ICDs.

How Are Impulse Control Disorders Treated?

Since a combination of factors causes ICDs, treatment also typically involves a combination of methods and usually involves medication, psychotherapy, and behavioral-modification therapy (BMT).

- **Cognitive therapy** will encourage the individual to identify negative behavioral patterns and the negative consequences associated with those behaviors.

- **BMT** will teach new coping mechanisms and techniques on how to avoid situations leading to impulsive behaviors. Cognitive-behavioral therapy (CBT) has been widely used and it is found to be an effective therapy.

- **Exposure therapy** places the individual in the situations leading to impulsive behaviors while working with her or him to exercise self-control. This helps the person to build tolerance to the situation gradually and respond appropriately.

- **Other complimentary methods**, such as mindfulness techniques, yoga or meditation, hypnotism, and herbal remedies, can also be beneficial in helping people learn how to improve willpower and control emotions when faced with stressors.

Although no drugs are specially approved in the treatment of ICD, some medications have proven effective in some cases. Selective serotonin reuptake inhibitors (SSRIs) are antidepressant medications that have shown effectiveness in treating ICDs.

Before starting a medication to treat an ICD, patient should be screened for drug and alcohol addiction. This will help avoid unnecessary complications and ensure safe care for the individual. If an individual is addicted, she or he should undergo a detox program before starting medication for ICD.

References

1. "Impulse Control Disorder and Abuse," American Addiction Centers, n.d.

2. "The State of Mental Health in America," Mental Health America (MHA), n.d.

3. "Impulse Control Disorders," Disorders.org, n.d.

4. Patricelli, Kathryn. "Impulse Control Disorder," Gulf Bend Center, n.d.

5. "Impulse Control Disorder," East Central Mental Health Center, n.d.

Section 19.2

Disruptive Behavior Disorders

This section includes text excerpted from "Disruptive Behavior Disorders," Substance Abuse and Mental Health Services Administration (SAMHSA), April 5, 2017.

It is common for children and adolescents to sometimes argue, be uncooperative, and defy parents or teachers. This is more likely when they are overwhelmed or stressed. When angry or hostile behavior persists and leads to problems at home, school, or with friends, there may be a more serious issue.

Disruptive behavior disorders (DBD) involve an ongoing pattern of uncooperative or hostile actions, such as temper tantrums, fighting, cruelty, arguing, and defiance toward parents, teachers, or other authority figures. Young people with these disorders finds it hard to control their emotions and actions. This leads to problems at school and in relationships with family or friends.

The two most common DBDs are oppositional defiant disorder (ODD) and conduct disorder (CD).

Signs and Symptoms of Oppositional Defiant Disorder

Children and adolescents with oppositional defiant disorder (ODD) show ongoing hostility. They are irritable. They argue with parents, teachers, and friends. They often rebel, defy rules, and hold grudges. They often have problems behaving at school. All young people behave this way at times. A young person with ODD shows these symptoms regularly.

In ODD, a young person's actions are worse than in other children of the same age. The symptoms interfere with daily life. Young people with ODD may show symptoms only at home at first. Over time, they may show symptoms in other settings such as school, activities outside of school, and relating to authority figures. Young people with ODD are at higher risk for depression or anxiety as they get older.

The three main types of ODD symptoms are an angry and irritable mood, argumentative and defiant behavior, and vindictiveness. The symptoms are different in children younger than age five than in older children and adolescents.

Angry and Irritable Mood

Examples of angry and irritable mood include:

- Losing one's temper often

- Being easily annoyed by others

  Showing outbursts of rage or resentment toward others

Argumentative and Defiant Behavior

Examples of argumentative and defiant behavior include:

- Arguing with adults or other authority figures

- Defying rules or refusing to do things that an adult authority figure requests

- Deliberately annoying or upsetting others

- Blaming others for their own mistakes or misbehaviors

Vindictiveness

Examples of vindictiveness include:

- Showing a spiteful, nasty, or cruel attitude toward others

- Being mean, vengeful, or punishing toward others

Signs and Symptoms of Conduct Disorder

Conduct disorder (CD) involves ongoing disruptive and violent actions that violate the rights of others, hurt others, or are not age appropriate. For example, a school-aged child might bully and physically fight with classmates, or an adolescent might destroy someone's property.

Children who develop CD at a young age tend to have long-term behavior problems that last into adulthood. Often, young people with CD had ODD at a younger age. The symptoms of CD cause problems in daily life, such as at school, in friendships, or at home. Young people with CD have problems considering others' needs or feelings.

The four main types of CD symptoms are: aggression to people and animals, destruction of property, deceit or theft, and serious violation of rules.

Aggression to People and Animals

Examples of aggression to people and animals include:

- Bullying, threatening, or intimidating others
- Starting physical fights
- Using weapons that can harm others
- Being physically cruel to people or animals
- Stealing from others, such as mugging or purse snatching
- Forcing others into sexual activity

Destruction of Property

Examples of destruction of property include:

- Setting fires
- Destroying others' property

Deceit or Theft

Examples of deceit or theft include:

- Lying to get things from others
- Stealing things without others knowing, such as shoplifting
- Breaking into someone's home, car, or building

Serious Violation of Rules

Examples of serious rule violations include:

- Breaking family rules, such as when to be home at night
- Running away from home overnight at least twice, or once without returning for a long time
- Often skipping school

Risk Factors of Oppositional Defiant Disorder

ODD usually starts in preschool or childhood, and sometimes in early adolescence. About three percent of children have ODD. In young children, ODD is more common in males than females. In school-age children and adolescents, ODD occurs about equally in males and females.

Risk Factors of Conduct Disorder

About eight percent of children and adolescents have CD at some point. Symptoms may start in preschool, but they usually start in middle childhood or adolescence. CD becomes more common in adolescence. It is more common in males than females. Males with CD usually have problems such as fighting, stealing, vandalism, and school discipline. Females with CD tend to show symptoms such as lying, running away, truancy, spreading rumors, and misusing friendships.

Risk Factors across Disruptive Behavior Disorders

There is no single cause for these disorders. It is unclear why some children develop them. Biological, environmental, and psychological factors may play a role.

Biological Factors

Young people are more likely to develop DBD if they have:

- A parent who had ODD or CD

- A parent who had other behavioral disorders, such as schizophrenia, depression or bipolar disorder, attention deficit hyperactivity disorder (ADHD), or a severe alcohol use disorder

- Differences in parts of the brain involved in mood, judgment, problem-solving, perceptions of threats, and impulse control

Environmental Factors

In some cases, the following may be risk factors for a DBD:

- Abuse or neglect
- Being abandoned by parents or guardians
- Chaotic environments, including lack of structure or rules
- Exposure to violence
- Parental criminality

Psychological Factors

The following may be risk factors for a DBD:

- High emotional reactivity

- Difficulties controlling emotions

- Problems dealing with frustration

Co-Occurring Disorders

Many children and adolescents with DBDs have other disorders such as ADHD, anxiety disorders, depression, bipolar disorder, substance-use disorders (SUDs), or learning problems. Disruptive behaviors can be hard to treat if other disorders are not treated.

ADHD is the most common disorder tied to disruptive behaviors. Young people with both ADHD and disruptive behaviors tend to have more severe symptoms. ADHD combined with ODD tends to lead to more problems with aggression, misbehavior, and school performance. Delinquency in adolescence, aggression in adolescence, and serious violent offenses in adulthood are more likely in people with both CD and ADHD than with CD alone.

Evidence-Based Treatments for Disruptive Behavior Disorders

Early treatment is best. A trained professional should do a full evaluation to make the diagnosis. No single treatment works best. Treatments must address each person's needs and symptoms. Treatment must consider the child's age and development, the severity of symptoms, any co-occurring disorder, and the child's ability to participate in treatment. The treatment plan should consider the goals and abilities of family members.

A young person or caregiver should consult a healthcare professional when choosing the right treatment and consider the patient's own gender, race, ethnicity, language, and culture.

Intervention Programs

Parent training, behavioral family therapy (BFT), and skills-based interventions are common approaches.

Parent Training

Parent training programs teach skills that family members can use to manage a child's behavior. Skills include rewarding positive actions, communicating well, giving clear instruction, using discipline and supervision, and managing outbursts and aggression.

Examples of effective parent training programs include:

- Helping the Noncompliant Child (for children ages three to eight)

- Parent-Child Interaction Therapy (PCIT) (for children ages two to eight)

- Incredible Years Program (for children up to age 12)

- Triple P-Positive Parenting Program (for children up to age 16)

- Parent Management Training—Oregon Model (PMTO) (for children ages 2–18)

- The Kadin Method for Parenting the Defiant Child

- Familia Adelante (FA) (for high-risk Latino/Latina youth and their families)

Behavioral Family Therapy

Behavioral family therapy (BFT) programs involve working with the family and the child or adolescent. The family learns how to support wellness. The programs can include parent training and ways to deal with complex behavior problems.

Multisystemic therapy (MST) focuses on all areas of life that might affect a person's actions. This includes home, family, teachers, neighborhoods, and friends. The idea is that each area plays a role in how the person acts and reacts. Focusing on these areas helps improve a person's life.

Functional family therapy (FFT) is a strength-based approach. It focuses on risk factors and protective factors within and outside of the family. The person learns to avoid risk factors and build protective factors.

Brief strategic family therapy (BSFT) is a problem-focused approach. It focuses on skill building. It helps families overcome individual and family-wide behavior patterns. It provides strategies for bringing families into therapy.

Multidimensional treatment foster care (MTFC) gives young people a place to stay in the community instead of hospital care, group homes, juvenile justice centers, or residential care. Families learn to provide treatment and supervision at home, in school, and in the community. The program emphasizes clear rules with follow-through on consequences and rewards for good behavior. It also includes guidance from a mentoring adult and avoiding friends who may influence bad behaviors.

Skills-Based Interventions

Skills-based interventions teach young people to deal with problematic events and actions. This includes how to relate to others, interpret situations, and respond to upsetting events. The interventions may be combined with other treatments to address severe disruptive behaviors:

- **Cognitive behavioral therapy (CBT)** teaches young people skills to reduce behavior problems.

- **Social skills training (SST)** helps young people learn how to interact with peers.

- **Cognitive problem-solving training (CPSST)** and coping skills training teach young people positive ways to respond to stressful events, cope with difficulty, and change thought patterns that lead to bad behaviors.

- **Anger management** is individual therapy that helps young people learn how to manage anger and respond better to situations.

- **Aggression replacement training (ART)** is a structured program for aggressive youth that teaches social skills and anger control and builds awareness of fairness, justice, and concern for the rights and needs of others.

Medication

Medication alone is not used to treat DBDs. It may be useful as part of a treatment plan that includes treating ADHD, mood disorders, or anxiety disorders, or other physical or mental disorders. For example, when medication is used to treat ADHD, disruptive behaviors tend to decrease.

Complementary Therapies and Activities for Disruptive Behavior Disorders

Complementary therapies and activities can help young people improve their well-being, and are meant to be used along with evidence-based treatments (EBT).

Early Intervention and Prevention Programs

Dealing with early symptoms can help reduce or prevent problems tied to DBDs. Effective prevention programs and early assessment and treatment can help improve children's actions and stop symptoms from getting worse.

Early identification screening for disruptive behaviors is sometimes done with preschool children who have behavior problems at school or at home. Identifying the child's needs early and providing treatment and supports may improve outcomes for the child and family.

Parent training programs can prevent aggressive, disruptive, and antisocial actions by young people. Such programs teach parents how to:

- Develop warm, nurturing relationships with their children
- Replace harsh parenting with consistent discipline that sets boundaries for misbehavior
- Use positive parenting methods to reward good behavior

School-Wide Positive Behavioral Supports (SWPBS) focus on improving classroom management and improving students' relationships, self-awareness, decision-making, and social skills. The programs include consequences for misbehavior and rewards for good behavior. Students with severe behavioral needs may receive team-based services.

Other Services

Stress management for families can help caregivers and families of young people with disruptive behaviors deal with frustration and respond calmly to misbehavior.

Mentoring programs for at-risk youth, community-based programs, and programs lasting a year or more can help young people with disruptive behaviors.

Solution-focused therapy helps young people with disruptive behaviors learn to achieve goals. This approach assumes that the person knows what would make life better. The sessions help the person take steps to improve their life.

Wraparound services can address the needs of young people with disruptive behaviors. This involves a team that plans community-based services (CBS). The team may include family members, service providers, teachers, and agency staff. They work together to create and use a personal care plan.

SUD treatment is often needed for children and especially adolescents with disruptive behaviors. Alcohol and drug use is common in this group and must be dealt with for other treatments to work.

Yoga, meditation, mindfulness activities, and participation in sports with an involved coach can help reduce disruptive behaviors.

Recovery and Support Services and Activities for Disruptive Behavior Disorders

Self-help and support groups can provide youth and their families with knowledge and support to make treatment decisions that work for them. Organizations and websites provide self-help information and help youth and families find local support groups. They can help foster hope and promote outreach and engagement. This includes both youth peer-to-peer and family-to-family supports provided by a certified peer or family support specialist who can promote hope, foster recovery, and build resiliency skills.

Finding Treatment for Disruptive Behavior Disorders

Consult a healthcare professional who has training and experience working with DBDs.

Section 19.3

Self-Harm

This section includes text excerpted from "Hurtful Emotions," *NIH News in Health*, National Institutes of Health (NIH), September 7, 2017.

Understanding Self-Harm

People deal with difficult feelings in all sorts of ways. They may talk with friends, go work out, or listen to music. But some people may feel an urge to hurt themselves when distressed. Harming or thinking about harming yourself doesn't mean you have a mental disorder. But it is an unhealthy way to cope with strong feelings. Finding new ways to cope can help you get through difficult times.

Some unhealthy ways people may try to relieve emotional pain include cutting, burning, or hitting themselves. These behaviors can be difficult to detect. People usually keep them a secret. Wounds can often be treated at home and covered with clothing or jewelry.

"The largest percentage of people who engage in nonsuicidal self-injuring behaviors are teenagers," says Dr. Jennifer Muehlenkamp, National Institutes of Health (NIH)-funded psychologist at the University of Wisconsin—Eau Claire. Around two out of ten teens and college-aged students report trying this behavior at least once.

Those are the key ages because youths are changing environments, Muehlenkamp explains. "Transitioning into college or from junior high into high school creates a lot of potential change. You lose the familiarity of your social group, and your social support might shift. There's a lot of new stress and pressures."

People who are anxious, depressed, or have an eating disorder are also more likely to turn to self-injuring behaviors. So are those in sexual minority groups who experience discrimination and bullying, such as those who identify as gay, lesbian, bisexual, or transsexual.

"Self-injury is a sign that someone is struggling," says Muehlenkamp. "Many youths transition out of it. But those who engage in it more repetitively and chronically may benefit from a direct clinical intervention."

If you're a parent or caregiver who's concerned, look for frequent unexplained injuries and clues like bandages in trash cans. Watch to see if the person wears appropriate clothing for the weather. Someone who is self-harming may wear long pants or sleeves to cover their injuries, even when it's hot.

"The way most people find out is the person who is self-injuring will disclose it," Muehlenkamp says. They often tell a friend or a sibling first.

If someone confides in you, "your first reaction is essential to whether or not they will seek help," Muehlenkamp explains. "Be as nonreactive and nonjudgmental as possible."

Not everyone who self-injures is suicidal. But the only way to know is to ask. If they express any suicidal thinking, get them connected with a mental-health provider. You can also call the National Suicide Prevention Lifeline (NSPL) at 800-273-8255 for advice.

Parents can open conversations with their kids by asking them if they've heard of self-harming behaviors or if they know friends who do it. If a friend has confided in them, they can offer to go talk to a trusted adult with their friend to get them help.

There are no medications for treating self-injuring behaviors. But some medications can help treat mental disorders that the person may be dealing with, like depression or anxiety. Mental-health counseling or therapy can also help you learn new ways to cope with emotion.

Ways to Cope

There's no right or wrong way to deal with intense emotions. If you're feeling distressed:

- Talk with friends.
- Watch a funny movie or read a comforting book.
- Listen to music.
- Get active. Go for a walk or get some exercise.
- Distract yourself with any activity or hobby you love.
- Avoid smoking, drinking, and other risky behaviors.
- Take care of your body. Eat and drink well. Get enough sleep.
- Realize it's okay to cry it out.

Section 19.4

Problem Gambling

This section includes text excerpted from "When the Stakes Turn Toxic," *NIH News in Health*, National Institutes of Health (NIH), May 2011. Reviewed December 2018.

About Problem Gambling

Anyone who's bought a lottery ticket or played bingo has gambled. Gambling is any game of chance in which money changes hands. It's common in most cultures around the world. Many people enjoy gambling as recreation without causing harm to themselves or others. Yet some people can't control their impulse to gamble, even when it takes a terrible toll on their lives.

For these gamblers and their families, researchers have been making progress in several areas. Scientists are learning why people have problems with gambling: how common it is, what goes on inside the gambler's brain, who is at risk and what kinds of treatment can help.

Problem gambling is defined by some researchers as gambling that causes harm to the gambler or someone else, in spite of a desire to stop. Between two percent and four percent of Americans struggle with this condition. Problem gambling can progress to a recognized psychiatric diagnosis called pathological gambling.

Pathological gambling may affect from 0.4 to 2 percent of Americans. "Pathological gambling comes with a constellation of problems that contribute to chaos," says Dr. Donald Black of the University of Iowa (UI). "It's associated with worse physical health, excessive smoking, excessive drinking, not exercising, not seeing primary care doctors and worse dental care. It also fuels depression, family dysfunction, crime, bankruptcy, and suicide."

Together, pathological and problem gambling may affect up to five percent of Americans. That number may rise, though. Laws in many states are creating more options for legal gambling, and Internet gambling are becoming more common.

Still, gambling is often done in family settings, condoned or encouraged by parents. And the younger you start, the more likely you are to get into trouble later on. From three to eight percent of adolescents have a problem with gambling.

Dr. John Welte of the University of Buffalo has found that, across the lifespan, gambling problems are even more common than alcohol dependence. They are also much more common in males, in young people, and in people who live in relatively poor neighborhoods. "That's not true of the prevalence of alcoholism," says Welte. "Alcoholism is much more democratic. So think about motives for gambling. People are hoping that winning will improve their lot. That makes them more vulnerable to developing a gambling problem."

In a study of mostly African-American inner-city youth, Dr. Silvia Martins of Johns Hopkins University has found that about 15 percent have some form of problem gambling. Most at-risk were adolescents and young adults who began showing symptoms of depression at age 12. They were highly impulsive, although not hyperactive or aggressive. As the African-American boys developed into their teens and early adulthood, gambling appeared to be a separate risk factor for early fatherhood and criminal arrest.

"We are following up with these inner-city kids every single year as they enter adulthood," says Martins.

But why is gambling irresistible to some folks and not others? Using advanced imaging techniques, Dr. Alexander Neumeister of Mount Sinai School of Medicine looked at the brains of people with gambling problems and alcohol problems. He measured the number of special receptors involved in regulating impulse control and other factors.

"A key feature of addiction is impaired impulse control," says Neumeister. "Abnormal function of the forebrain leads to reduced tolerance to waiting." The resulting impatience may cause people to act without considering the consequences. "Our imaging clearly points toward the importance of impaired forebrain function in addiction."

Pinpointing areas in the brain's reward center, Neumeister's team found that people with alcohol addiction and gambling problems show different functioning of these special receptors compared to healthy people. The differences were related to the severity of addiction. Other researchers are trying to develop drugs that could treat the affected areas.

Talk therapy can also help. Dr. Nancy Petry at the University of Connecticut Health Center works with pathological gamblers and people seeking treatment for drug use disorders. Gambling problems arise in about 10 to 20 percent of substance abusers. Petry compared the use of different types of talk therapy, including very brief interventions and cognitive-behavioral therapy (CBT). CBT teaches people how to think differently about problems and then act on that knowledge.

"We found very brief interventions and CBT were effective in reducing gambling and gambling-related problems," Petry says. "There was a significant improvement relative to usual care or standard forms of treatment like Gamblers Anonymous (a 12-step program)."

Anybody can have a gambling problem, and no one should feel ashamed or be afraid to seek treatment. "Pathological gambling is a medical disorder, not a sin or a vice," says Dr. Carlos Blanco of Columbia University and the New York State Psychiatric Institute (NYSPI). "There is no stereotype. The main predictor of outcome is really motivation."

In other words, what counts most is a strong drive or desire to take action. Blanco offers gamblers motivational interviewing, which helps them explore their mixed feelings about trying to quit gambling. This primes them to be ready and willing to begin CBT. Using both therapies together can be very effective.

If you have concerns about your gambling, ask for help. Your health provider can work with you to find the treatment that's best for you.

Signs of Problem Gambling

Are you troubled by gambling? Seek help if:

- You always think about gambling.

- You gamble with money you need for other things.

- You keep gambling even though you may feel bad afterward.

- You get nervous when you try to quit.

- You need to gamble with increasing amounts of money to get the same buzz.

- You lose money, but you return to "chase" losses by gambling even more.

- You spend work, school or family time gambling.

- You tell lies to hide your gambling.

- You lose a job, educational opportunity or relationship because of gambling.

- You find that no matter how hard you try, you can't stop.

Chapter 20

Tourette Syndrome

Tourette syndrome (TS) is a condition of the nervous system. TS causes people to have "tics."

Tics are sudden twitches, movements, or sounds that people do repeatedly. People who have tics cannot stop their body from doing these things. For example, a person might keep blinking over and over again. Or, a person might make a grunting sound unwillingly.

Having tics is a little bit like having hiccups. Even though you might not want to hiccup, your body does it anyway. Sometimes people can stop themselves from doing a certain tic for a while, but it's hard. Eventually, the person has to do the tic.

Types of Tics

There are two types of tics—motor and vocal:

Motor Tics

Motor tics are movements of the body. Examples of motor tics include blinking, shrugging the shoulders, or jerking an arm.

Vocal Tics

Vocal tics are sounds that a person makes with her or his voice. Examples of vocal tics include humming, clearing the throat, or yelling out a word or phrase.

This chapter includes text excerpted from "Facts about Tourette Syndrome," Centers for Disease Control and Prevention (CDC), April 13, 2018.

Tics can be either simple or complex:

Simple Tics

Simple tics involve just a few parts of the body. Examples of simple tics include squinting the eyes or sniffing.

Complex Tics

Complex tics usually involve several different parts of the body and can have a pattern. An example of a complex tic is bobbing the head while jerking an arm and then jumping up.

Symptoms of Tourette Syndrome

The main symptoms of TS are tics. Symptoms usually begin when a child is five to ten years of age. The first symptoms often are motor tics that occur in the head and neck area. Tics usually are worse during times that are stressful or exciting. They tend to improve when a person is calm or focused on an activity.

The types of tics and how often a person has tics changes a lot over time. Even though the symptoms might appear, disappear, and reappear, these conditions are considered chronic.

In most cases, tics decrease during adolescence and early adulthood and sometimes disappear entirely. However, many people with TS experience tics into adulthood and, in some cases, tics can become worse during adulthood.

Although the media often portray people with TS as involuntarily shouting out swear words (called coprolalia) or constantly repeating the words of other people (called echolalia), these symptoms are rare and are not required for a diagnosis of TS.

Diagnosis of Tourette Syndrome

There is no single test, like a blood test, to diagnose TS. Health professionals look at the person's symptoms to diagnose TS and other tic disorders. The tic disorders differ from each other in terms of the type of tic present (motor or vocal, or a combination of the both), and how long the symptoms have lasted. TS can be diagnosed if a person has both motor and vocal tics, and has had tic symptoms for at least a year.

Treatment for Tourette Syndrome

Although there is no cure for TS, there are treatments available to help manage the tics. Many people with TS have tics that do not get in the way of their daily life and, therefore, do not need any treatment. However, medication and behavioral treatments are available if tics cause pain or injury; interfere with school, work, or social life; or cause stress.

Other Concerns and Conditions Related to Tourette Syndrome

TS often occurs with other conditions (called co-occurring conditions). Almost 9 out of 10 children diagnosed with TS, 86 percent also have been diagnosed with at least one additional mental, behavioral, or developmental condition. The two most common conditions are attention deficit hyperactivity disorder (ADHD) and obsessive-compulsive disorder (OCD). It is important to find out if a person with TS has any other conditions, and treat those conditions properly.

TS often occurs with other related conditions (also called co-occurring conditions). These conditions can include ADHD, OCD, and other behavioral or conduct problems. People with TS and related conditions can be at higher risk for learning, behavioral, and social problems.

The symptoms of other disorders can complicate the diagnosis and treatment of TS and create extra challenges for people with TS and their families, educators, and health professionals.

Findings from a Centers for Disease Control and Prevention (CDC) study indicated that 86 percent of children who had been diagnosed with TS also had been diagnosed with at least one additional mental health, behavioral, or developmental condition based on parent report. Among children with TS:

- 63 percent had attention deficit hyperactivity disorder (ADHD)
- 26 percent had behavioral problems, such as oppositional defiant disorder (ODD) or conduct disorder (CD)
- 49 percent had anxiety problems
- 25 percent had depression
- 35 percent had an autism spectrum disorder (ASD)
- 47 percent had a learning disability
- 29 percent had a speech or language problem.

- 30 percent had a developmental delay

- 12 percent had an intellectual disability

Because co-occurring conditions are so common among people with TS, it is important for doctors to assess every child with TS for other conditions and problems.

Attention Deficit Hyperactivity Disorder

ADHD was the most common co-occurring condition among children with TS.

Children with ADHD have trouble paying attention and controlling impulsive behaviors. They might act without thinking about what the result will be and, in some cases, they are also overly active. It is normal for children to have trouble focusing and behaving at one time or another. However, for children with ADHD. symptoms can continue, can be severe, and cause difficulty at school, at home, or with friends.

Obsessive-Compulsive Behaviors

People with obsessive-compulsive behaviors have unwanted thoughts (obsessions) that they feel a need to respond to (compulsions). Obsessive-compulsive behaviors and OCD have been shown to occur among more than one-third of people with TS.

Sometimes it is difficult to tell the difference between complex tics that a child with TS may have and obsessive-compulsive behaviors.

Behavior or Conduct Problems

About one in four children with TS have disruptive behavior problems, such as oppositional defiant disorder (ODD) or conduct disorder (CD).

Oppositional Defiant Disorder

Children with ODD show negative, defiant and hostile behaviors toward adults or authority figures. ODD usually starts before a child is eight years of age, but no later than early adolescence. Children with ODD might show symptoms most often with people they know well, such as family members or a regular care provider. The behavior problems associated with ODD are more severe or persistent than what might be expected for the child's age and result in major problems in school, at home, or with peers.

Examples of ODD behaviors include:

- Losing one's temper a lot

- Arguing with adults or refusing to comply with adults' rules or requests

- Getting angry or being resentful or vindictive often

- Annoying others on purpose or easily becoming annoyed with others

- Blaming other people often for one's own mistakes or misbehavior

Conduct Disorder

Children with CD act aggressive toward others and break rules, laws, and social norms. They might have more injuries and difficulty with friends. In addition, the symptoms of CD happen in more than one area in the child's life (for example, at home, in the community, and at school).

Behavior problems can be highly disruptive for the child and others in the child's life. It is important to get a diagnosis and treatment plan from a mental-health professional as soon as possible. Effective treatments for disruptive behaviors include behavior therapy training for parents.

Rage

Some people with TS have anger that is out of control or episodes of "rage." The rage that happens repeatedly and is disproportionate to the situation that triggers it may be diagnosed as a mood disorder, like intermittent explosive disorder. Symptoms might include extreme verbal or physical aggression. Examples of verbal aggression include extreme yelling, screaming, and cursing. Examples of physical aggression include extreme shoving, kicking, hitting, biting, and throwing objects. Rage symptoms are more likely to occur among those with other behavioral disorders such as ADHD, ODD, or CD.

Among people with TS, symptoms of rage are more likely to occur at home than outside the home. Treatment can include behavior therapy, learning how to relax, and social skills training. Some of these methods will help individuals and families better understand what can cause the symptoms of rage, how to avoid encouraging these behaviors, and how to use appropriate discipline for these behaviors. In addition, treating other behavioral disorders that the person might have, such as ADHD, ODD, or CD can help to reduce symptoms of rage.

Anxiety

There are many different types of anxiety disorders with many different causes and symptoms. These include generalized anxiety disorder, OCD, panic disorder, posttraumatic stress disorder (PTSD), separation anxiety, and different types of phobias. Separation anxiety is most common among young children. These children feel very worried when they are apart from their parents.

Depression

Everyone feels worried, anxious, sad, or stressed from time to time. However, if these feelings do not go away and they interfere with daily life (for example, keeping a child home from school or other activities, or keeping an adult from working or attending social activities), a person might have depression. Having either a depressed mood or a loss of interest or pleasure for at least two weeks might mean that someone has depression. Children and teens with depression might be irritable instead of sad.

To be diagnosed with depression, other symptoms also must be present, such as:

- Changes in eating habits or weight gain or loss
- Changes in sleep habits
- Changes in activity level (others notice increased activity or that the person has slowed down)
- Less energy
- Feelings of worthlessness or guilt
- Difficulty thinking, concentrating, or making decisions
- Repeated thoughts of death
- Thoughts or plans about suicide, or a suicide attempt

Depression can be treated with counseling and medication.

Other Health Concerns

Children with TS can also have other health conditions that require care. Findings from the CDC study found that 43 percent of children who had been diagnosed with TS also had been diagnosed with at least one additional chronic health condition.

Among children with TS:

- 28 percent had asthma

- 13 percent had hearing or vision problems

- 12 percent had a bone, joint, or muscle problems.

- 9 percent had suffered a brain injury or concussion

The rates of asthma and hearing or vision problems were similar to children with TS, but bone, joint, or muscle problems as well as brain injury or concussion were higher for children with TS. Children with TS were also less likely to receive effective coordination of care or have a medical home, which means a primary care setting where a team of providers provides healthcare and preventive services.

Educational Concerns

As a group, people with TS have levels of intelligence similar to those of people without TS. However, people with TS might be more likely to have learning differences, a learning disability, or a developmental delay that affects their ability to learn.

Many people with TS have problems with writing, organizing, and paying attention. People with TS might have problems processing what they hear or see. This can affect a person's ability to learn by listening to or watching a teacher. Or, the person might have problems with their other senses (such as how things feel, smell, taste, and movement) that affects learning and behavior. Children with TS might have trouble with social skills that affect their ability to interact with others.

As a result of these challenges, children with TS might need extra help in school. Many times, these concerns can be addressed with accommodations and behavioral interventions (for example, help with social skills).

Accommodations can include things such as providing a different testing location or extra testing time, providing tips on how to be more organized, giving the childless homework, or letting the child use a computer to take notes in class. Children also might need behavioral interventions, therapy, or they may need to learn strategies to help with stress, paying attention, or other symptoms.

Risk Factors and Causes of Tourette Syndrome

Doctors and scientists do not know the exact cause of TS. Research suggests that it is an inherited genetic condition. That means it is passed on from parent to child through genes.

Who Is Affected?

In the United States, 1 of every 360 children 6 through 17 years of age has been diagnosed with TS. Other studies that also included children with undiagnosed TS have estimated that 1 of every 162 children have TS. This suggests that about half of children with TS are not diagnosed.

TS can affect people of all racial and ethnic groups. Boys are affected three to five times more often than girls.

Part Three

Mental-Health Treatments

Chapter 21

Recognizing a Mental-Health Emergency

As a parent or caregiver, you want the best for your children or other dependents. You may be concerned or have questions about certain behaviors they exhibit and how to ensure they get help.

What to Look For

It is important to be aware of warning signs that your child may be struggling. You can play a critical role in knowing when your child may need help.

Consult with a school counselor, school nurse, mental-health provider, or another healthcare professional if your child shows one or more of the following behaviors:

- Feeling very sad or withdrawn for more than two weeks

- Seriously trying to harm or kill herself or himself, or making plans to do so

- Experiencing sudden overwhelming fear for no reason, sometimes with a racing heart or fast breathing

- Getting in many fights or wanting to hurt others

This chapter includes text excerpted from "For Parents and Caregivers," MentalHealth.gov, U.S. Department of Health and Human Services (HHS), September 26, 2017.

- Showing severe out-of-control behavior that can hurt oneself or others
- Not eating, throwing up, or using laxatives to make themselves lose weight
- Having intense worries or fears that get in the way of daily activities
- Experiencing extreme difficulty in controlling behavior, putting themselves in physical danger, or causing problems in school
- Using drugs or alcohol repeatedly
- Having severe mood swings that cause problems in relationships
- Showing drastic changes in behavior or personality

Because children often can't understand difficult situations on their own, you should pay particular attention if they experience:

- Loss of a loved one
- Divorce or separation of their parents
- Any major transition—new home, new school, etc.
- Traumatic life experiences, such as living through a natural disaster
- Teasing or bullying
- Difficulties in school or with classmates

What to Do

If you are concerned about your child's behaviors, it is important to get appropriate care. You should:

- Talk to your child's doctor, school nurse, or another healthcare provider and seek further information about the behaviors or symptoms that worry you
- Ask your child's primary-care physician if your child needs further evaluation by a specialist with experience in child behavioral problems
- Ask if your child's specialist is experienced in treating the problems you are observing

- Talk to your medical provider about any medication and treatment plans

How to Talk about Mental Health

Do you need help starting a conversation with your child about mental health? Try leading with these questions. Make sure you actively listen to your child's response.

- Can you tell me more about what is happening?

- How you are feeling?

- Have you had feelings like this in the past?

- Sometimes you need to talk to an adult about your feelings. I'm here to listen. How can I help you feel better?

- Do you feel like you want to talk to someone else about your problem?

- I'm worried about your safety. Can you tell me if you have thoughts about harming yourself or others?

When talking about mental-health problems with your child you should:

- Communicate in a straightforward manner

- Speak at a level that is appropriate to a child or adolescents' age and development level (preschool children need fewer details than teenagers)

- Discuss the topic when your child feels safe and comfortable

- Watch for reactions during the discussion and slow down or back up if your child becomes confused or looks upset

- Listen openly and let your child tell you about their feelings and worries

Get Help for Your Child

People often don't get the mental-health services they need because they don't know where to start. Talk to your primary-care doctor or another health professional about mental-health problems. Ask them to connect you with the right mental-health services.

If you do not have a health professional who is able to assist you, use these resources to find help for yourself, your friends, your family, or your students.

Emergency Medical Services—911

If the situation is potentially life-threatening, get immediate emergency assistance by calling 911, available 24 hours a day.

National Suicide Prevention Lifeline (NSPL) 800-273-8255 or Live Online Chat

If you or someone you know is suicidal or in emotional distress, contact the NSPL. Trained crisis workers are available to talk 24 hours a day, 7 days a week. Your confidential and toll-free call goes to the nearest crisis center in the lifeline national network. These centers provide crisis counseling and mental-health referrals.

Substance Abuse and Mental Health Services Administration (SAMHSA) Treatment Referral Helpline, 877-726-4727

Get general information on mental health and locate treatment services in your area. Speak to a live person, Monday through Friday from 8 a.m. to 8 p.m. EST.

Chapter 22

Recovery Is Possible

The adoption of recovery by behavioral health systems over the years has signaled a dramatic shift in the expectation for positive outcomes for individuals who experience mental and/or substance-use conditions. When individuals with mental and/or substance-use disorders (SUDs) seek help, they are met with the knowledge and belief that anyone can recover and/or manage their conditions successfully. The value of recovery and recovery-oriented behavioral health systems is widely accepted by states, communities, healthcare providers, peers, families, researchers, and advocates including the U.S. Surgeon General, the Institute of Medicine (IOM), and others.

Substance Abuse and Mental Health Services Administration (SAMHSA) has established a working definition of recovery that defines recovery as a process of change through which individuals improve their health and wellness, live self-directed lives, and strive to reach their full potential. Recovery is built on access to evidence-based clinical treatment and recovery support services for all populations.

SAMHSA has delineated four major dimensions that support a life in recovery:

- **Health**—overcoming or managing one's disease(s) or symptoms—for example, abstaining from the use of alcohol, illicit drugs, and nonprescribed medications if one has an addiction problem—and, for everyone in recovery, making

---

This chapter includes text excerpted from "Recovery and Recovery Support," Substance Abuse and Mental Health Services Administration (SAMHSA), October 12, 2018.

informed, healthy choices that support physical and emotional well-being

- **Home**—having a stable and safe place to live
- **Purpose**—conducting meaningful daily activities, such as a job, school volunteerism, family caretaking, or creative endeavors, and the independence, income, and resources to participate in society
- **Community**—having relationships and social networks that provide support, friendship, love, and hope

Hope, the belief that these challenges and conditions can be overcome, is the foundation of recovery. A person's recovery is built on their strengths, talents, coping abilities, resources, and inherent values. It is holistic, addresses the whole person and their community, and is supported by peers, friends, and family members.

The process of recovery is highly personal and occurs via many pathways. It may include clinical treatment, medications, faith-based approaches, peer support, family support, self-care, and other approaches. Recovery is characterized by continual growth and improvement in one's health and wellness that may involve setbacks. Because setbacks are a natural part of life, resilience becomes a key component of recovery.

Resilience refers to an individual's ability to cope with adversity and adapt to challenges or change. Resilience develops over time and gives an individual the capacity not only to cope with life's challenges, but also to be better prepared for the next stressful situation. Optimism and the ability to remain hopeful are essential to resilience and the process of recovery.

Because recovery is a highly individualized process, recovery services and supports must be flexible to ensure cultural relevancy. What may work for adults in recovery may be very different for youth or older adults in recovery. For example, the promotion of resilience in young people, and the nature of social supports, peer mentors, and recovery coaching for adolescents and transitional age youth are different than recovery support services for adults and older adults.

The process of recovery is supported through relationships and social networks. This often involves family members who become the champions of their loved one's recovery. They provide essential support to their family member's journey of recovery and similarly experience the moments of positive healing as well as the difficult challenges. Families of people in recovery may experience adversities in their social, occupational, and financial lives, as well as in their overall quality of family life. These experiences can lead to increased family stress, guilt, shame, anger, fear, anxiety, loss, grief, and isolation. The concept of resilience in recovery is also vital for family members who need access to intentional supports that promote their health and well-being. The support of peers and friends is also crucial in engaging and supporting individuals in recovery.

Recovery Support

Recovery support is provided through treatment, services, and community-based programs by behavioral healthcare providers, peer providers, family members, friends and social networks, the faith community, and people with experience in recovery. Recovery support services help people enter into and navigate systems of care, remove barriers to recovery, stay engaged in the recovery process, and live full lives in communities of their choice.

Recovery support services include culturally and linguistically appropriate services that assist individuals and families working toward recovery from mental and/or substance-use problems. They incorporate a full range of social, legal, and other services that facilitate recovery, wellness, and linkage to and coordination among service providers, and other supports shown to improve quality of life for people in and seeking recovery and their families.

Recovery support services also include access to evidence-based practices such as supported employment, education, and housing; assertive community treatment; illness management; and peer-operated services. Recovery support services may be provided before, during, or after clinical treatment or may be provided to individuals who are not in treatment but seek support services. These services, provided by professionals and peers, are delivered through a variety of community and faith-based groups, treatment providers, schools, and other specialized services. For example, in the United States, there are 22 recovery high schools that help reduce the risk environment for youth with substance-use disorders. These schools typically have high retention rates and low relapse rates. The broad range of service delivery options ensures the life experiences of all people are valued and represented.

Cultural Awareness and Competency

Supporting recovery requires that mental health and addiction services:

- Be responsive and respectful to the health beliefs, practices, and cultural and linguistic needs of diverse people and groups.

- Actively address diversity in the delivery of services.

- Seek to reduce health disparities in access and outcomes.

Cultural competence describes the ability of an individual or organization to interact effectively with people of different cultures. To produce positive change, practitioners must understand the cultural context of the community they serve, and have the willingness and skills to work within this context. This means drawing on community-based values, traditions, and customs, and working with knowledgeable people from the community to plan, implement, and evaluate prevention activities.

Individuals, families, and communities that have experienced social and economic disadvantages are more likely to face greater obstacles to overall health. Characteristics such as race or ethnicity, religion, low socioeconomic status, gender, age, mental health, disability, sexual orientation or gender identity, geographic location, or other characteristics historically linked to exclusion or discrimination are known to influence health status.

A recovery focus is also a preventive approach that simultaneously supports building resiliency, wellness, measurable recovery, and quality of life.

Chapter 23

Mental-Healthcare Services

Chapter Contents

Section 23.1

Types of Mental-Health Professionals

This section contains text excerpted from the following sources: Text under the heading "Types of Therapists" is excerpted from "Types of Therapists," U.S. Department of Veterans Affairs (VA), August 14, 2015. Reviewed December 2018; Text under the heading "What Education, Skills, and Attributes Should a Mental-Health Provider Have?" is excerpted from "Finding a Mental Health Provider for Children and Families in Your Early Head Start/ Head Start Program," U.S. Department of Health and Human Services (HHS), June 16, 2017.

Types of Therapists

Mental-health professionals can have different training, credentials, or licenses. Providers can also offer different services, based on their expertise. If you are looking for a particular type of treatment (such as medications) or expert focus, the license and specialized training of the mental-health provider is important.

The information below reviews the most common types of licensed mental-health providers and generally explains their education, training, and services offered. Whether or not a therapist needs a license to provide psychotherapy and the requirements to be licensed varies by state. Your health-insurance provider may also allow you to see only certain types of mental-health providers. Check your policy for details.

Psychologists

Licensed clinical psychologists focus on mental-health assessment and treatment. They have a doctoral degree (e.g., Ph.D., PsyD, EdD) from four or more years of graduate training in clinical or counseling psychology. To be licensed to practice, psychologists must have another one to two years of supervised clinical experience. Psychologists have the title of "doctor" because of their doctoral degree, but in most states, they cannot prescribe medicine.

Clinical Social Workers

The purpose of social work is to enhance human well-being by helping people meet basic human needs. Licensed social workers also focus on diagnosis and treatment, and specialize in areas such as mental health, aging, and family and children. Most licensed social workers have a master's degree from two years of graduate training (e.g., MSW) or a doctoral degree in social work (e.g., DSW or Ph.D.).

Master's-Level Clinicians

Master's-level clinicians have a master's degree in counseling, psychology, or marriage and family therapy (e.g., MA, MFT). To be licensed to provide individual and/or group counseling, master's-level clinicians must meet requirements that vary by state.

Psychiatrists

Psychiatrists have either a Doctor of Allopathic Medicine (MD) or Doctor of Osteopathic Medicine (DO) degree in addition to specialized training in the diagnosis and treatment of mental-health problems. Since they are medical doctors, psychiatrists can prescribe medicine. Some may also provide psychotherapy.

Psychiatric Nurses or Nurse Practitioners

Psychiatric-mental-health nurses (PMHN) can have different levels of training. Most are registered nurses (RN) with additional training in psychiatry or psychology. Psychiatric-mental-health advanced practice registered nurses (PMH-APRN) have a graduate degree. Psychiatric nurse practitioners are registered nurse practitioners with specialized training in the diagnosis and treatment of mental-health problems. In most states, psychiatric nurses and psychiatric nurse practitioners can prescribe medicine.

What Education, Skills, and Attributes Should a Mental-Health Provider Have?

Mental-health providers should have the licensure, education, experience, and attributes that support high-quality services.

Education

Typically, a mental-health provider has a minimum of a master's degree in a human services field with licensure or certification from an accredited state board. Common types of mental-health professionals include marriage and family therapists, social workers, psychiatrists, and psychologists. Table 23.1 describes the level of education and licensure each type of mental-health provider requires.

Table 23.1. Common Types of Mental-Health Providers and Level of Education

Marriage and family therapist	Marriage and family therapists (MFT) have a master's degree and clinical experience in marriage and family therapy.
Social worker	Licensed clinical social workers (LCSW/LICSW) have a master's in social work (MSW) along with additional clinical training.
Psychiatrist	A psychiatrist is a physician (MD or DO) who specializes in mental health. Because they are medical doctors, psychiatrists can prescribe Medication.
Psychologist	Psychologists have a doctoral degree in psychology (PhD or PsyD) and are licensed in clinical psychology
Counselor	Licensed professional counselors (LPC) or licensed mental-health counselors (LMHC) have a master's degree in counseling

Experience

Services for children and families are likely to be more successful when a mental-health provider is experienced in treating the specific challenges the family is facing. Often, a mental-health provider has a special area of focus, such as depression, childhood trauma, or substance abuse. Experienced providers have seen the problems faced repeatedly by children and families, which can broaden their view and give them added insight.

Important to early child and family work is the mental-health providers' experience with an ability to:

- Conduct and interpret mental-health screenings and assessment's for very young children

- Facilitate a family-centered approach to services

- Use evidence-based practices

- Have knowledge of and sensitivity to the first language of families

- Use treatment methods that reflect the culture-specific values and treatment needs of clients

Attributes

Mental-health providers are typically required to have training in ethical conduct covering topics such as tolerance, integrity, boundaries, and self-awareness. Yet, a mental-health professional's "way of being" can greatly affect the success of a child and family's experience with therapeutic work. Important attributes to look for in any mental-health provider include:

Strong communication skills with the ability to listen and engage in shared decision-making.

- A strength-based perspective that supports a family's sense of hope.

- Flexibility to adjust one's schedule and expectations to the needs of the family.

- Dependability—showing up on time and regularly.

- Open-mindedness—accepting where families are in the process.

Approach / Orientation

Another important component to consider when looking for mental-health providers is their approach to mental-health work (often referred to as their "orientation"). Mental-health providers have very different approaches to their work based on their training and experience. Some therapists adopt a particular approach to their work that may be informed by a specific theoretical perspective and others use a more eclectic approach—drawing from multiple theories and orientations. Some therapists might provide their clients with guidance on how to change specific behaviors that are problematic while others may focus more on the quality of the relationships that a parent or child has with other family members. Knowing what a family expects or is most comfortable with before a referral can assist program staff in linking a family to the right mental-health provider. For example, one family may prefer a therapist with a more behavioral approach who might suggest specific strategies. Another family may be more comfortable with a therapist who spends more time listening, reflecting, and asking questions about their relationships.

Section 23.2

Psychotherapies

This section includes text excerpted from "Psychotherapies," National Institute of Mental Health (NIMH), November 2016.

"Psychotherapy," sometimes called "talk therapy," is a term for a variety of treatment techniques that aim to help a person identify and change troubling emotions, thoughts, and behavior. Most psychotherapy takes place with a licensed and trained mental-healthcare professional and a patient meeting one on one or with other patients in a group setting.

Someone might seek out psychotherapy for different reasons:

- You might be dealing with severe or long-term stress from a job or family situation, the loss of a loved one, or relationship or other family issues. Or you may have symptoms with no physical explanation: changes in sleep or appetite, low energy, a lack of interest or pleasure in activities that you once enjoyed, persistent irritability, or a sense of discouragement or hopelessness that won't go away.

- A health professional may suspect or have diagnosed a condition such as depression, bipolar disorder, or posttraumatic stress or other disorder and recommended psychotherapy as a first treatment or to go along with medication.

- You may be seeking treatment for a family member or child who has been diagnosed with a condition affecting mental health and for whom a health professional has recommended treatment.

An exam by your primary-care practitioner can ensure there is nothing in your overall health that would explain your or a loved one's symptoms.

What to Consider When Looking for a Therapist

Therapists have different professional backgrounds and specialties. There are resources at the end of this material that can help you find out about the different credentials of therapists and resources for locating therapists.

There are many different types of psychotherapy. Different therapies are often variations on an established approach, such as cognitive behavioral therapy. There is no formal approval process for psychotherapies as there is for the use of medications in medicine. For many therapies, however, research involving large numbers of patients has provided evidence that treatment is effective for specific disorders. These "evidence-based therapies" have been shown in research to reduce symptoms of depression, anxiety, and other disorders.

The particular approach a therapist uses depends on the condition being treated and the training and experience of the therapist. Also, therapists may combine and adapt elements of different approaches. The health information pages for specific disorders on the NIMH website list some of the evidence-based therapies for those disorders.

One goal of establishing an evidence base for psychotherapies is to prevent situations in which a person receives therapy for months or years with no benefit. If you have been in therapy and feel you are not getting better, talk to your therapist, or look into other practitioners or approaches. The object of therapy is to gain relief from symptoms and improve quality of life.

Once you have identified one or more possible therapists, a preliminary conversation with a therapist can help you get an idea of how treatment will proceed and whether you feel comfortable with the therapist. Rapport and trust are important. Discussions in therapy are deeply personal and it's important that you feel comfortable and trusting with the therapist and have confidence in her or his expertise. Consider asking the following questions:

- What are the credentials and experience of the therapist? Does she or he have a specialty?

- What approach will the therapist take to help you? Does she or he practice a particular type of therapy? What can the therapist tell you about the rationale for the therapy and the evidence base?

- Does the therapist have experience in diagnosing and treating the age group (for example, a child) and the specific condition for which treatment is being sought? If a child is the patient, how will parents be involved in treatment?

- What are the goals of therapy? Does the therapist recommend a specific time frame or number of sessions? How will progress be assessed and what happens if you (or the therapist) feel you aren't starting to feel better?

- Will there be homework?

- Are medications an option? How will medications be prescribed if the therapist is not an M.D.?

- Are our meetings confidential? How can this be assured?

Psychotherapies and Other Treatment Options

Psychotherapy can be an alternative to medication or can be used along with other treatment options, such as medications. Choosing the right treatment plan should be based on a person's individual needs and medical situation and under a mental-health professional's care.

Even when medications relieve symptoms, psychotherapy and other interventions can help a person address specific issues. These might include self-defeating ways of thinking, fears, problems with interactions with other people, or dealing with situations at home or at school or with employment.

Elements of Psychotherapy

A variety of different kinds of psychotherapies and interventions have been shown to be effective for specific disorders. Psychotherapists may use one primary approach or incorporate different elements depending on their training, the condition being treated, and the needs of the person receiving treatment.

Here are examples of the elements that psychotherapies can include.

- Helping a person become aware of ways of thinking that may be automatic but are inaccurate and harmful. (An example might be someone who has a low opinion of her or his own abilities.) The therapist helps the person find ways to question these thoughts, understand how they affect emotions and behavior, and try ways to change self-defeating patterns. This approach is central to cognitive behavioral therapy (CBT).

- Identifying ways to cope with stress.

- Examining in depth a person's interactions with others and offering guidance with social and communication skills, if needed.

- Relaxation and mindfulness techniques.

- Exposure therapy for people with anxiety disorders. In exposure therapy, a person spends brief periods in a supportive environment, learning to tolerate the distress certain items, ideas, or imagined scenes cause. Over time the fear associated with these things dissipates.

- Tracking emotions and activities and the impact of each on the other.

- Safety planning can include helping a person recognize warning signs and think about coping strategies, such as contacting friends, family, or emergency personnel.

- Supportive counseling to help a person explore troubling issues and provide emotional support.

eHealth

Telephones, the Internet, and mobile devices have opened up new possibilities for providing interventions that can reach people in areas where mental-health professionals may not be easily available and can be on hand 24/7. Some of these approaches involve a therapist providing help from a distance, but others—such as web-based programs and cell phone apps—are designed to provide information and feedback in the absence of a therapist.

Some approaches that use electronic media to provide help for mental health-related conditions have been shown by research to be helpful in some situations, but not yet others. The American Psychological Association (APA) has information to consider before choosing online therapy.

Taking the First Step

The symptoms of mental disorders can have a profound effect on someone's quality of life and ability to function. Treatment can address symptoms as well as assist someone experiencing severe or ongoing stress. Some of the reasons that you might consider seeking out psychotherapy include:

- Overwhelming sadness or helplessness that doesn't go away
- Serious, unusual insomnia or sleeping too much
- Difficulty focusing on work or carrying out other everyday activities

- Constant worry and anxiety

- Drinking to excess or any behavior that harms yourself or others

- Dealing with a difficult transition, such as a divorce, children leaving home, job difficulties, or the death of someone close

- Children's behavior problems that interfere with school, family, or peers

Seeking help is not an admission of weakness, but a step toward understanding and obtaining relief from distressing symptoms.

Finding a Therapist

Many different professionals offer psychotherapy. Examples include psychiatrists, psychologists, social workers, counselors, and psychiatric nurses. Information on the credentials of providers is available from the National Alliance on Mental Illness (NAMI). Resources to help find a practitioner are listed on the Help for Mental Illnesses page on the National Institute of Mental Health (NIMH) website.

Your health plan may have a list of mental-health practitioners who participate in the plan. Other resources on the "Help for Mental Illnesses" page can help you look for reduced-cost health services. The resources listed there include links to help find reduced-cost treatment. When talking with a prospective therapist, ask about treatment fees, whether the therapist participates in insurance plans, and whether there is a sliding scale for fees according to income.

Chapter 24

Mental-Health Medications

Chapter Contents

Section 24.1

Mental-Health Medications: An Overview

This section includes text excerpted from "Mental Health
Medications," National Institute of Mental
Health (NIMH), October 2016.

Medications can play a role in treating several mental disorders
and conditions. Treatment may also include psychotherapy (also called
"talk therapy") and brain stimulation therapies (less common). In some
cases, psychotherapy alone may be the best treatment option. Choosing the right treatment plan should be based on a person's individual
needs and medical situation, and under a mental-health professional's
care.

Information about medications changes frequently. Check the U.S.
Food and Drug Administration (FDA) website for the latest warnings,
patient medication guides, or newly approved medications. You can
search by the brand name of drugs, herbs, and supplements drugs on
the MedlinePlus website (medlineplus.gov/druginformation.html). This
website also provides additional information about each medication,
including side effects and FDA warnings.

Understanding Your Medications

If you are prescribed a medication, be sure that you:

- Tell the doctor about all medications and vitamin supplements
  you are already taking

- Remind your doctor about any allergies and any problems you
  have had with medicines

- Understand how to take the medicine before you start using it
  and take your medicine as instructed

- Don't take medicines prescribed for another person or give yours
  to someone else

- Call your doctor right away if you have any problems with your
  medicine or if you are worried that it might be doing more harm
  than good. Your doctor may be able to adjust the dose or change
  your prescription to a different one that may work better for
  you.

- Report serious side effects to the FDA MedWatch Adverse Event Reporting program online at www.fda.gov/Safety/MedWatch] or by phone [800-332-1088]. You or your doctor may send a report.

Section 24.2

Antidepressants

This section includes text excerpted from "Mental Health Medications," National Institute of Mental Health (NIMH), October 2016.

What Are Antidepressants?

Antidepressants are medications commonly used to treat depression. Antidepressants are also used for other health conditions, such as anxiety, pain, and insomnia. Although antidepressants are not U.S. Food and Drug Administration (FDA)-approved specifically to treat attention deficit hyperactivity disorder (ADHD), antidepressants are sometimes used to treat ADHD in adults.

The most popular types of antidepressants are called selective serotonin reuptake inhibitors (SSRIs). Examples of SSRIs include:

- Fluoxetine

- Citalopram

- Sertraline

- Paroxetine

- Escitalopram

Other types of antidepressants are serotonin and norepinephrine reuptake inhibitors (SNRIs). SNRIs are similar to SSRIs and include venlafaxine and duloxetine.

Another antidepressant that is commonly used is bupropion. Bupropion is a third type of antidepressant which works differently than either SSRIs or SNRIs. Bupropion is also used to treat seasonal affective disorder and to help people stop smoking.

SSRIs, SNRIs, and bupropion are popular because they do not cause as many side effects as older classes of antidepressants, and seem to help a broader group of depressive and anxiety disorders. Older antidepressant medications include tricyclics, tetracyclics, and monoamine oxidase inhibitors (MAOIs). For some people, tricyclics, tetracyclics, or MAOIs may be the best medications.

How Do People Respond to Antidepressants?

According to a research review by the Agency for Healthcare Research and Quality (AHRQ), all antidepressant medications work about as well as each other to improve symptoms of depression and to keep depression symptoms from coming back. For reasons not yet well understood, some people respond better to some antidepressant medications than to others. Therefore, it is important to know that some people may not feel better with the first medicine they try and may need to try several medicines to find the one that works for them. Others may find that a medicine helped for a while, but their symptoms came back. It is important to carefully follow your doctor's directions for taking your medicine at an adequate dose and over an extended period of time (often four to six weeks) for it to work.

Once a person begins taking antidepressants, it is important to not stop taking them without the help of a doctor. Sometimes people taking antidepressants feel better and stop taking the medication too soon, and the depression may return. When it is time to stop the medication, the doctor will help the person slowly and safely decrease the dose. It's important to give the body time to adjust to the change. People don't get addicted (or "hooked") on these medications, but stopping them abruptly may also cause withdrawal symptoms.

What Are the Possible Side Effects of Antidepressants?

Some antidepressants may cause more side effects than others. You may need to try several different antidepressant medications before finding the one that improves your symptoms and that causes side effects that you can manage.

The most common side effects listed by the FDA include:

- Nausea and vomiting

- Weight gain

- Diarrhea

- Sleepiness

- Sexual problems

Call your doctor right away if you have any of the following symptoms, especially if they are new, worsening, or worry you:

- Thoughts about suicide or dying

- Attempts to commit suicide

- New or worsening depression

- New or worsening anxiety

- Feeling very agitated or restless

- Panic attacks

- Trouble sleeping (insomnia)

- New or worsening irritability

- Acting aggressively, being angry, or violent

- Acting on dangerous impulses

- An extreme increase in activity and talking (mania)

- Other unusual changes in behavior or mood

Combining the newer SSRI or SNRI antidepressants with one of the commonly-used "triptan" medications used to treat migraine headaches could cause a life-threatening illness called "serotonin syndrome." A person with serotonin syndrome may be agitated, have hallucinations (see or hear things that are not real), have a high temperature, or have unusual blood pressure changes. Serotonin syndrome is usually associated with the older antidepressants called MAOIs, but it can happen with the newer antidepressants as well, if they are mixed with the wrong medications.

Antidepressants may cause other side effects that were not included in this list. To report any serious adverse effects associated with the use of antidepressant medicines, please contact the FDA MedWatch program (www.fda.gov/Safety/MedWatch).

Section 24.3

Antianxiety Medications

This section includes text excerpted from
"Mental Health Medications," National Institute
of Mental Health (NIMH), October 2016.

What Are Antianxiety Medications?

Antianxiety medications help reduce the symptoms of anxiety, such as panic attacks, or extreme fear and worry. The most common antianxiety medications are called benzodiazepines. Benzodiazepines can treat generalized anxiety disorder. In the case of panic disorder or social phobia (social anxiety disorder (SAD)), benzodiazepines are usually second-line treatments, behind selective serotonin reuptake inhibitors (SSRIs) or other antidepressants.

Benzodiazepines used to treat anxiety disorders include:

- Clonazepam

- Alprazolam

- Lorazepam

Short half-life (or short-acting) benzodiazepines (such as Lorazepam) and beta-blockers are used to treat the short-term symptoms of anxiety. Beta-blockers help manage physical symptoms of anxiety, such as trembling, rapid heartbeat, and sweating that people with phobias (an overwhelming and unreasonable fear of an object or situation, such as public speaking) experience in difficult situations. Taking these medications for a short period of time can help the person keep physical symptoms under control and can be used "as needed" to reduce acute anxiety.

Buspirone (which is unrelated to the benzodiazepines) is sometimes used for the long-term treatment of chronic anxiety. In contrast to the benzodiazepines, buspirone must be taken every day for a few weeks to reach its full effect. It is not useful on an "as-needed" basis.

How Do People Respond to Antianxiety Medications?

Antianxiety medications such as benzodiazepines are effective in relieving anxiety and take effect more quickly than the antidepressant medications (or buspirone) often prescribed for anxiety. However, people can build up a tolerance to benzodiazepines if they are taken over a long period of time and may need higher and higher doses to get the same effect. Some people may even become dependent on them. To avoid these problems, doctors usually prescribe benzodiazepines for short periods, a practice that is especially helpful for older adults, people who have substance-abuse problems and people who become dependent on medication easily. If people suddenly stop taking benzodiazepines, they may have withdrawal symptoms or their anxiety may return. Therefore, benzodiazepines should be tapered off slowly.

What Are the Possible Side Effects of Antianxiety Medications?

Like other medications, antianxiety medications may cause side effects. Some of these side effects and risks are serious. The most common side effects for benzodiazepines are drowsiness and dizziness. Other possible side effects include:

- Nausea
- Blurred vision
- Headache
- Confusion
- Tiredness
- Nightmares

Tell your doctor if any of these symptoms are severe or do not go away:

- Drowsiness
- Dizziness
- Unsteadiness
- Problems with coordination
- Difficulty thinking or remembering
- Increased saliva
- Muscle or joint pain
- Frequent urination
- Blurred vision

- Changes in sex drive or ability

If you experience any of the symptoms below, call your doctor immediately:

- Rash
- Hives
- Swelling of the eyes, face, lips, tongue, or throat
- Difficulty breathing or swallowing
- Hoarseness
- Seizures
- Yellowing of the skin or eyes
- Depression
- Difficulty speaking
- Yellowing of the skin or eyes
- Thoughts of suicide or harming yourself
- Difficulty breathing

Common side effects of beta-blockers include:

- Fatigue
- Cold hands
- Dizziness or lightheadedness
- Weakness

Beta-blockers generally are not recommended for people with asthma or diabetes because they may worsen symptoms related to both.

Possible side effects from buspirone include:

- Dizziness
- Headaches
- Nausea
- Nervousness
- Lightheadedness
- Excitement
- Trouble sleeping

Antianxiety medications may cause other side effects that are not included in the lists above. To report any serious adverse effects associated with the use of these medicines, please contact the FDA MedWatch program (www.fda.gov/Safety/MedWatch).

Section 24.4

Stimulants

This section includes text excerpted from
"Mental Health Medications," National Institute
of Mental Health (NIMH), October 2016.

What Are Stimulants?

As the name suggests, stimulants increase alertness, attention, and energy, as well as elevate blood pressure, heart rate, and respiration. Stimulant medications are often prescribed to treat children, adolescents, or adults diagnosed with attention deficit hyperactivity disorder (ADHD).

Stimulants used to treat ADHD include:

- Methylphenidate

- Amphetamine

- Dextroamphetamine

- Lisdexamfetamine dimesylate

Note: In 2002, the U.S. Food and Drug Administration (FDA) approved the nonstimulant medication atomoxetine for use as a treatment for ADHD. Two other nonstimulant antihypertensive medications, clonidine, and guanfacine are also approved for the treatment of ADHD in children and adolescents. One of these nonstimulant medications is often tried first in a young person with ADHD, and if the response is insufficient, then a stimulant is prescribed.

Stimulants are also prescribed to treat other health conditions, including narcolepsy, and occasionally depression (especially in older or chronically medically ill people and in those who have not responded to other treatments).

How Do People Respond to Stimulants?

Prescription stimulants have a calming and "focusing" effect on individuals with ADHD. Stimulant medications are safe when given under a doctor's supervision. Some children taking them may feel slightly different or "funny."

Some parents worry that stimulant medications may lead to drug abuse or dependence, but there is little evidence of this when they are used properly as prescribed. Additionally, research shows that teens with ADHD who took stimulant medications were less likely to abuse drugs than those who did not take stimulant medications.

What Are the Possible Side Effects of Stimulants?

Stimulants may cause side effects. Most side effects are minor and disappear when dosage levels are lowered. The most common side effects include:

- Difficulty falling asleep or staying asleep

  - Loss of appetite

  - Stomach pain

  - Headache

  - Less common side effects include:

- Motor tics or verbal tics (sudden, repetitive movements or sounds)

  - Personality changes, such as appearing "flat" or without emotion

  - Call your doctor right away if you have any of these symptoms, especially if they are new, become worse, or worry you.

Stimulants may cause other side effects that are not included in the list above. To report any serious adverse effects associated with the use of stimulants, please contact the FDA MedWatch program (www. fda.gov/Safety/MedWatch).

Section 24.5

Antipsychotics

This section includes text excerpted from
"Mental Health Medications," National Institute
of Mental Health (NIMH), October 2016.

What Are Antipsychotics?

Antipsychotic medicines are primarily used to manage psychosis. The word "psychosis" is used to describe conditions that affect the mind, and in which there has been some loss of contact with reality, often including delusions (false, fixed beliefs) or hallucinations (hearing or seeing things that are not really there). It can be a symptom of a physical condition such as drug abuse or a mental disorder such as schizophrenia, bipolar disorder, or very severe depression (also known as "psychotic depression").

Antipsychotic medications are often used in combination with other medications to treat delirium, dementia, and mental-health conditions, including:

- Attention deficit hyperactivity disorder (ADHD)

- Severe depression

- Eating disorders

- Posttraumatic stress disorder (PTSD)

- Obsessive-compulsive disorder (OCD)

- Generalized anxiety disorder (GAD)

Antipsychotic medicines do not cure these conditions. They are used to help relieve symptoms and improve quality of life.

Older or first-generation antipsychotic medications are also called conventional "typical" antipsychotics or "neuroleptics." Some of the common typical antipsychotics include:

- Chlorpromazine

- Haloperidol

- Perphenazine

- Fluphenazine

Newer or second generation medications are also called "atypical" antipsychotics. Some of the common atypical antipsychotics include:

- Risperidone

- Olanzapine

- Quetiapine

- Ziprasidone

- Aripiprazole

- Paliperidone

- Lurasidone

According to a research review by the Agency for Healthcare Research and Quality (AHRQ), typical and atypical antipsychotics both work to treat symptoms of schizophrenia and the manic phase of bipolar disorder.

Several atypical antipsychotics have a "broader spectrum" of action than the older medications and are used for treating bipolar depression or depression that has not responded to an antidepressant medication alone.

How Do People Respond to Antipsychotics?

Certain symptoms, such as feeling agitated and having hallucinations, usually go away within days of starting an antipsychotic medication. Symptoms like delusions usually go away within a few weeks, but the full effects of the medication may not be seen for up to six weeks. Every patient responds differently, so it may take several trials of different antipsychotic medications to find the one that works best.

Some people may have a relapse—meaning their symptoms come back or get worse. Usually, relapses happen when people stop taking their medication, or when they only take it sometimes. Some people stop taking the medication because they feel better or they may feel that they don't need it anymore, but no one should stop taking an antipsychotic medication without talking to her or his doctor. When a doctor says it is okay to stop taking a medication, it should be gradually tapered off—never stopped suddenly. Many people must stay on an antipsychotic continuously for months or years in order to stay well; treatment should be personalized for each individual.

What Are the Possible Side Effects of Antipsychotics?

Antipsychotics have many side effects (or adverse events) and risks. The U.S. Food and Drug Administration (FDA) lists the following side effects of antipsychotic medicines:

- Drowsiness
- Dizziness
- Restlessness
- Weight gain (the risk is higher with some atypical antipsychotic medicines)
- Dry mouth
- Constipation
- Nausea
- Vomiting
- Blurred vision
- Low blood pressure
- Uncontrollable movements, such as tics and tremors (the risk is higher with typical antipsychotic medicines)
- Seizures
- A low number of white blood cells, which fight infections

A person taking an atypical antipsychotic medication should have her or his weight, glucose levels, and lipid levels monitored regularly by a doctor.

Typical antipsychotic medications can also cause additional side effects related to physical movement, such as:

- Rigidity
- Persistent muscle spasms
- Tremors
- Restlessness

Long-term use of typical antipsychotic medications may lead to a condition called tardive dyskinesia (TD). TD causes muscle movements, commonly around the mouth, that a person can't control. TD can range

275

from mild to severe, and in some people, the problem cannot be cured. Sometimes people with TD recover partially or fully after they stop taking typical antipsychotic medication. People who think that they might have TD should check with their doctor before stopping their medication. TD rarely occurs while taking atypical antipsychotics.

Antipsychotics may cause other side effects that are not included in this list above. To report any serious adverse effects associated with the use of these medicines, please contact the FDA MedWatch program (www.fda.gov/Safety/MedWatch).

Section 24.6

Mood Stabilizers

This section includes text excerpted from
"Mental Health Medications," National Institute
of Mental Health (NIMH), October 2016.

What Are Mood Stabilizers?

Mood stabilizers are used primarily to treat bipolar disorder, mood swings associated with other mental disorders, and in some cases, to augment the effect of other medications used to treat depression. Lithium, which is an effective mood stabilizer, is approved for the treatment of mania and the maintenance treatment of bipolar disorder. A number of cohort studies describe anti-suicide benefits of lithium for individuals on long-term maintenance. Mood stabilizers work by decreasing abnormal activity in the brain and are also sometimes used to treat:

- Depression (usually along with an antidepressant)
- Schizoaffective disorder
- Disorders of impulse control
- Certain mental illnesses in children

Anticonvulsant medications are also used as mood stabilizers. They were originally developed to treat seizures, but they were found to help control unstable moods as well. One anticonvulsant commonly used as a mood stabilizer is valproic acid (also called divalproex sodium). For some people, especially those with "mixed" symptoms of mania and depression or those with rapid-cycling bipolar disorder, valproic acid may work better than lithium. Other anticonvulsants used as mood stabilizers include:

- Carbamazepine
- Lamotrigine
- Oxcarbazepine

What Are the Possible Side Effects of Mood Stabilizers?

Mood stabilizers can cause several side effects, and some of them may become serious, especially at excessively high blood levels. These side effects include:

- Itching, rash
- Excessive thirst
- Frequent urination
- Tremor (shakiness) of the hands
- Nausea and vomiting
- Slurred speech
- Fast, slow, irregular, or pounding heartbeat
- Blackouts
- Changes in vision
- Seizures
- Hallucinations (seeing things or hearing voices that do not exist)
- Loss of coordination
- Swelling of the eyes, face, lips, tongue, throat, hands, feet, ankles, or lower legs.

If a person with bipolar disorder is being treated with lithium, should visit the doctor regularly to check the lithium levels her or his blood, and make sure the kidneys and the thyroid are working normally.

Lithium is eliminated from the body through the kidney, so the dose may need to be lowered in older people with reduced kidney function. Also, loss of water from the body, such as through sweating or diarrhea, can cause the lithium level to rise, requiring a temporary lowering of the daily dose. Although kidney functions are checked periodically during lithium treatment, actual damage of the kidney is uncommon in people whose blood levels of lithium have stayed within the therapeutic range.

Mood stabilizers may cause other side effects that are not included in this list. To report any serious adverse effects associated with the use of these medicines, please contact the FDA MedWatch program (www.fda.gov/Safety/MedWatch).

For the side effects of Carbamazepine, Lamotrigine, and Oxcarbazepine, please visit MedlinePlus Drugs, Herbs, and Supplements (medlineplus.gov/druginformation.html).

Some possible side effects linked anticonvulsants (such as valproic acid) include:

- Drowsiness

- Dizziness

- Headache

- Diarrhea

- Constipation

- Changes in appetite

- Weight changes

- Back pain

- Agitation

- Mood swings

- Abnormal thinking

- Uncontrollable shaking of a part of the body

- Loss of coordination

- Uncontrollable movements of the eyes

- Blurred or double vision

- Ringing in the ears

- Hair loss

These medications may also:

- Cause damage to the liver or pancreas, so people taking it should see their doctors regularly

- Increase testosterone (a male hormone) levels in teenage girls and lead to a condition called polycystic ovarian syndrome (a disease that can affect fertility and make the menstrual cycle become irregular)

Medications for common adult health problems, such as diabetes, high blood pressure, anxiety, and depression may interact badly with anticonvulsants. In this case, a doctor can offer other medication options.

Section 24.7

Special Groups: Children, Older Adults, and Pregnant Women

This section includes text excerpted from
"Mental Health Medications," National Institute
of Mental Health (NIMH), October 2016.

All types of people take psychiatric medications, but some groups have special needs, including:

- Children and adolescents

- Older adults

- Women who are pregnant or who may become pregnant

Children and Adolescents

Many medications used to treat children and adolescents with mental illness are safe and effective. However, some medications have not been studied or approved for use with children or adolescents. Still, a doctor can give a young person an U.S. Food and Drug Administration

(FDA)-approved medication on an "off-label" basis. This means that the doctor prescribes the medication to help the patient even though the medicine is not approved for the specific mental disorder that is being treated or for use by patients under a certain age. Remember:

- It is important to watch children and adolescents who take these medications on an "off-label" basis.

- Children may have different reactions and side effects than adults.

- Some medications have current FDA warnings about potentially dangerous side effects for younger patients.

In addition to medications, other treatments for children and adolescents should be considered, either to be tried first, with medication added later if necessary, or to be provided along with medication. Psychotherapy, family therapy, educational courses, and behavior management techniques can help everyone involved cope with disorders that affect a child's mental health.

Older Adults

People over 65 have to be careful when taking medications, especially when they're taking many different drugs. Older adults have a higher risk for experiencing bad drug interactions, missing doses, or overdosing.

Older adults also tend to be more sensitive to medications. Even healthy older people react to medications differently than younger people because older people's bodies process and eliminate medications more slowly. Therefore, lower or less frequent doses may be needed for older adults. Before starting a medication, older people and their family members should talk carefully with a physician about whether a medication can affect alertness, memory, or coordination, and how to help ensure that prescribed medications do not increase the risk of falls.

Sometimes memory problems affect older people who take medications for mental disorders. An older adult may forget her or his regular dose and take too much or not enough. A good way to keep track of medicine is to use a seven-day pill box, which can be bought at any pharmacy. At the beginning of each week, older adults and their caregivers fill the box so that it is easy to remember what medicine to take. Many pharmacies also have pill boxes with sections for medications that must be taken more than once a day.

Women Who Are Pregnant or Who May Become Pregnant

The research on the use of psychiatric medications during pregnancy is limited. The risks are different depending on which medication is taken, and at what point during the pregnancy the medication is taken. Decisions on treatments for all conditions during pregnancy should be based on each woman's needs and circumstances, and based on a careful weighing of the likely benefits and risks of all available options, including psychotherapy (or "watchful waiting" during part or all of the pregnancy), medication, or a combination of the two. While no medication is considered perfectly safe for all women at all stages of pregnancy, this must be balanced for each woman against the fact that untreated serious mental disorders themselves can pose a risk to a pregnant woman and her developing fetus. Medications should be selected based on available scientific research, and they should be taken at the lowest possible dose. Pregnant women should have a medical professional who will watch them closely throughout their pregnancy and after delivery.

Most women should avoid certain medications during pregnancy. For example:

- Mood stabilizers are known to cause birth defects. Benzodiazepines and lithium have been shown to cause "floppy baby syndrome," in which a baby is drowsy and limp, and cannot breathe or feed well. Benzodiazepines may cause birth defects or other infant problems, especially if taken during the first trimester.

- According to research, taking antipsychotic medications during pregnancy can lead to birth defects, especially if they are taken during the first trimester and in combination with other drugs, but the risks vary widely and depend on the type of antipsychotic taken. The conventional antipsychotic haloperidol has been studied more than others, and has been found not to cause birth defects. Research on the newer atypical antipsychotics is ongoing.

Antidepressants, especially selective serotonin reuptake inhibitor (SSRIs), are considered to be safe during pregnancy. However, antidepressant medications do cross the placental barrier and may reach the fetus. Birth defects or other problems are possible, but they are very rare. The effects of antidepressants on childhood development remain under study.

Studies have also found that fetuses exposed to SSRIs during the third trimester may be born with "withdrawal" symptoms such as breathing problems, jitteriness, irritability, trouble feeding, or hypoglycemia (low blood sugar). Most studies have found that these symptoms in babies are generally mild and short-lived, and no deaths have been reported. Risks from the use of antidepressants need to be balanced with the risks of stopping medication; if a mother is too depressed to care for herself and her child, both may be at risk for problems.

In 2004, the FDA issued a warning against the use of certain antidepressants in the late third trimester. The warning said that doctors may want to gradually taper pregnant women off antidepressants in the third trimester so that the baby is not affected. After a woman delivers, she should consult with her doctor to decide whether to return to a full dose during the period when she is most vulnerable to postpartum depression.

After the baby is born, women and their doctors should watch for postpartum depression, especially if a mother stopped taking her medication during pregnancy. In addition, women who nurse while taking psychiatric medications should know that a small amount of the medication passes into the breast milk. However, the medication may or may not affect the baby depending s on the medication and when it is taken. Women taking psychiatric medications and who intend to breastfeed should discuss the potential risks and benefits with their doctors.

Chapter 25

Brain Stimulation Therapies

Brain stimulation therapies (BST) can play a role in treating certain mental disorders. Brain stimulation therapies involve activating or inhibiting the brain directly with electricity. The electricity can be given directly by electrodes implanted in the brain, or noninvasively through electrodes placed on the scalp. The electricity can also be induced by using magnetic fields applied to the head. While these types of therapies are less frequently used than medication and psychotherapies, they hold promise for treating certain mental disorders that do not respond to other treatments.

Electroconvulsive therapy (ECT) is the best-studied brain stimulation therapy and has the longest history of use. Other stimulation therapies discussed here are newer, and in some cases, still experimental methods. These include:

- Vagus nerve stimulation (VNS)

- Repetitive transcranial magnetic stimulation (rTMS)

- Magnetic seizure therapy (MST)

- Deep brain stimulation (DBS)

A treatment plan may also include medication and psychotherapy. Choosing the right treatment plan should be based on a person's individual needs and medical situation and under a doctor's care.

This chapter includes text excerpted from "Brain Stimulation Therapies," National Institute of Mental Health (NIMH), June 2016.

Electroconvulsive Therapy

ECT uses an electric current to treat serious mental disorders. This type of therapy is usually considered only if a patient's illness has not improved after other treatments (such as antidepressant medication or psychotherapy) are tried, or in cases where rapid response is needed (as in the case of suicide risk and catatonia, for example).

Why Electroconvulsive Therapy Is Done

ECT is most often used to treat severe, treatment-resistant depression (TRD), but it may also be medically indicated in other mental disorders, such as bipolar disorder or schizophrenia. It also may be used in life-threatening circumstances, such as when a patient is unable to move or respond to the outside world (e.g., catatonia), is suicidal, or is malnourished as a result of severe depression.

ECT can be effective in reducing the chances of relapse when patients undergo follow-up treatments. Two major advantages of ECT overmedication are that ECT begins to work quicker, often starting within the first week, and older individuals respond especially quickly.

How Electroconvulsive Therapy Works

Before ECT is administered, a person is sedated with general anesthesia and given a medication called a muscle relaxant to prevent movement during the procedure. An anesthesiologist monitors breathing, heart rate and blood pressure during the entire procedure, which is conducted by a trained medical team, including physicians and nurses. During the procedure:

- Electrodes are placed at precise locations on the head

- Through the electrodes, an electric current pass through the brain, causing a seizure that lasts generally less than one minute. Because the patient is under anesthesia and has taken a muscle relaxant, it is not painful and the patient cannot feel the electrical impulses.

- Five to ten minutes after the procedure ends, the patient awakens. May feel groggy at first as the anesthesia wears off. But after about an hour, the patient usually is alert and can resume normal activities.

- A typical course of ECT is administered about three times a week until the patient's depression improves (usually within 6 to 12 treatments). After that, maintenance ECT treatment is sometimes needed to reduce the chances that symptoms will return. ECT maintenance treatment varies depending on the needs of the individual and may range from one session per week to one session every few months. Frequently, a person who undergoes ECT also takes antidepressant medication or a mood stabilizing medication.

Side Effects of Electroconvulsive Therapy

The most common side effects associated with ECT include:

- A headache
- Upset stomach
- Muscle aches
- Memory loss

Some people may experience memory problems, especially of memories around the time of the treatment. Sometimes the memory problems are more severe, but usually, they improve over the days and weeks following the end of an ECT course.

Research has found that memory problems seem to be more associated with the traditional type of ECT called bilateral ECT, in which the electrodes are placed on both sides of the head.

In unilateral ECT, the electrodes are placed on just one side of the head—typically the right side because it is opposite the brain's learning and memory areas. Unilateral ECT has been found to be less likely to cause memory problems, and therefore, is preferred by many doctors, patients, and families.

Vagus Nerve Stimulation

Vagus nerve stimulation (VNS) works through a device implanted under the skin that sends electrical pulses through the left vagus nerve, half of a prominent pair of nerves that run from the brainstem through the neck and down to each side of the chest and abdomen. The vagus nerves carry messages from the brain to the body's major organs (e.g., heart, lungs, and intestines) and to areas of the brain that control mood, sleep, and other functions.

Why Vagus Nerve Stimulation Is Done

VNS was originally developed as a treatment for epilepsy. However, scientists noticed that it also had favorable effects on mood, especially depressive symptoms. Using brain scans, scientists found that the device affected areas of the brain that are involved in mood regulation. The pulses appeared to alter the levels of certain neurotransmitters (brain chemicals) associated with mood, including serotonin, norepinephrine, gamma-aminobutyric acid (GABA), and glutamate.

In 2005, the U.S. Food and Drug Administration (FDA) approved VNS for use in treating treatment-resistant depression in certain circumstances:

- If the patient is 18 years of age or over; and

- If the illness has lasted two years or more; and

- if it is severe or recurrent; and

- if the depression has not eased after trying at least four other treatments.

According to the FDA, it is not intended to be a first-line treatment, even for patients with severe depression. And, despite FDA approval, VNS remains an infrequently used because the results of early studies testing its effectiveness for major depression were mixed. But a newer study, which pooled together findings from controlled clinical trials, found that 32 percent of depressed people responded to VSN and 14 percent had a full remission of symptoms after being treated for nearly two years.

How Vagus Nerve Stimulation Works

A device called a pulse generator, about the size of a stopwatch, is surgically implanted in the upper left side of the chest. Connected to the pulse generator is an electrical lead wire, which is connected from the generator to the left vagus nerve.

Typically, 30-second electrical pulses are sent about every five minutes from the generator to the vagus nerve. The duration and frequency of the pulses may vary depending on how the generator is programmed. The vagus nerve, in turn, delivers those signals to the brain. The pulse generator, which operates continuously, is powered by a battery that lasts around ten years, after which it must be replaced. Normally, people do not feel pain or any other sensations as the device operates.

The device also can be temporarily deactivated by placing a magnet over the chest where the pulse generator is implanted. A person may want to deactivate it if side effects become intolerable, or before engaging in strenuous activity or exercise because it may interfere with breathing. The device reactivates when the magnet is removed.

VNS treatment is intended to reduce symptoms of depression. It may be several months before the patient notices any benefits and not all patients will respond to VNS. It is important to remember that VNS is intended to be given along with other traditional therapies, such as medications, and patients should not expect to discontinue these other treatments, even with the device in place.

Side Effects of Vagus Nerve Stimulation

VNS is not without risk. There may be complications such as infection from the implant surgery, or the device may come loose, move around or malfunction, which may require additional surgery to correct. Some patients have no improvement in symptoms and some actually get worse.

Other potential side effects include:

- Voice changes or hoarseness

- A cough or a sore throat

- Neck pain

- Discomfort or tingling in the area where the device is implanted

- Breathing problems, especially during exercise

- Difficulty swallowing

Long-term side effects are unknown.

Repetitive Transcranial Magnetic Stimulation

Repetitive transcranial magnetic stimulation (rTMS) uses a magnet to activate the brain. First developed in 1985, rTMS has been studied as a treatment for depression, psychosis, anxiety, and other disorders.

Unlike ECT, in which electrical stimulation is more generalized, rTMS can be targeted to a specific site in the brain. Scientists believe that focusing on a specific site in the brain reduces the chance for the types of side effects associated with ECT. But opinions vary as to what site is best.

Why Repetitive Transcranial Magnetic Stimulation Is Done

In 2008, rTMS was approved for use by the FDA as a treatment for major depression for patients who do not respond to at least one antidepressant medication in the current episode. It is also used in other countries as a treatment for depression in patients who have not responded to medications and who might otherwise be considered for ECT.

The evidence supporting rTMS for depression was mixed until the first large clinical trial, funded by the National Institute of Mental Health (NIMH), was published in 2010. The trial found that 14 percent achieved remission with rTMS compared to 5 percent with an inactive (sham) treatment. After the trial ended, patients could enter a second phase in which everyone, including those who previously received the sham treatment, was given rTMS. Remission rates during the second phase climbed to nearly 30 percent. A sham treatment is like a placebo, but instead of being an inactive pill, it's an inactive procedure that mimics real rTMS.

How Repetitive Transcranial Magnetic Stimulation Works

A typical rTMS session lasts 30 to 60 minutes and does not require anesthesia.

During the procedure an electromagnetic (EM) coil is held against the forehead near an area of the brain that is thought to be involved in mood regulation. Then, short electromagnetic pulses are administered through the coil. The magnetic pulses easily pass through the skull and cause small electrical currents that stimulate nerve cells in the targeted brain region.

Because this type of pulse generally does not reach further than two inches into the brain, scientists can select which parts of the brain will be affected and which will not be. The magnetic field is about the same strength as that of a magnetic resonance imaging (MRI) scan. Generally, the person feels a slight knocking or tapping on the head as the pulses are administered.

Not all scientists agree on the best way to position the magnet on the patient's head or give the electromagnetic pulses. They also do not yet know if rTMS works best when given as a single treatment or combined with medication and/or psychotherapy. More research is underway to determine the safest and most effective uses of rTMS.

Side Effects of Repetitive Transcranial Magnetic Stimulation

Sometimes a person may have discomfort at the site on the head where the magnet is placed. The muscles of the scalp, jaw or face may contract or tingle during the procedure. Mild headaches or brief lightheadedness may result. It is also possible that the procedure could cause a seizure, although documented incidences of this are uncommon. Two large-scale studies on the safety of rTMS found that most side effects, such as headaches or scalp discomfort, were mild or moderate, and no seizures occurred. Because the treatment is relatively new, however, long-term side effects are unknown.

Magnetic Seizure Therapy
How Magnetic Seizure Therapy Works

Magnetic seizure therapy (MST) borrows certain aspects from both ECT and rTMS. Like rTMS, MST uses magnetic pulses instead of electricity to stimulate a precise target in the brain. However, unlike rTMS, MST aims to induce a seizure-like ECT. So the pulses are given at a higher frequency than that used in rTMS. Therefore, like ECT, the patient must be anesthetized and given a muscle relaxant to prevent movement. The goal of MST is to retain the effectiveness of ECT while reducing its cognitive side effects.

MST is in the early stages of testing for mental disorders, but initial results are promising. A review article that examined the evidence from eight clinical studies found that MST triggered remission from major depression or bipolar disorder in 30 to 40 percent of individuals.

Side Effects of Magnetic Seizure Therapy

Like ECT, MST carries the risk of side effects that can be caused by anesthesia exposure and the induction of a seizure. Studies in both animals and humans have found that MST produces

- Fewer memory side effects
- Shorter seizures
- Allows for a shorter recovery time than ECT

Deep Brain Stimulation

Deep brain stimulation (DBS) was first developed as a treatment for Parkinson disease (PD) to reduce tremor, stiffness, walking problems, and uncontrollable movements. In DBS, a pair of electrodes is implanted in the brain and controlled by a generator that is implanted in the chest. Stimulation is continuous and its frequency and level are customized to the individual.

DBS has been studied as a treatment for depression or obsessive-compulsive disorder (OCD). As of now, there is a Humanitarian Device Exemption (HDE) for the use of DBS to treat OCD, but its use in depression remains only on an experimental basis. A review of all 22 published studies testing DBS for depression found that only three of them were of high quality because they not only had a treatment group but also a control group which did not receive DBS. The review found that across the studies, 40 to 50 percent of people showed receiving DBS greater than 50 percent improvement.

How Deep Brain Stimulation Works

DBS requires brain surgery. The head is shaved and then attached with screws to a sturdy frame that prevents the head from moving during the surgery. Scans of the head and brain using MRI are taken. The surgeon uses these images as guides during the surgery. Patients are awake during the procedure to provide the surgeon with feedback, but they feel no pain because the head is numbed with a local anesthetic and the brain itself does not register pain.

Once ready for surgery, two holes are drilled into the head. From there, the surgeon threads a slender tube down into the brain to place electrodes on each side of a specific area of the brain. In the case of depression, the first area of the brain targeted by DBS is called Area 25, or the subgenual cingulate cortex. This area has been found to be overactive in depression and other mood disorders. But later research targeted several other areas of the brain affected by depression. So DBS is now targeting several areas of the brain for treating depression. In the case of OCD, the electrodes are placed in an area of the brain (the ventral capsule (VC)/ventral striatum (VS)) believed to be associated with the disorder.

After the electrodes are implanted and the patient provides feedback about their placement, the patient is put under general anesthesia. The electrodes are then attached to wires that are run inside the body from the head down to the chest, where a pair of battery-operated generators is implanted. From here, electrical pulses are continuously delivered over the wires to the electrodes in the brain. Although it is unclear exactly how the device works to reduce depression or OCD, scientists believe that the pulses help to "reset" the area of the brain that is malfunctioning so that it works normally again.

Side Effects of Deep Brain Stimulation

DBS carries risks associated with any type of brain surgery. For example, the procedure may lead to:

- Bleeding in the brain or stroke
- Infection
- Disorientation or confusion
- Unwanted mood changes
- Movement disorders
- Lightheadedness
- Trouble sleeping

Because the procedure is still being studied, other side effects not yet identified may be possible. Long-term benefits and side effects are unknown.

Chapter 26

Complementary and Alternative Medicine for Mental Healthcare

Chapter Contents

Section 26.1

Anxiety and Complementary Health Approaches

This section includes text excerpted from "Anxiety and Complementary Health Approaches," National Center for Complementary and Integrative Health (NCCIH), August 21, 2018.

Researchers are studying a variety of complementary health approaches to see whether they might be helpful for occasional anxiety or anxiety disorders. There is some evidence that mindfulness and other forms of meditation, music, relaxation techniques, and melatonin may be efficacious for anxiety, especially anxiety associated with medical procedures or chronic medical problems. However, there is not enough evidence on other complementary health approaches for anxiety to draw definitive conclusions about their efficacy.

Mind and Body Approaches for Treating Anxiety Disorders

Acupuncture

Although some studies of acupuncture for anxiety have had positive outcomes, in general, many of the studies on acupuncture for anxiety have been of poor methodological quality or not of statistical significance. In addition, because the research is extremely variable (e.g., number and variety of acupuncture points, the frequency of sessions, and duration of treatment), it is difficult to draw firm conclusions about potential benefits.

Acupuncture is generally considered safe when performed by an experienced practitioner using sterile needles. Reports of serious adverse events related to acupuncture are rare, but include infections and punctured organs.

Massage Therapy

In some studies massage therapy helped to reduce anxiety for people with cancer or other comorbid medical conditions; however, other studies did not find a statistically significant beneficial effect. Little research has been done on massage for anxiety disorders, and results have been conflicting.

Massage therapy appears to have few risks if it is used appropriately and provided by a trained massage professional.

Mindfulness Meditation

Meditation therapy is commonly used and has been shown to be of small to modest benefit for people with anxiety-related symptoms. There is some evidence that transcendental meditation (TM) may have a beneficial effect on anxiety. However, there is a lack of studies with adequate statistical power in patients with clinically diagnosed anxiety disorders, which makes it difficult to draw firm conclusions about its efficacy for anxiety disorders.

Meditation is generally considered to be safe for healthy people. However, people with physical limitations may not be able to participate in certain meditative practices involving movement.

Relaxation Techniques

Relaxation techniques may reduce anxiety in individuals with chronic medical problems and those who are having medical procedures. However, research demonstrates that conventional psychotherapy, for individuals with generalized anxiety disorder (GAD), may be more effective than relaxation techniques.

Relaxation techniques are generally considered safe for healthy people. People with serious physical or mental-health problems should discuss relaxation techniques with their healthcare providers.

Natural Products for Treating Anxiety Disorders
Chamomile

There is some research that suggests that a chamomile extract may be helpful for GAD, but the studies are preliminary and their findings are not conclusive. There have been reports of allergic reactions, including rare cases of anaphylaxis, in people who have consumed or come into contact with chamomile products. People are more likely to experience allergic reactions to chamomile if they're allergic to related plants such as ragweed, chrysanthemums, marigolds, or daisies. Interactions between chamomile and cyclosporine and warfarin have been reported, and there are theoretical reasons to suspect that chamomile might interact with other drugs as well.

Kava

Kava extract may produce moderately beneficial effects on anxiety symptoms; however, the use of kava supplements has been linked to a risk of severe liver damage. It has been associated with several cases of dystonia and may interact with several drugs, including drugs used to treat Parkinson disease (PD).

However, a 2013 randomized controlled trial of 75 participants who received kava extract over a six-week period found no significant differences across groups for liver function tests, nor any significant adverse reactions associated with kava administration. Long-term safety studies of kava are needed.

Melatonin

There is some research that suggests melatonin may help reduce anxiety in patients who are about to have surgery and may be as effective as standard treatment with midazolam in reducing preoperative anxiety. Melatonin supplements appear to be safe when used short-term; less is known about long-term safety.

Lavender

Although some studies of lavender preparations for anxiety have shown some therapeutic effects, in general, many of these studies have been of poor methodological quality. When lavender teas and extracts are taken by mouth, they may cause headache, changes in appetite, and constipation.

Using lavender supplements with sedative medications may increase drowsiness.

Section 26.2

Autism and Complementary Health Approaches

This section includes text excerpted from "Autism Spectrum Disorder and Complementary Health Approaches," National Center for Complementary and Integrative Health (NCCIH), July 25, 2017.

Estimates of the prevalence of autism in the United States vary, but U.S. government statistics estimate that about one in 68 children (or 1.5 percent of eight-year-old children) have autism spectrum disorder (ASD). There is no cure for ASD, but research shows that early diagnosis and interventions, such as during preschool or before, are more likely to have major positive effects on symptoms and later skills. Many parents choose complementary health approaches for their children with ASD to help manage symptoms; however, despite this use, there is a paucity of high-quality research focused on complementary approaches for ASD. Of the ASD research that has been conducted, most have been in the pediatric population; very few trials of complementary health approaches have been conducted in adults with ASD.

The existing evidence base indicates that melatonin may be beneficial for sleep disorders associated with ASD. Music therapy may have a positive effect on social interaction, and communication and behavioral skills in those affected by ASD. However, there is insufficient evidence to determine whether other complementary health approaches such as modified diets, supplementation with omega-3 fatty acids or vitamin B_6, or chelation are efficacious for ASD symptoms.

Natural Products and Biologics for People with Autism
Melatonin

There is some limited evidence that suggests melatonin may help with sleep problems in children with ASD. A 2014 review of melatonin as an option for managing sleep disorders in children with ASD found no serious safety concerns attributed to melatonin use in this population in the evaluated studies. Some reported adverse effects associated with melatonin use in children with ASD include morning drowsiness, increased enuresis, headache, dizziness, diarrhea, rash, and hypothermia. Melatonin is primarily metabolized by CYP1A2 and CYP2C19, so inhibitors of CYP1A2 may increase melatonin concentrations.

Melatonin may decrease blood pressure or serum glucose, so patients who are being treated with agents that affect blood pressure or serum glucose concentrations should be monitored closely.

Findings from a 2012 study in 24 children indicated that melatonin in dosages of 1 or 3 mg per day was well tolerated and safe over a 14-week duration.

Most studies of melatonin have examined short-term use; however, there is a lack of long-term safety data.

Omega-3 Fatty Acid Supplementation

There is insufficient evidence that omega-3 fatty acid supplementation is an effective treatment for ASD. Omega-3 fatty acid supplements usually do not have negative side effects. When side effects do occur, they typically consist of minor gastrointestinal (GI) symptoms.

It is uncertain whether people with fish or shellfish allergies can safely consume fish oil supplements.

Probiotics

The clinical evidence does not support the use of probiotics to modify behavior in children with ASD. None of the studies reported any adverse effects. However, there have been reports linking probiotics to severe side effects, such as dangerous infections, in people with serious underlying medical problems.

Secretin

Evidence suggests that single- or multiple-dose intravenous secretin, a gastrointestinal hormone, is not effective as a treatment for ASD. The 2012 Cochrane review also analyzed the studies for adverse effect and found that no serious events, such anaphylaxis, were reported. However, several studies reported some adverse events following secretin administration, including tantrums, hyperactivity, aggression, flushing, and other behavioral symptoms.

Vitamin B_6 and Magnesium

To date, there is insufficient evidence to support the use of vitamin B6 and magnesium as a treatment option for ASD. The studies included in the Cochrane review had no reported clinically significant side effects during administration of high doses of vitamin B_6 and magnesium.

Chelation

There is no evidence that indicates the effectiveness of pharmaceutical chelation as an intervention for ASD. Furthermore, there is substantial evidence that there is no link between heavy metals and autism. There have been previous reports of serious adverse events from intravenous chelation, including hypocalcemia, renal impairment, and reported death. There have been previous reports of serious adverse events from intravenous chelation, including hypocalcemia, renal impairment and reported death. The 2015 Cochrane review concluded that given these reports, the risks of chelation for ASD outweigh any possible (or potential) benefits.

Special Diets for People with Autism
Gluten-Free and Casein-Free Diet

There is evidence that parents commonly put their children with ASD on exclusion diets. Despite this common practice, there is insufficient evidence to support the use of gluten-free and/or casein-free diets as an effective treatment for children with ASD. Nutritionists have raised concerns about potential harms and risks of such diets, but evidence to support these risks is lacking. None of the studies included in the Cochrane review reported on adverse outcomes or potential adverse effects of gluten-free and/or casein-free diets in this population.

Ketogenic Diet

There is limited evidence that the high-fat, very-low-carbohydrate "ketogenic" diet may help individuals with seizure disorders, which are sometimes associated with autism. The mechanism of action of the ketogenic diet is not fully understood, and caution should be taken to avoid deleterious adverse effects or refractory outcomes. Ketogenic diets should be supervised by a nutritionist to ensure that children get the appropriate nutritional requirements for growth. Reported adverse effects include short-term gastrointestinal-related disturbances, to longer-term cardiovascular complications.

Mind and Body Practices for People with Autism
Acupuncture

Results of clinical trials on the effectiveness of acupuncture for ASD have been mixed, but there is no conclusive evidence available to support the use of acupuncture for the treatment of ASD. Relatively few complications from using acupuncture have been reported. Still, complications have resulted from the use of nonsterile needles and improper delivery of treatments.

A few studies in children with ASD included in the reviews above reported either no adverse events or minor side effects, but relevance between these reported adverse effects and acupuncture were unclear.

Music Therapy

There is some evidence that music therapy may help to improve some social and behavioral skills in children with ASD. Music therapy for people with ASD appears to be safe. None of the studies included in the Cochrane review reported any side effects caused by music therapy.

Other Approaches for People with Autism

Hyperbaric Oxygen Therapy

Available evidence does not support the use of hyperbaric oxygen therapy as an effective treatment for ASD. There are known risks of barotrauma and exacerbation of pulmonary disease at higher atmospheric pressures.

Section 26.3

Depression and Complementary Health Approaches

This section includes text excerpted from "Depression and Complementary Health Approaches," National Center for Complementary and Integrative Health (NCCIH), May 3, 2018.

Many individuals with depression turn to complementary health approach as an adjunct to or in place of conventional treatment. Although these approaches are commonly used and readily available in the marketplace, many of these treatments have not been rigorously studied for depression. For this reason, it's important that you understand the benefits and risks of these complementary approaches to advising your patients.

A task force on complementary and alternative medicine (CAM) tried and found that, based on the quality of available evidence, there is enough evidence to support further research on some complementary approaches, including omega-3 fatty acids, St. John's wort (*Hypericum perforatum*), folate, S-adenosyl-l-methionine (SAMe), light therapy, physical exercise, and mindfulness-based therapies for augmenting treatments of depression in adults. However, the task force noted the need for more rigorous and larger studies before employing these complementary approaches.

Natural Products for People with Depression
Omega-3 Fatty Acids

Some evidence suggests that omega-3 fatty acid supplementation may provide a small effect in adjunctive therapy in patients with a diagnosis of major depressive disorder (MDD) and on depressive patients without a diagnosis of MDD. Most trials have been adjunctive studies. Although the data are promising, controlled trials of omega-3 fatty acids as a monotherapy are inconclusive compared to standard antidepressant medicines, and it remains unclear that a mechanism is present to suggest that a pharmacological or biological antidepressant effect exists.

Omega-3 fatty acid supplements are generally safe and well-tolerated. When side effects do occur, they typically consist of minor gastrointestinal symptoms and fishy aftertaste.

There is some concern that omega-3 supplements may extend bleeding time. The risk appears to be minimal, and should never be used in patients who take drugs that affect platelet function. It is important to discuss any potential herb-drug interactions with patients if they are considering using omega-3 fatty acids.

It is uncertain whether people with fish or shellfish allergies can safely consume fish oil supplements and should not be used in such patients.

St. John's Wort

There is some evidence that suggests St. John's wort (*Hypericum perforatum*) may have an effect on mild to moderate major depressive disorder (MDD) for a limited number of patients, similar to standard antidepressants, but the evidence is far from definitive. Although some studies have demonstrated a slight efficacy over placebo, others contradict these findings.

The significant herb-drug interactions of St. John's wort are important safety considerations.

Drug interactions with St. John's wort limit use and are important safety considerations. Combining St. John's wort and certain antidepressants can lead to serotonin syndrome, with dangerous symptoms ranging from tremor and diarrhea to very dangerous confusion, muscle stiffness, drop in body temperature, and even death.

Other side effects of St. John's wort are usually minor and uncommon and may include upset stomach and sensitivity to sunlight. Also, St. John's wort may worsen feelings of anxiety in some people.

A rare, but possible side effect of taking St. John's wort is psychosis. Those with certain mental-health disorders, such as bipolar disorder, are at risk of experiencing this rare side effect. Therefore, it is important to discuss this potential side effect with patients who are considering using St. John's wort and encourage discontinuation of the herb if they experience a worsening of symptoms.

Taking St. John's wort increases the activity of cytochrome P450 3A4 (CYP3A4) enzyme and reduces plasma concentrations and can weaken many prescription medicines, such as:

- Antidepressants
- Oral contraceptives
- Cyclosporine
- Digoxin
- Some human immunodeficiency virus (HIV) drugs including indinavir
- Some chemotherapeutic agents including irinotecan
- Warfarin and other anticoagulants

S-Adenosyl-L-Methionine

Available scientific evidence does not support the use of S-Adenosyl-L-Methionine (SAMe) for the treatment of depression. Information on the long-term safety of SAMe is limited and inconclusive. However, in one study of alcohol-related liver disease in which participants took SAMe for two years, no serious side effects were reported.

SAMe may decrease the effects of levodopa. It is also possible that SAMe might interact with drugs and dietary supplements that increase levels of serotonin, including some antidepressants, L-tryptophan, and St. John's wort, but the evidence for such interactions are very limited.

SAMe promotes the growth of *Pneumocystis*, a fungus that can cause pneumonia in people with suppressed immune systems. It is possible that taking SAMe might increase the likelihood or severity of *Pneumocystis* infection in people who are HIV positive and should never be used in these patients.

Side effects of SAMe appear to be uncommon, and when they do occur they are usually problems such as nausea or digestive upsets.

Inositol

Available scientific evidence does not support the use of Inositol for the treatment of depression. There is a paucity of data on the safety and side effects of inositol. A 2014 meta-analysis of inositol for depression and anxiety disorders found that inositol marginally caused gastrointestinal upset compared with placebo. A 2011 European review on the safety of inositol had similar findings in that inositol induced gastrointestinal side effects such as nausea, flatus, and diarrhea.

Mind and Body Practices for People with Depression
Acupuncture

Available scientific evidence does not support the use of acupuncture for the treatment of depression. Relatively few complications from using acupuncture have been reported. Still, complications have resulted from the use of nonsterile needles and improper delivery of treatments. When not delivered properly, acupuncture can cause serious adverse effects, including skin infections, punctured organs, pneumothoraces, and injury to the central nervous system.

Music Therapy

There is some limited evidence that suggests music therapy may provide an improvement in mood. There are no adverse effects associated with music therapy.

Relaxation Training

Evidence suggests that relaxation training is better than no treatment in reducing symptoms of depression, but is not as beneficial as psychological therapies (e.g., cognitive-behavioral therapy (CBT)).

Relaxation techniques are generally considered safe for healthy people. However, occasionally, people report unpleasant experiences such as increased anxiety, intrusive thoughts, or fear of losing control.

There have been rare reports that certain relaxation techniques might cause or worsen symptoms in people with epilepsy or certain psychiatric conditions, or with a history of abuse or trauma.

Section 26.4

Seasonal Affective Disorder and Complementary Health Approaches

This section includes text excerpted from "Complementary Health Approaches for Seasonal Affective Disorder," National Center for Complementary and Integrative Health (NCCIH), December 27, 2017.

Seasonal affective disorder (SAD), a type of depression that comes and goes with the seasons, typically starts in the late fall and early winter and goes away during the spring and summer. Depressive episodes linked to the summer can occur but are much less common than winter episodes of SAD. To be diagnosed with SAD, people must meet full criteria for major depression coinciding with specific seasons for at least two years. Some of the symptoms of the winter pattern of SAD include having low energy, overeating, craving carbohydrates, and social withdrawal. Light therapy has become a standard treatment of SAD, and antidepressants have also been shown to improve SAD symptoms.

Some people turn to complementary health approaches to prevent SAD, including St. John's wort, melatonin, and vitamin D.

Mind and Body Practices for People with Seasonal Affective Disorder
Light Therapy

There is some evidence that light therapy may be useful as a preventive treatment for people with a history of season affect disorder.

The idea behind light therapy is to replace the diminished sunshine of the fall and winter months using daily exposure to a light box. Most typically, light boxes filter out the ultraviolet rays and require 20 to 60 minutes of exposure to 10,000 lux of cool-white fluorescent light, an amount that is about 20 times greater than ordinary indoor lighting.

A 2015 Cochrane review of one study involving 46 people concluded that there is limited evidence on light therapy as a preventive treatment for patients with a history of SAD. Evidence is limited based on methodological limitations and small sample sizes of studies. The review authors noted that the decision for or against initiating preventive treatment of SAD or using other preventive options should be strongly based on patient preferences. Ultraviolet (UV) lights should be avoided because of the increased risk of skin cancer. People should avoid staring directly into the light to avoid possible retinal injury. Side effects are typically mild and include vision issues such as blurry vision, photophobia, or headache. Light therapy may induce mania in patients with unrecognized or undertreated bipolar disorder.

Cognitive Behavioral Therapy

Cognitive behavioral therapy (CBT) is a type of psychotherapy that is effective for SAD. Traditional cognitive behavioral therapy has been adapted for use with SAD (CBT-SAD). CBT-SAD relies on basic techniques of CBT such as identifying negative thoughts and replacing them with more positive thoughts along with a technique called behavioral activation. Behavioral activation seeks to help the person identify activities that are engaging and pleasurable, whether indoors or outdoors, to improve coping with winter. CBT is generally considered safe for most people.

Natural Products for People with Seasonal Affective Disorder
St. John's Wort

There is limited evidence that St. John's wort may improve some symptoms of SAD; however, the studies have been small. It can weaken the effects of many medicines, including antidepressants, contraceptives, cyclosporine, digoxin, indinavir, irinotecan, and anticoagulants.

Taking St. John's wort with certain antidepressants or other drugs that affect serotonin may lead to increased serotonin-related side effects, which may be potentially serious. It may cause increased sensitivity to sunlight. Other side effects can include anxiety, dry mouth, dizziness, gastrointestinal symptoms, fatigue, headache, or sexual dysfunction.

Melatonin

There is some limited evidence (small trials involving few patients) that suggests melatonin improves sleep in some patients with SAD. Melatonin appears to be safe when used short term, but the lack of long-term studies means it's not yet known if it's safe for extended use. Side effects of melatonin are uncommon but can include drowsiness, headache, dizziness, or nausea. There have been no reports of significant side effects of melatonin in children.

Vitamin D

Vitamin D supplementation by itself is not considered an effective SAD treatment. Low blood levels of vitamin D are often found in people with SAD; however, the evidence for its use has been mixed. Although some studies suggest vitamin D supplementation may be as effective as light therapy, others found vitamin D had no effect. High doses of vitamin D may cause fatigue, abdominal cramps, nausea, vomiting, renal damage, and other adverse effects.

Section 26.5

Sleep Disorders and Complementary Health Approaches

This section includes text excerpted from "Sleep Disorders: In Depth," National Center for Complementary and Integrative Health (NCCIH), November 20, 2018.

What Are Sleep Disorders and How Important Are They?

There are more than 80 different sleep disorders. Chronic, long-term sleep disorders affect millions of Americans each year. These disorders and the sleep deprivation they cause can interfere with work, driving, social activities, and overall quality of life, and can have serious health implications. Sleep disorders account for an estimated $16 billion in medical costs each year, plus indirect costs due to missed days of work, decreased productivity, and other factors.

Is It a Sleep Disorder or Not Enough Sleep?

Some people who feel tired during the day have a true sleep disorder, but for others, the real problem is not allowing enough time for sleep. Adults need at least seven to eight hours of sleep each night to be well rested, but the average adult sleeps for less than seven hours a night.

Sleep is a basic human need, like eating, drinking, and breathing, and is vital to good health and well-being. Shortchanging yourself on sleep slows your thinking and reaction time, makes you irritable and increases your risk of injury. It may even decrease your resistance to infections, increase your risk of obesity, and increase your risk of heart disease.

What the Science Says about Complementary Health Approaches and Insomnia

Research has produced promising results for some complementary health approaches for insomnia, such as relaxation techniques. However, evidence of effectiveness is still limited for most products and practices, and safety concerns have been raised about a few.

Mind and Body Practices

There is evidence that **relaxation techniques** can be effective in treating chronic insomnia. **Progressive relaxation** may help people with insomnia and nighttime anxiety. **Music-assisted relaxation** may be moderately beneficial in improving sleep quality in people with sleep problems, but the number of studies has been small.

Various forms of relaxation are sometimes combined with components of cognitive-behavioral therapy (CBT) (such as sleep restriction and stimulus control), with good results. Using relaxation techniques before bedtime can be part of a strategy to improve sleep habits that also includes other steps, such as maintaining a consistent sleep schedule; avoiding caffeine, alcohol, heavy meals, and strenuous exercise too close to bedtime; and sleeping in a quiet, cool, dark room.

Relaxation techniques are generally safe. However, rare side effects have been reported in people with serious physical or mental-health conditions. If you have a serious underlying health problem, it would be a good idea to consult your healthcare provider before using relaxation techniques.

In a preliminary study, **mindfulness-based stress reduction**, a type of meditation, was as effective as a prescription drug in a small group of people with insomnia. Several other studies have also reported that mindfulness-based stress reduction improved sleep, but the people who participated in these studies had other health problems, such as cancer.

Preliminary studies in postmenopausal women and women with osteoarthritis suggest that **yoga** may be helpful for insomnia. Some practitioners who treat insomnia have reported that **hypnotherapy** enhanced the effectiveness of cognitive-behavioral therapy and relaxation techniques in their patients, but very little rigorous research has been conducted on the use of hypnotherapy for insomnia.

A small 2012 study on **massage therapy** showed promising results for insomnia in postmenopausal women. However, conclusions cannot be reached on the basis of a single study.

Most of the studies that have evaluated **acupuncture** for insomnia have been of poor scientific quality. Available evidence is not rigorous enough to show whether acupuncture is helpful for insomnia.

Dietary Supplements
Melatonin and Related Supplements

Melatonin may help with jet lag and sleep problems related to shift work.

A 2013 evaluation of the results of 19 studies concluded that melatonin may help people with insomnia fall asleep faster, sleep longer, and sleep better, but the effect of melatonin is small compared to that of other treatments for insomnia.

Studies of melatonin in children with sleep problems suggest that it may be helpful, both in generally healthy children and in those with conditions such as autism or attention deficit hyperactivity disorder (ADHD). However, both the number of studies and the number of children who participated in the studies are small, and all of the studies tested melatonin only for short periods of time.

Melatonin supplements appear to be relatively safe for short-term use, although the use of melatonin was linked to bad moods in elderly people (most of whom had dementia) in one study. The long-term safety of melatonin supplements has not been established.

Dietary supplements containing substances that can be changed into melatonin in the body—**L-tryptophan** and **5-hydroxytryptophan** (5-HTP)—have been researched as sleep aids.

Studies of L-tryptophan supplements as an insomnia treatment have had inconsistent results, and the effects of 5-HTP supplements on insomnia have not been established. The use of L-tryptophan supplements may be linked to eosinophilia-myalgia syndrome (EMS), a complex, potentially fatal disorder with multiple symptoms including severe muscle pain. It is uncertain whether the risk of EMS associated with L-tryptophan supplements is due to impurities in L-tryptophan preparations or to L-tryptophan itself.

Herbs

Although **chamomile** has traditionally been used for insomnia, often in the form of a tea, there is no conclusive evidence from clinical trials showing whether it is helpful. Some people, especially those who are allergic to ragweed or related plants, may have allergic reactions to chamomile.

Although **kava** is said to have sedative properties, very little research has been conducted on whether this herb is helpful for insomnia. More importantly, kava supplements have been linked to a risk of severe liver damage.

Clinical trials of **valerian** (another herb said to have sedative properties) have had inconsistent results, and its value for insomnia has not been demonstrated. Although few people have reported negative side effects from valerian, it is uncertain whether this herb is safe for long-term use.

Some "sleep formula" dietary supplements combine valerian with other herbs such as **hops, lemon balm, passionflower**, and **kava** or other ingredients such as **melatonin** and **5-HTP**. There is little evidence on these preparations from studies in people.

Other Complementary Health Approaches

Aromatherapy is the therapeutic use of essential oils from plants. It is uncertain whether aromatherapy is helpful for treating insomnia because little rigorous research has been done on this topic. A systematic review concluded that available evidence does not demonstrate significant effects of **homeopathic medicines** for insomnia.

If You're Considering Complementary Health Approaches for Sleep Problems

Talk to your healthcare providers. Tell them about the complementary health approach you are considering and ask any questions you may have. Because trouble sleeping can be an indication of a more serious condition, and because some prescription and over-the-counter (OTC) drugs can contribute to sleep problems, it is important to discuss your sleep-related symptoms with your healthcare providers before trying any complementary health product or practice.

Be cautious about using any sleep product—prescription medications, OTC medications, dietary supplements, or homeopathic remedies. Find out about potential side effects and any risks from long-term use or combining products.

Keep in mind that "natural" does not always mean safe. For example, kava products can cause serious harm to the liver. Also, a manufacturer's use of the term "standardized" (or "verified" or "certified") does not necessarily guarantee product quality or consistency. Natural products can cause health problems if not used correctly. The healthcare providers you see about your sleep problems can advise you.

If you are pregnant, nursing a child, or considering giving a child a dietary supplement or other natural health product, it is especially important to consult your (or your child's) healthcare provider. If you are considering a practitioner-provided complementary health practice, check with your insurer to see if the services will be covered, and ask a trusted source (such as your healthcare provider or a nearby hospital or medical school) to recommend a practitioner.

Tell all your healthcare providers about any complementary health approaches you use. Give them a full picture of what you do to manage your health. This will help ensure coordinated and safe care.

Section 26.6

Substance-Use Disorders and Complementary Health Approaches

This section includes text excerpted from "Mind and Body Approaches for Substance Use Disorders," National Center for Complementary and Integrative Health (NCCIH), April 16, 2018.

Mindfulness-based approaches have shown some success when applied to the treatment of substance abuse and addiction. Mindfulness-based approaches for substance-abuse treatment, in part, attempt to decrease the impact of negative affect, which is thought to serve as a trigger for substance use. Improving distress tolerance is an important aspect of mindfulness-based substance-abuse treatment. These approaches can be part of a comprehensive addiction treatment plan that includes behavioral modifications and may include pharmaceuticals to decrease cravings, group therapy, or counseling.

Mind and Body Practices for People with Substance-Use Disorders
Acupuncture

To date, there is not enough consistent data to support the use of acupuncture for substance-use outcomes; however, there are some findings that suggest acupuncture may have positive effects as an adjunctive therapy for withdrawal/craving and anxiety symptoms. Only a few high-quality studies on acupuncture for smoking cessation have been conducted, so firm conclusions about its effectiveness cannot be drawn.

Relatively few complications from the use of acupuncture have been reported to the U.S. Food and Drug Administration (FDA), in light of the millions of people treated each year and the number of acupuncture needles used. Still, complications have resulted from inadequate sterilization of needles and from improper delivery of treatments. When not delivered properly, acupuncture can cause serious adverse effects, including infections and punctured organs.

Hypnotherapy

There is some evidence to suggest that hypnotherapy may improve smoking cessation, but data are not definitive. It is considered safe when performed by a health professional trained in hypnotherapy. Self-hypnosis also appears to be safe for most people. There are no reported cases of injury resulting from self-hypnosis.

Mindfulness Meditation

Available data suggest that mindfulness-based interventions may help significantly reduce the consumption of several substances including alcohol, cigarettes, opiates, and others compared to control groups; however, many studies have had small sample sizes, methodological problems, and a lack of consistently replicated findings. Meditation is considered to be safe for healthy people. There have been rare reports that meditation could cause or worsen symptoms in people who have certain psychiatric problems, but this question has not been fully researched.

Music Therapy

Although there is some evidence that music therapy may have an effect on emotional and motivational outcomes and perceived helpfulness, the efficacy of music therapy for substance-abuse disorders (SUD) is unclear.

Yoga

Only a few studies have been conducted on the effects of yoga for smoking cessation. Although preliminary results have been positive, larger, high-quality studies are needed to determine rigorously if yoga is an effective treatment. Yoga is generally low-impact and safe for healthy people when practiced appropriately under the guidance of a well-trained instructor.

Overall, those who practice yoga have a low rate of side effects, and the risk of serious injury from yoga is quite low. However, certain types of stroke as well as pain from nerve damage are among the rare possible side effects of practicing yoga. Women who are pregnant and people with certain medical conditions, such as high blood pressure, glaucoma, and sciatica should modify or avoid some yoga poses.

Chapter 27

Technology and the Future of Mental-Health Treatment

Technology has opened a new frontier in mental-health support and data collection. Mobile devices like cell phones, smartphones, and tablets are giving the public, doctors, and researchers new ways to access help, monitor progress, and increase understanding of mental well-being.

Mobile mental-health support can be very simple but effective. For example, anyone with the ability to send a text message can contact a crisis center. New technology can also be packaged into an extremely sophisticated app for smartphones or tablets. Such apps might use the device's built-in sensors to collect information on a user's typical behavior patterns. If the app detects a change in behavior, it may provide a signal that help is needed before a crisis occurs. Some apps are stand-alone programs that promise to improve memory or thinking skills. Others help the user connect to a peer counselor or to a healthcare professional.

Excitement about the huge range of opportunities has led to a burst of app development. There are thousands of mental-health apps available in iTunes and Android app stores, and the number is growing every year. However, this new technology frontier includes a lot of uncertainty. There are very little industry regulation and very little

This chapter includes text excerpted from "Technology and the Future of Mental Health Treatment," National Institute of Mental Health (NIMH), February 2017.

information on app effectiveness, which can lead consumers to wonder which apps they should trust.

Before focusing on the state of the science and where it may lead, it's important to look at the advantages and disadvantages of expanding mental-health treatment and research into a mobile world.

The Pros and Cons of Mental-Health Apps

Experts believe that technology has a lot of potential for clients and clinicians alike. A few of the advantages of mobile care include:

- **Convenience.** Treatment can take place anytime and anywhere (e.g., at home in the middle of the night or on a bus on the way to work) and may be ideal for those who have trouble with in-person appointments.

- **Anonymity.** Clients can seek treatment options without involving other people.

- **An introduction to care.** Technology may be a good first step for those who have avoided mental healthcare in the past.

- **Lower cost.** Some apps are free or cost less than traditional care.

- **Service to more people.** Technology can help mental-health providers offer treatment to people in remote areas or to many people in times of sudden need (e.g., following a natural disaster or terror attack).

- **Interest.** Some technologies might be more appealing than traditional treatment methods, which may encourage clients to continue therapy.

- **24-hours service.** Technology can provide round-the-clock monitoring or intervention support.

- **Consistency.** Technology can offer the same treatment program to all users.

- **Support.** Technology can complement traditional therapy by extending an in-person session, reinforcing new skills, and providing support and monitoring.

This new era of mental-health technology offers great opportunities but also raises a number of concerns. Tackling potential problems will be an important part of making sure new apps provide benefits without causing harm. That is why the mental-health community and software developers are focusing on:

- **Effectiveness.** The biggest concern with technological interventions is obtaining scientific evidence that they work and that they work as well as traditional methods.

- **For whom and for what.** Another concern is understanding if apps work for all people and for all mental-health conditions.

- **Guidance.** There are no industry-wide standards to help consumers know if an app or other mobile technology is proven effective.

- **Privacy.** Apps deal with very sensitive personal information so app makers need to be able to guarantee privacy for app users.

- **Regulation.** The question of who will or should regulate mental-health technology and the data it generates needs to be answered.

- **Overselling.** There is some concern that if an app or program promises more than it delivers, consumers may turn away from other, more effective therapies.

Trends in App Development

Creative research and engineering teams are combining their skills to address a wide range of mental-health concerns. Some popular areas of app development include:

Self-Management Apps

"Self-management" means that the user puts information into the app so that the app can provide feedback. For example, the user might set up medication reminders, or use the app to develop tools for managing stress, anxiety, or sleep problems. Some software can use additional equipment to track heart rate, breathing patterns, blood pressure, etc., and may help the user track progress and receive feedback.

Apps for Improving Thinking Skills

Apps that help the user with cognitive remediation (improved thinking skills) are promising. These apps are often targeted toward people with serious mental illnesses.

Skill-Training Apps

Skill-training apps may feel more like games than other mental-health apps as they help users learn new coping or thinking skills. The user might watch an educational video about anxiety management or the importance of social support. Next, the user might pick some new strategies to try and then use the app to track how often those new skills are practiced.

Illness Management, Supported Care

This type of app technology adds additional support by allowing the user to interact with another human being. The app may help the user connect with peer support or may send information to a trained healthcare provider who can offer guidance and therapy options. Researchers are working to learn how much human interaction people need for app-based treatments to be effective.

Passive Symptom Tracking

A lot of effort is going into developing apps that can collect data using the sensors built into smartphones. These sensors can record movement patterns, social interactions (such as the number of texts and phone calls), behavior at different times of the day, vocal tone and speed, and more. In the future, apps may be able to analyze these data to determine the user's real-time state of mind. Such apps may be able to recognize changes in behavior patterns that signal a mood episode such as mania, depression, or psychosis before it occurs. An app may not replace a mental-health professional, but it may be able to alert caregivers when a client needs additional attention. The goal is to create apps that support a range of users, including those with serious mental illnesses.

Data Collection

Data collection apps can gather data without any help from the user. Receiving information from a large number of individuals at the same time can increase researchers' understanding of mental health and help them develop better interventions.

Research via Smartphone?

Dr. Patricia Areán's pioneering BRIGHTEN study, showed that research via smartphone app is already a reality. The BRIGHTEN study was remarkable because it used technology to both deliver treatment interventions and also to actually conduct the research trial. In other words, the research team used technology to recruit, screen, enroll, treat, and assess participants. BRIGHTEN was especially exciting because the study showed that technology can be an efficient way to pilot test promising new treatments, and that those treatments need to be engaging.

A New Partnership: Clinicians and Engineers

Researchers have found that interventions are most effective when people like them, are engaged, and want to continue using them. Behavioral health apps will need to combine the engineers' skills for making an app easy to use and entertaining with the clinician's skills for providing effective treatment options.

Researchers and software engineers are developing and testing apps that do everything from managing medications to teaching coping skills to when someone may need more emotional help. Intervention apps may help someone give up smoking, manage symptoms, or overcome anxiety, depression, posttraumatic stress disorder (PTSD), or insomnia. While the apps are becoming more appealing and user-friendly, there still isn't a lot of information on their effectiveness.

Evaluating Apps

There are no review boards, checklists, or widely accepted rules for choosing a mental-health app. Most apps do not have peer-reviewed research to support their claims, and it is unlikely that every mental-health app will go through a randomized, controlled research trial to test effectiveness. One reason is that testing is a slow process and technology evolves quickly. By the time an app has been put through rigorous scientific testing, the original technology may be outdated.

As of now, there are no national standards for evaluating the effectiveness of the hundreds of mental-health apps that are available. Consumers should be cautious about trusting a program. However, there are a few suggestions for finding an app that may work for you:

- Ask a trusted healthcare provider for a recommendation. Some larger providers may offer several apps and collect data on their use.

- Check to see if the app offers recommendations for what to do if symptoms get worse or if there is a psychiatric emergency.

- Decide if you want an app that is completely automated or an app that offers opportunities for contact with a trained person.

- Search for information on the app developer. Can you find helpful information about her or his credentials and experience?

- Beware of misleading logos. The National Institute of Mental Health (NIMH) has not developed and does not endorse any apps. However, some app developers have unlawfully used the NIMH logo to market their products.

- Search the PubMed database offered by National Library of Medicine (NLM) (www.ncbi.nlm.nih.gov/pubmed/). This resource contains articles on a wide range of research topics, including mental-health app development.

- If there is no information about a particular app, check to see if it is based on a treatment that has been tested. For example, research has shown that Internet-based cognitive behavior therapy (CBT) is as effective as conventional CBT for disorders that respond well to CBT, like depression, anxiety, social phobia, and panic disorder.

- Try it. If you're interested in an app, test it for a few days and decide if it's easy to use, holds your attention, and if you want to continue using it. An app is only effective if keeps users engaged for weeks or months.

Chapter 28

Health Insurance and Mental-Health Services

Do you have insurance questions about mental-health or addiction services?

Help is available if you have:

- Been denied coverage

- Reached a limit on your plan (such as copayments, deductibles, yearly visits, etc.)

- Have an overly large copay or deductible

You may be protected by Mental Health and Substance-Use Disorder Coverage Parity laws require most health plans to apply similar rules to mental-health benefits as they do for medical and surgical benefits. There are federal and state agencies who can provide assistance.

Frequently Asked Questions on Health Insurance and Mental-Health Services

Does the Affordable Care Act Require Insurance Plans to Cover Mental-Health Benefits?

Most individual and small group health insurance plans, including plans sold on the Marketplace are required to cover mental health and

---

This chapter includes text excerpted from "Health Insurance and Mental Health Services," MentalHealth.gov, U.S. Department of Health and Human Services (HHS), March 19, 2018.

substance-use disorder (SUD) services. Medicaid Alternative Benefit Plans (MABP) also must cover mental health and SUD services. These plans must have coverage of essential health benefits, which include ten categories of benefits as defined under the healthcare law. One of those categories is mental health and SUD services. Another is rehabilitative and habilitative services. Additionally, these plans must comply with mental health and substance-use parity requirements, as set forth in the Mental Health Parity and Addiction Equity Act (MHPAEA), meaning coverage for mental health and substance-abuse services generally cannot be more restrictive than coverage for medical and surgical services.

How Do You Find out If Your Health Insurance Plan Is Supposed to Be Covering Mental Health or Substance-Use Disorder Services in Parity with Medical and Surgical Benefits? What Do You Do If You Think Your Plan Is Not Meeting Parity Requirements?

In general, for those in large employer plans, if mental health or SUD services are offered, they are subject to the parity protections required under MHPAEA. The smallest employer and individual plans, mental health and SUD services must meet MHPAEA requirements.

If you have questions about your insurance plan, you first look at your plan's enrollment materials, or any other information you have on the plan, to see what the coverage levels are for all benefits. Because of the Affordable Care Act (ACA), health insurers are required to provide you with an easy-to-understand summary of your benefits including mental-health benefits, which should make it easier to see what your coverage is. More information also may be available via the Mental Health and Addiction Insurance Help consumer portal prototype and with your state Consumer Assistance Program (CAP).

Does Medicaid Cover Mental Health or Substance-Use Disorder Services?

All state Medicaid programs provide some mental-health services and some offer SUD services to beneficiaries, and the Children's Health Insurance Program (CHIP) beneficiaries receive a full-service array. These services often include counseling, therapy, medication management, social work services, peer support, and SUD treatment. While states determine which of these services to cover for adults, Medicaid and CHIP requires that children enrolled in Medicaid receive a wide range of medically necessary services, including mental-health services. In addition, coverage for the new Medicaid adult expansion populations is required to include essential-health benefits, including mental health and SUD benefits, and must meet mental health and substance-abuse parity requirements under MHPAEA in the same manner as health plans.

Does Medicare Cover Mental Health or Substance-Use Disorder Services?

Yes, Medicare covers a wide range of mental-health services.

- **Medicare Part A (Hospital Insurance)** covers inpatient mental-healthcare services you get in a hospital. Part A covers your room, meals, nursing care, and other related services and supplies.

- **Medicare Part B (Medical Insurance)** helps cover mental-health services that you would generally get outside of a hospital, including visits with a psychiatrist or other doctor, visits with a clinical psychologist or clinical social worker, and lab tests ordered by your doctor.

- **Medicare Part D (Prescription Drug)** helps cover drugs you may need to treat a mental-health condition. Each Part D plan has its own list of covered drugs, known as a formulary.

If you get your Medicare benefits through a Medicare Advantage Plan (like a health maintenance organization (HMO) or preferred provider organization (PPO)) or other Medicare health plan, check your plan's membership materials or call the plan for details about how to get your mental-health benefits.

What Can You Do If You Think That You Need Mental Health or Substance-Use Disorder Services for Yourself or Family Members?

Here are three steps you can take right now:

- Learn more about how you, your friends, and your family can obtain health insurance coverage provided by Medicaid or CHIP or the Health Insurance Marketplaces by visiting www. HealthCare.gov.

- Find out more about how the law is expanding coverage of mental health and SUD benefits and federal parity protections: www.aspe.hhs.gov/health/reports/2013/mental/rb_mental.cfm

- Find help in your area with the Behavioral Health Treatment Services Locator (BHTSL) or the Find a Health Center (www.findahealthcenter.hrsa.gov).

What Is the Health Insurance Marketplace?

The Health Insurance Marketplace is designed to make buying health coverage easier and more affordable. The Marketplace allows individuals to compare health plans, get answers to questions, find out if they are eligible for tax credits to help pay for private insurance or health programs such as the CHIP, and enroll in a health plan that meets their needs. The marketplace can help you:

- Look for and compare private health plans

- Get answers to questions about your health coverage options

- Get reduced costs, if you're eligible

- Enroll in a health plan that meets your needs

Part Four

Pediatric Mental-Health Concerns

Chapter 29

Childhood Mental Disorders

Mental health in childhood means reaching developmental and emotional milestones and learning healthy social skills and how to cope when there are problems. Mentally-healthy children have a positive quality of life (QOL) and can function well at home, in school, and in their communities. This chapter provides information about children's mental health.

Mental disorders among children are described as serious changes in the way children typically learn, behave, or handle their emotions, which cause distress and problems getting through the day.

Among the more common mental disorders that can be diagnosed in childhood are; attention deficit hyperactivity disorder (ADHD), anxiety, and behavior disorders. Other childhood disorders and concerns that affect how children learn, behave, or handle their emotions can include learning and developmental disabilities, autism, and risk factors like substance use and self-harm.

What Are the Symptoms of Childhood Mental Disorders?

Symptoms of mental disorders change over time as a child grows, and may include difficulties with how a child plays, learns, speaks, and acts or how the child handles their emotions. Symptoms often start in early childhood, although some disorders may develop during the teenage years. The diagnosis is often made in the school years and

This chapter includes text excerpted from "What Are Childhood Mental Disorders?" Centers for Disease Control and Prevention (CDC), March 14, 2018.

sometimes earlier. However, some children with a mental disorder may not be recognized or diagnosed as having one.

Can Childhood Mental Disorders Be Treated?

Childhood mental disorders can be treated and managed. There are many treatment options based on the best and most updated medical evidence, so parents and doctors should work closely with everyone involved in the child's treatment—teachers, coaches, therapists, and other family members. Taking advantage of all the resources available will help parents, health professionals, and educators guide the child towards success. Early diagnosis and appropriate services for children and their families can make a difference in the lives of children with mental disorders.

Get Help Finding Treatment

If you have concerns about a child, you can use these resources to help you find a healthcare provider familiar with treatment options.

- **Psychologist Locator** (locator.apa.org.), a service of the American Psychological Association (APA) Practice Organization

- **Child and Adolescent Psychiatrist** Finder (www.aacap.org/ AACAP/Families_and_Youth/Resources/CAP_Finder.aspx), a research tool by the American Academy of Child and Adolescent Psychiatry (AACAP)

- **Find a Cognitive Behavioral Therapist** (www.findcbt.org/ xFAT), a search tool by the Association for Behavioral and Cognitive Therapies (ABCT)

- If you need help finding treatment facilities, visit MentalHealth. gov

Who Is Affected?

Childhood mental disorders affect many children and families. Girls and boys of all ages, ethnic and racial backgrounds, and living in all regions of the United States experience mental disorders. Based on the National Research Council (NRC) and Institute of Medicine (IM) report that gathered findings from previous studies, it is estimated that 13 to 20 percent of children living in the United States (up to 1 out of 5 children) experience a mental disorder in a given year, and economic costs to individuals, families, and society were estimated to be $247 billion per year in 2007.

What Is the Impact of Mental Disorders in Children?

Mental health is important to overall health. Mental disorders are chronic health conditions—those that go on for a long time and often don't go away completely—that can continue through the lifespan. Without early diagnosis and treatment, children with mental disorders can have problems at home, in school, and in forming friendships. This can also interfere with their healthy development, and these problems can continue into adulthood.

What Can Be Done?

Parents. You know your child best. Talk to your child's healthcare professional if you have concerns about the way your child behaves at home, in school, or with friends.

Youth. It is just as important to take care of your mental health as it is to take care of your physical health. If you are angry, worried or sad, don't be afraid to talk about your feelings and reach out to a trusted friend or adult.

Healthcare professionals. Early diagnosis and appropriate treatment based on updated guidelines are very important. There are resources available to help diagnose and treat children's mental disorders.

Teachers and school administrators. Early identification is important so that children can get the help they need. Work with families and healthcare professionals if you have concerns about the mental health of a child in your school.

Chapter 30

Mental Healthcare for Children and Teens

When to Seek Help

Even under the best of circumstances, it can be hard to tell the difference between challenging behaviors and emotions that are consistent with typical child development and those that are cause for concern. It is important to remember that many disorders such as anxiety, attention deficit hyperactivity disorder (ADHD) and depression, do occur during childhood. In fact, many adults who seek treatment reflect back on how these disorders affected their childhood and wish that they had received help sooner. In general, if a child's behavior persists for a few weeks or longer, causes distress for the child or the child's family, and interferes with functioning at school, at home, or with friends, then consider seeking help. If a child's behavior is unsafe, or if a child talks about wanting to hurt or someone else, then seek help immediately.

Young children may benefit from an evaluation and treatment if they:

- Have frequent tantrums or are intensely irritable much of the time

- Often talk about fears or worries

This chapter includes text excerpted from "Children and Mental Health," National Institute of Mental Health (NIMH), June 30, 2018.

- Complain about frequent stomachaches or headaches with no known medical cause
- Are in constant motion and cannot sit quietly (except when they are watching videos or playing video games)
- Sleep too much or too little, have frequent nightmares, or seem sleepy during the day
- Are not interested in playing with other children or have difficulty making friends
- Struggle academically or have experienced a decline in grades
- Repeat actions or check things many times out of fear that something bad may happen

Older children and adolescents may benefit from an evaluation if they:

- Have lost interest in things that they used to enjoy
- Have low energy
- Sleep too much or too little, or seem sleepy throughout the day
- Are spending more and more time alone, and avoid social activities with friends or family
- Fear gaining weight, or diet or exercise excessively
- Engage in self-harm behaviors (e.g., cutting or burning their skin)
- Smoke, drink. or use drugs
- Engage in risky or destructive behavior alone or with friends
- Have thoughts of suicide
- Have periods of highly elevated energy and activity, and require much less sleep than usual
- Say that they think someone is trying to control their mind or that they hear things that other people cannot hear

First Steps for Parents

If you are concerned about your child, where do you begin?

- **Talk with your child's teacher.** What is the child's behavior such as in school, daycare, or on the playground?

- **Talk with your child's pediatrician.** Describe the behavior, and report what you have observed and learned from talking with others.

- **Ask for a referral to a mental-health professional** who has experience and expertise dealing with children.

Finding Answers

An evaluation by a health professional can help clarify problems that may be underlying a child's behavior and provide reassurance or recommendations for next steps. It provides an opportunity to learn about a child's strengths and weaknesses and determine which interventions might be most helpful.

A comprehensive assessment of a child's mental health includes the following:

- An interview with parents addressing a child's developmental history, temperament, relationships with friends and family, medical history, interests, abilities, and any prior treatment. It is important to get a picture of the child's current situation, for example: has changed schools recently, has there been an illness in the family or a change with an impact on the child's daily life.

- Information gathering from school, such as standardized tests, reports on behavior, capabilities, and difficulties

- An interview with the child about her or his experiences, as well as testing and behavioral observations, if needed

Treatment Options

Assessment results may suggest that a child's behavior is related to changes or stresses at home or school, or is the result of a disorder for which treatment would be recommended. Treatment recommendations may include:

- **Psychotherapy ("talk therapy").** There are many different approaches to psychotherapy, including structured psychotherapies directed at specific conditions. Effective psychotherapy for children always includes:

  - Parent involvement in the treatment (especially for children and adolescents)

- Teaching skills and practicing skills at home or at school (between session "homework assignments")

- Measures of progress (e.g., rating scales, improvements on homework assignments) that are tracked over time

- **Medications.** Medication may be used along with psychotherapy. As with adults, the type of medications used for children depends on the diagnosis and may include antidepressants, stimulants, mood stabilizers, and others. Medications are often used in combination with psychotherapy. If different specialists are involved, treatment should be coordinated.

- **Family counseling.** Including parents and other members of the family in treatment can help families understand how a child's individual challenges may affect relationships with parents and siblings and vice versa.

- **Support for parents.** Individual or group sessions that include training and the opportunity to talk with other parents can provide new strategies for supporting a child and managing difficult behavior in a positive way. The therapist can also coach parents on how to deal with schools.

Choosing a Mental-Health Professional

It's especially important to look for a child mental-health professional who has training and experience treating the specific problems that your child is experiencing. Ask the following questions when meeting with prospective treatment providers:

- Do you use treatment approaches that are supported by research?

- Do you involve parents in the treatment? If so, how are parents involved?

- Will there be homework between sessions?

- How will progress from treatment be evaluated?

- How soon can we expect to see progress?

- How long should treatment last?

Working with the School

If your child has behavioral or emotional challenges that interfere with her or his success in school, may be able to benefit from plans or accommodations that are provided under laws originally enacted to prevent discrimination against children with disabilities. The health professionals who are caring for your child can help you communicate with the school. A first step may be to ask the school whether an individualized education program (IEP) or a 504 plan is appropriate for your child. Accommodations might include simple measures such as providing a child with a tape recorder for taking notes, permitting flexibility with the amount of time allowed for tests, or adjusting seating in the classroom to reduce distraction. There are many sources of information on what schools can and, in some cases, must provide for children who would benefit from accommodations and how parents can request evaluation and services for their child:

- There are parent training and information centers (PTIC) and community parent resource centers (CPRC) throughout the United States. The center for parent information and resources website lists centers in each state.

- The U.S. Department of Education (DOE or ED) has detailed information on laws that establish mechanisms for providing children with accommodations tailored to their individual needs and aimed at helping them succeed in school. The ED also has a website on the Individuals with Disabilities Education Act (DEA), and the ED's Office of Civil Rights (OCR) has information on other federal laws that prohibit discrimination based on disability in public programs, such as schools.

Many of the organizations listed in this chapter as additional resources also offer information on working with schools as well as other more general information on disorders affecting children.

Chapter 31

Helping Children and Teens Cope with Violence and Disaster

Each year, children experience violence and disaster and face other traumas. Young people are injured, they see others harmed by violence, they suffer sexual abuse, and they lose loved ones or witness other tragic and shocking events. Community members—teachers, religious leaders, and other adults—can help children overcome these experiences and start the process of recovery.

What Is Trauma?

Trauma is often thought of as physical injuries. Psychological trauma is an emotionally painful, shocking, stressful, and sometimes life-threatening experience. It may or may not involve physical injuries, and can result from witnessing distressing events. Examples include a natural disaster, physical or sexual abuse, and terrorism.

Disasters such as hurricanes, earthquakes, and floods can claim lives, destroy homes or whole communities, and cause serious physical and psychological injuries. Trauma can also be caused by acts of violence. September 11, 2001, a terrorist attack is one example.

This chapter includes text excerpted from "Helping Children and Adolescents Cope with Violence and Disasters: What Community Members Can Do," National Institute of Mental Health (NIMH), 2014. Reviewed December 2018.

Mass shootings in schools or communities and physical or sexual assault are other examples. Traumatic events threaten people's sense of safety.

Reactions (responses) to trauma can be immediate or delayed. Reactions to trauma differ in severity and cover a wide range of behaviors and responses. Children with existing mental-health problems, past traumatic experiences, and/or limited family and social supports may be more reactive to trauma. Frequently experienced responses among children after trauma is a loss of trust and a fear of the event happening again.

It's Important to Remember:

- Children's reactions to trauma are strongly influenced by adults' responses to trauma.

- People from different cultures may have their own ways of reacting to trauma.

Commonly Experienced Responses to Trauma among Children

Children age five and under may react in a number of ways including:

- Showing signs of fear

- Clinging to parent or caregiver

- Crying or screaming

- Whimpering or trembling

- Moving aimlessly

- Becoming immobile

- Returning to behaviors common to being younger

- Thumbsucking

- Bedwetting

- Being afraid of the dark

Children age 6 to 11 may react by:

- Isolating themselves

- Becoming quiet around friends, family, and teachers

- Having nightmares or other sleep problems
- Refusing to go to bed
- Becoming irritable or disruptive
- Having outbursts of anger
- Starting fights
- Being unable to concentrate
- Refusing to go to school
- Complaining of physical problems
- Developing unfounded fears
- Becoming depressed
- Expressing guilt over what happened
- Feeling numb emotionally
- Doing poorly with school and homework
- Loss of interest in fun activities

Adolescents, age 12 to 17 may react by:

- Having flashbacks to the event (flashbacks are the mind reliving the event)
- Having nightmares or other sleep problems
- Avoiding reminders of the event
- Using or abusing drugs, alcohol, or tobacco
- Being disruptive, disrespectful, or behaving destructively
- Having physical complaints
- Feeling isolated or confused
- Being depressed
- Being angry
- Loss of interest in fun activities
- Having suicidal thoughts

Adolescents may feel guilty. They may feel guilty for not preventing injury or deaths. They also may have thoughts of revenge.

What Can Community Members Do Following a Traumatic Event?

Community members play important roles by helping children who experience violence or disaster. They help children cope with trauma and protect them from further trauma exposure.

It is important to remember:

- Children should be allowed to express their feelings and discuss the event, but not be forced.
- Community members should identify and address their own feelings; this may allow them to help others more effectively.
- Community members can also use their buildings and institutions as gathering places to promote support.
- Community members can help people identify resources and emphasize community strengths and resources that sustain hope.

Community members need to be sensitive to:

- Difficult behavior
- Strong emotions
- Different cultural responses

Community members can help in finding mental-health professionals to:

- Counsel children
- Help them see that fears are normal
- Offer play therapy
- Offer art therapy
- Help children develop coping skills, problem-solving skills, and ways to deal with fear

Finally, community members can hold parent meetings to discuss the event, their child's response, how help is being given to their child, how parents can help their child, and other available support.

How Can Adults Help Children and Adolescents Who Experienced Trauma?

Helping children can start immediately, even at the scene of the event. Most children recover within a few weeks of a traumatic experience, while some may need help longer. Grief, a deep emotional response to loss, may take months to resolve. Children may experience grief over the loss of a loved one, teacher, friend, or pet. Grief may be re-experienced or worsened by news reports or the event's anniversary.

Some children may need help from a mental-health professional. Some people may seek other kinds of help from community leaders. Identify children who need support and help them obtain it.

Examples of problematic behaviors could be:

- Refusal to go places that remind them of the event
- Emotional numbness
- Dangerous behavior
- Unexplained anger/rage
- Sleep problems including nightmares

Adult helpers should:

- Pay attention to children
- Listen to them
- Accept/do not argue about their feelings
- Help them cope with the reality of their experiences

Reduce the effects of other stressors, such as

- Frequent moving or changes in place of residence
- Long periods away from family and friends
- Pressures to perform well in school
- Transportation problems
- Fighting within the family
- Being hungry

Monitor healing

- It takes time
- Do not ignore severe reactions
- Pay attention to sudden changes in behaviors, speech, language use, or strong emotions.

Remind children that adults

- Love them

- Support them
- Will be with them when possible

Help for All People in the First Days and Weeks

There are steps adults can take following a disaster that can help them cope, making it easier to provide better care for children. These include creating safe conditions, remaining calm and friendly, and connecting with others. Being sensitive to people under stress and respecting their decisions is important.

When possible, help people:

- Get food
- Get a safe place to live
- Get help from a doctor or nurse if hurt
- Contact loved ones or friends
- Keep children with parents or relatives
- Understand what happened
- Understand what is being done
- Know where to get help

Don't:

- Force people to tell their stories
- Probe for personal details
- Say things like "everything will be okay," or "at least you survived"
- Say what you think people should feel or how people should have acted
- Say people suffered because they deserved it
- Be negative about available help
- Make promises that you can't keep such as "you will go home soon"

Chapter 32

Anxiety, Depression, and Children's Mental Health

Many children have fears and worries and will feel sad and hopeless from time to time. Strong fears will appear at different times in development. For example, toddlers are often very distressed about being away from their parents, even if they are safe and cared for. Although fears and worries are typical in children, persistent or extreme forms of fear and sadness feelings could be due to anxiety or depression. Because the symptoms primarily involve thoughts and feelings, they are called internalizing disorders.

Anxiety

When children do not outgrow the fears and worries that are typical in young children, or when there are so many fears and worries that they interfere with school, home, or play activities, the child may be diagnosed with an anxiety disorder. Examples of different types of anxiety disorders include:

- Being very afraid when away from parents (separation anxiety)

- Having extreme fear about a specific thing or situation, such as dogs, insects, or going to the doctor (phobias)

This chapter includes text excerpted from "Anxiety, Depression and Children's Mental Health," Centers for Disease Control and Prevention (CDC), March 15, 2018.

- Being very afraid of school and other places where there are people (social anxiety)

- Being very worried about the future and about bad things happening (general anxiety)

- Having repeated episodes of sudden, unexpected, intense fear that come with symptoms like heart pounding, having trouble breathing, or feeling dizzy, shaky, or sweaty (panic disorder)

Anxiety may present as fear or worry, but can also make children irritable and angry. Anxiety symptoms can also include trouble sleeping, as well as physical symptoms like fatigue, headaches, or stomachaches. Some anxious children keep their worries to themselves and, thus, the symptoms can be missed.

Depression

Occasionally being sad or feeling hopeless is a part of every child's life. However, some children feel sad or uninterested in things that they used to enjoy or feel helpless or hopeless in situations where they could do something to address the situations. When children feel persistent sadness and hopelessness, they may be diagnosed with depression.

Examples of behaviors often seen when children are depressed to include:

- Feeling sad, hopeless, or irritable a lot of the time

- Not wanting to do or enjoy doing fun things

- Changes in eating patterns—eating a lot more or a lot less than usual

- Changes in sleep patterns—sleeping a lot more or a lot less than normal

- Changes in energy—being tired and sluggish or tense and restless a lot of the time

- Having a hard time paying attention ·

- Feeling worthless, useless, or guilty

- Self-injury and self-destructive behavior

Extreme depression can lead a child to think about suicide or plan for suicide. For youth ages 10 to 14 years, suicide is the leading form of death.

Some children may not talk about helpless and hopeless thoughts, and they may not appear sad. Depression might also cause a child to make trouble or act unmotivated, so others might not notice that the child is depressed or may incorrectly label the child as a trouble-maker or lazy.

Treatment for Anxiety and Depression

The first step to treatment is to talk with a healthcare provider to get an evaluation. Some of the signs and symptoms of anxiety or depression are shared with other conditions, such as trauma. Specific symptoms like having a hard time focusing could be a sign of attention deficit hyperactivity disorder (ADHD). It is important to get a careful evaluation to get the best diagnosis and treatment. Consultation with a health provider can help determine if the medication should be part of the treatment. A mental-health professional can develop a therapy plan that works best for the child and family. Behavior therapy includes child therapy, family therapy, or a combination of both. The school can also be included in the treatment plan. For very young children, involving parents in treatment is key. Cognitive-behavioral therapy (CBT) is one form of therapy that is used to treat anxiety or depression, particularly in older children. It helps the child change negative thoughts into more positive, effective ways of thinking, leading to more effective behavior. Behavior therapy for anxiety may involve helping children cope with and manage anxiety symptoms while gradually exposing them to their fears so as to help them learn that bad things do not occur.

Treatments can also include a variety of ways to help the child feel less stressed and be healthier like nutritious food, physical activity, sufficient sleep, predictable routines, and social support.

Get Help Finding Treatment

Here are tools to find a healthcare provider familiar with treatment options:

- **Psychologist Locator** (locator.apa.org), a service of the American Psychological Association (APA) Practice Organization

- **Child and Adolescent Psychiatrist Finder** (www.aacap.org/AACAP/Families_and_Youth/Resources/CAP_Finder.aspx), a research tool by the American Academy of Child and Adolescent Psychiatry (AACAP)

- **Find a Cognitive Behavioral Therapist** (www.findcbt.org/ xFAT/), a search tool by the Association for Behavioral and Cognitive Therapies (ABCT)

- If you need help finding treatment facilities, visit MentalHealth. gov

Managing Symptoms: Staying Healthy

Being healthy is important for all children and can be especially important for children with depression or anxiety. In addition to getting the right treatment, leading a healthy lifestyle can play a role in managing symptoms of depression or anxiety. Here are some healthy behaviors that may help:

- Eating a healthful diet centered on fruits, vegetables, whole grains, legumes (for example, beans, peas, and lentils), lean protein sources, and nuts and seeds

- Participating in physical activity for at least 60 minutes each day

- Getting the recommended amount of sleep each night based on age

- Practicing mindfulness or relaxation techniques

Prevention of Anxiety and Depression

It is not known exactly why some children develop anxiety or depression. Many factors may play a role, including biology and temperament. But it is also known that some children are more likely to develop anxiety or depression when they experience trauma or stress when they are maltreated when they are bullied or rejected by other children, or when their own parents have anxiety or depression.

Although these factors appear to increase the risk of anxiety or depression, there are ways to decrease the chance that children experience them.

Chapter 33

Attention Deficit Hyperactivity Disorder

Attention deficit hyperactivity disorder (ADHD) is one of the most common neurodevelopmental disorders of childhood. It is usually first diagnosed in childhood and often lasts into adulthood. Children with ADHD may have trouble paying attention, controlling impulsive behaviors (may act without thinking about what the result will be), or be overly active.

Signs and Symptoms of Attention Deficit Hyperactivity Disorder

It is normal for children to have trouble focusing and behaving at one time or another. However, children with ADHD do not just grow out of these behaviors. The symptoms continue, can be severe, and can cause difficulty at school, at home, or with friends.

A child with ADHD might:

- Daydream a lot

- Forget or lose things a lot

- Squirm or fidget

- Talk too much

This chapter includes text excerpted from "Attention Deficit Hyperactivity Disorder (ADHD)," Centers for Disease Control and Prevention (CDC), September 19, 2018.

- Make careless mistakes or take unnecessary risks
- Have a hard time resisting the temptation
- Have trouble taking turns
- Have difficulty getting along with others

Types of Attention Deficit Hyperactivity Disorder

There are three different types of ADHD, depending on which types of symptoms are strongest in the individual:

- **Predominantly Inattentive Presentation (PIP).** It is hard for the individual to organize or finish a task, to pay attention to details, or to follow instructions or conversations. The person is easily distracted or forgets details of daily routines.

- **Predominantly Hyperactive-Impulsive Presentation (PHIP).** The person fidgets and talks a lot. It is hard to sit still for long (e.g., for a meal or while doing homework). Smaller children may run, jump, or climb constantly. The individual feels restless and has trouble with impulsivity. Someone who is impulsive may interrupt others a lot, grab things from people, or speak at inappropriate times. It is hard for the person to wait their turn or listen to directions. A person with impulsiveness may have more accidents and injuries than others.

- **Combined Presentation.** Symptoms of the above two types are equally present in the person.

- Because symptoms can change over time, the presentation may change over time as well.

Causes of Attention Deficit Hyperactivity Disorder

Scientists are studying cause(s) and risk factors in an effort to find better ways to manage and reduce the chances of a person having ADHD. The cause(s) and risk factors for ADHD are unknown, but current research shows that genetics plays an important role. Studies of twins link genes with ADHD.

In addition to genetics, scientists are studying other possible causes and risk factors including:

- Brain injury
- Exposure to environmental pollutants (e.g., lead) during pregnancy or at a young age

- Alcohol and tobacco use during pregnancy
- Premature delivery
- Low birth weight

Research does not support the popularly held views that ADHD is caused by eating too much sugar, watching too much television, parenting, or social and environmental factors such as poverty or family chaos. Of course, many things, including these, might make symptoms worse, especially in certain people. But the evidence is not strong enough to conclude that they are the main causes of ADHD.

Diagnosis of Attention Deficit Hyperactivity Disorder

Deciding if a child has ADHD is a process with several steps. There is no single test to diagnose ADHD, and many other problems, like anxiety, depression, sleep problems, and certain types of learning disabilities, can have similar symptoms. One step of the process involves having a medical exam, including hearing and vision tests, to rule out other problems with symptoms like ADHD. Another part of the process may include a checklist for rating ADHD symptoms and taking a history of the child from parents, teachers, and sometimes, the child.

Treatment for Attention Deficit Hyperactivity Disorder

In most cases, ADHD is best treated with a combination of behavior therapy and medication. For preschool-aged children (four to five years of age) with ADHD, behavior therapy, particularly training for parents, is recommended as the first line of treatment. What works best can depend on the child and family. Good treatment plans will include close monitoring, follow-ups, and making changes, if needed, along the way.

Managing Symptoms: Staying Healthy

Being healthy is important for all children and can be especially important for children with ADHD. In addition to behavioral therapy and medication, having a healthy lifestyle can make it easier for your child to deal with ADHD symptoms. Here are some healthy behaviors that may help:

- Eating a healthful diet centered on fruits, vegetables, whole grains, legumes (for example, beans, peas, and lentils), lean protein sources, and nuts and seeds

- Participating in physical activity for at least 60 minutes each day

- Limiting the amount of daily screen time from televisions (TVs), computers, phones, etc.

- Getting the recommended amount of sleep each night based on age

Get Help

If you or your doctor has concerns about ADHD, you can take your child to a specialist such as a child psychologist or developmental pediatrician, or you can contact your local early intervention agency (for children under three) or public school (for children three and older).

The Centers for Disease Control and Prevention (CDC) sponsors the National Resource Center (NRC) on ADHD, a program of CHADD— Children and Adults with ADHD. Their website has links to information for people with ADHD and their families. The National Resource Center operates a call center with trained staff to answer questions about ADHD. The number is 800-233-4050.

In order to make sure your child reaches her or his full potential, it is very important to get help for ADHD as early as possible.

Chapter 34

Autism Spectrum Disorder

Autism spectrum disorder (ASD) is a developmental disability that can cause significant social, communication, and behavioral challenges. There is often nothing about how people with ASD look that sets them apart from other people, but people with ASD may communicate, interact, behave, and learn in ways that are different from most other people. The learning, thinking, and problem-solving abilities of people with ASD can range from gifted to severely challenged. Some people with ASD need a lot of help in their daily lives; others need less.

A diagnosis of ASD now includes several conditions that used to be diagnosed separately: autistic disorder, a pervasive developmental disorder not otherwise specified (PDD-NOS), and Asperger syndrome (AS). These conditions are now all called autism spectrum disorder.

Signs and Symptoms of Autism Spectrum Disorder

People with ASD often have problems with social, emotional, and communication skills. They might repeat certain behaviors and might not want change in their daily activities. Many people with ASD also have different ways of learning, paying attention, or reacting to things. Signs of ASD begin during early childhood and typically last throughout a person's life.

This chapter includes text excerpted from "Autism Spectrum Disorder (ASD)—Basics about ASD," Centers for Disease Control and Prevention (CDC), May 3, 2018.

Children or adults with ASD might:

- Not point at objects to show interest (for example, not point at an airplane flying over)

- Not look at objects when another person points at them

- Have trouble relating to others or not have an interest in other people at all

- Avoid eye contact and want to be alone

- Have trouble understanding other people's feelings or talking about their own feelings

- Prefer not to be held or cuddled, or might cuddle only when they want to

- Appear to be unaware when people talk to them, but respond to other sounds

- Be very interested in people, but not know how to talk, play, or relate to them

- Repeat or echo words or phrases said to them, or repeat words or phrases in place of normal language

- Have trouble expressing their needs using typical words or motions

- Not play "pretend" games (for example, not pretend to "feed" a doll)

- Repeat actions over and over again

- Have trouble adapting when a routine changes

- Have unusual reactions to the way things smell, taste, look, feel, or sound

- Lose skills they once had (for example, stop saying words they were using)

Diagnosis of Autism Spectrum Disorder

Diagnosing ASD can be difficult since there is no medical test, like a blood test, to diagnose the disorders. Doctors look at the child's behavior and development to make a diagnosis.

ASD can sometimes be detected at 18 months or younger. By age two, a diagnosis by an experienced professional can be considered very reliable. However, many children do not receive a final diagnosis until much older. This delay means that children with ASD might not get the early help they need.

Treatment for Autism Spectrum Disorder

There is currently no cure for ASD. However, research shows that early intervention treatment (EIT) services can improve a child's development. Early intervention services help children from birth to three years old (36 months) learn important skills. Services can include therapy to help the child talk, walk, and interact with others. Therefore, it is important to talk to your child's doctor as soon as possible if you think your child has ASD or other developmental problem.

Even if your child has not been diagnosed with an ASD, may be eligible for early intervention treatment services. The Individuals with Disabilities Education Act (IDEA) says that children under the age of three years (36 months) who are at risk of having developmental delays may be eligible for services. These services are provided through an early intervention system in your state. Through this system, you can ask for an evaluation.

In addition, treatment for particular symptoms, such as speech therapy for language delays, often does not need to wait for a formal ASD diagnosis.

Causes and Risk Factors of Autism Spectrum Disorder

All of the causes of ASD are not known. However, the CDC has learned that there are likely many causes for multiple types of ASD. There may be many different factors that make a child more likely to have an ASD, including environmental, biologic, and genetic factors.

- Most scientists agree that genes are one of the risk factors that can make a person more likely to develop ASD.

- Children who have a sibling with ASD are at a higher risk of also having ASD.

- ASD tends to occur more often in people who have certain genetic or chromosomal conditions, such as fragile X syndrome or tuberous sclerosis.

- When taken during pregnancy, the prescription drugs valproic acid and thalidomide have been linked with a higher risk of ASD.

- There is some evidence that the critical period for developing ASD occurs before, during, and immediately after birth.

- Children born to older parents are at greater risk for having ASD.

ASD continues to be an important public health concern. Like the many families living with ASD, the Centers for Disease Control and Prevention (CDC) wants to find out what causes the disorder. Understanding the factors that make a person more likely to develop ASD will help us learn more about the causes. The CDC is currently working on one of the largest U.S. studies to date, called Study to Explore Early Development (SEED). SEED is looking at many possible risk factors for ASD, including genetic, environmental, pregnancy, and behavioral factors.

Who Is Affected?

ASD occurs in all racial, ethnic, and socioeconomic groups, but is about four times more common among boys than among girls.

For over a decade, the CDC's Autism and Developmental Disabilities Monitoring (ADDM) Network has been estimating the number of children with ASD in the United States. The CDC has learned a lot about how many U.S. children have ASD. It will be important to use the same methods to track how the number of children with ASD is changing over time in order to learn more about the disorder.

If You're Concerned

If you think your child might have ASD or you think there could be a problem with the way your child plays, learns, speaks, or acts, contact your child's doctor, and share your concerns.

If you or the doctor is still concerned, ask the doctor for a referral to a specialist who can do a more in-depth evaluation of your child. Specialists who can do a more in-depth evaluation and make a diagnosis include:

1. Developmental Pediatricians (doctors who have special training in child development and children with special needs)

2. Child Neurologists (doctors who work on the brain, spine, and nerves)

3. Child Psychologists or Psychiatrists (doctors who know about the human mind)

At the same time, call your state's public early childhood system to request a free evaluation to find out if your child qualifies for intervention services. This is sometimes called a Child Find evaluation. You do not need to wait for a doctor's referral or a medical diagnosis to make this call.

Where to call for a free evaluation from the state depends on your child's age:

- If your child is not yet three years old, contact your local early intervention system.

  - You can find the right contact information for your state by calling the Early Childhood Technical Assistance (ECTA) Center at 919-962-2001.

  - Or visit the ECTA website If your child is three years old or older, contact your local public school system.

- Even if your child is not yet old enough for kindergarten or enrolled in a public school, call your local elementary school or board of education and ask to speak with someone who can help you have your child evaluated.

- If you're not sure who to contact, call the ECTA Center at 919-962-2001.

- Or visit the ECTA website (ectacenter.org).

Research shows that early intervention services can greatly improve a child's development. In order to make sure your child reaches her or his full potential, it is very important to get help for an ASD as soon as possible.

Chapter 35

Behavior Disorders in Children

Children sometimes argue, are aggressive, or act angry or defiant around adults. A behavior disorder may be diagnosed when these disruptive behaviors are uncommon for the child's age at the time, persist over time, or are severe. Because disruptive behavior disorders involve acting out and showing unwanted behavior towards others they are often called externalizing disorders.

Oppositional Defiant Disorder

When children act out persistently so that it causes serious problems at home, in school, or with peers, they may be diagnosed with oppositional defiant disorder (ODD). ODD usually starts before 8 years of age, but no later than by about 12 years of age. Children with ODD are more likely to act oppositional or defiant around people they know well, such as family members, a regular-care provider, or a teacher. Children with ODD show these behaviors more often than other children their age.

Examples of ODD behaviors include:

- Often being angry or losing one's temper

- Often arguing with adults or refusing to comply with adults' rules or requests

This chapter includes text excerpted from "Children's Mental Health and Behavior or Conduct Problems," Centers for Disease Control and Prevention (CDC), April 20, 2018.

- Often resentful or spiteful

- Deliberately annoying others or becoming annoyed with others

- Often blaming other people for one's own mistakes or misbehavior

Conduct Disorder

Conduct disorder (CD) is diagnosed when children show an ongoing pattern of aggression toward others, and serious violations of rules and social norms at home, in school, and with peers. These rule violations may involve breaking the law and result in arrest. Children with CD are more likely to get injured and may have difficulties getting along with peers.
Examples of CD behaviors include:

- Breaking serious rules, such as running away, staying out at night when told not to, or skipping school

- Being aggressive in a way that causes harm, such as bullying, fighting, or being cruel to animals

- Lying, stealing, or damaging other people's property on purpose

Treatment for Behavior Disorders

Starting treatment early is important. Treatment is most effective if it fits the needs of the specific child and family. The first step to treatment is to talk with a healthcare provider. A comprehensive evaluation by a mental-health professional may be needed to get the right diagnosis. Some of the signs of behavior problems, such as not following rules in school, could be related to learning problems which may need additional intervention. For younger children, the treatment with the strongest evidence is behavior therapy training for parents, where a therapist helps the parent learn effective ways to strengthen the parent-child relationship and respond to the child's behavior. For school-age children and teens, an often-used effective treatment is a combination of training and therapy that includes the child, the family, and the school.

Get Help Finding Treatment

Here are tools to find a healthcare provider familiar with treatment options:

- **Psychologist Locator** (locator.apa.org), a service of the American Psychological Association (APA) Practice Organization

- **Child and Adolescent Psychiatrist Finder** (www.aacap.org/ AACAP/Families_and_Youth/Resources/CAP_Finder.aspx), a research tool by the American Academy of Child and Adolescent Psychiatry (AACAP)

- **Find a Cognitive Behavioral Therapist** (www.findcbt.org/ xFAT), a search tool by the Association for Behavioral and Cognitive Therapies (ABCT)

- If you need help finding treatment facilities, visit MentalHealth. gov

Managing Symptoms of Behavior or Conduct Problems

Being healthy is important for all children and can be especially important for children with behavior or conduct problems. In addition to behavioral therapy and medication, practicing certain healthy lifestyle behaviors may reduce challenging and disruptive behaviors your child might experience. Here are some healthy behaviors that may help:

- Engaging in regular physical activity, including aerobic and vigorous exercise

- Eating a healthful diet centered on fruits, vegetables, whole grains, legumes (for example, beans, peas, and lentils), lean protein sources, and nuts and seeds

- Getting the recommended amount of sleep each night based on age

- Strengthening relationships with family members

Prevention of Disruptive Behavior Disorders

It is not known exactly why some children develop disruptive behavior disorders. Many factors may play a role, including biological and social factors. It is known that children are at greater risk when they are exposed to other types of violence and criminal behavior, when they experience maltreatment or harsh or inconsistent parenting, or when their parents have mental-health conditions like substance-use disorders (SUDs), depression, or attention deficit hyperactivity disorder (ADHD). The quality of early childhood care also can impact whether a child develops behavior problems.

Although these factors appear to increase the risk for disruptive behavior disorders, there are ways to decrease the chance that children experience them.

Chapter 36

Bipolar Disorder in Children and Teens

Does your child go through intense mood changes? Does your child have extreme behavior changes? Does your child get much more excited and active than other kids her or his age? Do other people say your child is too excited or too moody? Do you notice has highs and lows much more often than other children? Do these mood changes affect how your child acts at school or at home?

Some children and teens with these symptoms may have bipolar disorder, a serious mental illness.

What Is Bipolar Disorder?

Bipolar disorder (BD) is a serious brain illness. It is also called manic-depressive illness or manic depression. Children with bipolar disorder go through unusual mood changes. Sometimes they feel very happy or "up," and are much more energetic and active than usual, or those other kids of their age. This is called a manic episode. Sometimes children with bipolar disorder feel very sad and "down," and are much less active than usual. This is called depression or a depressive episode.

Bipolar disorder is not the same as the normal ups and downs every kid goes through. Bipolar symptoms are more powerful than that. The mood swings are more extreme and are accompanied by changes in

This chapter includes text excerpted from "Bipolar Disorder in Children and Teens," National Institute of Mental Health (NIMH), 2015. Reviewed December 2018.

sleep, energy level, and the ability to think clearly. Bipolar symptoms are so strong, they can make it hard for a child to do well in school or get along with friends and family members. The illness can also be dangerous. Some young people with bipolar disorder try to hurt themselves or attempt suicide.

Children and teens with bipolar disorder should get treatment. With help, they can manage their symptoms and lead successful lives.

Who Develops Bipolar Disorder

Anyone can develop bipolar disorder, including children and teens. However, most people with bipolar disorder develop it in their late teen or early adult years. The illness usually lasts a lifetime.

Why Does Someone Develop Bipolar Disorder?

Doctors do not know what causes bipolar disorder, but several things may contribute to the illness. Family genes may be one factor because bipolar disorder sometimes runs in families. However, it is important to know that just because someone in your family has bipolar disorder, it does not mean other members of the family will have it as well.

Another factor that may lead to bipolar disorder is the brain structure or the brain function of the person with the disorder. Scientists are finding out more about the disorder by studying it. This research may help doctors do a better job of treating people. Also, this research may help doctors to predict whether a person will get bipolar disorder. One day, doctors may be able to prevent the illness in some people.

What Are the Symptoms of Bipolar Disorder?

Bipolar "mood episodes" include unusual mood changes along with unusual sleep habits, activity levels, thoughts, or behavior. In a child, these mood and activity changes must be very different from their usual behavior and from the behavior of other children. A person with bipolar disorder may have manic episodes, depressive episodes, or "mixed" episodes. A mixed episode has both manic and depressive symptoms. These mood episodes cause symptoms that last a week or two or sometimes longer. During an episode, the symptoms last every day for most of the day.

Children and teens having a manic episode may:

- Feel very happy or act silly in a way that's unusual for them and for other people their age
- Have a very short-temper
- Talk really fast about a lot of different things
- Have trouble sleeping but not feel tired
- Have trouble staying focused
- Talk and think about sex more often
- Do risky things

Children and teens having a depressive episode may:

- Feel very sad
- Complain about pain a lot, such as stomachaches and headaches
- Sleep too little or too much
- Feel guilty and worthless
- Eat too little or too much
- Have little energy and no interest in fun activities
- Think about death or suicide

Can Children and Teens with Bipolar Disorder Have Other Problems?

Young people with bipolar disorder can have several problems at the same time. These include:

- **Substance abuse.** Both adults and kids with bipolar disorder are at risk of drinking or taking drugs
- **Attention deficit hyperactivity disorder (ADHD).** Children who have both bipolar disorder and ADHD may have trouble staying focused
- **Anxiety disorders,** like separation anxiety

Sometimes behavior problems go along with mood episodes. Young people may take a lot of risks, such as driving too fast or spending too much money. Some young people with bipolar disorder think about suicide. Watch for any signs of suicidal thinking. Take these signs seriously and call your child's doctor.

How Is Bipolar Disorder Diagnosed?

An experienced doctor will carefully examine your child. There are no blood tests or brain scans that can diagnose bipolar disorder. Instead, the doctor will ask questions about your child's mood and sleeping patterns. The doctor will also ask about your child's energy and behavior. Sometimes doctors need to know about medical problems in your family, such as depression or alcoholism. The doctor may use tests to see if something other than bipolar disorder is causing your child's symptoms.

How Is Bipolar Disorder Treated?

Right now, there is no cure for bipolar disorder. Doctors often treat children who have the illness in much the same way they treat adults. Treatment can help control symptoms. Steady, dependable treatment works better than treatment that starts and stops. Treatment options include:

- **Medication.** There are several types of medication that can help. Children respond to medications in different ways, so the right type of medication depends on the child. Some children may need more than one type of medication because their symptoms are so complex. Sometimes they need to try different types of medicine to see which are best for them. Children should take the fewest number of medications and the smallest doses possible to help their symptoms. A good way to remember this is "start low, go slow." Medications can cause side effects. **Always tell your child's doctor about any problems with side effects.** Do not stop giving your child medication without a doctor's help. Stopping medication suddenly can be dangerous, and it can make bipolar symptoms worse.

- **Therapy.** Different kinds of psychotherapy, or "talk" therapy, can help children with bipolar disorder. Therapy can help children change their behavior and manage their routines. It can also help young people get along better with family and friends. Sometimes therapy includes family members.

What Can Children and Teens Expect from Treatment?

With treatment, children and teens with bipolar disorder can get better over time. It helps when doctors, parents, and young people work together.

Sometimes a child's bipolar disorder changes. When this happens, treatment needs to change too. For example, your child may need to try a different medication. The doctor may also recommend other treatment changes. Symptoms may come back after a while, and more adjustments may be needed. Treatment can take time, but sticking with it helps many children and teens have fewer bipolar symptoms.

You can help treatment be more effective. Try keeping a chart of your child's moods, behaviors, and sleep patterns. This is called a "daily life chart" or "mood chart." It can help you and your child understand and track the illness. A chart can also help the doctor see whether treatment is working.

How Can I Help My Child or Teen?

Help begins with the right diagnosis and treatment. If you think your child may have bipolar disorder, make an appointment with your family doctor to talk about the symptoms you notice.

If your child has bipolar disorder, here are some basic things you can do:

- Be patient.
- Encourage your child to talk, and listen to your child carefully.
- Be understanding of mood episodes.
- Help your child have fun.
- Help your child understand that treatment can make life better.

How Does Bipolar Disorder Affect Parents and Family?

Taking care of a child or teenager with bipolar disorder can be stressful for you, too. You have to cope with the mood swings and other problems, such as short-tempers and risky activities. This can challenge any parent. Sometimes the stress can strain your relationships with other people, and you may miss work or lose free time.

If you are taking care of a child with bipolar disorder, take care of yourself too. Find someone you can talk to about your feelings. Talk with the doctor about support groups for caregivers. If you keep your stress level down, you will do a better job. It might help your child get better too.

Where Do I Go for Help?

If you're not sure where to get help, call your family doctor. You can also check the phone book for mental-health professionals. Hospital doctors can help in an emergency. Finally, the Substance Abuse and Mental Health Services Administration (SAMHSA) has an online tool to help you find mental-health services in your area.

Chapter 37

Language and Speech Disorders

Helping Children Learn Language

Parents and caregivers are the most important teachers during a child's early years. Children learn language by listening to others speak and by practicing. Even young babies notice when others repeat and respond to the noises and sounds they make. Children's language and brain skills get stronger if they hear many different words. Parents can help their child learn in many different ways, such as:

- Responding to the first sounds, gurgles, and gestures a baby makes

- Repeating what the child says and adding to it

- Talking about the things that a child sees

- Asking questions and listening to the answers

- Looking at or reading books

- Telling stories

- Singing songs and sharing rhymes

- This can happen both during playtime and during daily routines

This chapter includes text excerpted from "Language and Speech Disorders," Centers for Disease Control and Prevention (CDC), May 23, 2018.

Parents can also observe the following:

- How their child hears and talks and compare it with typical milestones for communication skills

- How their child reacts to sounds and has their hearing tested if they have concerns

What to Do If There Are Concerns Related to Your Child's Speaking Abilities

Some children struggle with understanding and speaking and they need help. They may not master the language milestones at the same time as other children, and it may be a sign of a language or speech delay or disorder.

Language development has different parts, and children might have problems with one or more of the following:

- Understanding what others say (receptive language). This could be due to:

  - Not hearing the words (hearing loss)

  - Not understanding the meaning of the words

- Communicating thoughts using language (expressive language)

  This could be due to:

  - Not knowing the words to use

  - Not knowing how to put words together

  - Knowing the words to use but not being able to express them

Language and speech disorders can exist together or by themselves. Examples of problems with language and speech development include the following:

- Speech disorders:

  - The difficulty with forming specific words or sounds correctly

  - The difficulty with making words or sentences flow smoothly, such as stuttering or stammering

- Language delay: the ability to understand and speak develops more slowly than is typical

- Language disorders

  - Aphasia (difficulty understanding or speaking parts of language due to a brain injury or how the brain works)

  - Auditory processing disorder (difficulty understanding the meaning of the sounds that the ear sends to the brain)

Language or speech disorders can occur with other learning disorders that affect reading and writing. Children with language disorders may feel frustrated that they cannot understand others or make themselves understood, and they may act out, act helpless, or withdraw. Language or speech disorders can also be present with emotional or behavioral disorders, such as attention deficit hyperactivity disorder (ADHD) or anxiety. Children with developmental disabilities including autism spectrum disorder (ASD) may also have difficulties with speech and language. The combination of challenges can make it particularly hard for a child to succeed in school. Properly diagnosing a child's disorder is crucial so that each child can get the right kind of help.

Detecting Problems with Language or Speech

If a child has a problem with language or speech development, talk to a healthcare provider about an evaluation. An important first step is to find out if the child may have a hearing loss. Hearing loss may be difficult to notice particularly if a child has a hearing loss only in one ear or has a partial hearing loss, which means they can hear some sounds but not others.

A language development specialist like a speech-language pathologist will conduct a careful assessment to determine what type of problem with language or speech the child may have.

Overall, learning more than one language does not cause language disorders, but children may not follow exactly the same developmental milestones as those who learn only one language. Developing the ability to understand and speak in two languages depends on how much practice the child has using both languages, and the kind of practice. If a child who is learning more than one language has difficulty with language development, careful assessment by a specialist who understands the development of skills in more than one language may be needed.

Treatment for Language or Speech Disorders and Delays

Children with language problems often need extra help and special instruction. Speech-language pathologists can work directly with children and their parents, caregivers, and teachers.

Having a language or speech delay or disorder can qualify a child for early intervention (for children up to three years of age) and special education services (for children aged three years and older). Schools can do their own testing for language or speech disorders to see if a child needs intervention. An evaluation by a healthcare professional is needed if there are other concerns about the child's hearing, behavior, or emotions. Parents, healthcare providers, and the school can work together to find the right referrals and treatment.

What Every Parent Should Know

Children with specific learning disabilities, including language or speech disorders, are eligible for special education services or accommodations at school under the Individuals with Disabilities in Education Act (IDEA) and Section 504, an antidiscrimination law.

The Role of Healthcare Providers

Healthcare providers can play an important part in collaborating with schools to help a child with speech or language disorders and delay or other disabilities get the special services they need. The American Academy of Pediatrics (AAP) has created a report that describes the roles that healthcare providers can have in helping children with disabilities, including language or speech disorders.

Chapter 38

Learning Disorders

Many children may struggle in school with some topics or skills from time to time. When children try hard and still struggle with a specific set of skills over time, it could be a sign of a learning disorder. Having a learning disorder means that a child has difficulty in one or more areas of learning, even when overall intelligence or motivation is not affected.

Some of the symptoms of learning disorders are:

- Difficulty telling right from left
- Reversing letters, words, or numbers, after first or second grade
- Difficulties recognizing patterns or sorting items by size or shape
- Difficulty understanding and following instructions or staying organized
- Difficulty remembering what was just said or what was just read
- Lacking coordination when moving around
- Difficulty doing tasks with the hands, like writing, cutting, or drawing
- Difficulty understanding the concept of time

Examples of learning disorders include:

- Dyslexia—difficulty with reading

This chapter includes text excerpted from "Learning Disorders," Centers for Disease Control and Prevention (CDC), February 1, 2017.

- Dyscalculia—difficulty with math
- Dysgraphia—difficulty with writing

Children with learning disorders may feel frustrated that they cannot master a subject despite trying hard, and may act out, act helpless, or withdraw. Learning disorders can also be present with emotional or behavioral disorders, such as attention deficit hyperactivity disorder (ADHD), or anxiety. The combination of problems can make it particularly hard for a child to succeed in school. Properly diagnosing each disorder is crucial, so that the child can get the right kind of help for each.

Treatment for Learning Disorders

Children with learning disorders often need extra help and instruction that are specialized for them. Having a learning disorder can qualify a child for special education services in school. Schools usually do their own testing for learning disorders to see if a child needs intervention. An evaluation by a healthcare professional is needed if there are other concerns about the child's behavior or emotions. Parents, healthcare providers, and the school can work together to find the right referrals and treatment.

What Every Parent Should Know Regarding Learning Disorders

Children with specific learning disabilities are eligible for special education services or accommodations at school under the Individuals with Disabilities in Education Act (IDEA) and an antidiscrimination law known as Section 504. Learn more about education services and accommodations that are available for children with specific learning disabilities. You should also read the guidelines from the U.S. Department of Justice (DOJ) Disability Rights Section about testing accommodations for individuals with disabilities. Get help from your state's Parent Training and Information Center (PTI) at www.parent-centerhub.org/find-your-center.

The Role of Healthcare Providers

Healthcare providers can play an important part in collaborating with schools to help a child with learning disorders or other disabilities get the special services they need. The American Academy of

Pediatrics (AAP) has created a report that describes the roles that healthcare providers can have in helping children with disabilities, including learning disorders:

- Identifying children in need of early intervention or special education services

- Sharing relevant information with early intervention or school personnel

- Meeting with early intervention or school personnel and parents or guardians

- Using early intervention or school information in medical diagnostic or treatment plans

- Working within an early intervention, school, or school-based health clinic

- Working at an administrative level to improve school functioning around children with special needs

Chapter 39

Obsessive-Compulsive Disorder among Children

Many children occasionally have thoughts that bother them, and they might feel like they have to do something about those thoughts, even if their actions don't actually make sense. For example, they might worry about having bad luck if they don't wear a favorite piece of clothing. For some children, the thoughts and the urges to perform certain actions persist, even if they try to ignore them or make them go away. Children may have an obsessive-compulsive disorder (OCD) when unwanted thoughts, and the behaviors they feel they must do because of the thoughts, happen frequently, take up a lot of time (more than an hour a day), interfere with their activities, or make them very upset. The thoughts are called obsessions. The behaviors are called compulsions.

Symptoms of Obsessive-Compulsive Disorder

Having OCD means having obsessions, compulsions, or both. Examples of obsessive or compulsive behaviors include:

- Having unwanted thoughts, impulses, or images that occur over and over and which cause anxiety or distress

---

This chapter includes text excerpted from "Obsessive-Compulsive Disorder and Children's Mental Health," Centers for Disease Control and Prevention (CDC), March 14, 2018.

- Having to think about or say something over and over (for example, counting, or repeating words over and over silently or out loud)

- Having to do something over and over (for example, handwashing, placing things in a specific order, or checking the same things over and over, like whether a door is locked)

- Having to do something over and over according to certain rules that must be followed exactly in order to make an obsession go away

Children do these behaviors because they have the feeling that the behaviors will prevent bad things from happening or will make them feel better. However, the behavior is not typically connected to actual danger of something bad happening, or the behavior is extreme, such as washing hands multiple times per hour.

A common myth is that OCD means being really neat and orderly. Sometimes, OCD behaviors may involve cleaning, but many times someone with OCD is too focused on one thing that must be done over and over, rather than on being organized. Obsessions and compulsions can also change over time.

Treatment for Obsessive-Compulsive Disorder

The first step to treatment is to talk with a healthcare provider to arrange an evaluation. A comprehensive evaluation by a mental-health professional will determine if the anxiety or distress involves memories of a traumatic event that actually happened, or if the fears are based on other thoughts or beliefs. The mental-health professional should also determine whether someone with OCD has a current or past tic disorder. Anxiety or depression and disruptive behaviors may also occur with OCD.

Treatments can include behavior therapy and medication. Behavior therapy, specifically cognitive-behavioral therapy (CBT), helps the child change negative thoughts into more positive, effective ways of thinking, leading to more effective behavior. Behavior therapy for OCD can involve gradually exposing children to their fears in a safe setting; this helps them learn that bad things do not really occur when they don't do the behavior, which eventually decreases their anxiety. Behavior therapy alone can be effective, but some children are treated with a combination of behavior therapy and medication. Families and schools can help children manage stress by being part of the therapy process and learning how to respond supportively without accidentally making obsessions or compulsions more likely to happen again.

Prevention of Obsessive-Compulsive Disorder

It is not known exactly why some children develop OCD. There is likely to be a biological and neurological component, and some children with OCD also have Tourette syndrome or other tic disorders. There are some studies that suggest that health problems during pregnancy and birth may make OCD more likely, which is one of many important reasons to support the health of women during pregnancy.

Chapter 40

Pediatric Autoimmune Neuropsychiatric Disorders Associated with Streptococcal Infections

What Is PANDAS?

PANDAS is short for pediatric autoimmune neuropsychiatric disorders associated with streptococcal infections. A child may be diagnosed with PANDAS when:

- Obsessive-compulsive disorder (OCD) and/or tic disorders suddenly appear following a strep infection (such as strep throat or scarlet fever); or

- The symptoms of OCD or tic symptoms suddenly become worse following a strep infection.

The symptoms are usually dramatic, happen "overnight and out of the blue," and can include motor and/or vocal tics, obsessions, and/or compulsions. In addition to these symptoms, children may also become moody or irritable, experience anxiety attacks, or show concerns about separating from parents or loved ones.

This chapter includes text excerpted from "PANDAS—Questions and Answers," National Institute of Mental Health (NIMH), September 2016.

What Causes PANDAS

The strep bacteria are very ancient organisms that survive in the human host by hiding from the immune system as long as possible. It hides itself by putting molecules on its cell wall so that it looks nearly identical to molecules found on the child's heart, joints, skin, and brain tissues. This hiding is called "molecular mimicry" and allows the strep bacteria to evade detection for a long time.

However, the molecules on the strep bacteria are eventually recognized as foreign to the body and the child's immune system reacts to them by producing antibodies. Because of the molecular mimicry by the bacteria, the immune system reacts not only to the strep molecules but also to the human host molecules that were mimicked; antibodies system "attack" the mimicked molecules in the child's own tissues.

Studies at the National Institute of Mental Health (NIMH) and elsewhere have shown that some cross-reactive "anti-brain" antibodies target the brain—causing OCD, tics, and the other neuropsychiatric symptoms of PANDAS.

Could an Adult Develop PANDAS?

PANDAS is considered a pediatric disorder and typically first appears in childhood from age three to puberty. Reactions to strep infections are rare after age 12, but researchers recognize that PANDAS could occur, though rarely, among adolescents. It is unlikely that someone would experience these post-strep neuropsychiatric symptoms for the first time as an adult, but it has not been fully studied.

It is possible that adolescents and adults may have immune-mediated OCD, but this is not known. The research studies on immune-mediated OCD at the NIMH are restricted to children.

Signs and Symptoms of PANDAS
How Is PANDAS Diagnosed?

The diagnosis of PANDAS is a clinical diagnosis, which means that there are no lab tests that can diagnose PANDAS. Instead, healthcare providers use diagnostic criteria for the diagnosis of PANDAS (see below). At the present time, the clinical features of the illness are the only means of determining whether or not a child might have PANDAS.

The diagnostic criteria are:

- Presence of obsessive-compulsive disorder and/or a tic disorder

- Pediatric onset of symptoms (age three years to puberty)

- Episodic course of symptom severity (see information below)

- Association with group A beta-hemolytic streptococcal infection (a positive throat culture for strep or history of scarlet fever)

- Association with neurological abnormalities (physical hyperactivity, or unusual, jerky movements that are not in the child's control)

- Very abrupt onset or worsening of symptoms

If the symptoms have been present for more than a week, blood tests may be done to document a preceding streptococcal infection.

Are There Any Other Symptoms Associated with PANDAS Episodes?

Yes. Children with PANDAS often experience one or more of the following symptoms in conjunction with their OCD and/or tics:

- Attention deficit hyperactivity disorder (ADHD) symptoms (hyperactivity, inattention, fidgety)

- Separation anxiety (child is "clingy" and has difficulty separating from her/his caregivers; for example, the child may not want to be in a different room in the house from her or his parents)

- Mood changes, such as irritability, sadness, emotional lability (tendency to laugh or cry unexpectedly at what might seem the wrong moment)

- Trouble sleeping, night-time bed-wetting, day-time frequent urination, or both

- Changes in motor skills (e.g., changes in handwriting)

- Joint pain

What Is an Episodic Course of Symptoms?

Children with PANDAS seem to have dramatic ups and downs in the severity of their OCD and/or tics. OCD or tics that are almost always present at a relatively consistent level do not represent an episodic course. Many children with OCD or tics have good days and bad days, or even good weeks and bad weeks. However, children with PANDAS have a very sudden onset or worsening of their symptoms, followed by a slow, gradual improvement. If children with PANDAS get another strep infection, their symptoms suddenly worsen again. The increased symptom severity usually persists for at least several weeks, but may last for several months or longer.

My Child Has Had Strep Throat Before, and Has Tics, OCD, or Both. Does That Mean My Child Has PANDAS?

No. Many children have OCD and/or tics, and almost all school-aged children get strep throat at some point. In fact, the average grade-school student will have two or three strep throat infections each year. PANDAS is considered as a diagnosis when there is a very close relationship between the abrupt onset or worsening of OCD and/or tics and a strep infection. If strep is found in conjunction with two or three episodes of OCD, tics, or both, then it may be that the child has PANDAS.

What Does an Elevated Antistreptococcal Antibody Titer Mean? Is This Bad for My Child?

The anti-streptococcal antibody titer (amount of molecules in blood that indicate a previous infection) is a test that determines whether the child has had a previous strep infection.

An elevated anti-strep titer means the child has had a strep infection sometime within the past few months, and her or his body created antibodies to fight the strep bacteria.

Some children create lots of antibodies and have very high titers (up to 2,000), while others have more modest elevations. The height of the titer elevation doesn't matter and elevated titers are not necessarily bad for your child. They are measuring a normal, healthy response—the production of antibodies to fight off an infection. The antibodies stay in the body for some time after the infection is gone, but the amount of time that the antibodies persist varies greatly between different individuals. Some children have "positive" antibody titers for many months after a single infection.

When Is a Strep Titer Considered to Be Abnormal, or "Elevated"?

The lab at National Institutes of Health considers strep titers between 0–400 to be normal. Other labs set the upper limit at 150 or

200. Since each lab measures titers in different ways, it is important to know the range used by the laboratory where the test was done—just ask where they draw the line between negative or positive titers.

What If My Child's Doctor Does Not Understand or Does Not Want to Consider PANDAS?

Contact the International OCD Foundation (www.iocdf.org/find-help) or the PANDAS Network (www.pandasnetwork.org) to find a doctor who may be knowledgeable about PANDAS.

Treatment for PANDAS
What Are the Treatment Options for Children with PANDAS?

The best treatment for acute episodes of PANDAS is to treat the strep infection causing the symptoms (if it is still present) with antibiotics.

- A throat culture should be done to document the presence of strep bacteria in the throat.

- If the throat culture is positive, a single course of antibiotics will usually get rid of the strep infection and allow the PANDAS symptoms to subside.

If a properly obtained throat culture is negative, the clinician should make sure that the child doesn't have an occult (hidden) strep infection, such as a sinus infection (often caused by strep bacteria) or strep bacteria infecting the anus, vagina, or urethral opening of the penis. Although the latter infections are rare, they have been reported to trigger PANDAS symptoms in some patients and can be particularly problematic because they will linger for longer periods of time and continue to provoke the production of cross-reactive antibodies.

The strep bacteria can be harder to eradicate in the sinuses and other sites, so the course of antibiotic treatment may need to be longer than that used for strep throat.

How Can You Manage Neuropsychiatric Symptoms of PANDAS?

Children with PANDAS-related obsessive-compulsive symptoms will benefit from standard medications and/or behavioral therapies, such as cognitive behavioral therapy (CBT). OCD symptoms are treated best with a combination of CBT and a selective serotonin reuptake inhibitor (SSRI) medication, and tics respond to a variety of medications.

Children with PANDAS appear to be unusually sensitive to the side-effects of SSRIs and other medications, so it is important to "START LOW AND GO SLOW!!" when using these medications. In other words, clinicians should prescribe a very small starting dose of the medication and increase it slowly enough that the child experiences as few side-effects as possible. If PANDAS symptoms worsen, the SSRI dosage should be decreased promptly. However, SSRIs and other medications should not be stopped abruptly, as that could also cause difficulties.

What about Treating PANDAS with Plasma Exchange or Immunoglobulin?

Plasma exchange or immunoglobulin (IVIG) may be a consideration for acutely and severely affected children with PANDAS. Research suggests that both active treatments can improve global functioning, depression, emotional ups and downs, and obsessive-compulsive symptoms. However, there are a number of side-effects associated with the treatments, including nausea, vomiting, headaches, and dizziness.

In addition, there is a risk of infection with any invasive procedure, such as these. **Thus, the treatments should be reserved for severely ill patients, and administered by a qualified team of healthcare professionals.** Clinicians considering such an intervention are invited to contact the PANDAS research group at the NIMH for consultation.

Should an Elevated Strep Titer Be Treated with Antibiotics?

No. Elevated titers indicate that a patient has had a past strep exposure but the titers can't tell you precisely when the strep infection occurred. Children may have "positive" titers for many months after one infection. Since these elevated titers are merely a marker of a prior infection and not proof of an ongoing infection it is not appropriate to give antibiotics for elevated titers. Antibiotics are recommended only when a child has a positive rapid strep test or positive strep throat culture.

Can Penicillin Be Used to Treat PANDAS or Prevent Future PANDAS Symptom Exacerbations?

Penicillin does not specifically treat the symptoms of PANDAS. Penicillin and other antibiotics treat a sore throat caused by the strep by getting rid of the bacteria. In PANDAS, research suggests that it is the antibodies produced by the body in response to the strep infection that may cause PANDAS symptoms, not the bacteria itself.

Researchers at the NIMH have been investigating the use of antibiotics as a form of prophylaxis or prevention of future problems. At this time, however, there isn't enough evidence to recommend the long-term use of antibiotics.

My Child Has PANDAS. Should He Have His Tonsils Removed?

Current research does not suggest that tonsillectomies for children with PANDAS are helpful. If a tonsillectomy is recommended because of frequent episodes of tonsillitis, it would be useful to discuss the pros and cons of the procedure with your child's healthcare provider because of the role that the tonsils play in fighting strep infections.

Chapter 41

Posttraumatic Stress Disorder and Children

All children may experience very stressful events that affect how they think and feel. Most of the time, children recover quickly and well. However, sometimes children who experience severe stress, such as from an injury, from the death or threatened death of a close family member or friend, or from violence, will be affected long term. The child could experience this trauma directly or could witness it happening to someone else. When children develop long-term symptoms (longer than a month) from such stress, which are upsetting or interfere with their relationships and activities, they may be diagnosed with posttraumatic stress disorder (PTSD).

Examples of PTSD symptoms include:

- Reliving the event over and over in thought or in play

- Nightmares and sleep problems

- Becoming very upset when something causes memories of the event

- Lack of positive emotions

- Intense ongoing fear or sadness

- Irritability and angry outbursts

This chapter includes text excerpted from "Post-Traumatic Stress Disorder and Children's Mental Health," Centers for Disease Control and Prevention (CDC), March 14, 2018.

- Constantly looking for possible threats, being easily startled
- Acting helpless, hopeless, or withdrawn
- Denying that the event happened or feeling numb
- Avoiding places or people associated with the event

Because children who have experienced traumatic stress may seem restless, fidgety, or have trouble paying attention and staying organized, the symptoms of traumatic stress can be confused with symptoms of attention deficit hyperactivity disorder (ADHD).

Examples of events that could cause PTSD include:

- Physical, sexual, or emotional maltreatment
- Being a victim or witness to violence or crime
- Serious illness or death of a close family member or friend
- Natural or manmade disasters
- Severe car accidents

Treatment of Posttraumatic Stress Disorder

The first step to treatment is to talk with a healthcare provider to arrange an evaluation. For a PTSD diagnosis, a specific event must have triggered the symptoms. Because the event was distressing, children may not want to talk about the event, so a health provider who is highly skilled in talking with children and families may be needed. Once the diagnosis is made, the first step is to make the child feel safe by getting support from parents, friends, and school, and by minimizing the chance of another traumatic event to the extent possible. Psychotherapy in which the child can speak, draw, play, or write about the stressful event can be done with the child, the family, or a group. Behavior therapy, specifically cognitive-behavioral therapy (CBT), helps children learn to change thoughts and feelings by first changing behavior in order to reduce the fear or worry. Medication may also be used to decrease symptoms.

Get Help Finding Treatment

Here are tools to find a healthcare provider familiar with treatment options:

- **Psychologist Locator** (locator.apa.org.), a service of the American Psychological Association (APA) Practice Organization

- **Child and Adolescent Psychiatrist Finder** (www.aacap.org/AACAP/Families_and_Youth/Resources/CAP_Finder.aspx), a research tool by the American Academy of Child and Adolescent Psychiatry (AACAP)

- **Find a Cognitive Behavioral Therapist** (www.findcbt.org/xFAT), a search tool by the Association for Behavioral and Cognitive Therapies (ABCT)

- If you need help finding treatment facilities, visit MentalHealth.gov

Prevention of Posttraumatic Stress Disorder

It is not known exactly why some children develop PTSD after experiencing stressful and traumatic events, and others do not. Many factors may play a role, including biology and temperament. But preventing risks for trauma, such as maltreatment, violence, or injuries, or lessening the impact of unavoidable disasters on children, can help protect a child from PTSD.

Part Five

Other Populations with Distinctive Mental-Health Concerns

Chapter 42

Mental-Health Issues among Men

Chapter Contents

Section 42.1

Mental Health for Men

This section includes text excerpted from "Men and Mental Health,"
National Institute of Mental Health (NIMH), May 2016.

Many mental illnesses affect both men and women however men
may be less likely to talk about their feelings and seek help. Recognizing the signs that someone may have a mood or mental disorder is the
first step toward getting treatment and living a better life.

Warning Signs of Mental-Health Disorders

Men and women experience many of the same mental-disorders but
their willingness to talk about their feelings may be very different. This
is one of the reasons that their symptoms may be very different as well.
For example, some men with depression or an anxiety disorder hide
their emotions and may appear to be angry or aggressive while many
women will express sadness. Some men may turn to drugs or alcohol
to try to cope with their emotional issues. Sometimes mental-health
symptoms appear to be physical issues. For example, a racing heart,
tightening chest, ongoing headaches, and digestive issues can be a
sign of an emotional problem.
Warning signs include:

- Anger, irritability, or aggressiveness

- Noticeable changes in mood, energy level, or appetite

- Difficulty sleeping or sleeping too much

- Difficulty concentrating, feeling restless, or on edge

- Increased worry or feeling stressed

- A need for alcohol or drugs

- Sadness or hopelessness

- Suicidal thoughts

- Feeling flat or having trouble feeling positive emotions

- Engaging in high-risk activities

- Ongoing headaches, digestive issues, or pain

- Obsessive thinking or compulsive behavior

- Thoughts or behaviors that interfere with work, family, or social life

- Unusual thinking or behaviors that concern other people

  Some of the mental-disorders affecting men include:

- Anxiety disorders including social phobia

- Attention deficit hyperactivity disorder (ADHD, ADD)

- Autism spectrum disorder (ASD)

- Bipolar disorder

- Borderline personality disorder (BPD)

- Depression

- Eating disorders

- Obsessive-compulsive disorder (OCD)

- Posttraumatic stress disorder (PTSD)

- Psychosis

- Schizophrenia

- Substance-use disorder (SUD)

- Suicidal thoughts

Section 42.2

Men and Depression

This section includes text excerpted from "Men and Depression,"
National Institute of Mental Health (NIMH), January 2017.

Men and women both experience depression but their symptoms can be very different. Because men who are depressed may appear to be angry or aggressive instead of sad, their families, friends, and even their doctors may not always recognize the anger or aggression as depression symptoms. In addition, men are less likely than women to recognize, talk about, and seek treatment for depression. Yet depression affects a large number of men.

What Is Depression?

Everyone feels sad or irritable and has trouble sleeping once in a while. But these feelings and troubles usually pass after a couple of days. Depression is a common but serious mood disorder that may cause severe symptoms. Depression affects the ability to feel, think, and handle daily activities. Also known as a major depressive disorder (MDD) or clinical depression, a man must have symptoms for at least two weeks to be diagnosed with depression.

Both men and women get depression but their willingness to talk about their feelings may be very different. This is one of the reasons that depression symptoms for men and women may be very different as well.

For example, some men with depression hide their emotions and may seem to be angry, irritable, or aggressive while many women seem sad or express sadness. Men with depression may feel very tired and lose interest in work, family, or hobbies. They may be more likely to have difficulty sleeping than women who have depression. Sometimes mental-health symptoms appear to be physical issues. For example, a racing heart, tightening chest, ongoing headaches, or digestive issues can be signs of a mental-health problem. Many men are more likely to see their doctor about physical symptoms than emotional symptoms.

Some men may turn to drugs or alcohol to try to cope with their emotional symptoms. Also, while women with depression are more likely to attempt suicide, men are more likely to die by suicide because they tend to use more lethal methods.

Depression can affect any man at any age. With the right treatment, most men with depression can get better and gain back their interest in work, family, and hobbies.

What Are the Signs and Symptoms of Depression in Men?

Different men have different symptoms, but some common depression symptoms include:

- Anger, irritability, or aggressiveness
- Feeling anxious, restless, or "on edge"
- Loss of interest in work, family, or once-pleasurable activities

- Problems with sexual desire and performance
- Feeling sad, "empty," flat, or hopeless
- Not being able to concentrate or remember details
- Feeling very tired, not being able to sleep, or sleeping too much
- Overeating or not wanting to eat at all
- Thoughts of suicide or suicide attempts
- Physical aches or pains, headaches, cramps, or digestive problems
- Inability to meet the responsibilities of work, caring for family, or other important activities
- Engaging in high-risk activities
- A need for alcohol or drugs
- Withdrawing from family and friends or becoming isolated

Not every man who is depressed experiences every symptom. Some men experience only a few symptoms while others may experience many.

What Are the Different Types of Depression?

The most common types of depression are:

- **Major depression**—depressive symptoms that interfere with a man's ability to work, sleep, study, eat, and enjoy most aspects of life. An episode of major depression may occur only once in a person's lifetime. But it is common for a person to have several episodes. Special forms (subtypes) of major depression include:

  - **Psychotic depression**—severe depression associated with delusions (false, fixed beliefs) or hallucinations (hearing or seeing things that are not really there). These psychotic symptoms are depression-themed. For example, a man may believe he is sick or poor when he is not, or he may hear voices that are not real that say that he is worthless.

  - **Seasonal affective disorder (SAD)**—characterized by depression symptoms that appear every year during the winter months when there is less natural sunlight.

397

- **Persistent depressive disorder (PDD)** (also called dysthymia)—depressive symptoms that last a long time (two years or longer) but are less severe than those of major depression.

- **Minor depression**—similar to major depression and persistent depressive disorder, but symptoms are less severe and may not last as long.

- **Bipolar disorder** is different from depression. It is included in this list because a person with bipolar disorder experiences episodes of extreme low moods (depression). But a person with bipolar disorder also experiences extreme high moods (called "mania").

What Causes Depression in Men

Depression is one of the most common mental disorders in the United States. Available research suggests that depression is caused by a combination of risk factors including:

- **Genetic factors.** Men with a family history of depression may be more likely to develop it than those whose family members do not have the illness.

- **Environmental stress.** Financial problems, loss of a loved one, a difficult relationship, major life changes, work problems, or any stressful situation may trigger depression in some men.

- **Illness.** Depression can occur with other serious medical illnesses, such as diabetes, cancer, heart disease, or Parkinson disease (PD). Depression can make these conditions worse and vice versa. Sometimes, medications taken for these illnesses may cause side effects that trigger or worsen depression.

How Is Depression Treated?

Men often avoid addressing their feelings and, in many cases, friends and family members are the first to recognize that their loved one is depressed. It is important that friends and family support their loved one and encourage him to visit a doctor or mental-health professional for an evaluation. A health professional can do an exam or lab tests to rule out other conditions that may have symptoms that are like those of depression. She or he also can tell if certain medications are affecting the depression.

The doctor needs to get a complete history of symptoms, such as when they started, how long they have lasted, how bad they are, whether they have occurred before, and if so, how they were treated. It is important that the man seeking help be open and honest about any efforts at "self-medication" with alcohol, nonprescribed drugs, gambling, or high-risk activities. A complete history should include information about a family history of depression or other mental disorders.

After a diagnosis, depression is usually treated with medications or psychotherapy, or a combination of the two. The increasingly-popular "collaborative care" approach combines physical and behavioral healthcare. Collaborative care involves a team of healthcare providers and managers, including a primary-care doctor and specialists.

Medication

Medications called antidepressants can work well to treat depression, but they can take several weeks to be effective. Often with medication, symptoms such as sleep, appetite, and concentration problems improve before mood lifts, so it is important to give medication a chance before deciding whether it is effective or not.

Antidepressants can have side effects including:

• Headache

• Nausea or feeling sick to your stomach

• Difficulty sleeping and nervousness

• Agitation or restlessness

• Sexual problems

Most side effects lessen over time but it is important to talk with your doctor about any side effects that you may have. Starting antidepressant medication at a low dose and gradually increasing to a full therapeutic dose may help minimize adverse effects.

It's important to know that although antidepressants can be safe and effective for many people, they may present serious risks to some, especially children, teens, and young adults. A "black box" warning—the most serious type of warning that a prescription drug can have—has been added to the labels of antidepressant medications to warn people that antidepressants may cause some young people to have suicidal thoughts or may increase the risk for suicide attempts. This is especially true for those who become agitated when they first start taking the medication and before it begins to work. Anyone taking antidepressants should be monitored closely, especially when they first start taking them.

For most people, though, the risks of untreated depression far outweigh those of taking antidepressant medications under a doctor's supervision. Careful monitoring by a health professional will also minimize any potential risks.

For reasons that are not well-understood, many people respond better to some antidepressants than to others. If a man does not respond to one medication, his doctor may suggest trying another. Sometimes, a medication may be only partially effective. In that case, another medication might be added to help make the antidepressant more effective.

If you begin taking antidepressants, do not stop taking them without the help of a doctor. Sometimes people taking antidepressants feel better and then stop taking the medication on their own, and the depression returns. When it is time to stop the medication, usually after a course of 6 to 12 months, the doctor will help you slowly and safely decrease your dose. Stopping them abruptly can cause withdrawal symptoms.

Some people who relapse back into depression after stopping an antidepressant benefit from staying on medication for additional months or years.

Psychotherapy

Several types of psychotherapy or "talk therapy" can help treat depression. Some therapies are just as effective as medications for certain types of depression. Therapy helps by teaching new ways of thinking and behaving, and changing habits that may be contributing to the depression. Therapy can also help men understand and work through difficult situations or relationships that may be causing their depression or making it worse.

Cognitive-behavioral therapy (CBT), interpersonal therapy (IPT), and problem-solving therapy (PST) are examples of evidence-based talk therapy treatments for depression.

Treatment for depression should be personalized. Some men might try therapy first and add antidepressant medication later if it is needed. Others might start treatment with both medication and psychotherapy.

How Can You Help a Loved One Who Is Depressed?

It's important to remember that a person with depression cannot simply "snap out of it." It is also important to know that he may not recognize his symptoms and may not want to get professional treatment.

If you think someone has depression, you can support him by helping him find a doctor or mental-health professional and then helping him make an appointment. Even men who have trouble recognizing that they are depressed may agree to seek help for physical symptoms, such as feeling tired or run down. They may be willing to talk with their regular health professional about a new difficulty they are having at work or losing interest in doing things they usually enjoy. Talking with a primary-care provider may be a good first step toward learning about and treating possible depression.

Other ways to help include:

- Offering him support, understanding, patience, and encouragement

- Listening carefully and talking with him

- Never ignoring comments about suicide, and alerting his therapist or doctor

- Helping him increase his level of physical and social activity by inviting him out for hikes, games, and other events. If he says, "no," keep trying, but don't push him to take on too much too soon.

- Encouraging him to report any concerns about medications to his healthcare provider

- Ensuring that he gets to his doctor's appointments

- Reminding him that with time and treatment, the depression will lift

How Can You Help Yourself If You Are Depressed?

Than later can relieve symptoms quicker and reduce the length of time treatment is needed.

Other things that may help include:

- Spending time with other people and talking with a friend or relative about your feelings

- Increasing your level of physical activity. Regular exercise can help people with mild to moderate depression and may be one part of a treatment plan for those with severe depression. Talk with your healthcare professional about what kind of exercise is right for you.

- Breaking up large tasks into small ones, and tackling what you can as you can. Don't try to do too many things at once

- Delaying important decisions until you feel better. Discuss decisions with others who know you well.

- Keeping stable daily routines. For example, eating and going to bed at the same time every day.

- Avoiding alcohol

As you continue treatment, gradually you will start to feel better. Remember that if you are taking an antidepressant, it may take several weeks for it to start working. Try to do things that you used to enjoy before you had depression. Go easy on yourself.

Where Can You Go for Help?

If you are unsure of where to go for help, ask your family doctor or healthcare provider. You can also find resources online including the National Institute of Mental Health (NIMH) website at www. nimh.nih.gov/FindHelp, or check with your insurance carrier to find someone who participates in your plan. Hospital doctors can help in an emergency.

What If You or Someone You Know Is in Crisis?

Men with depression are at risk for suicide. If you or someone you know is in crisis, get help quickly.

- Call your doctor.

- Call 911 for emergency services.

- Go to the nearest hospital emergency room.

- Call the toll-free, 24-hour hotline of the National Suicide Prevention Lifeline (NSPL) at 800-273-8255; TTY: 800-799-4889.

- Veterans can call the Veterans Crisis Line at 800-273-8255, then press 1.

In many instances, a crisis can be avoided when friends or family members are involved in the treatment and can recognize crisis warning signs. Crisis warning signs are different for different people. One person may have more trouble sleeping and become more agitated. Another person may sleep more, stop eating, and focus on disturbing thoughts. Creating a plan that lists the loved one's warning signs—those actions that usually occur before a crisis—and the healthcare provider's contact information may help avoid a crisis.

Chapter 43

Mental-Health Issues among Women

Chapter Contents

Section 43.1

Mental Health for Women

This section includes text excerpted from "Women and Mental Health," National Institute of Mental Health (NIMH), July 2016.

Mental disorders can affect women and men differently. Some disorders, such as depression and anxiety, are more common in women. There are also certain types of depression that are unique to women. Some women may experience symptoms of mental disorders at times of hormone change, such as perinatal depression, premenstrual dysphoric disorder (PMDD), and perimenopause-related depression. When it comes to other mental disorders such as schizophrenia and bipolar disorder, research has not found differences in rates that men and women experience these illnesses. But, women may experience these illnesses differently–certain symptoms may be more common in women than in men, and the course of the illness can be affected by the sex of the individual. Researchers are only now beginning to tease apart the various biological and psychosocial factors that may impact the mental health of both women and men.

Signs and Symptoms of Mental-Health Issues

Women and men can develop most of the same mental disorders and conditions, but may experience different symptoms. Some symptoms include:

- Persistent sadness or feelings of hopelessness

- Abuse of alcohol and/or drugs

- Dramatic changes in eating or sleeping habits

- Appetite and/or weight changes

- Decreased energy or fatigue

- Excessive fear or worry

- Seeing or hearing things that are not there

- Extremely high and low moods

- Aches, headaches, or digestive problems without a clear cause

- Irritability

- Social withdrawal
- Thoughts of suicide

Section 43.2

Anxiety Disorders among Women

This section includes text excerpted from "Anxiety Disorders," Office on Women's Health (OWH), U.S. Department of Health and Human Services (HHS), August 28, 2018.

Anxiety is a normal response to stress. But when it becomes hard to control and affects your day-to-day life, it can be disabling. Anxiety disorders affect nearly one in five adults in the United States. Women are more than twice as likely as men to get an anxiety disorder in their lifetime. Anxiety disorders are often treated with counseling, medicine, or a combination of both. Some women also find that yoga or meditation helps with anxiety disorders.

Who Gets Anxiety Disorders

Anxiety disorders affect about 40 million American adults every year. Anxiety disorders also affect children and teens. About 8 percent of teens ages 13 to 18 have an anxiety disorder, with symptoms starting around age 6.

Women are more than twice as likely as men to get an anxiety disorder in their lifetime. Also, some types of anxiety disorders affect some women more than others:

- **Generalized anxiety disorder (GAD)** affects more American Indian and Alaskan Native women than women of other races and ethnicities. GAD also affects more white women and Hispanic women than Asian or African-American women.

- **Social phobia and panic disorder** affect more white women than women of other races and ethnicities.

How Does Counseling Help Treat Anxiety Disorders?

Your doctor may refer you for a type of counseling for anxiety disorders called cognitive-behavioral therapy (CBT). You can talk to a trained mental-health professional about what caused your anxiety disorder and how to deal with the symptoms.

For example, you can talk to a psychiatrist, psychologist, social worker, or counselor. CBT can help you change the thinking patterns around your fears. It may help you change the way you react to situations that may create anxiety. You may also learn ways to reduce feelings of anxiety and improve specific behaviors caused by chronic anxiety. These strategies may include relaxation therapy and problem-solving.

What Types of Medicine Treat Anxiety Disorders?

Several types of medicine treat anxiety disorders. These include:

- **Antianxiety (benzodiazepines).** These medicines are usually prescribed for short periods of time because they are addictive. Stopping this medicine too quickly can cause withdrawal symptoms.

- **Beta-blockers.** These medicines can help prevent the physical symptoms of an anxiety disorder, like trembling or sweating.

- **Selective serotonin reuptake inhibitors (SSRIs).** SSRIs change the level of serotonin in the brain. They increase the amount of serotonin available to help brain cells communicate with each other. Common side effects can include insomnia or sedation, stomach problems, and a lack of sexual desire.

- **Tricyclics.** Tricyclics work like SSRIs. But sometimes they cause more side effects than SSRIs. They may cause dizziness, drowsiness, dry mouth, constipation, or weight gain.

- **Monoamine oxidase inhibitors (MAOIs).** People who take MAOIs must avoid certain foods and drinks (like Parmesan or cheddar cheese and red wine) that contain an amino acid called "tyramine." Taking an MAOI and eating these foods can cause blood pressure levels to spike dangerously. Women who take MAOIs must also avoid certain medicines, such as some types of birth control pills, pain relievers, and cold and allergy medicines. Talk to your doctor about any medicine you take.

All medicines have risks. You should talk to your doctor about the benefits and risks of all medicines.

What If Your Anxiety Disorder Treatment Is Not Working?

Sometimes, you may need to work with your doctor to try several different treatments or combinations of treatments before you find one that works for you.

If you are having trouble with side effects from medicines, talk to your doctor or nurse. Do not stop taking your medicine without talking to a doctor or nurse. Your doctor may adjust how much medicine you take and when you take it.

What If Your Anxiety Disorder Comes Back?

Sometimes symptoms of an anxiety disorder come back after you have finished treatment. This may happen during or after a stressful event. It may also happen without any warning.

Many people with anxiety disorders do get better with treatment. But, if your symptoms come back, your doctor will work with you to change or adjust your medicine or treatment plan.

You can also talk to your doctor about ways to identify and prevent anxiety from coming back. This may include writing down your feelings or meeting with your counselor if you think your anxiety is uncontrollable.

Will Your Anxiety Disorder Treatment Affect Pregnancy?

If your treatment is counseling, it will not affect your pregnancy. If you are on medicine to treat your anxiety disorder, talk to your doctor. Some medicines used to treat anxiety can affect your unborn baby.

If You Are Taking Medicine to Treat Anxiety Disorder, Can You Breastfeed Your Baby?

It depends. Some medicines used to treat anxiety can pass through breast milk. Certain antidepressants, such as some SSRIs, are safe to take during breastfeeding. Do not stop taking your medicine too quickly. Talk to your doctor to find out what medicine is best for you and your baby.

How Do Anxiety Disorders Affect Other Health Conditions?

Anxiety disorders may affect other health problems that are common in women. These include:

- **Depression.** Anxiety disorders can happen at the same time as depression. When this happens, treatment for both anxiety and depression may not be as effective. You may need a combination of treatments, such as counseling and medicine.

- **Irritable bowel syndrome (IBS).** IBS symptoms are common in people with anxiety disorders. Generalized anxiety disorder is also common among people with IBS. Worry can make IBS symptoms worse, especially gastrointestinal (GI) symptoms such as upset stomach or gas. GI symptoms can also be stressful and lead to more anxiety. Although treatments for IBS can help treat anxiety, it's important that you treat both conditions.

- **Chronic pain.** Anxiety disorders are common in women with certain diseases that cause chronic pain, including rheumatoid arthritis (RA), fibromyalgia, and migraine.

- **Cardiovascular disease (CVD).** Anxiety and depression increase the risk for heart disease, the leading cause of death for American women. Anxiety can also make recovery harder after a heart attack or stroke.

- **Asthma.** Studies link asthma to anxiety disorders. Stress and anxiety can trigger asthma attacks while the shortness of breath and wheezing during asthma attacks can cause anxiety. Studies show that breathing retraining may help asthma control and ease anxiety.

What Is the Latest Research on Anxiety Disorders and Women?

Researchers are studying why women are more than twice as likely as men to develop anxiety disorders and depression. Changes in levels of the hormone estrogen throughout a woman's menstrual cycle and reproductive life (during the years a woman can have a baby) probably play a role.

Researchers also studied the male hormone testosterone, which is found in women and men but typically in higher levels in men. They found that treatment with testosterone had similar effects as antianxiety and antidepressant medicine for the women in the study.

Other research focuses on anxiety disorders and depression during and after pregnancy and among overweight and obese women.

Section 43.3

Bipolar Disorder among Women

This section includes text excerpted from "Bipolar Disorder," Office on Women's Health (OWH), U.S. Department of Health and Human Services (HHS), August 28, 2018.

Bipolar disorder, formerly known as manic-depressive illness, is a serious medical condition. Someone with bipolar disorder has extreme episodes of mania, or being very "up" or energetic and active, and episodes of depression, or being very "down" and sad. Changing hormones during the menstrual cycle, pregnancy, and menopause can affect how severe a woman's bipolar disorder is, but menstrual cycle conditions (like premenstrual syndrome) are not the same as bipolar disorder.

What Is Bipolar Disorder?

Bipolar disorder is a serious medical condition that causes extreme swings in a person's mood, energy, and ability to function. These mood changes, called manic and depressive episodes, are not the same as the typical ups and downs that everyone goes through from time to time. These mood changes are also different from those caused by premenstrual syndrome (PMS) or premenstrual dysphoric disorder (PMDD).

There are different types of bipolar disorder. The two most common types are bipolar I (pronounced "bipolar one") and bipolar II

411

(pronounced "bipolar two"). The different types of bipolar disorder are based on how severe a person's mood and behavior changes are and how quickly they come and go. Some types of bipolar disorder are more severe than others, but all types of bipolar disorder can be treated.

What Is Bipolar I Disorder?

Bipolar I (pronounced "bipolar one") disorder is the most severe type of bipolar disorder. It affects women and men equally, but it is often diagnosed later in life for women than for men. Bipolar I disorder causes severe swings in mood and energy, from highs (manic episodes) to lows (depressive episodes).

What Is Bipolar II Disorder?

Bipolar II (pronounced "bipolar two") disorder is the most common type of bipolar disorder. It affects more women than men.

Women with bipolar II disorder experience similar mood changes to people with bipolar I, but the manic episodes are less severe. These less intense episodes are called hypomania. However, women with bipolar II tend to have depressive episodes more often.

Because hypomanic episodes are less severe than manic episodes, women with bipolar II may be more able than women with bipolar I to live in the community with family and complete everyday tasks at work, school, or home. Bipolar II disorder can usually be treated without hospitalization.

What Does It Mean to Have an Episode of Bipolar Disorder?

The term "episode" may be used to describe what happens when a person with bipolar disorder has several manic or depressive symptoms for most of the day, nearly every day, for at least one to two weeks. Sometimes symptoms are so severe that the person cannot do everyday tasks at work, school, or home.

What Is a Hypomanic Episode?

A hypomanic episode, also called hypomania, has fewer or milder symptoms than a manic episode. Women who have mood changes with hypomanic episodes may have a milder but still serious condition called bipolar II disorder.

What Is a Manic Episode?

Symptoms of mania or a manic episode include:
Mood changes:

- Feeling "high," or having an overly happy or outgoing mood with a lot of energy
- Having an extremely irritable mood, feeling agitated, or feeling jumpy or wired

Behavioral changes:

- Talking very fast, jumping from one idea to another, or having racing thoughts
- Being easily distracted all of the time
- Taking on many new projects without getting others completed
- Being unusually "wired" or restless
- Getting little to no sleep
- Having an unrealistic positive belief in one's abilities (such as being able to fly or read minds)
- Behaving impulsively and taking part in a lot of pleasurable, high-risk behaviors, such as spending sprees, impulsive sex, and impulsive business investments

A manic episode can be followed by a depressive episode. A person can also experience a "mixed state" in which she or he feels symptoms of both mania and depression.

What Is a Depressive Episode?

Symptoms of depression or a depressive episode include:

- Mood changes:
  - A long period (more than two weeks) of feeling worried, empty, hopeless, or sad
  - Loss of interest in activities once enjoyed
- Behavioral changes:
  - Feeling tired or "slowed down"
  - Having problems concentrating, remembering, and making decisions

- Being restless or irritable

- Changing eating, sleeping, or other daily habits

- Thinking of death or suicide or attempting suicide

A person can also experience a "mixed state" in which she or he feels symptoms of both mania and depression.

What Causes Bipolar Disorder

Experts do not know what causes bipolar disorder. Some possible causes include:

- **Biology.** The way the brain is shaped and how it functions may be different in people with bipolar disorder.

- **Chemistry.** In people with bipolar disorder, levels of brain chemicals may not be balanced correctly. These chemicals usually help regulate thoughts, moods, and behaviors so that a person does not feel so high or low.

- **Family history.** Bipolar disorder is more common in people who have a sibling, parent, or child with the condition. Certain genes may be involved in causing bipolar disorder.

How Does Bipolar Disorder Affect Women?

Women and men are equally likely to have bipolar I disorder, but women are more likely to have bipolar II disorder and may experience more rapid cycling between highs and lows.

Women with bipolar disorder are also more likely than men with bipolar disorder to have other physical and mental-health conditions, including problems with alcohol use, depression caused by bipolar disorder, thyroid disease, obesity caused by medicines that treat bipolar disorder, and migraine headaches.

Changing hormones during the menstrual cycle and menopause can also affect how severe a woman's bipolar disorder is, but they do not cause bipolar disorder.

How Does Pregnancy Affect Bipolar Disorder?

Women who have bipolar disorder are at risk for experiencing an episode after giving birth, especially a depressive episode. Women who experience a depressive or manic episode after giving birth are also more likely to have episodes after other pregnancies. Women with bipolar disorder are at high risk of developing postpartum psychosis (PP), which is a medical emergency.

Talk to your doctor or nurse if you are trying to get pregnant or are pregnant. Some medicines are not safe to take during pregnancy.

Can You Take Medicine for Bipolar Disorder While Breastfeeding?

Yes. Certain medicines to treat bipolar disorder are safe to take while breastfeeding. Talk to your doctor about what medicines you can take after giving birth.

Section 43.4

Depression among Women

This section includes text excerpted from "Depression," Office on Women's Health (OWH), U.S. Department of Health and Human Services (HHS),, October 18, 2018.

Life is full of ups and downs, but when you feel sad, empty, or hopeless most of the time for at least two weeks or those feelings keep you from your regular activities, you may have depression. Depression is a serious mental-health condition. Women are twice as likely as men to be diagnosed with depression. Depression is not a normal part of being a woman. Most women, even those with the most severe depression, can get better with treatment.

Who Gets Depression

Women are twice as likely as men to be diagnosed with depression. It is more than twice as common for African-American, Hispanic, and white women to have depression compared to Asian-American women. Depression is also more common in women whose families live below the federal poverty line.

What Causes Depression

There is no single cause of depression. Also, different types of depression may have different causes. There are many reasons why a woman may have depression:

- **Family history**. Women with a family history of depression may be more at risk. But depression can also happen in women who don't have a family history of depression.

- **Brain changes.** The brains of people with depression look and function differently from those of people who don't have depression.

- **Chemistry.** In someone who has depression, parts of the brain that manage mood, thoughts, sleep, appetite, and behavior may not have the right balance of chemicals.

- **Hormone levels.** Changes in the female hormones—estrogen and progesterone—during the menstrual cycle, pregnancy, postpartum period, perimenopause, or menopause may all raise a woman's risk for depression. Having a miscarriage can also put a woman at higher risk for depression.

- **Stress.** Serious and stressful life events, or the combination of several stressful events, such as trauma, loss of a loved one, a bad relationship, work responsibilities, caring for children and aging parents, abuse, and poverty, may trigger depression in some people.

- **Medical problems.** Dealing with a serious health problem, such as stroke, heart attack, or cancer, can lead to depression. Research shows that people who have a serious illness and depression are more likely to have more serious types of both conditions. Some medical illnesses, like Parkinson disease (PD), hypothyroidism, and stroke, can cause changes in the brain that can trigger depression.

- **Pain.** Women who feel emotional or physical pain for long periods are much more likely to develop depression. The pain can come from a chronic (long-term) health problem, accident, or trauma such as sexual assault or abuse.

What Are the Symptoms of Depression?

Not all people with depression have the same symptoms. Some people might have only a few symptoms, while others may have many.

How often symptoms happen, how long they last, and how severe they are may be different for each person.

If you have any of the following symptoms for at least two weeks, talk to a doctor or nurse or mental-health professional:

- Feeling sad, "down," or empty, including crying often

- Feeling hopeless, helpless, worthless, or useless

- Loss of interest in hobbies and activities that you once enjoyed

- Decreased energy

- Difficulty staying focused, remembering, or making decisions

- Sleeplessness, early morning awakening, or oversleeping and not wanting to get up

- Lack of appetite, leading to weight loss, or eating to feel better, leading to weight gain

- Thoughts of hurting yourself

- Thoughts of death or suicide

- Feeling easily annoyed, bothered, or angered

- Constant physical symptoms that do not get better with treatment, such as headaches, upset stomach, and pain that doesn't go away

How Is Depression Linked to Other Health Problems?

Depression is linked to many health problems in women, including:

- **Heart disease.** People with heart disease are about twice as likely to have depression as people who don't have heart disease.

- **Obesity.** Studies show that 43 percent of adults with depression have obesity. Women, especially white women, with depression are more likely to have obesity than women without depression are. Women with depression are also more likely than men with depression to have obesity.

- **Cancer.** Up to one in four people with cancer may also experience depression. More women with cancer than men with cancer experience depression.

Get Help for Depression

Talk to someone like a doctor, nurse, psychiatrist, mental-health professional, or social worker about your symptoms.

What If You Have Thoughts of Hurting Yourself?

If you are thinking about hurting or even killing yourself, get help now. Call 911 or the National Suicide Prevention Lifeline (NSPL) at 800-273-8255.

You might feel like your pain is too overwhelming to bear, but those feelings don't last forever. People do make it through suicidal thoughts. Many thoughts of suicide are impulses that go away after a short period of time.

Does Exercise Help Treat Depression?

For some people, yes. Researchers think that exercise may work better than no treatment at all to treat depression. They also think that exercise can help make depression symptoms happen less often or be less severe. Researchers do not know whether exercise works as well as therapy or medicine to treat depression. People with depression often find it very difficult to exercise, even though they know it will help make them feel better. Walking is a good way to begin exercising if you haven't exercised recently.

Will Treatment for Depression Affect Your Chances of Getting Pregnant?

Maybe. Some medicines, such as some types of antidepressants, may make it more difficult for you to get pregnant, but more research is needed. Talk to your doctor about other treatments for depression that don't involve medicine if you are trying to get pregnant. For example, a type of talk therapy called cognitive-behavioral therapy (CBT) helps women with depression. This type of therapy has little to no risk for women trying to get pregnant. During CBT, you work with a mental-health professional to explore why you are depressed and train yourself to replace negative thoughts with positive ones. Certain mental-healthcare professionals specialize in depression related to infertility.

Women who are already taking an antidepressant and who are trying to get pregnant should talk to their doctor or nurse about the risks and benefits of stopping the medicine.

Section 43.5

Eating Disorders among Women

This section contains text excerpted from the following sources: Text in this section begins with excerpts from "Eating Disorders," Office on Women's Health (OWH), U.S. Department of Health and Human Services (HHS), May 17, 2018; Text under the heading "Anorexia Nervosa" is excerpted from "Anorexia Nervosa," Office on Women's Health (OWH), U.S. Department of Health and Human Services (HHS), August 28, 2018; Text under the heading "Binge Eating Disorder" is excerpted from "Binge Eating Disorder," Office on Women's Health (OWH), U.S. Department of Health and Human Services (HHS), August 28, 2018; Text under the heading "Bulimia Nervosa" is excerpted from "Bulimia Nervosa," Office on Women's Health (OWH), U.S. Department of Health and Human Services (HHS), August 28, 2018.

Eating disorders, such as anorexia, bulimia, and binge eating disorder, are serious mental-health conditions that can happen to anyone but are much more common in women. People with eating disorders eat too little or too much. Extreme eating or dieting is not a normal or healthy part of being a woman. Some eating disorders also involve people making themselves throw up or taking laxatives to get rid of the food, or extreme exercise to burn off the calories. All eating disorders are dangerous if left untreated.

Anorexia Nervosa
What Is Anorexia?

Anorexia nervosa, often called anorexia, is a type of eating disorder. Eating disorders are mental-health problems that cause extreme and dangerous eating behaviors. These extreme eating behaviors cause other serious health problems and sometimes death. Some eating disorders also involves extreme exercise.

Women with anorexia severely limit the amount of food they eat to prevent weight gain. People with anorexia usually have an intense fear of gaining weight and may think they are fat even when they are thin. Women with anorexia may also exercise too much so that they do not gain weight. Over time, eating so little food leads to serious health problems and sometimes death.

What Is the Difference between Anorexia and Other Eating Disorders?

Women with eating disorders, such as anorexia, bulimia, and binge eating disorder, have a mental-health condition that affects how they eat, and sometimes how they exercise. These eating disorders threatens their health.

Unlike women with bulimia and binge eating disorder, girls and women with anorexia do not eat enough to sustain basic bodily functions. Women with bulimia and binge eating disorder usually binge, or eat too much while feeling out of control.

It is possible to have more than one eating disorder in your lifetime. Regardless of what type of eating disorder you may have, you can get better with treatment.

Who Is at Risk for Anorexia?

Anorexia is more common among girls and women than boys and men.

Anorexia is also more common among girls and younger women than older women. On average, girls develop anorexia at 16 or 17. Teen girls between 13 and 19 and young women in their early twenties are most at risk. But eating disorders are happening more often in older women. In a study, 13 percent of American women over 50 had signs of an eating disorder.

What Causes Anorexia

Researchers are not sure exactly what causes anorexia and other eating disorders. Researchers think that eating disorders might happen because of a combination of a person's biology and life events. This combination includes having specific genes, a person's biology, body image and self-esteem, social experiences, family health history, and sometimes other mental-health illnesses.

Researchers are also studying unusual activity in the brain, such as changing levels of serotonin or other chemicals, to see how it may affect eating.

How Does Anorexia Affect a Woman's Health?

With anorexia, your body doesn't get the energy that it needs from food, so it slows down and stops working normally. Over time, anorexia can affect your body in the following ways:

- Heart problems, including low blood pressure, a slower heart rate, irregular heartbeat, heart attack, and sudden death from heart problems

- Anemia (when your red blood cells do not carry enough oxygen to your body) and other blood problems

- Thinning of the bones (osteopenia or osteoporosis)

- Kidney stones or kidney failure

- Lack of periods, which can cause problems getting pregnant

- During pregnancy, a higher risk for miscarriage, cesarean delivery, or having a baby with low birth weight

Anorexia is a serious illness that can also lead to death. Studies have found that more women and girls die from anorexia than any other eating disorder or serious mental-health problem such as depression. Many people with anorexia also have other mental-health problems such as depression or anxiety.

Long-term studies of 20 years or more show that women who had an eating disorder in the past usually reach and maintain a healthy weight after treatment.

How Does Anorexia Affect Pregnancy?

Anorexia can cause problems getting pregnant and during pregnancy.

Extreme weight loss can cause missed menstrual periods because you may not ovulate, or release an egg from the ovary. When you do not weigh enough to ovulate, it is difficult to get pregnant. However, if you do not want to have children right now and you have sex, you should use birth control.

Anorexia can also cause problems during pregnancy. Anorexia raises your risk for:

- Miscarriage (pregnancy loss)

- Premature birth (also called preterm birth), or childbirth before 37 weeks of pregnancy

- Delivery by cesarean section (C-section)

- Having a low birth weight baby (less than five pounds, eight ounces at birth)

- Depression after the baby is born (postpartum depression)

If You Had an Eating Disorder in the Past, Can You Still Get Pregnant?

Yes. Women who have recovered from anorexia, are at a healthy weight, and have normal menstrual cycles have a better chance of getting pregnant and having a safe and healthy pregnancy.

If you had an eating disorder in the past, it may take you a little longer to get pregnant (about six months to a year) compared to women who never had an eating disorder.

Tell your doctor if you had an eating disorder in the past and are trying to become pregnant.

If You Take Medicine to Treat Anorexia, Can You Breastfeed Your Baby?

Maybe. Some medicines used to treat anorexia can pass through breast milk. Certain antidepressants can be used safely during breastfeeding.

Talk to your doctor to find out which medicine works best for you.

Binge Eating Disorder

Binge eating disorder (BED) is the most common type of eating disorder in the United States. People with binge eating disorder often feel out of control and eat a large amount of food at one time (called a binge). Unlike other eating disorders, people who have binge eating disorder do not throw up the food or exercise too much. Binge eating disorder is a serious health problem, but people with binge eating disorder can get better with treatment.

What Is Binge Eating Disorder?

Binge eating disorder is a type of eating disorder. Eating disorders are mental-health problems that cause extreme and dangerous eating behaviors. These extreme eating behaviors cause other serious health problems and sometimes death. Some eating disorders also involves extreme exercise.

According to the American Psychiatric Association (APA), women with binge eating disorder feel out of control and eat too much (binge), at least once a week for at least three months. During binges women with binge eating disorder usually eat faster than normal, eat until they are uncomfortable, eat when they are not physically hungry, and feel embarrassed, disgusted, or depressed because of the binges. Women with this type of eating disorder may be overweight or obese

What Is the Difference between Binge Eating Disorder and Other Eating Disorders?

Women with eating disorders, such as binge eating disorder, bulimia, and anorexia, have a mental-health condition that affects how they eat, and sometimes how they exercise. These eating disorders threatens their health.

Unlike people with anorexia or bulimia, people with binge eating disorder do not throw up their food, exercise a lot, or starve themselves. People with binge eating disorder are often overweight or obese. But not all people with binge eating disorder are overweight, and being overweight does not always mean you have binge eating disorder.

It is possible to have more than one eating disorder in your lifetime. Regardless of what type of eating disorder you may have, you can get better with treatment.

Who Is at Risk for Binge Eating Disorder?

Binge eating disorder affects more than three percent of women in the United States. More than half of people with binge eating disorder are women.

Binge eating disorder affects women of all races and ethnicities. It is the most common eating disorder among Hispanic, Asian-American, and African-American women.

Some women may be more at risk for binge eating disorder.

- Women and girls who diet often are 12 times more likely to binge eat than women and girls who do not diet.

- Binge eating disorder affects more young and middle-aged women than older women. On average, women develop binge eating disorder in their early to mid-twenties. But eating disorders are happening more often in older women. In one study, 13 percent of American women over 50 had signs of an eating disorder.

What Are the Symptoms of Binge Eating Disorder?

It can be difficult to tell whether someone has binge eating disorder. Many women with binge eating disorder hide their behavior because they are embarrassed.

You may have binge eating disorder if, for at least once a week over the past three months, you have binged. Binge eating disorder means you have at least three of these symptoms while binging:

- Eating faster than normal

- Eating until uncomfortably full

- Eating large amounts of food when not hungry

- Eating alone because of embarrassment

- Feeling disgusted, depressed, or guilty afterward

People with binge eating disorder may also have other mental-health problems, such as depression, anxiety, or substance abuse.

What Causes Binge Eating Disorder

Researchers are not sure exactly what causes binge eating disorder and other eating disorders. Researchers think that eating disorders might happen because of a combination of a person's biology and life events. This combination includes having specific genes, a person's biology, body image and self-esteem, social experiences, family health history, and sometimes other mental-health illnesses.

Studies suggest that people with binge eating disorder may use overeating as a way to deal with anger, sadness, boredom, anxiety, or stress.

Researchers are studying how changing levels of brain chemicals may affect eating habits. Neuroimaging, or pictures of the brain, may lead to a better understanding of binge eating disorder.

How Does Binge Eating Disorder Affect a Woman's Health?

Many, but not all, women with binge eating disorder are overweight or obese. Obesity raises your risk for many serious health problems:

- Type 2 diabetes

- Heart disease

- High blood pressure

- High cholesterol

- Gallbladder disease

- Certain types of cancer, including breast, endometrial (a type of uterine cancer), colorectal, kidney, esophageal, pancreatic, thyroid, and gallbladder cancer

- Problems with your menstrual cycle, including preventing ovulation, which can make it harder to get pregnant

People with binge eating disorder often have other serious mental-health illnesses such as depression, anxiety, or substance abuse. These problems can seriously affect a woman's everyday life and can be treated.

How Does Binge Eating Disorder Affect Pregnancy?

Binge eating disorder can cause problems getting pregnant and during pregnancy. Pregnancy can also trigger binge eating disorder.

Obesity raises the level of the hormone estrogen in your body. Higher levels of estrogen can stop you from ovulating, or releasing an egg from the ovary. This can make it more difficult to get pregnant. However, if you do not want to have children right now and have sex, you should use birth control.

Overweight or obesity may also cause problems during pregnancy. Overweight and obesity raises your risk for:

- Gestational hypertension (high blood pressure during pregnancy) and preeclampsia (high blood pressure and kidney problems during pregnancy). If not controlled, both problems can threaten the life of the mother and the baby.

- Gestational diabetes (diabetes that starts during pregnancy). If not controlled, gestational diabetes can cause you to have a large baby. This raises your risk for a C-section.

Pregnancy can raise the risk for binge eating disorder in women who are at higher risk for eating disorders. In one study, almost half of the women with binge eating disorder got the condition during pregnancy. The research suggests that binge eating during pregnancy may be caused by:

- Worry over pregnancy weight gain. Women may binge because they feel a loss of control over their bodies because of the pregnancy weight.

- Greater stress during pregnancy

- Depression

425

- History of smoking and alcohol abuse

- Lack of social support

After pregnancy, postpartum depression and weight from pregnancy can trigger binge eating disorder in women with a history of binge eating. Women with binge eating disorder before pregnancy often gain more weight during pregnancy than women without an eating disorder. Researchers think that weight gain during pregnancy may cause some women who had binge eating disorder before pregnancy to binge eat during pregnancy.

If You Take Medicine to Treat Binge Eating Disorder, Can You Breastfeed Your Baby?

Maybe. Some medicines used to treat binge eating disorder can pass through breast milk. Certain antidepressants can be used safely during breastfeeding. Talk to your doctor to find out what medicine works best for you.

Bulimia Nervosa

Bulimia nervosa, often called bulimia, is a type of eating disorder. People with bulimia eat large amounts of food at one time, then try to get rid of the food or weight gain by throwing up, taking laxatives, fasting (not eating anything), or exercising a lot more than normal. Bulimia affects more girls and women than boys and men. Bulimia is a serious health problem, but people with bulimia can get better with treatment.

What Is Bulimia?

Bulimia nervosa, often called bulimia, is a type of eating disorder. Eating disorders are mental-health problems that cause extreme and dangerous eating behaviors. These extreme eating behaviors cause other serious health problems and sometimes death. Some eating disorders also involves extreme exercise.

Women with bulimia eat a lot of food in a short amount of time and feel a lack of control over eating during this time (called binging). People with bulimia then try to prevent weight gain by getting rid of the food (called purging). Purging may be done by:

- Making yourself throw up

- Taking laxatives. Laxatives can include pills or liquids that speed up the movement of food through your body and lead to bowel movements.

Women with bulimia may also try to prevent weight gain after binging by exercising a lot more than normal, eating very little or not at all (fasting), or taking pills to urinate often.

Women with bulimia usually have self-esteem that is closely linked to their body image.

What Is the Difference between Bulimia and Other Eating Disorders?

Women with eating disorders, such as bulimia, anorexia, and binge eating disorder, have a mental-health condition that affects how they eat, and sometimes how they exercise. These eating disorders threatens their health.

Unlike women with anorexia, women with bulimia often have a normal weight. Unlike women with binge eating disorder, women with bulimia purge, or try to get rid of the food or weight after binging. Binging and purging are usually done in private. This can make it difficult to tell if a loved one has bulimia or another eating disorder.

It is possible to have more than one eating disorder in your lifetime. Regardless of what type of eating disorder you may have, you can get better with treatment.

Who Is at Risk for Bulimia?

Bulimia affects more women than men. It affects up to two percent of women and happens to women of all races and ethnicities.

Bulimia affects more girls and younger women than older women. On average, women develop bulimia at 18 or 19. Teen girls between 15 and 19 and young women in their early twenties are most at risk. But eating disorders are happening more often in older women. In a study, 13 percent of American women over 50 had signs of an eating disorder.

What Are the Symptoms of Bulimia?

Someone with bulimia may be thin, overweight, or have a normal weight. It can be difficult to tell based on a person's weight whether someone has bulimia. This is because binging and purging are most often done in private. However, family or friends may see empty food wrappers in unexpected places or vomit in the home.

Over time, some symptoms of bulimia may include:

- Swollen cheeks or jaw area

- Calluses or scrapes on the knuckles (if using fingers to induce vomiting)

- Teeth that look clear instead of white and are increasingly sensitive and decaying

- Broken blood vessels in the eyes

- Acid reflux, constipation, and other gastrointestinal problems

- Severe dehydration

Girls or women with bulimia may also have behavior changes such as:

- Often going to the bathroom right after eating (to throw up)

- Exercising a lot, even in bad weather or when hurt or tired

- Acting moody or sad, hating the way she looks, or feeling hopeless

- Having problems expressing anger

- Not wanting to go out with friends or do activities she once enjoyed

People with bulimia often have other mental-health problems, including depression, anxiety, or substance abuse.

What Causes Bulimia

Researchers are not sure exactly what causes bulimia and other eating disorders. Researchers think that eating disorders might happen because of a combination of a person's biology and life events. This combination includes having specific genes, a person's biology, body image and self-esteem, social experiences, family health history, and sometimes other mental-health illnesses.

Researchers are also studying unusual activity in the brain, such as changing levels of serotonin or other chemicals, to see how it may affect eating.

How Does Bulimia Affect a Woman's Health?

Purging through vomiting or taking laxatives can prevent your body from getting the important nutrients it needs from food. Over time, bulimia can affect your body in the following ways:

- Stomach damage from overeating

- Electrolyte imbalance (having levels of sodium, potassium, or other minerals that are too high or too low, which can lead to heart attack or heart failure)
- Ulcers and other damage to your throat from vomiting
- Irregular periods or not having periods, which can cause problems getting pregnant
- Tooth decay from vomiting
- Dehydration
- Problems having bowel movements or damage to the intestines from laxative abuse

Long-term studies of 20 years or more show that women who had an eating disorder in the past usually reach and maintain a healthy weight after treatment.

If You Had an Eating Disorder in the Past, Can You Still Get Pregnant?

Women who have recovered from bulimia and have normal menstrual cycles have a better chance of getting pregnant and having a safe and healthy pregnancy. If you had an eating disorder in the past, it may take you a little longer to get pregnant (about six months to one year) compared to women who never had an eating disorder. Tell your doctor if you had an eating disorder in the past and are trying to become pregnant.

If You Take Medicine to Treat Bulimia, Can You Breastfeed Your Baby?

Maybe. Some medicines used to treat bulimia can pass through breast milk. Certain antidepressants can be used safely during breastfeeding. Talk to your doctor to find out what medicine works best for you.

Section 43.6

Premenstrual Dysphoric Disorder

This section includes text excerpted from "Premenstrual Dysphoric
Disorder (PMDD)," Office on Women's Health (OWH), U.S.
Department of Health and Human Services (HHS), March 16, 2018.

Premenstrual dysphoric disorder (PMDD) is a health problem that
is similar to premenstrual syndrome (PMS) but is more serious. PMDD
causes severe irritability, depression, or anxiety in the week or two
before your period starts. Symptoms usually go away two to three days
after your period starts. You may need medicine or other treatment to
help with your symptoms.

What Is Premenstrual Dysphoric Disorder?

PMDD is a condition similar to PMS that also happens in the week
or two before your period starts as hormone levels begin to fall after
ovulation. PMDD causes more severe symptoms than PMS, including
severe depression, irritability, and tension.

Who Gets Premenstrual Dysphoric Disorder

PMDD affects up to five percent of women of childbearing age. Many
women with PMDD may also have anxiety or depression.

What Are the Symptoms of Premenstrual Dysphoric Disorder?

Symptoms of PMDD include:

- Lasting irritability or anger that may affect other people
- Feelings of sadness or despair, or even thoughts of suicide
- Feelings of tension or anxiety
- Panic attacks
- Mood swings or crying often
- Lack of interest in daily activities and relationships
- Trouble thinking or focusing
- Tiredness or low energy

- Food cravings or binge eating

- Trouble sleeping

- Feeling out of control

- Physical symptoms, such as cramps, bloating, breast tenderness, headaches, and joint or muscle pain

What Causes Premenstrual Dysphoric Disorder

Researchers do not know for sure what causes PMDD or PMS. Hormonal changes throughout the menstrual cycle may play a role. A brain chemical called serotonin may also play a role in PMDD. Serotonin levels change throughout the menstrual cycle. Some women may be more sensitive to these changes.

How Is Premenstrual Dysphoric Disorder Diagnosed?

Your doctor will talk to you about your health history and do a physical examination. You will need to keep a calendar or diary of your symptoms to help your doctor diagnose PMDD.

You must have five or more PMDD symptoms, including one mood-related symptom, to be diagnosed with PMDD.

How Is Premenstrual Dysphoric Disorder Treated?

Treatments for PMDD include:

- Antidepressants called selective serotonin reuptake inhibitors (SSRIs). SSRIs change serotonin levels in the brain. The U.S. Food and Drug Administration (FDA) approved three SSRIs to treat PMDD:

  - Sertraline

  - Fluoxetine

  - Paroxetine HCI

- Birth control pills. The U.S. Food and Drug Administration (FDA) has approved a birth control pill containing drospirenone and ethinyl estradiol, to treat PMDD.

- Over-the-counter (OTC) pain relievers may help relieve physical symptoms, such as cramps, joint pain, headaches, backaches, and breast tenderness. These include:

  - Ibuprofen

  - Naproxen

  - Aspirin

- Stress management, such as relaxation techniques and spending time on activities you enjoy

Making healthy changes, such as eating a healthy combination of foods across the food groups, cutting back on salty and sugary foods, and getting more physical activity, may also help relieve some PMDD symptoms. But PMDD can be serious enough that some women should go to a doctor or nurse to discuss treatment options. And, if you are thinking of hurting yourself or others, call 911 right away.

Section 43.7

Premenstrual Syndrome

This section includes text excerpted from "Premenstrual Syndrome (PMS)," Office on Women's Health (OWH), U.S. Department of Health and Human Services (HHS), March 16, 2018.

Premenstrual syndrome (PMS) is a combination of symptoms that many women get about a week or two before their period. Most women, over 90 percent, say they get some premenstrual symptoms, such as bloating, headaches, and moodiness. For some women, these symptoms may be so severe that they miss work or school, but other women are not bothered by milder symptoms. On average, women in their 30s are most likely to have PMS. Your doctor can help you find ways to relieve your symptoms.

What Is Premenstrual Syndrome?

PMS is a combination of physical and emotional symptoms that many women get after ovulation and before the start of their menstrual period. Researchers think that PMS happens in the days after ovulation because estrogen and progesterone levels begin falling dramatically if you are not pregnant. PMS symptoms go away within a few days after a woman's period starts as hormone levels begin rising again.

Some women get their periods without any signs of PMS or only very mild symptoms. For others, PMS symptoms may be so severe that it makes it hard to do everyday activities like going to work or school. Severe PMS symptoms may be a sign of premenstrual dysphoric disorder (PMDD). PMS goes away when you no longer get a period, such as after menopause. After pregnancy, PMS might come back, but you might have different PMS symptoms.

Who Gets Premenstrual Syndrome

As many as three in four women say they get PMS symptoms at some point in their lifetime. For most women, PMS symptoms are mild. Less than five percent of women of childbearing age get a more severe form of PMS, called PMDD.

PMS may happen more often in women who:

- Have high levels of stress

- Have a family history of depression

- Have a personal history of either postpartum depression or depression

Does Premenstrual Syndrome Change with Age?

Yes. PMS symptoms may get worse as you reach your late 30s or 40s and approach menopause and are in the transition to menopause, called perimenopause.

This is especially true for women whose moods are sensitive to changing hormone levels during the menstrual cycle. In the years leading up to menopause, your hormone levels also go up and down in an unpredictable way as your body slowly transitions to menopause. You may get the same mood changes, or they may get worse.

PMS stops after menopause when you no longer get a period.

What Are the Symptoms of Premenstrual Syndrome?

PMS symptoms are different for every woman. You may get physical symptoms, such as bloating or gassiness, or emotional symptoms, such as sadness, or both. Your symptoms may also change throughout your life.

Physical symptoms of PMS can include:

- Swollen or tender breasts
- Constipation or diarrhea
- Bloating or a gassy feeling
- Cramping
- Headache or backache
- Clumsiness
- Lower tolerance for noise or light

Emotional or mental symptoms of PMS include:

- Irritability or hostile behavior
- Feeling tired
- Sleep problems (sleeping too much or too little)
- Appetite changes or food cravings
- Trouble with concentration or memory
- Tension or anxiety
- Depression, feelings of sadness, or crying spells
- Mood swings
- Less interest in sex

Talk to your doctor or nurse if your symptoms bother you or affect your daily life.

What Causes Premenstrual Syndrome

Researchers do not know exactly what causes PMS. Changes in hormone levels during the menstrual cycle may play a role. These changing hormone levels may affect some women more than others.

How Is Premenstrual Syndrome Diagnosed?

There is no single test for PMS. Your doctor will talk with you about your symptoms, including when they happen and how much they affect your life.

You probably have PMS if you have symptoms that:

- Happen in the five days before your period for at least three menstrual cycles in a row

- End within four days after your period starts

- Keep you from enjoying or doing some of your normal activities

- Keep track of which PMS symptoms you have and how severe they are for a few months. Write down your symptoms each day on a calendar or with an app on your phone. Take this information with you when you see your doctor.

How Does Premenstrual Syndrome Affect Other Health Problems?

About half of women who need relief from PMS also have another health problem, which may get worse in the time before their menstrual period. These health problems share many symptoms with PMS and include:

- **Depression and anxiety disorders.** These are the most common conditions that overlap with PMS. Depression and anxiety symptoms are similar to PMS and may get worse before or during your period.

- **Myalgic encephalomyelitis (ME)/chronic fatigue syndrome (CFS).** Some women report that their symptoms often get worse right before their period. Research shows that women with ME/CFS may also be more likely to have heavy menstrual bleeding and early or premature menopause.

- **Irritable bowel syndrome (IBS).** IBS causes cramping, bloating, and gas. Your IBS symptoms may get worse right before your period.

- **Bladder pain syndrome.** Women with bladder pain syndrome are more likely to have painful cramps during PMS.

PMS may also worsen some health problems, such as asthma, allergies, and migraines.

What Can You Do at Home to Relieve Premenstrual Syndrome Symptoms?

These tips will help you be healthier in general, and may relieve some of your PMS symptoms.

- **Get regular aerobic physical activity throughout the month.** Exercise can help with symptoms such as depression, difficulty concentrating, and fatigue.

- **Choose healthy foods most of the time.** Avoiding foods and drinks with caffeine, salt, and sugar in the two weeks before your period may lessen many PMS symptoms.

- **Get enough sleep.** Try to get about eight hours of sleep each night. Lack of sleep is linked to depression and anxiety and can make PMS symptoms such as moodiness worse.

- **Find healthy ways to cope with stress.** Talk to your friends or write in a journal. Some women also find yoga, massage, or meditation helpful.

- **Don't smoke.** In one large study, women who smoked reported more PMS symptoms and worse PMS symptoms than women who did not smoke.

What Medicines Can Treat Premenstrual Syndrome Symptoms?

Over-the-counter (OTC) and prescription medicines can help treat some PMS symptoms.

OTC pain relievers you can buy in most stores may help lessen physical symptoms, such as cramps, headaches, backaches, and breast tenderness. These include:

- Ibuprofen

- Naproxen

- Aspirin

Some women find that taking an OTC pain reliever right before their period starts lessens the amount of pain and bleeding they have during their period.

Prescription medicines may help if OTC pain medicines don't work:

- **Hormonal birth control** may help with the physical symptoms of PMS, but it may make other symptoms worse. You may need to try several different types of birth control before you find one that helps your symptoms.

- **Antidepressants** can help relieve emotional symptoms of PMS for some women when other medicines don't help. Selective serotonin reuptake inhibitors, or SSRIs, are the most common type of antidepressant used to treat PMS.

- **Diuretics** ("water pills") may reduce symptoms of bloating and breast tenderness.

- **Antianxiety medicine** may help reduce feelings of anxiousness.

All medicines have risks. Talk to your doctor or nurse about the benefits and risks.

Should You Take Vitamins or Minerals to Treat Premenstrual Syndrome Symptoms?

Maybe. Studies show that certain vitamins and minerals may help relieve some PMS symptoms. The U.S. Food and Drug Administration (FDA) does not regulate vitamins or mineral and herbal supplements in the same way they regulate medicines. Talk to your doctor before taking any supplement.

Studies have found benefits for:

- **Calcium.** Studies show that calcium can help reduce some PMS symptoms, such as fatigue, cravings, and depression. Calcium is found in foods such as milk, cheese, and yogurt. Some foods, such as orange juice, cereal, and bread, have calcium added (fortified). You can also take a calcium supplement.

- **Vitamin B$_6$.** Vitamin B$_6$ may help with PMS symptoms, including moodiness, irritability, forgetfulness, bloating, and anxiety. Vitamin B$_6$ can be found in foods such as fish, poultry, potatoes, fruit (except for citrus fruits), and fortified cereals. You can also take it as a dietary supplement.

Studies have found mixed results for:

- **Magnesium.** Magnesium may help relieve some PMS symptoms, including migraines. If you get menstrual migraines, talk to your doctor about whether you need more magnesium. Magnesium is found in green, leafy vegetables such as spinach, as well as in nuts, whole grains, and fortified cereals. You can also take a supplement.

- **Polyunsaturated fatty acids (omega-3 and omega-6).** Studies show that taking a supplement with one to two grams of polyunsaturated fatty acids may help reduce cramps and other PMS symptoms. Good sources of polyunsaturated fatty acids include flaxseed, nuts, fish, and green leafy vegetables.

What Complementary or Alternative Medicines May Help Relieve Premenstrual Syndrome Symptoms?

Some women report relief from their PMS symptoms with yoga or meditation. Others say herbal supplements help relieve symptoms. Talk with your doctor or nurse before taking any of these supplements. They may interact with other medicines you take, making your other medicine not work or cause dangerous side effects. The FDA does not regulate herbal supplements at the same level that it regulates medicines.

Some research studies show relief from PMS symptoms with these herbal supplements, but other studies do not. Many herbal supplements should not be used with other medicines. Some herbal supplements women use to ease PMS symptoms include:

- **Black cohosh.** The underground stems and root of black cohosh are used fresh or dried to make tea, capsules, pills, or liquid extracts. Black cohosh is most often used to help treat menopausal symptoms, and some women use it to help relieve PMS symptoms.

- **Chasteberry.** Dried ripe chasteberry is used to prepare liquid extracts or pills that some women take to relieve PMS symptoms. Women taking hormonal birth control or hormone therapy for menopause symptoms should not take chasteberry.

- **Evening primrose oil.** The oil is taken from the plant's seeds and put into capsules. Some women report that the pill helps relieve PMS symptoms, but the research results are mixed.

Section 43.8

Postpartum Depression and Postpartum Psychosis

This section includes text excerpted from "Postpartum Depression," Office on Women's Health (OWH), U.S. Department of Health and Human Services (HHS), August 28, 2018.

Your body and mind go through many changes during and after pregnancy. If you feel empty, emotionless, or sad all or most of the time for longer than two weeks during or after pregnancy, reach out for help. If you feel like you don't love or care for your baby, you might have postpartum depression. Treatment for depression, such as therapy or medicine, works and will help you and your baby be as healthy as possible in the future.

What Is Postpartum Depression?

"Postpartum" means the time after childbirth. Most women get the "baby blues," or feel sad or empty, within a few days of giving birth. For many women, the baby blues go away in three to five days. If your baby blues don't go away or you feel sad, hopeless, or empty for longer than two weeks, you may have postpartum depression. Feeling hopeless or empty after childbirth is not a regular or expected part of being a mother.

Postpartum depression is a serious mental illness that involves the brain and affects your behavior and physical health. If you have depression, then sad, flat, or empty feelings don't go away and can interfere with your day-to-day life. You might feel unconnected to your baby, as if you are not the baby's mother, or you might not love or care for the baby. These feelings can be mild to severe.

Mothers can also experience anxiety disorders during or after pregnancy.

How Common Is Postpartum Depression?

Depression is a common problem after pregnancy. One in nine new mothers has postpartum depression.

How Do You Know If You Have Postpartum Depression?

Some normal changes after pregnancy can cause symptoms similar to those of depression. Many mothers feel overwhelmed when a new baby comes home. But if you have any of the following symptoms of depression for more than two weeks, call your doctor, nurse, or midwife:

- Feeling restless or moody
- Feeling sad, hopeless, or overwhelmed
- Crying a lot
- Having thoughts of hurting the baby
- Having thoughts of hurting yourself
- Not having any interest in the baby, not feeling connected to the baby, or feeling as if your baby is someone else's baby
- Having no energy or motivation
- Eating too little or too much
- Sleeping too little or too much
- Having trouble focusing or making decisions
- Having memory problems
- Feeling worthless, guilty, or like a bad mother
- Losing interest or pleasure in activities you used to enjoy
- Withdrawing from friends and family
- Having headaches, aches, and pains, or stomach problems that don't go away

Some women don't tell anyone about their symptoms. New mothers may feel embarrassed, ashamed, or guilty about feeling depressed when they are supposed to be happy. They may also worry they will be seen as bad mothers. Any woman can become depressed during pregnancy or after having a baby. It doesn't mean you are a bad mom. You and your baby don't have to suffer. There is help. Your doctor can help you figure out whether your symptoms are caused by depression or something else.

What Causes Postpartum Depression

Hormonal changes may trigger symptoms of postpartum depression. When you are pregnant, levels of the female hormones estrogen and progesterone are the highest they'll ever be. In the first 24 hours after childbirth, hormone levels quickly drop back to normal, prepregnancy levels. Researchers think this sudden change in hormone levels may lead to depression. This is similar to hormone changes before a woman's period but involves much more extreme swings in hormone levels.

Levels of thyroid hormones may also drop after giving birth. The thyroid is a small gland in the neck that helps regulate how your body uses and stores energy from food. Low levels of thyroid hormones can cause symptoms of depression. A simple blood test can tell whether this condition is causing your symptoms. If so, your doctor can prescribe thyroid medicine.

Other feelings may contribute to postpartum depression. Many new mothers say they feel:

- Tired after labor and delivery
- Tired from a lack of sleep or broken sleep
- Overwhelmed with a new baby
- Doubts about their ability to be a good mother
- Stress from changes in work and home routines
- An unrealistic need to be a perfect mom
- Grief about loss of who they were before having the baby
- Less attractive
- A lack of free time

These feelings are common among new mothers. But postpartum depression is a serious health condition and can be treated. Postpartum depression is not a regular or expected part of being a new mother.

Are Some Women More at Risk of Postpartum Depression?

Yes. You may be more at risk of postpartum depression if you:

- Have a personal history of depression or bipolar disorder
- Have a family history of depression or bipolar disorder
- Do not have support from family and friends
- Were depressed during pregnancy
- Had problems with a previous pregnancy or birth

- Have relationship or money problems
- Are younger than twenty
- Have alcoholism, use illegal drugs, or have some other problem with drugs
- Have a baby with special needs
- Have difficulty breastfeeding
- Had an unplanned or unwanted pregnancy

The U.S. Preventive Services Task Force (USPSTF) recommends that doctors look for and ask about symptoms of depression during and after pregnancy, regardless of a woman's risk of depression.

What Is the Difference between "Baby Blues" and Postpartum Depression?

Many women have the baby blues in the days after childbirth. If you have the baby blues, you may:

- Have mood swings
- Feel sad, anxious, or overwhelmed
- Have crying spells
- Lose your appetite
- Have trouble sleeping

The baby blues usually go away in three to five days after they start. The symptoms of postpartum depression last longer and are more severe. Postpartum depression usually begins within the first month after childbirth, but it can begin during pregnancy or for up to a year after birth.

Postpartum depression needs to be treated by a doctor or nurse.

What Is Postpartum Psychosis?

Postpartum psychosis is rare. It happens in up to 4 new mothers out of every 1,000 births. It usually begins in the first two weeks after childbirth. It is a medical emergency. Women who have bipolar disorder or another mental-health condition called schizoaffective disorder have a higher risk of postpartum psychosis. Symptoms may include:

- Seeing or hearing things that aren't there

- Feeling confused most of the time
- Having rapid mood swings within several minutes (for example, crying hysterically, then laughing a lot, followed by extreme sadness)
- Trying to hurt yourself or your baby
- Paranoia (thinking that others are focused on harming you)
- Restlessness or agitation
- Behaving recklessly or in a way that is not normal for you

What Should You Do If You Have Symptoms of Postpartum Depression?

Call your doctor, nurse, midwife, or pediatrician if:

- Your baby blues don't go away after two weeks
- Symptoms of depression get more and more intense
- Symptoms of depression begin within one year of delivery and last more than two weeks
- It is difficult to work or get things done at home
- You cannot care for yourself or your baby (e.g., eating, sleeping, bathing)
- You have thoughts about hurting yourself or your baby

Ask your partner or a loved one to call for you if necessary. Your doctor, nurse, or midwife can ask you questions to test for depression. They can also refer you to a mental-health professional for help and treatment.

What Can You Do at Home to Feel Better While Seeing a Doctor for Postpartum Depression?

Here are some ways to begin feeling better or getting more rest, in addition to talking to a healthcare professional:

- Rest as much as you can. Sleep when the baby is sleeping.
- Don't try to do too much or to do everything by yourself. Ask your partner, family, and friends for help.
- Make time to go out, visit friends, or spend time alone with your partner.

- Talk about your feelings with your partner, supportive family members, and friends.

- Talk with other mothers so that you can learn from their experiences.

- Join a support group. Ask your doctor or nurse about groups in your area.

Don't make any major life changes right after giving birth. More major life changes in addition to a new baby can cause unneeded stress. Sometimes big changes can't be avoided. When that happens, try to arrange support and help in your new situation ahead of time.

It can also help to have a partner, a friend, or another caregiver who can help take care of the baby while you are depressed. If you are feeling depressed during pregnancy or after having a baby, don't suffer alone. Tell a loved one and call your doctor right away.

How Is Postpartum Depression Treated?

The common types of treatment for postpartum depression are:

- **Talk therapy.** This involves talking to a therapist, psychologist, or social worker to learn strategies to change how depression makes you think, feel, and act.

- **Medicine.** Your doctor or nurse can prescribe an antidepressant medicine. These medicines can help relieve symptoms of depression and some can be taken while you're breastfeeding. You can enter a medicine into the LactMed® database to find out whether the medicine passes through breastmilk and, if so, whether it has any possible side effects for your nursing baby.

- **Electroconvulsive therapy (ECT).** This can be used in extreme cases to treat postpartum depression.

These treatments can be used alone or together. Your depression can affect your baby. Getting treatment is important for you and your baby. Taking medicines for depression or going to therapy does not make you a bad mother or a failure. Getting help is a sign of strength. Talk with your doctor or nurse about the benefits and risks of taking medicine to treat depression when you are pregnant or breastfeeding.

What Can Happen If Postpartum Depression Is Not Treated?

Untreated postpartum depression can affect your ability to parent. You may:

- Not have enough energy
- Have trouble focusing on the baby's needs and your own needs
- Feel moody
- Not be able to care for your baby
- Have a higher risk of attempting suicide

Feeling like a bad mother can make depression worse. It is important to reach out for help if you feel depressed.

Researchers believe postpartum depression in a mother can affect her child throughout childhood, causing:

- Delays in language development and problems learning
- Problems with mother-child bonding
- Behavior problems
- More crying or agitation
- Shorter height and higher risk of obesity in preschoolers
- Problems dealing with stress and adjusting to school and other social situations

Chapter 44

Mental-Health Issues among Older Adults

Chapter Contents

Section 44.1

Mental Health and Aging

This section includes text excerpted from "Older Adults and Mental Health," National Institute of Mental Health (NIMH), March 2018.

It's just as important for an older person with symptoms of depression to seek treatment as it is for someone younger. The impact of depression on health in older adults can be severe: much research has reported that depression is associated with worse health in people with conditions like heart disease, diabetes, and stroke. Depression can complicate the treatment of these conditions, including making it more difficult for someone to care for her or himself and to seek treatment when needed. In older adults, depression may be disregarded as frailty, or it may be viewed as an inevitable result of life changes, chronic illness, and disability. Recognizing the signs and seeing a mental-health practitioner is the first step to getting treatment, which can make a real difference in someone's quality of life (QOL).

Warning Signs for Mental-Health Issues among Older Adults

If you are noticing any of the following signs then you must seek the help of a mental-health practitioner.

- Noticeable changes in mood, energy level, or appetite
- Feeling flat or having trouble feeling positive emotions
- Difficulty sleeping or sleeping too much
- Difficulty concentrating, feeling restless, or on edge
- Increased worry or feeling stressed
- Anger, irritability or aggressiveness
- Ongoing headaches, digestive issues, or pain
- A need for alcohol or drugs
- Sadness or hopelessness
- Suicidal thoughts
- Feeling flat or having trouble feeling positive emotions
- Engaging in high-risk activities

- Obsessive thinking or compulsive behavior

- Thoughts or behaviors that interfere with work, family, or social life

- Unusual thinking or behaviors that concern other people

Section 44.2

Alzheimer Disease among Older Adults

This section includes text excerpted from "Alzheimer's Disease," Centers for Disease Control and Prevention (CDC), May 2013. Reviewed December 2018.

What Is Alzheimer Disease?

Alzheimer disease (AD) is:

- The most common type of dementia

- A progressive disease beginning with mild memory loss possibly leading to loss of the ability to carry on a conversation and respond to the environment

- Involves parts of the brain that control thought, memory, and language

- Can seriously affect a person's ability to carry out daily activities

Although scientists are learning more every day, right now, they still do not know what causes AD.

Who Has Alzheimer Disease

In 2014, as many as five million Americans were living with AD. Younger people may get AD, but it is less common. The number of people living with the disease doubles every 5 years beyond age 65. This number is projected to nearly triple to 14 million people by 2060. The symptoms of the disease can first appear after age 60 and the risk increases with age.

What Is Known about Alzheimer Disease?

Scientists do not yet fully understand what causes AD. There probably is not one single cause, but several factors that affect each person differently.

- **Age** is the best-known risk factor for AD.

- **Family history.** Researchers believe that genetics may play a role in developing AD.

- **Changes in the brain** can begin years before the first symptoms appear.

Researchers are studying whether education, diet, and environment play a role in developing AD. Scientists are finding more evidence that some of the risk factors for heart disease and stroke, such as high blood pressure and high cholesterol may also increase the risk of AD. There is growing evidence that physical, mental, and social activities may reduce the risk of AD.

How Do You Know If It's Alzheimer Disease?

AD is not a normal part of aging. Memory problems are typically one of the first warning signs of cognitive loss.

According to the National Institute on Aging (NIA), in addition to memory problems, someone with AD may experience one or more of the following signs:

- Memory loss that disrupts daily life, such as getting lost in a familiar place or repeating questions

- Trouble handling money and paying bills

- Difficulty completing familiar tasks at home, at work or at leisure

- Decreased or poor judgment

- Misplaces things and being unable to retrace steps to find them

- Changes in mood, personality, or behavioral

If you or someone you know has several or even most of the signs listed above, it does not mean that you or they have AD. It is important to consult a mental-healthcare provider when you or someone you know has concerns about memory loss, thinking skills, or behavioral changes.

- Some causes for symptoms, such as depression and drug interactions, are reversible. However, they can be serious and should be identified and treated by a mental-healthcare provider as soon as possible.

- Early and accurate diagnosis provides opportunities for you and your family to consider or review financial planning, develop advance directives, enroll in clinical trials, and anticipate care needs.

How Is Alzheimer Disease Treated?

Medical management can improve the quality of life (QOL) for individuals living with AD and their caregivers. As of now there is no known cure for AD.

Treatment addresses several different areas:

- Helping people maintain mental function

- Managing behavioral symptoms

- Slowing or delaying the symptoms of the disease

Support for Family and Friends

At present, many people living with AD are cared for at home by family members.

Caregiving can have positive aspects for the caregiver as well as the person being cared for. It may bring personal fulfillment to the caregiver, such as satisfaction from helping a family member or friend, and lead to the development of new skills and improved family relationships.

Although most people willingly provide care to their loved ones and friends, caring for a person with AD at home can be a difficult task and might become overwhelming at times. Each day brings new challenges as the caregiver copes with changing levels of ability and new patterns of behavior. As the disease gets worse, people living with AD often need more intensive care.

What Is the Burden of Alzheimer Disease in the United States?

Alzheimer disease is:

- One of the top ten leading causes of death in the United States.

- The sixth leading cause of death among U.S. adults.

- The fifth leading cause of death among adults aged sixty-five years or older.

In 2014, an estimated 5 million Americans aged 65 years or older had AD. This number is projected to nearly triple to 14 million people by 2060.

In 2010, the costs of treating AD were projected to fall between $159 and $215 billion. By 2040, these costs are projected to jump to between $379 and more than $500 billion annually.

Death rates for AD are increasing, unlike heart disease and cancer death rates that are on the decline. Dementia, including AD, has been shown to be underreported in death certificates, and therefore, the proportion of older people who die from Alzheimer may be considerably higher.

Section 44.3

Depression in Late Life

This section includes text excerpted from "Depression and Older Adults," National Institute on Aging (NIA), National Institutes of Health (NIH), May 1, 2017.

Depression is more than just feeling sad or blue. It is a common but serious mood disorder that needs treatment. It causes severe symptoms that affect how you feel, think, and handle daily activities, such as sleeping, eating, and working.

When you have depression, you have trouble with daily life for weeks at a time. Doctors call this condition "depressive disorder" or "clinical depression."

Depression is a real illness. It is not a sign of a person's weakness or a character flaw. You can't "snap out of" clinical depression. Most people who experience depression need treatment to get better.

Depression Is Not a Normal Part of Aging

Depression is a common problem among older adults, but it is not a normal part of aging. In fact, studies show that most older adults feel satisfied with their lives, despite having more illnesses or physical problems. However, important life changes that happen as we get older may cause feelings of uneasiness, stress, and sadness.

For instance, the death of a loved one, moving from work into retirement, or dealing with a serious illness can leave people feeling sad or anxious. After a period of adjustment, many older adults can regain their emotional balance, but others do not and may develop depression.

Recognizing Symptoms of Depression in Older Adults

Depression in older adults may be difficult to recognize because they may show different symptoms than younger people. For some older adults with depression, sadness is not their main symptom. They may have other, less obvious symptoms of depression, or they may not be willing to talk about their feelings. Therefore, doctors may be less likely to recognize that their patient has depression.

Sometimes older people who are depressed appear to feel tired, have trouble sleeping, or seem grumpy and irritable. Confusion or attention problems caused by depression can sometimes look like Alzheimer disease (AD) or other brain disorders. Older adults also may have more medical conditions, such as heart disease, stroke, or cancer, which may cause depressive symptoms. Or they may be taking medications with side effects that contribute to depression.

Types of Depression

There are several types of depressive disorders.

Major depression involves severe symptoms that interfere with the ability to work, sleep, study, eat, and enjoy life. An episode can occur only once in a person's lifetime, but more often, a person has several episodes.

Persistent depressive disorder (PDD) is a depressed mood that lasts for at least two years. A person diagnosed with persistent depressive disorder (PDD) may have episodes of major depression along with periods of less severe symptoms, but symptoms must last for two years to be considered PDD.

Other forms of depression include psychotic depression, postpartum depression, and seasonal affective disorder (SAD).

Causes and Risk Factors for Depression

Several factors, or a combination of factors, may contribute to depression.

- **Genes.** People with a family history of depression may be more likely to develop it than those whose families do not have the illness.

- **Personal history.** Older adults who had depression when they were younger are more at risk for developing depression in late life than those who did not have the illness earlier in life.

- **Brain chemistry.** People with depression may have different brain chemistry than those without the illness.

- **Stress.** Loss of a loved one, a difficult relationship, or any stressful situation may trigger depression.

Vascular Depression

For older adults who experience depression for the first time later in life, the depression may be related to changes that occur in the brain and body as a person ages. For example, older adults may suffer from restricted-blood flow, a condition called ischemia. Over time, blood vessels may stiffen and prevent blood from flowing normally to the body's organs, including the brain.

If this happens, an older adult with no family history of depression may develop what is sometimes called "vascular depression." Those with vascular depression also may be at risk for heart disease, stroke, or other vascular illness.

Depression Can Co-Occur with Other Illnesses

Depression, especially in middle-aged or older adults, can co-occur with other serious medical illnesses such as diabetes, cancer, heart disease, and Parkinson disease (PD). Depression can make these conditions worse and vice versa. Sometimes medications taken for these physical illnesses may cause side effects that contribute to depression. A doctor experienced in treating these complicated illnesses can help work out the best treatment strategy.

All these factors can cause depression to go undiagnosed or untreated in older people. Yet, treating the depression will help an older adult better manage other conditions she or he may have.

Common Symptoms of Depression

There are many symptoms associated with depression, and some will vary depending on the individual. However, some of the most common symptoms are listed below. If you have several of these symptoms for more than two weeks, you may have depression.

- Persistent sad, anxious, or "empty" mood
- Feelings of hopelessness, guilt, worthlessness, or helplessness
- Irritability, restlessness, or having trouble sitting still
- Loss of interest in once pleasurable activities, including sex
- Decreased energy or fatigue
- Moving or talking more slowly
- Difficulty concentrating, remembering, making decisions
- Difficulty sleeping, early-morning awakening, or oversleeping
- Eating more or less than usual, usually with unplanned-weight gain or loss
- Thoughts of death or suicide, or suicide attempts
- Aches or pains, headaches, cramps, or digestive problems without a clear physical cause and/or that do not ease with treatment
- Frequent crying

Treatments for Depression

Depression, even severe depression, can be treated. If you think you may have depression, start by making an appointment to see your doctor or mental-healthcare provider. This could be your primary doctor or a provider who specializes in diagnosing and treating mental-health conditions (a psychologist or psychiatrist). Certain medications and some medical conditions can cause the same symptoms as depression. A doctor can rule out these possibilities by doing a physical exam, interview, and lab tests. If the doctor can find no medical condition that may be causing the depression, the next step is a psychological evaluation.

Treatment choices differ for each person, and sometimes multiple treatments must be tried to find one that works. It is important to keep trying until you find something that works for you.

The most common forms of treatment for depression are medication and psychotherapy.

Therapy for Depression

Psychotherapy, also called "talk therapy," can help people with depression. Some treatments are short term, lasting 10 to 20 weeks; others are longer, depending on the person's needs.

Cognitive-behavioral therapy (CBT) is one type of talk therapy used to treat depression. It focuses on helping people change negative thinking and any behaviors that may be making depression worse. Interpersonal therapy can help an individual understand and work through troubled relationships that may cause the depression or make it worse. Other types of talk therapy, like problem-solving therapy, can be helpful for people with depression.

Medications for Depression

Antidepressants are medicines that treat depression. There are many different types of antidepressants. They may help improve the way your brain uses certain chemicals that control mood or stress. You may need to try several different antidepressant medicines before finding one that improves your symptoms and has manageable side effects.

Antidepressants take time, usually two to four weeks, to work. Often symptoms such as sleep, appetite, and concentration problems improve before mood lifts, so it is important to give the medication a chance to work before deciding whether it works for you.

If you begin taking antidepressants, do not stop taking them without the help of a doctor. Sometimes people taking antidepressants feel better and then stop taking the medication on their own, but then the depression returns. When you and your doctor have decided it is time to stop the medication, usually after 6 to 12 months, the doctor will help you slowly and safely decrease your dose. Stopping antidepressants abruptly can cause withdrawal symptoms.

Most antidepressants are generally safe, but the U.S. Food and Drug Administration (FDA) requires that all antidepressants carry black box warnings, the strictest warnings for prescriptions. The warning says that patients of all ages taking antidepressants should be watched closely, especially during the first few weeks of treatment. Talk to your doctor about any side effects of your medication that you should watch for.

For older adults who are already taking several medications for other conditions, it is important to talk with a doctor about any adverse drug interactions that may occur while taking antidepressants.

Do not use herbal medicines such as St. John's wort before talking with your healthcare provider. It should never be combined with a prescription antidepressant, and you should not use it to replace conventional care or to postpone seeing a healthcare provider.

Preventing Depression

What can be done to lower the risk of depression?

How can people cope?

There are a few steps you can take. Try to prepare for major changes in life, such as retirement or moving from your home of many years. Stay in touch with family. Let them know when you feel sad.

Regular exercise may also help prevent depression or lift your mood if you are depressed. Pick something you like to do. Being physically fit and eating a balanced diet may help avoid illnesses that can bring on disability or depression.

Chapter 45

Lesbian, Gay, Bisexual, and Transsexual Mental-Health Issues

Chapter Contents

Section 45.1

Mental Health and Gay and Bisexual Men

This section includes text excerpted from "Gay and Bisexual Men's Health—Mental Health," Centers for Disease Control and Prevention (CDC), February 29, 2016.

The majority of gay and bisexual men have and maintain good mental health, even though research has shown that they are at greater risk for mental-health problems. Like everyone else, the majority of gay and bisexual men are able to cope successfully if connected to the right resources.

However, ongoing homophobia, stigma (negative and usually unfair beliefs), and discrimination (unfairly treating a person or group of people) can have negative effects on your health. Research also shows that, compared to other men, gay and bisexual men have higher chances of having:

- Major depression

- Bipolar disorder

- Generalized anxiety disorder (GAD)

Gay and bisexual men may also face other health threats that usually happen along with mental-health problems. These include more use of illegal drugs and a greater risk for suicide. Gay and bisexual men are more likely than other men to have tried to commit suicide as well as to have succeeded at suicide. Human immunodeficiency virus (HIV) is another issue that has had a huge impact on the mental health of gay and bisexual men. It affects men who are living with HIV; those who are at high risk, but HIV negative; and loved ones of those living with, or who have died from HIV.

Revealing Sexual Orientation

Keeping your sexual orientation hidden from others (being "in the closet") and fear of having your sexual orientation disclosed (being "outed") can add to the stress of being gay or bisexual. In general, research has shown that gay and bisexual men who are open about their sexual orientation with others have better health outcomes than gay and bisexual men who do not. However, being "out" in some settings and to people who react negatively can add to the stress experienced by gay and bisexual men, and can lead to poorer mental health and discrimination.

Keys to Maintaining Good Mental Health

Having a supportive group of friends and family members is often key to successfully dealing with the stress of day-to-day life and maintaining good mental health. If you are unable to get social support from your friends and families, you can try finding support by becoming involved in community, social, athletic, religious, and other groups. Mental-health counseling and support groups that are sensitive to the needs of gay and bisexual men can be especially useful if you are coming to terms with your sexual orientation or are experiencing depression, anxiety, or other mental-health problems.

While many gay, bisexual, and other men who have sex with men may not seek care from a mental-health provider because of a fear of discrimination or homophobia, it is important to keep this as an option and to find a provider that is trustworthy and compatible. The HIV Treatment Works Campaign also has helpful resources to address common issues and questions.

Section 45.2

Substance-Use Disorders and Lesbian, Gay, Bisexual, and Transsexual

This section includes text excerpted from "Substance Use and SUDs in LGBT Populations," National Institute on Drug Abuse (NIDA), September 2017.

People who identify as lesbian, gay, bisexual, or transgender (LGBT) often face social stigma, discrimination, and other challenges not encountered by people who identify as heterosexual. They also face a greater risk of harassment and violence. As a result of these and other stressors, sexual minorities are at increased risk for various behavioral-health issues.

Many federally-funded surveys have started to ask about sexual orientation and gender identification in their data collections. Surveys thus far have found that sexual minorities have higher rates of substance misuse and substance-use disorders (SUDs) than people who identify as heterosexual. Therefore, it is not yet possible to establish long-term trends about substance use and SUD prevalence in LGBT populations.

Substance Use and Misuse

According to 2015 data from the National Survey on Drug Use and Health (NSDUH), adults defined as "sexual minority" (in this survey, meaning lesbian, gay, or bisexual) were more than twice as likely as heterosexual adults (39.1 versus 17.1%) to have used any illicit drug in the past year. Nearly a third of sexual minority adults (30.7%) used marijuana in 2014, compared to 12.9 percent of heterosexual adults, and about 1 in 10 (10.4%) misused prescription pain relievers, compared to 4.5 percent of heterosexual adults.

A 2013 survey conducted by the U.S. Census Bureau (USCB) found that a higher percentage of LGBT adults between 18 and 64 reported being involved in binge drinking (five or more drinks on a single occasion) than heterosexual adults. LGBT people in treatment for SUDs initiated alcohol consumption earlier than their heterosexual counterparts.

Lesbian, gay, and bisexual adolescents also reported higher rates of substance use compared to heterosexual adolescents. In one meta-analysis, LGB adolescents were 90 percent more likely to use substances than heterosexual adolescents, and the difference was particularly pronounced in some subpopulations; bisexual adolescents used substances at 3.4 times the rate of heterosexual adolescents, and lesbian and bisexual females used at four times the rate of their heterosexual counterparts.

Substance-Use Disorders and Comorbidities

LGBT persons also have a greater likelihood than non-LGBT persons of experiencing a SUD in their lifetime, and they often enter treatment with more severe SUDs. Some common SUD treatment modalities have been shown to be effective for gay or bisexual men including motivational interviewing, social support therapy, contingency management, and cognitive-behavioral therapy (CBT).

Addiction treatment programs offering specialized groups for gay and bisexual men showed better outcomes for those clients compared to gay and bisexual men in nonspecialized programs; but in one study, only 7.4 percent of programs offered specialized services for LGBT patients. As of now, research is limited on rates of SUD among transgender populations, although research shows that transgender individuals are more likely to seek SUD treatment than the nontransgender population. Available research suggests that treatment should address unique factors in these patients' lives that may include homophobia and transphobia, family problems, violence, and social isolation.

Sexual minorities with SUDs are more likely to have additional (comorbid or co-occurring) psychiatric disorders. For example, gay and bisexual men and lesbian and bisexual women report greater odds of frequent mental distress and depression than their heterosexual counterparts. Transgender children and adolescents have higher levels of depression, suicidality, self-harm, and eating disorders than their nontransgender counterparts. Thus, it is particularly important that LGBT people in SUD treatment be screened for other psychiatric problems (as well as vice versa) and all identifiable conditions should be treated concurrently.

LGBT people are also at increased risks for human immunodeficiency virus (HIV) due to both intravenous drug use and risky sexual behaviors. HIV infection is particularly prevalent among gay and bisexual men (men who have sex with men, or MSM) and transgender women who have sex with men. SUD treatment can also help prevent HIV transmission among those at high risk. For example, addiction treatment is associated not only with reduced drug use but also with less risky sexual behavior among MSM, and those with HIV report improvements in viral load.

Chapter 46

Victims of Trauma and Disaster

Chapter Contents

Section 46.1

Abuse, Trauma, and Mental Health

This section includes text excerpted from "Abuse, Trauma, and Mental Health," Office on Women's Health (OWH), U.S. Department of Health and Human Services (HHS), August 28, 2018.

Abuse, whether physical, emotional, verbal, or sexual, can have long-term effects on your mental health. Trauma can affect how you feel about yourself and how you relate to others. Women who have gone through abuse or other trauma have a higher risk of developing a mental-health condition, such as depression, anxiety, or posttraumatic stress disorder (PTSD). Trauma and abuse are never your fault. You can get help to heal the physical, mental, and emotional scars of trauma and abuse.

How Are Abuse and Trauma Related to Mental Health?

Trauma can happen after you experience an event or events that hurt you physically or emotionally. Trauma can have lasting effects on your mental, physical, and emotional health. Experiencing abuse or other trauma puts people at risk of developing mental-health conditions, such as:

- Anxiety disorders

- Depression

- PTSD

- Misusing alcohol or drugs

- Borderline personality disorder (BPD)

Abuse may have happened during childhood or as an adult. It can be emotional, verbal, physical, or sexual. Trauma can include dangerous, frightening, or extremely stressful situations or events, such as sexual assault, war, an accident or natural disaster, the sudden or violent death of a close loved one, or a serious physical health problem.

The long-term effects of abuse or trauma can include:

- Severe anxiety, stress, or fear

- Abuse of alcohol or drugs

- Depression

- Eating disorders

- Self-injury

- Suicide

How Can Being in the Military Affect My Mental Health?

If you were or are in the military, you may have experienced or witnessed a life-threatening event. You may have been on missions that exposed you to traumatic combat-related experiences, such as incoming fire, explosive devices, or dead bodies. Other military experiences, like military sexual trauma, can also affect mental health.

About one in four veterans of the wars in Iraq and Afghanistan has been diagnosed with a mental-health condition, such as PTSD, depression, and anxiety. Left untreated, mental-health issues can cause long-term problems for you, your family, and your community. Reach out to someone for help if you're experiencing the signs of a mental-health condition.

What Is Military Sexual Trauma?

Military sexual trauma (MST) is a term used by the U.S. Department of Veterans Affairs (VA) to describe sexual assault or repeated, threatening sexual harassment that happens while the victim is in the military. MST can happen to both men and women, but female service members are at higher risk of MST. MST can also lead to depression, PTSD, and substance abuse. Studies show that one in four or five women in the military experiences MST.

MST can happen during war, peace, or training. It can happen between people of the same sex or different sexes. If you've experienced MST, you may feel fear, shame, anger, embarrassment, or guilt. You may have trouble trusting people. You may even have physical symptoms like headaches, diarrhea, chronic fatigue, or gynecological problems.

When you're actively serving, it can be difficult to report or talk about MST. The U.S. Department of Defense (DoD) has two ways for you to report an assault if you are on active duty:

- **Restricted reporting** lets you confidentially report the assault to someone and get medical treatment and counseling, but it won't trigger an actual investigation. This is intended to make it easier to report an assault and to give you time to heal mentally and physically. You can decide later if you want the military to begin a criminal investigation.

- **Unrestricted reporting** means that you will still receive medical treatment and counseling, but the assault will be reported through your chain of command. It will trigger an investigation.

If you have been assaulted or are unsure about what to do, you can call a confidential helpline that works specifically with the DoD community at the Safe Helpline. Call 877-995-5247, or visit safehelpline.org.

If you have experienced MST, you can also contact your nearest VA facility to speak with the MST coordinator. VA facilities have healthcare providers who are trained to treat the effects of MST. Many have specialized outpatient mental-health services focusing on sexual trauma.

How Do You Know If Your Mental Health Is Affected by past Abuse or Trauma?

It can be difficult to tell whether or how much your mental health is affected by past abuse or trauma. Sometimes the symptoms of trauma or abuse don't start to affect your life for many months or years after the event took place. If you have any of the following symptoms, talk to your doctor or nurse or reach out for help:

- Anxiety

- Trouble sleeping

- Anger

- Depression

- Changes in mood or appetite

- Abusing drugs or alcohol

What Should You Do If You have Been Abused or Traumatized?

The sooner you can get professional help for abuse or trauma, the sooner you can begin to get better. If you have been physically hurt, visit a hospital or doctor right away. You may also need to call the police. The doctor and the police can help document what has happened to you. This documentation may be important later if you decide to press charges against someone who attacked you.

If you are experiencing changes in how you think, feel, or behave that are interfering with your ability to work or live your life normally, reach out to a mental-health professional. Find a mental-health professional near you. A mental-health professional can help make sense of any symptoms you may be having that are related to your abuse or trauma. The professional can help you find the best kinds of treatment to help manage symptoms of the abuse or trauma.

If you're in immediate danger, **call 911.**

You can also call helplines to talk about what happened to you or get guidance about what to do:

- **National Domestic Violence Hotline**

    Phone number: 800-799-7233

- **National Sexual Assault Hotline**

    Phone number: 800-656-4673

- **Safe Helpline** (for members of the military)

    Phone number: 877-995-5247

Abuse or trauma you have suffered is not your fault. You can get better with treatment.

How Are Abuse and Trauma Treated?

Symptoms caused by abuse or trauma can usually be treated with different types of talk therapy, medicine, or both. Therapy with a professional counselor can help you work through your feelings and learn healthy ways to cope. Medicines might include antidepressants or antianxiety medicine.

Now a days, complementary mind and body therapies, such as mindfulness and yoga, may be offered along with traditional treatments such as medicines and therapy.

Section 46.2

Coping with Traumatic Events

This section includes text excerpted from "Coping with
Traumatic Events," National Institute of Mental
Health (NIMH), February 2017.

A traumatic event is a shocking, scary, or dangerous experience that
affects someone emotionally. These situations may be natural, like a
tornado or earthquake. They can also be caused by other people, like
a car accident, crime, or terror attack.

How individuals respond to traumatic events is an important
area of research for the National Institute of Mental Health (NIMH).
Researchers are exploring the factors that help people cope as well as
the factors that increase their risk for problems following the event.

Warning Signs

There are many different responses to potentially traumatic events.
Most people have intense responses immediately following, and often
for several weeks or even months after, a traumatic event. These
responses can include:

- Feeling anxious, sad, or angry

- Trouble concentrating and sleeping

- Continually thinking about what happened

For most people, these are normal and expected responses and
generally lessen with time. Healthy ways of coping in this time period
include avoiding alcohol and other drugs, spending time with loved
ones and trusted friends who are supportive, trying to maintain normal
routines for meals, exercise, and sleep. In general, staying active is a
good way to cope with stressful feelings.

However, in some cases, the stressful thoughts and feelings after a
trauma continue for a long time and interfere with everyday life. For
people who continue to feel the effects of the trauma, it is important
to seek professional help. Some signs that an individual may need
help include:

- Worrying a lot or feeling very anxious, sad, or fearful

- Crying often

- Having trouble thinking clearly
- Having frightening thoughts, reliving the experience
- Feeling angry
- Having nightmares or difficulty sleeping
- Avoiding places or people that bring back disturbing memories and responses.

Physical responses to trauma may also mean that an individual needs help. Physical symptoms may include:

- Headaches
- Stomach pain and digestive issues
- Feeling tired
- Racing heart and sweating
- Being very jumpy and easily startled

Those who already had mental-health problems or who have had traumatic experiences in the past, who are faced with ongoing stress, or who lack support from friends and family may be more likely to develop stronger symptoms and need additional help. Some people turn to alcohol or other drugs to cope with their symptoms. Although substance use can temporarily cover up symptoms, it can also make life more difficult.

Mental-health problems can be treated. If you or someone you know needs help, talk with your mental-healthcare provider.

Section 46.3

Disaster Survivors and Mental Health

This section includes text excerpted from "Recovering from
Disasters," Substance Abuse and Mental Health Services
Administration (SAMHSA), October 1, 2018.

Disaster Reactions

Disasters, both natural and human-caused, affect people and
communities in different ways. As you begin to rebuild and recover,
remember that it is very common for disaster survivors to have reactions to their experiences. Disaster survivors may show physical and
emotional signs of stress, and disasters may affect them financially.
Sadness, grief, and anger are just some of the common emotions survivors may experience. Reactions to the disaster may occur not only
in people with direct experience of a disaster but also in those who
were indirectly affected through repeated exposure to media coverage
of the incident.

Most disaster survivors are resilient and will recover with no additional assistance. However, some people may need a little extra help
during the recovery process. Certain groups or populations may be at
greater risk for developing severe reactions to a disaster or traumatic
event.

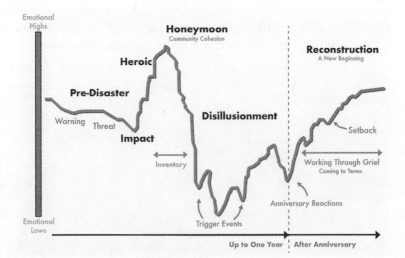

Figure 46.1. *Phases of Disaster*

Phases of Disaster

Phase 1. The predisaster phase is characterized by fear and uncertainty. The specific reactions a community experiences depend on the type of disaster. Disasters with no warning can cause feelings of vulnerability and lack of security; fears of future, unpredicted tragedies; and a sense of loss of control or the loss of the ability to protect yourself and your family. On the other hand, disasters with warning can cause guilt or self-blame for failure to heed the warnings. The predisaster phase may be as short as hours, or even minutes, such as during a terrorist attack, or it may be as long as several months, such as during a hurricane season.

Phase 2. The impact phase is characterized by a range of intense emotional reactions. As with the predisaster phase, the specific reactions also depend on the type of disaster that is occurring. Slow, low-threat disasters have psychological effects that are different from those of rapid, dangerous disasters. As a result, these reactions can range from shock to overt panic. Initial confusion and disbelief typically are followed by a focus on self-preservation and family protection. The impact phase is usually the shortest of the six phases of a disaster.

Phase 3. The heroic phase is characterized by a high level of activity with a low level of productivity. During this phase, there is a sense of altruism, and many community members exhibit adrenaline-induced rescue behavior. As a result, risk assessment may be impaired. The heroic phase often passes quickly into phase 4.

Phase 4. The honeymoon phase is characterized by a dramatic shift in emotion. During the honeymoon phase, disaster assistance is readily available. Community bonding occurs. Optimism exists that everything will return to normal quickly. As a result, numerous opportunities are available for providers and organizations to establish and build rapport with affected people and groups, and for them to build relationships with stakeholders. The honeymoon phase typically lasts only a few weeks.

Phase 5. The disillusionment phase is a stark contrast to the honeymoon phase. During the disillusionment phase, communities and individuals realize the limits of disaster assistance. As optimism turns to discouragement and stress continues to take a toll, negative reactions, such as physical exhaustion or substance use, may begin to surface. The increasing gap between need and assistance leads to

473

feelings of abandonment. Especially as the larger community returns to business as usual, there may be an increased demand for services, as individuals and communities become ready to accept support. The disillusionment phase can last months and even years. It is often extended by one or more trigger events, usually including the anniversary of the disaster.

Phase 6. The reconstruction phase is characterized by an overall feeling of recovery. Individuals and communities begin to assume responsibility for rebuilding their lives, and people adjust to a new "normal" while continuing to grieve losses. The reconstruction phase often begins around the anniversary of the disaster and may continue for some time beyond that. Following catastrophic events, the reconstruction phase may last for years.

Chapter 47

Mental-Health Issues among Minority and Immigrant Populations

Chapter Contents

Section 47.1

Mental Health and Minority Populations

This section includes text excerpted from "Minorities and Mental
Health: Moving beyond Stigma," National Institute on Minority
Health and Health Disparities (NIMHD), July 13, 2017.

Demographic trends in the United States have continued to change
rapidly. Projections indicate that within the next 30 years, the majority
of the United States will be non-White. Among the racial and ethnic
groups that will make up the majority, there is significant heteroge-
neity, making healthcare delivery even more challenging.

Mental illness is one of the most prevalent health problems in the
United States and one of the most taxing on the healthcare system. In
addition, mental illness carries the highest disease burden among all
diseases, with devastating effects on daily functioning; personal, social,
and occupational impairment; and premature death if left untreated.
One in ten children and one in five adults are affected by mental
illness.

Mental illness does not discriminate. It occurs in all racial, ethnic,
and socioeconomic groups and is the leading cause of disability in the
United States. However, two-thirds of individuals with a diagnosable
mental-health disorder do not seek treatment. Most ethnic minorities have similar prevalence rates of mental-health issues to those of
Whites, but they have less access to mental-health services, are less
likely to seek and receive needed care, and, when they do receive it, are
more likely to get poorer-quality care. This combination of disparities
leads to racial and ethnic minorities having a higher proportion of
unmet mental-healthcare needs compared with majority populations.

In 1999, health disparities in mental health were highlighted in the
U.S. Surgeon General's report on mental health. Dr. David Satcher,
former U.S. Surgeon General, called on all Americans to educate themselves and challenge the stigma, attitudes, fear, and misunderstanding
that remain barriers to truly addressing mental illness. In 2008, in an
effort to sustain dialogue on mental health in minority populations, the
U.S. House of Representatives established July as National Minority
Mental Health Awareness Month.

"Brother, You're on My Mind," created as a partnership between
Omega Psi Phi Fraternity, Inc., and the National Institute on Minority
Health and Health Disparities (NIMHD), is an example of an initiative
designed to increase awareness about mental health among African

American men. The focus of the initiative is on starting a conversation to dispel the myths associated with mental-health problems and assert the importance of seeking treatment. Expectations that men be "tough," coupled with poor access to mental-health services, leave men of color who struggle with mental illness especially susceptible to substance abuse, homelessness, incarceration, and homicide.

Particularly for populations of color, existing stigmas and the lack of discussion on mental health are major barriers to individuals seeking proper treatment. It is important to remember that mental health is fundamental to overall health and well-being at every stage of life.

Section 47.2

Mental Health and African Americans

This section includes text excerpted from "Mental Health and African Americans," Office of Minority Health (OMH), U.S. Department of Health and Human Services (HHS), September 15, 2017.

Facts on African American Mental Health

- Poverty level affects mental-health status. African Americans living below the poverty level, as compared to those over twice the poverty level, are three times more likely to report psychological distress.

- African Americans are ten percent more likely to report having serious psychological distress than non-Hispanic whites.

- The death rate from suicide for African American men was more than four times greater than for African American women, in 2014.

- However, the suicide rate for African Americans is 70 percent lower than that of the non-Hispanic white population.

- A report from the U.S. Surgeon General found that from 1980 to 1995, the suicide rate among African Americans ages 10 to 14 increased 233 percent, as compared to 120 percent of non-Hispanic whites.

Mental-Health Status

Table 47.1. Serious Psychological Distress among Adults 18 Years of Age and Over, Percent, 2013–2014

Non-Hispanic Black	Non-Hispanic White	Non-Hispanic Black/Non-Hispanic White Ratio
3.4	3.2	1.1

(Source: CDC, 2016. Health United States, 2015.)

Table 47.2. Serious Psychological Distress among Adults 18 Years of Age and Over, Percent of Poverty Level, 2013–2014

	African American	Non-Hispanic White	African American/Non-Hispanic White Ratio
Below 100%	7.4	10.7	0.7
100% – less than 200%	3.5	6.5	0.5
200% – less than 400%	2.3	2.7	0.9

(Source: CDC, 2016. Health United States, 2015.)

Table 47.3. Percent of Population with Feelings of Sadness, Hopelessness, Worthlessness, or That Everything Is an Effort, All of the Time, among Persons 18 Years of Age and Over, 2014

	Non-Hispanic Black	Non-Hispanic White	Non-Hispanic Black/Non-Hispanic White Ratio
Sadness	3.6	2.4	1.5
Hopelessness	2.3	1.7	1.4
Worthlessness	1.7	1.5	1.1
Everything is an effort	9.5	5	1.9

(Source: CDC 2016. Summary Health Statistics: National Health Interview Survey: 2014.)

Table 47.4. Percent of Population with Feelings of Sadness, Hopelessness, Worthlessness, or That Everything Is an Effort All of the Time, among Men 18 Years of Age and Over, 2014

	Non-Hispanic Black Men	Non-Hispanic White Men	Non-Hispanic Black Men/Non-Hispanic White Men Ratio
Sadness	3.1	1.8	1.7
Hopelessness	2.1	1.5	1.4
Worthlessness	1.5	1.4	1.1
Everything is an effort	8.9	4.3	2.1

(Source: CDC 2016. Summary Health Statistics: National Health Interview Survey: 2014.)

Table 47.5. Percent of Population with Feelings of Sadness, Hopelessness, Worthlessness, or That Everything Is an Effort All of the Time, among Women 18 Years of Age and Over, 2014

	Non-Hispanic Black Women	Non-Hispanic White Women	Non-Hispanic Black Women/Non-Hispanic White Women Ratio
Sadness	3.9	2.9	1.3
Hopelessness	2.4	1.9	1.3
Worthlessness	1.8	1.6	1.1
Everything is an effort	9.9	5.8	1.7

(Source: CDC 2016. Summary Health Statistics: National Health Interview Survey: 2014.)

Table 47.6. Percent of Population with Feelings of Nervousness or Restlessness, among Persons 18 Years of Age and Over, 2014

	Non-Hispanic Black	Non-Hispanic White	Non-Hispanic Black/ Non-Hispanic White Ratio
Nervousness, all or most of the time	4	4.6	0.9
Restlessness, all or most of the time	5.4	6	0.9

(Source: CDC 2016. Summary Health Statistics: National Health Interview Survey: 2014.)

Death Rates

Table 47.7. Age-Adjusted Death Rates for Suicide, by Sex, Race and Hispanic Origin, 2014

	Non-Hispanic Black	Non-Hispanic White	Non-Hispanic Black/ Non-Hispanic White Ratio
Male	9.7	25.8	0.4
Female	2.1	7.5	0.3
Total	5.7	16.4	0.3

(Source: CDC, 2016. National Vital Statistic Report.)

Table 47.8. Age-Adjusted Death Rates for Suicide, by Race, 2014

African American	Non-Hispanic White	African American/Non-Hispanic White Ratio
5.5	16.4	0.3

(Source: CDC, 2016. Health United States, 2015.)

Table 47.9. Death Rates for Suicide, Age, Race and Hispanic Origin Men, 2014

	African American Men	Non-Hispanic White Men	African American Men/Non-Hispanic White Men Ratio
15–24 years	12	22.4	0.5
25–44 years	14.3	31.7	0.5
45–64 years	9.9	37.1	0.3

Table 47.9. Continued

	African American Men	Non-Hispanic White Men	African American Men/Non-Hispanic White Men Ratio
65 years and over	8.9	36.1	0.2
All ages	9.4	25.8	0.4

(Source: CDC, 2016. Health United States, 2015.)

Table 47.10. Death Rates for Suicide, Age, Race and Hispanic Origin Women, 2014

	African American Women	Non-Hispanic White Women	African American Women/Non-Hispanic White Women Ratio
15–24 years	2.6	5.4	0.5
25–44 years	2.9	9.8	0.3
45–64 years	2.7	12.6	0.2
65 years and over	1.3	5.8	0.2
All ages	2.1	7.5	0.3

(Source: CDC, 2016. Health United States, 2015.)

Adolescents

Table 47.11. Death Rates for Suicide: Ages 15 to 19, 2014

	Non-Hispanic Black	Non-Hispanic White	Non-Hispanic Black/Non-Hispanic White Ratio
Male	6.8	16.6	0.4
Female	2.2	4.8	0.5
Total	4.5	10.9	0.4

(Source: CDC, 2016. National Center for Injury Prevention and Control. Web-Based Injury Statistics Query and Reporting System (WISQARS).)

Table 47.12. Suicidal Ideation among Students in Grades 9 to 12, 2015 Percent of Students Who Seriously Considered Suicide

	Non-Hispanic Black	Non-Hispanic White	Non-Hispanic Black/ Non-Hispanic White Ratio
Men	11	11.5	1
Women	18.7	22.8	0.8
Total	14.5	17.2	0.8

(Source: CDC 2016. High School Youth Risk Behavior Survey Data.)

Table 47.13. Suicidal Ideation among Students in Grades 9 to 12, 2015 Percent of Students Who Attempted Suicide

	Non-Hispanic Black	Non-Hispanic White	Non-Hispanic Black/ Non-Hispanic White Ratio
Men	7.2	3.7	1.9
Women	10.2	9.8	1
Total	8.9	6.8	1.3

(Source: CDC, 2016. High School Youth Risk Behavior Survey Data.)

Access to Healthcare

Table 47.14. Percent of Adults Age 18 and over Who Received Mental-Health Treatment or Counseling in 2014

	Non-Hispanic Black	Non-Hispanic White	Non-Hispanic Black/Non-Hispanic White Ratio
Total	9.4	18.8	0.5

(Source: SAMHSA, 2015. Results from the 2014 National Survey on Drug Use and Health: Mental Health Detailed Tables.)

Table 47.15. Percent of Adults Age 18 and over Who Received Prescription Medications for Mental-Health Treatment or Counseling, 2014

	Non-Hispanic Black	Non-Hispanic White	Non-Hispanic Black/ Non-Hispanic White Ratio
Total	6.6	15.7	0.4

(Source: SAMHSA, 2015. Results from the 2014 National Survey on Drug Use and Health: Mental Health Detailed Tables.)

Table 47.16. Adults Age 18 and over with past Year Major Depressive Episode Who Received Treatment for the Depression, 2012

Non-Hispanic Black	Non-Hispanic White	Non-Hispanic Black/ Non-Hispanic White Ratio
62.1	72	0.9

(Source: National Healthcare Quality and Disparities Reports.)

Section 47.3

Mental Health and American Indians/Alaska Natives

This section includes text excerpted from "Mental Health and American Indians/Alaska Natives," Office of Minority Health (OMH), U.S. Department of Health and Human Services (HHS), October 2, 2018.

Facts on Mental Health of American Indians and Alaska Natives

- In 2014, suicide was the second leading cause of death for American Indian and Alaska Natives between the ages of 10 and 34.

- In 2014, suicide was the leading cause of death for American Indian and Alaska Native girls between the ages of 10 and 14.

- American Indian and Alaska Natives are 50 percent more likely to experience feelings of nervousness or restlessness as compared to non-Hispanic whites.

- Violent deaths—unintentional injuries, homicide, and suicide—account for 75 percent of all mortality in the second decade of life for American Indian and Alaska Natives.

- While the overall death rate from suicide for American Indian and Alaska Natives is comparable to the White population, adolescent American Indian and Alaska Native females have death rates at almost four times the rate for White females in the same age groups.

Mental-Health Status

Table 47.17. Serious Psychological Distress among Adults 18 Years of Age and Over, Percent, 2013–2014

American Indian/Alaska Native	Non-Hispanic White	American Indian/Alaska Native/Non-Hispanic White Ratio
5.4	3.2	1.7

(Source: CDC, 2016. Health United States, 2015.)

Table 47.18. Percent of Population with Feelings of Sadness, Hopelessness, Worthlessness, or That Everything Is an Effort, All of the Time, among Persons 18 Years of Age and Over, 2014

	American Indian/ Alaska Native	Non-Hispanic White	American Indian/ Alaska Native/Non-Hispanic White Ratio
Sadness	4.4*	2.4	1.8
Hopelessness	2.5*	1.7	1.5
Worthlessness	2.4*	1.5	1.6
Everything is an effort	6.2	5	1.2

(Source: CDC 2016. Summary Health Statistics: National Health Interview Survey: 2014.)

Table 47.19. Percent of Population with Feelings of Nervousness or Restlessness, among Persons 18 Years of Age and Over, 2014

	American Indian/ Alaska Native	Non-Hispanic White	American Indian/ Alaska Native/Non-Hispanic White Ratio
Nervousness, all or most of the time	7.4	4.6	1.6
Restlessness, all or most of the time	9.2	6	1.5

(Source: CDC 2016. Summary Health Statistics: National Health Interview Survey: 2014.)

Death Rates

Table 47.20. Age-Adjusted Death Rates for Suicide, by Sex, Race and Hispanic Origin, 2014

	American Indian/ Alaska Native	Non-Hispanic White	American Indian/ Alaska Native/Non-Hispanic White Ratio
Male	16.4	25.8	0.6
Female	5.5	7.5	0.7
Total	10.9	16.4	0.7

(Source: CDC, 2016. National Vital Statistic Report.)

Table 47.21. Age-Adjusted Death Rates for Suicide, by Race, 2014

American Indian/Alaska Native	Non-Hispanic White	American Indian/Alaska Native/White Ratio
10.9	16.4	0.7

(Source: CDC, 2016. Health United States, 2015.)

Table 47.22. Death Rates for Suicide, Age, Race and Hispanic Origin Men, 2014

	American Indian/ Alaska Native Men	Non-Hispanic White Men	American Indian/ Alaska Native Men/ Non-Hispanic White Men Ratio
15–24 years	23.5	22.4	1
25–44 years	26.2	31.7	0.8
45–64 years	15.1	37.1	0.4
65 years and over	13.4	36.1	0.4
All ages	16.4	25.8	0.6

(Source: CDC, 2016. Health United States, 2015.)

Table 47.23. Death Rates for Suicide, Age, Race and Hispanic Origin Women, 2014

	American Indian/ Alaska Native Women	Non-Hispanic White Women	American Indian/ Alaska Native Women/Non-Hispanic White Women Ratio
15–24 years	9.6	5.4	1.8
25–44 years	9.7	9.8	1
45–64 years	—	12.6	—
65 years and over	—	5.8	—
All ages	5.5	7.5	0.7

(Source: CDC, 2016. Health United States, 2015.)

Adolescents

Table 47.24. Death Rates for Suicide: Ages 15 to 19, 2014

	American Indian/ Alaska Native	Non-Hispanic White	American Indian/ Alaska Native/ Non-Hispanic White Ratio
Male	31.7	16.6.	1.9
Female	18.2*	4.8	3.8
Total	25.1	10.9	2.3

(Source: CDC, 2016. National Center for Injury Prevention and Control. Web-based Injury Statistics Query and Reporting System (WISQARS).)

Table 47.25. Suicidal Ideation among Students in Grades 9 to 12, 2015 Percent of Students Who Seriously Considered Suicide

	American Indian/ Alaska Native	Non-Hispanic White	American Indian/Alaska Native/Non-Hispanic White Ratio
Men	—	11.5	—
Women	—	22.8	—
Total	20.9	17.2	1.2

(Source: CDC, 2016. High School Youth Risk Behavior Survey Data.)

Table 47.26. Suicidal Ideation among Students in Grades 9 to 12, 2015 Percent of Students Who Attempted Suicide

	American Indian/ Alaska Native	Non-Hispanic White	American Indian/ Alaska Native/ Non-Hispanic White Ratio
Men	—	3.7	—
Women	—	9.8	—
Total	15	6.8	2.2

(Source: CDC, 2016. High School Youth Risk Behavior Survey Data.)

Access to Healthcare

Table 47.27. Percent of Adults Who Received Mental-Health Treatment or Counseling in 2014

	American Indian/ Alaska Native	Non-Hispanic White	American Indian/ Alaska Native/ Non-Hispanic White Ratio
Total	14.1	18	0.8

(Source: SAMHSA, 2015. Results from the 2014 National Survey on Drug Use and Health: Mental Health Detailed Tables.)

Table 47.28. Percent of Adults Who Received Prescription Medications for Mental-Health Treatment or Counseling, 2014

	American Indian/ Alaska Native	Non-Hispanic White	American Indian/ Alaska Native/ Non-Hispanic White Ratio
Total	12.7	15.7	0.8

(Source: SAMHSA, 2015. Results from the 2014 National Survey on Drug Use and Health: Mental Health Detailed Tables.)

Section 47.4

Mental Health and Asian Americans

This section includes text excerpted from "Mental Health and Asian Americans," Office of Minority Health (OMH), U.S. Department of Health and Human Services (HHS), October 2, 2018.

Facts on Mental Health of Asian Americans

- Suicide was the ninth leading cause of death for Asian Americans, and the tenth leading cause of death for White Americans, in 2014.

- Southeast Asian refugees are at risk for posttraumatic stress disorder (PTSD) associated with trauma experienced before and after immigration to the United States. One study found that 70 percent of Southeast Asian refugees receiving mental healthcare were diagnosed with PTSD.

- For Asian Americans, the rate of serious psychological distress increases with lower levels of income, as it does in most other ethnic populations.

- The overall suicide rate for Asian Americans is half that of the White population.

Mental-Health Status

Table 47.29. Serious Psychological Distress among Adults 18 Years of Age and Over, Percent, 2009–2010

Asian American	Non-Hispanic White	Asian American/Non-Hispanic White Ratio
1.9	3.2	0.6

(Source: CDC, 2016. Health United States, 2015.)

Table 47.30. Serious Psychological Distress among Adults 18 Years of Age and Over, Percent of Poverty Level, 2012–2014

	Asian American	Non-Hispanic White	Asian American/Non-Hispanic White Ratio
Below 100%	4.1	10.2	0.4
100%–less than 200%	2.6	6.5	0.4
200% or greater	1.4	1.7	0.8

(Source: CDC. Health Data Interactive.)

Table 47.31. Percent of Population with Feelings of Sadness, Hopelessness, Worthlessness, or That Everything Is an Effort, All of the Time, among Persons 18 Years of Age and Over, 2014

	Asian American	Non-Hispanic White	Asian American/Non-Hispanic White Ratio
Sadness	2.4	2.4	1
Hopelessness	1.4	1.7	1
Worthlessness	0.6	1.5	0.4
Everything is an effort	3.3	5	0.7

(Source: CDC 2016. Summary Health Statistics: National Health Interview Survey: 2014.)

Table 47.32. Percent of Population with Feelings of Nervousness or Restlessness, among Persons 18 Years of Age and Over, 2010

	Asian American	Non-Hispanic White	Asian American/ Non-Hispanic White Ratio
Nervousness, all or most of the time	2.3	4.6	0.5
Restlessness, all or most of the time	3.7	6	0.6

(Source: CDC 2016. Summary Health Statistics: National Health Interview Survey: 2014.)

Table 47.33. Age-Adjusted Percent Distributions of Adults 18 Years of Age and Over, with Serious Psychological Distress, Most or All of the Time, 2004–2006

Population	Serious distress	Ratio/All Asian Population	Ratio/Whites
All Whites	2.9	—	—
All Asians	1.9	—	1.7
Chinese	1.6	0.8	0.6
Filipino	2.5	1.3	0.9
Asian Indian	1.4	0.7	0.5
Japanese	1.1	0.6	0.4
Vietnamese	2.5	1.3	0.9
Korean	1.3	0.7	0.4
Other Asian and NHOPI*	2.6	1.4	0.9

(Source: CDC, 2008. Health Characteristics of the Asian Adult Population: United States, 2004–2006.)

Death Rates

Table 47.34. Age-Adjusted Death Rates for Suicide, by Sex, Race and Hispanic Origin, 2013

	Asian/Pacific Islander	Non-Hispanic White	Asian/Pacific Islander/Non-Hispanic White Ratio
Male	8.9	25.8	0.3
Female	3.4	7.5	0.5
Total	6	16.4	0.4

(Source: CDC, 2008. Health Characteristics of the Asian Adult Population: United States, 2004-2006.)

Table 47.35. Age-Adjusted Death Rates for Suicide, by Race, 2014

Asian American	Non-Hispanic White	Asian American/Non-Hispanic White Ratio
6	16.4	0.4

(Source: CDC, 2016. Health United States, 2015.)

Table 47.36. Death Rates for Suicide, Age, Race and Hispanic Origin Men, 2014

	Asian American Men	Non-Hispanic White Men	Asian American Men/Non-Hispanic White Men Ratio
15–24 years	12.9	22.4	0.6
25–44 years	9.7	31.7	0.3
45–64 years	12.1	37.1	0.3
65 years and over	11.6	36.1	0.3
All ages	8.9	25.8	0.3

(Source: CDC, 2016. Health United States, 2015.)

Table 47.37. Death Rates for Suicide, Age, Race and Hispanic Origin Women, 2014

	Asian American Women	Non-Hispanic White Women	Asian American Women/Non-Hispanic White Women Ratio
15–24 years	4.1	5.4	0.8
25–44 years	4	9.8	0.4
45–64 years	4.2	12.6	0.3
65 years and over	5.2	5.8	0.9
All ages	3.4	7.5	0.5

(Source: CDC, 2016. Health United States, 2015.)

Adolescents

Table 47.38. Death Rates for Suicide: Ages 15 to 19, 2014

	Asian/Pacific Islander	Non-Hispanic White	Asian/Pacific Islander/Non-Hispanic White Ratio
Male	6.3	16.6	0.4
Female	5	4.8	1
Total	5.6	10.9	0.5

(Source: CDC, 2016. National Center for Injury Prevention and Control. Web-Based Injury Statistics Query and Reporting System (WISQARS).)

Table 47.39. Suicidal Ideation among Students in Grades 9 to 12, 2015 Percent of Students Who Seriously Considered Suicide

	Asian	Non-Hispanic White	Asian/Non-Hispanic White Ratio
Men	14.9	11.5	1.3
Women	21.3	22.8	0.9
Total	17.7	17.2	1

(Source: CDC, 2016. High School Youth Risk Behavior Survey Data.)

Table 47.40. Suicidal Ideation among Students in Grades 9 to12, 2015 Percent of Students Who Attempted Suicide

	Asian	Non-Hispanic White	Asian/Non-Hispanic White Ratio
Men	5.2	3.7	1.4
Women	11.1	9.8	1.1
Total	7.8	6.8	1.1

(Source: CDC, 2016. High School Youth Risk Behavior Survey Data.)

Access to Healthcare

Table 47.41. Percent of Adults Age 18 and over Who Received Mental-Health Treatment or Counseling in 2014

	Asian American	Non-Hispanic White	Asian American/ Non-Hispanic White Ratio
Total	6.8	18	0.4

(Source: SAMHSA, 2015. Results from the 2014 National Survey on Drug Use and Health: Mental Health Detailed Tables.)

Table 47.42. Percent of Adults Age 18 and over Who Received Prescription Medications for Mental-Health Treatment or Counseling, 2014

	Asian American	Non-Hispanic White	Asian American/ Non-Hispanic White Ratio
Total	4.9	15.7	0.3

(Source: SAMHSA, 2015. Results from the 2014 National Survey on Drug Use and Health: Mental Health Detailed Tables.)
Note: *NHOPI = Native Hawaiian or Other Pacific Islander.

Section 47.5

Mental Health and Hispanics

This section includes text excerpted from "Mental Health and Hispanics," Office of Minority Health (OMH), U.S. Department of Health and Human Services (HHS), February 24, 2017.

Facts on Mental Health of Hispanics

Poverty level affects mental-health status. Hispanics living below the poverty level, as compared to Hispanics over twice the poverty level, are over twice as likely to report psychological distress.

The death rate from suicide for Hispanic men was four times the rate for Hispanic women, in 2014.

However, the suicide rate for Hispanics is half that of the non-Hispanic white population.

Suicide attempts for Hispanic girls, grades 9 to 12, were 50 percent higher than for White girls in the same age group, in 2015.

Non-Hispanic whites received mental-health treatment two times more often than Hispanics, in 2014.

Mental-Health Status

Table 47.43. Serious Psychological Distress among Adults 18 Years of Age and Over, Percent, 2013–2014

Hispanic	Mexican American	Non-Hispanic White	Mexican/ Non-Hispanic White Ratio	Hispanic/ Non-Hispanic White Ratio
4.5	4.6	3.2	1.4	1.4

(Source: CDC, 2016. Health United States, 2015.)

Table 47.44. Serious Psychological Distress among Adults 18 Years of Age and Over, Percent of Poverty Level, 2013–2014

	Hispanic	Non-Hispanic White	Hispanic/Non-Hispanic White Ratio
Below 100%	8.2	10.7	0.8
100%–less than 200%	5	6.5	0.8
200%–less than 400%	3.2	2.7	1.2

(Source: CDC, 2016. Health United States, 2015.)

Table 47.45. Percent of Population with Feelings of Sadness, Hopelessness, Worthlessness, or That Everything Is an Effort, All of the Time, among Persons 18 Years of Age and Over, 2014

	Hispanic	Non-Hispanic White	Hispanic/Non-Hispanic White Ratio
Sadness	4.6	2.4	1.8
Hopelessness	3.9	1.7	2.3
Worthlessness	2.3	1.5	1.5
Everything is an effort	6.8	5	1.4

(Source: CDC 2016. Summary Health Statistics: National Health Interview Survey: 2014.)

Table 47.46. Percent of Population with Feelings of Sadness, Hopelessness, Worthlessness, or That Everything Is an Effort All of the Time, among Men 18 Years of Age and Over, 2014

	Hispanic Men	Non-Hispanic White Men	Hispanic Men/Non-Hispanic White Men Ratio
Sadness	3.9	1.8	2.2
Hopelessness	3.2	1.5	2.1
Worthlessness	1.9	1.4	1.4
Everything is an effort	6.5	4.3	1.5

(Source: CDC 2016. Summary Health Statistics: National Health Interview Survey: 2014.)

Table 47.47. Percent of Population with Feelings of Sadness, Hopelessness, Worthlessness, or That Everything Is an Effort All of the Time, among Women 18 Years of Age and Over, 2014

	Hispanic Women	Non-Hispanic White Women	Hispanic Women/Non-Hispanic White Women Ratio
Sadness	5.3	2.9	1.8
Hopelessness	4.6	1.9	2.4
Worthlessness	2.5	1.6	1.6
Everything is an effort	7.1	5.8	1.2

(Source: CDC 2016. Summary Health Statistics: National Health Interview Survey: 2014.)

Table 47.48. Percent of Population with Feelings of Nervousness or Restlessness, among Persons 18 Years of Age and Over, 2014

	Hispanic	Non-Hispanic White	Hispanic/Non-Hispanic White Ratio
Nervousness, all or most of the time	5.3	4.6	1.2
Restlessness, all or most of the time	7	6	1.2

(Source: CDC 2016. Summary Health Statistics: National Health Interview Survey: 2014.)

Death Rates

Table 47.49. Age-Adjusted Death Rates for Suicide, by Sex, Race, and Hispanic Origin, 2014

	Hispanic	Non-Hispanic White	Hispanic/Non-Hispanic White Ratio
Male	10.3	25.8	0.4
Female	2.5	7.5	0.3
Total	6.3	16.4	0.4

(Source: CDC, 2016. National Vital Statistic Report.)

Table 47.50. Age-Adjusted Death Rates for Suicide, by Race, 2014

Hispanic	Non-Hispanic White	Hispanic/Non-Hispanic White Ratio
6.3	16.4	0.4

(Source: CDC, 2016. Health United States, 2015.)

Table 47.51. Death Rates for Suicide, Age, Race, and Hispanic Origin Men, 2014

	Hispanic Men	Non-Hispanic White Men	Hispanic Men/Non-Hispanic White Men Ratio
15–24 years	11.5	22.4	0.5
25–44 years	12.6	31.7	0.4
45–64 years	12.4	37.1	0.3

Table 47.51. Continued

	Hispanic Men	Non-Hispanic White Men	Hispanic Men/ Non-Hispanic White Men Ratio
65 years and over	15.9	36.1	0.4
All ages	10.3	25.8	0.4

(Source: CDC, 2016. Health United States, 2015.)

Table 47.52. Death Rates for Suicide, Age, Race and Hispanic Origin Women, 2014

	Hispanic Women	Non-Hispanic White Women	Hispanic Women/ Non-Hispanic White Women Ratio
15–24 years	3.4	5.4	0.6
25–44 years	3	9.8	0.3
45–64 years	3.5	12.6	0.3
65 years and over	2.1	5.8	0.4
All ages	2.5	7.5	0.3

(Source: CDC, 2016. Health United States, 2015.)

Adolescents

Table 47.53. Age-Adjusted Death Rates for Suicide: Ages 15 to 19, 2014.

	Hispanic	Non-Hispanic White	Hispanic/Non-Hispanic White Ratio
Male	9.2	16.6	0.6
Female	2.4	4.8	0.5
Total	5.7	10.9	0.5

(Source: CDC, 2016. National Center for Injury Prevention and Control. Web-Based Injury Statistics Query and Reporting System (WISQARS).)

Table 47.54. Suicidal Ideation among Students in Grades 9 to 12, 2015 Percent of Students Who Seriously Considered Suicide

	Hispanic	Non-Hispanic White	Hispanic/Non-Hispanic White Ratio
Male	12.4	11.5	1.1
Female	25.6	22.8	1.1
Total	18.8	17.2	1.1

(Source: CDC 2016. High School Youth Risk Behavior Survey Data.)

Table 47.55. Suicidal Ideation among Students in Grades 9 to 12, 2015 Percent of Students Who Attempted Suicide

	Hispanic	Non-Hispanic White	Hispanic/Non-Hispanic White Ratio
Male	7.6	3.7	2.1
Female	15.1	9.8	1.5
Total	11.3	6.8	1.7

(Source: CDC 2016. High School Youth Risk Behavior Survey Data.)

Access to Healthcare

Table 47.56. Percent of Adults Age 18 and over Who Received Mental-Health Treatment or Counseling in 2014

	Hispanic	Non-Hispanic White	Hispanic/Non-Hispanic White Ratio
Total	8.3	18	0.5

(Source: SAMHSA, 2015. Results from the 2014 National Survey on Drug Use and Health: Mental Health Detailed Tables.)

Table 47.57. Percent of Adults Age 18 and over Who Received Prescription Medications for Mental-Health Treatment or Counseling, 2014

	Hispanic	Non-Hispanic White	Hispanic/Non-Hispanic White Ratio
Total	6.5	15.7	0.4

(Source: SAMHSA, 2015. Results from the 2014 National Survey on Drug Use and Health: Mental Health Detailed Tables.)

Table 47.58. Adults age 18 and over with Past Year Major Depressive Episode Who Received Treatment for the Depression, 2012

Hispanic	Non-Hispanic White	Hispanic/Non-Hispanic White Ratio
55.6	72	0.8

(Source: National Healthcare Quality and Disparities Reports. Data Query.)

Part Six

Mental Illness Co-Occurring with Other Disorders

Chapter 48

Cancer and Mental Health

Chapter Contents

Section 48.1

Psychological Stress and Cancer

This section includes text excerpted from "Psychological
Stress and Cancer," National Cancer Institute (NCI),
December 10, 2012. Reviewed December 2018.

What Is Psychological Stress?

Psychological stress describes what people feel when they are under
mental, physical, or emotional pressure. Although it is normal to experience some psychological stress from time to time, people who experience
high levels of psychological stress or who experience it repeatedly over a
long period of time may develop health problems (mental and/or physical).

Stress can be caused both by daily responsibilities and routine
events, as well as by more unusual events, such as a trauma or illness
in oneself or a close family member. When people feel that they are
unable to manage or control changes caused by cancer or normal life
activities, they are in distress. Distress has become increasingly recognized as a factor that can reduce the quality of life of cancer patients.
There is even some evidence that extreme distress is associated with
poorer clinical outcomes. Clinical guidelines are available to help doctors and nurses assess levels of distress and help patients manage it.

How Does the Body Respond during Stress?

The body responds to physical, mental, or emotional pressure by
releasing stress hormones (such as epinephrine and norepinephrine)
that increase blood pressure, speed heart rate, and raise blood sugar
levels. These changes help a person act with greater strength and
speed to escape a perceived threat.

Research has shown that people who experience intense and long-
term (i.e., chronic) stress can have digestive problems, fertility problems, urinary problems, and a weakened immune system. People who
experience chronic stress are also more prone to viral infections such
as the flu or common cold and to have headaches, sleep trouble, depression, and anxiety.

Can Psychological Stress Cause Cancer?

Although stress can cause a number of physical health problems,
the evidence that it can cause cancer is weak. Some studies have

indicated a link between various psychological factors and an increased risk of developing cancer, but others have not.

Apparent links between psychological stress and cancer could arise in several ways. For example, people under stress may develop certain behaviors, such as smoking, overeating, or drinking alcohol, which increase a person's risk for cancer. Or someone who has a relative with cancer may have a higher risk for cancer because of a shared inherited risk factor, not because of the stress induced by the family member's diagnosis.

How Does Psychological Stress Affect People Who Have Cancer?

People who have cancer may find the physical, emotional, and social effects of the disease to be stressful. Those who attempt to manage their stress with risky behaviors such as smoking or drinking alcohol or who become more sedentary may have a poorer quality of life after cancer treatment. In contrast, people who are able to use effective coping strategies to deal with stress, such as relaxation and stress management techniques, have been shown to have lower levels of depression, anxiety, and symptoms related to cancer and its treatment. However, there is no evidence that successful management of psychological stress improves cancer survival.

Evidence from experimental studies does suggest that psychological stress can affect a tumors ability to grow and spread. For example, some studies have shown that when mice bearing human tumors were kept confined or isolated from other mice—conditions that increase stress—their tumors were more likely to grow and spread (metastasize). In one set of experiments, tumors transplanted into the mammary fat pads of mice had much higher rates of spread to the lungs and lymph nodes if the mice were chronically stressed than if the mice were not stressed. Studies in mice and in human cancer cells grown in the laboratory have found that the stress hormone norepinephrine, part of the body's fight-or-flight response system, may promote angiogenesis and metastasis.

In another study, women with triple-negative breast cancer who had been treated with neoadjuvant chemotherapy were asked about their use of beta-blockers, which are medications that interfere with certain stress hormones, before and during chemotherapy. Women who reported using beta-blockers had a better chance of surviving their cancer treatment without a relapse than women who did not report beta-blocker use. There was no difference between the groups, however, in terms of overall survival.

Although there is still no strong evidence that stress directly affects cancer outcomes, some data do suggest that patients can develop a sense of helplessness or hopelessness when stress becomes overwhelming. This response is associated with higher rates of death, although the mechanism for this outcome is unclear. It may be that people who feel helpless or hopeless do not seek treatment when they become ill, give up prematurely on or fail to adhere to potentially helpful therapy, engage in risky behaviors such as drug use, or do not maintain a healthy lifestyle, resulting in premature death.

How Can People Who Have Cancer Learn to Cope with Psychological Stress?

Emotional and social support can help patients learn to cope with psychological stress. Such support can reduce levels of depression, anxiety, disease, and treatment-related symptoms among patients. Approaches can include the following:

- Training in relaxation, meditation, or stress management
- Counseling or talk therapy
- Cancer education sessions
- Social support in a group setting
- Medications for depression or anxiety
- Exercise

Some expert organizations recommend that all cancer patients be screened for distress early in the course of treatment. A number also recommend re-screening at critical points along the course of care. Healthcare providers can use a variety of screening tools, such as a distress scale or questionnaire, to gauge whether cancer patients need help managing their emotions or with other practical concerns. Patients who show moderate to severe distress are typically referred to appropriate resources, such as a clinical health psychologist, social worker, chaplain, or psychiatrist.

Section 48.2

Depression in Cancer Patients

This section includes text excerpted from "Depression
(PDQ®)—Patient Version," National Cancer
Institute (NCI), September 8, 2017.

Depression Is Different from Normal Sadness

Depression is not feeling sad. Depression is a disorder with specific symptoms that can be diagnosed and treated. For every ten patients diagnosed with cancer, about two patients become depressed. The numbers of men and women affected are about the same.

A person diagnosed with cancer faces many stressful issues. These may include:

- Fear of death

- Changes in life plans

- Changes in body image and self-esteem

- Changes in day to day living

- Worry about money and legal issues

Sadness and grief are common reactions to a cancer diagnosis. A person with cancer may also have other symptoms of depression, such as:

- Feelings of disbelief, denial, or despair

- Trouble sleeping

- Loss of appetite

- Anxiety or worry about the future

Not everyone who is diagnosed with cancer reacts in the same way. Some cancer patients may not have depression or anxiety, while others may have major depression or an anxiety disorder.

Signs that you have adjusted to the cancer diagnosis and treatment include the following:

- Being able to stay active in daily life

- Continuing in your roles as spouse, parent, or employee

- Being able to manage your feelings and emotions related to your cancer

Some Cancer Patients May Have a Higher Risk of Depression

There are known risk factors for depression after a cancer diagnosis. Anything that increases your chance of developing depression is called a "risk factor" for depression. Factors that increase the risk of depression are not always related to cancer.

Risk factors related to cancer that may cause depression include the following:

- Learning you have cancer when you are already depressed

- Having cancer pain that is not well controlled

- Being physically weakened by the cancer

- Having pancreatic cancer

- Having advanced cancer or a poor prognosis

- Feeling you are a burden to others

- Taking certain medicines, such as:

  - Corticosteroids

  - Procarbazine

  - L-asparaginase

  - Interferon alfa

  - Interleukin-2 (IL-2)

  - Amphotericin B

Risk factors not related to cancer that may cause depression include the following:

- A personal history of depression or suicide attempts

- A family history of depression or suicide

- A personal history of mental problems, alcoholism, or drug abuse

- Not having enough support from family or friends

- Stress caused by life events other than cancer

- Having other health problems, such as stroke or heart attack that may also cause depression

Medical Conditions That Can Cause Depression

There are many medical conditions that may cause depression. Some of them are listed below.

- Pain that doesn't go away with treatment

- Abnormal levels of calcium, sodium, or potassium in the blood

- Not enough vitamin B_{12} or folate in your diet

- Anemia

- Fever

- Too much or too little thyroid hormone

- Too little adrenal hormone

- Side effects caused by certain medicines

Family Members Also Have a Risk of Depression

Anxiety and depression may occur in family members who are caring for loved ones with cancer. Family members who talk about their feelings and solve problems together are less likely to have high levels of depression and anxiety.

Section 48.3

Cognitive Disorders and Delirium in Advanced Cancer

This section includes text excerpted from "Delirium (PDQ®)—Patient Version," National Cancer Institute (NCI), March 9, 2016.

What Is Delirium?

Delirium is a confused mental state that can occur in patients who have cancer, especially advanced cancer. Patients with delirium have problems with the following:

- Attention
- Thinking
- Awareness
- Behavior
- Emotions
- Judgment
- Memory
- Muscle control
- Sleeping and waking

There are three types of delirium:

- **Hypoactive.** The patient is not active and seems sleepy, tired, or depressed.
- **Hyperactive.** The patient is restless or agitated.
- **Mixed.** The patient changes back and forth between being hypoactive and hyperactive.

Delirium May Come and Go during the Day

The symptoms of delirium usually occur suddenly. They often occur within hours or days and may come and go. Delirium is often temporary and can be treated. However, in the last 24 to 48 hours of life, delirium may be permanent because of problems such as organ failure. Most advanced cancer patients have delirium that occurs in the last hours to days before death.

What Causes Delirium

There is often more than one cause of delirium in a cancer patient, especially when the cancer is advanced and the patient has many medical conditions. It may be caused by cancer, cancer treatment, or other medical conditions.

Causes of delirium include the following:

- Organ failures, such as liver or kidney failure

- **Electrolyte imbalances.** Electrolytes are important minerals (including salt, potassium, calcium, and phosphorous) in blood and body fluids. These electrolytes are needed to keep the heart, kidneys, nerves, and muscles working the way they should.

- Infections

- **Paraneoplastic syndromes.** Symptoms that occur when cancer-fighting antibodies or white blood (WB) cells attack normal cells in the nervous system by mistake.

- **Side effects of medicines and treatments.** Patients with cancer may take medicines with side effects that include delirium and confusion. The effects usually go away after the medicine is stopped.

- Withdrawal from medicines that depress (slow down) the CNS or central nervous system (brain and spinal cord)

Risk Factors for Delirium

Patients with cancer are likely to have more than one risk factor for delirium. Identifying risk factors early may help prevent delirium or decrease the time it takes to treat it. Risk factors include the following:

- Serious illness

- Having more than one disease

- Older age

- Dementia

- Low level of albumin (protein) in the blood, which is often caused by liver problems.

- Infection

- High level of nitrogen waste products in the blood, which is often caused by kidney problems

- Taking medicines that affect the mind or behavior

- Taking high doses of pain medicines, such as opioids

The risk increases when the patient has more than one risk factor. Older patients with advanced cancer who are hospitalized often have more than one risk factor for delirium.

Effects of Delirium on the Patient, Family, and Healthcare Providers

Delirium may be dangerous to the patient if her or his judgment is affected. Delirium can cause the patient to behave in unusual ways. Even a quiet or calm patient can have a sudden change in mood or become agitated and need more care.

Delirium can be upsetting to the family and caregivers. When the patient becomes agitated, family members often think the patient is in pain, but this may not be the case. Learning about differences between the symptoms of delirium and pain may help the family and caregivers understand how much pain medicine is needed. Healthcare providers can help the family and caregivers learn about these differences.

Delirium may affect physical health and communication. Patients with delirium are:

- More likely to fall

- Sometimes unable to control bladder and/or bowels

- More likely to become dehydrated (drink too little water to stay healthy)

They often need a longer hospital stay than patients without delirium.

The confused mental state of these patients may make them:

- Unable to talk with family members and caregivers about their needs and feelings

- Unable to make decisions about care

This makes it harder for healthcare providers to assess the patient's symptoms. The family may need to make decisions for the patient.

Diagnosing Delirium

Possible signs of delirium include sudden personality changes, problems thinking, and unusual anxiety or depression. When the following symptoms occur suddenly, they may be signs of delirium:

- Agitation
- Not cooperating
- Changes in personality or behavior
- Problems thinking
- Problems paying attention
- Unusual anxiety or depression

Early symptoms of delirium are like symptoms of depression and dementia. Delirium that causes the patient to be inactive may appear to be depression. Delirium and dementia both cause problems with memory, thinking, and judgment. Dementia may be caused by a number of medical conditions, including Alzheimer disease (AD). Differences in the symptoms of delirium and dementia include the following:

- Patients with delirium often show changes in how alert or aware they are. Patients who have dementia usually stay alert and aware until dementia becomes very advanced.
- Delirium occurs suddenly (within hours or days). Dementia appears gradually (over months to years) and gets worse over time.

Older patients with cancer may have both dementia and delirium. This can make it hard for the doctor to diagnose the problem. If treatment for delirium is given and the symptoms continue, then the diagnosis is more likely dementia. Checking the patient's health and symptoms over time can help diagnose delirium and dementia.

Physical exams and other laboratory tests are used to diagnose the causes of delirium.

Doctors will try to determine the causes of delirium.

- **Physical exam and history.** An exam of the body to check general signs of health, including checking for signs of disease, such as lumps or anything else that seems unusual. A history of the patient's health habits, past illnesses including depression, and treatments will also be taken. A physical exam can help rule out a physical condition that may be causing symptoms.

- **Laboratory tests.** Medical procedures that test samples of tissue, blood, urine, or other substances in the body. These tests help to diagnose disease, plan and check treatment, or monitor the disease over time.

Treatment of Delirium

Treatment includes looking at the causes and symptoms of delirium. Both the causes and the symptoms of delirium may be treated. Treatment depends on the following:

- Where the patient is living, such as home, hospital, or nursing home

- How advanced the cancer is

- How the delirium symptoms are affecting the patient

- The wishes of the patient and family

Treating the causes of delirium usually includes the following:

- Stopping or lowering the dose of medicines that cause delirium

- Giving fluids to treat dehydration

- Giving drugs to treat hypercalcemia (too much calcium in the blood)

- Giving antibiotics for infections

In a terminally ill patient with delirium, the doctor may treat just the symptoms. The doctor will continue to watch the patient closely during treatment.

Treatment without Medicines Can Also Help Relieve Symptoms

Controlling the patient's surroundings may help with mild symptoms of delirium. The following may help:

- Keep the patient's room quiet and well-lit, and put familiar objects in it

- Put a clock or calendar where the patient can see it

- Have family members around

- Keep the same caregivers as much as possible

Patients who may hurt themselves or others may need to have physical restraints.

Treatment May Include Medicines

Medicines may be used to treat the symptoms of delirium depending on the patient's condition and heart health. These medicines have serious side effects and the patient will be watched closely by a doctor. These medicines include the following:

• Haloperidol

• Olanzapine

• Risperidone

• Lorazepam

• Midazolam

Sedation

When the symptoms of delirium are not relieved with standard treatments and the patient is near death, in pain, or has trouble breathing, other treatment may be needed. Sometimes medicines that will sedate (calm) the patient will be used. The family and the healthcare team will make this decision together.

The decision to use sedation for delirium may be guided by the following:

• The patient will have repeated assessments by experts before the delirium is considered to be refractory (doesn't respond to treatment).

• The decision to sedate the patient is reviewed by a team of healthcare professionals and not made by one doctor.

• Temporary sedation, for short periods of time such as overnight, is considered before continuous sedation is used.

• The team of healthcare professionals will work with the family to make sure the team understands the family's views and that the family understands palliative sedation.

Chapter 49

Diabetes and Mental Health

Is mental health pretty low on your list of priorities for managing diabetes? This may change your mind. Mental health affects so many aspects of daily life—how you think and feel, handle stress, relate to others, and make choices. You can see how having a mental-health problem could make it harder to stick to your diabetes care plan.

The Mind–Body Connection

Thoughts, feelings, beliefs, and attitudes can affect how healthy your body is. Untreated mental-health issues can make diabetes worse, and problems with diabetes can make mental-health issues worse. But fortunately if one gets better, the other tends to get better, too.

Depression: More than Just a Bad Mood

Depression is a medical illness that causes feelings of sadness and often a loss of interest in activities you used to enjoy. It can get in the way of how well you function at work and home, including taking care of your diabetes. When you aren't able to manage your diabetes well, your risk goes up for diabetes complications like heart disease and nerve damage.

People with diabetes are two to three times more likely to have depression than people without diabetes. Only 25 to 50 percent of

---

This chapter includes text excerpted from "Diabetes and Mental Health," Centers for Disease Control and Prevention (CDC), August 6, 2018.

people with diabetes who have depression get diagnosed and treated. But treatment—therapy, medicine, or both—is usually very effective. And without treatment, depression often gets worse, not better.

Symptoms of depression can be mild to severe and include:

- Feeling sad or empty

- Losing interest in favorite activities

- Overeating or not wanting to eat at all

- Not being able to sleep or sleeping too much

- Having trouble concentrating or making decisions

- Feeling very tired

- Feeling hopeless, irritable, anxious, or guilty

- Having aches or pains, headaches, cramps, or digestive problems

- Having thoughts of suicide or death

If you think you might have depression, get in touch with your doctor right away for help getting treatment. The earlier depression is treated, the better for you, your quality of life, and your diabetes.

Stress and Anxiety

Stress is part of life, from traffic jams to family demands to everyday diabetes care. You can feel stress as an emotion, such as fear or anger, as a physical reaction like sweating or a racing heart, or both.

If you're stressed, you may not take as good care of yourself as usual. Your blood sugar levels can be affected too—stress hormones make blood sugar rise or fall unpredictably, and stress from being sick or injured can make your blood sugar go up. Being stressed for a long time can lead to other health problems or make them worse.

Anxiety—feelings of worry, fear, or being on edge—is how your mind and body react to stress. People with diabetes are 20 percent more likely than those without diabetes to have anxiety at some point in their life. Managing a long-term condition like diabetes is a major source of anxiety for some.

Studies show that therapy for anxiety usually works better than medicine, but sometimes both together works best. You can also help lower your stress and anxiety by:

- A quick walk can be calming, and the effect can last for hours

- Doing some relaxation exercises, like meditation or yoga

- Calling or texting a friend who understands you (not someone who is causing you stress!)

- Grabbing some "you" time. Take a break from whatever you're doing. Go outside, read something fun—whatever helps you recharge.

- Limiting alcohol and caffeine, eating healthy food, and getting enough sleep

- Anxiety can feel like low blood sugar and vice versa. It may be hard for you to recognize which it is and treat it effectively. If you're feeling anxious, try checking your blood sugar and treat it if it's low.

There will always be some stress in life. But if you feel overwhelmed, talking to a mental-health counselor can help. Ask your doctor for a referral.

Diabetes Distress

You may sometimes feel discouraged, worried, frustrated, or tired of dealing with daily diabetes care or like diabetes is controlling you instead of the other way around. Maybe you've been trying hard but not seeing results. Or you've developed a health problem related to diabetes in spite of your best efforts.

Those overwhelming feelings, known as diabetes distress, may cause you to slip into unhealthy habits, stop checking your blood sugar, even skip doctor's appointments. It happens to many—if not most—people with diabetes, often after years of good management. In any 18-month period, 33 to 50 percent of people with diabetes have diabetes distress.

Diabetes distress can look like depression or anxiety, but it can't be treated effectively with medication. Instead, these approaches have been shown to help:

- Make sure you're seeing an endocrinologist for your diabetes care. She or he is likely to have a deeper understanding of diabetes challenges than your regular doctor.

- Ask your doctor to refer you to a mental-health counselor who specializes in chronic health conditions.

- Get some one-on-one time with a diabetes educator so you can problem-solve together.

- Focus on one or two small diabetes management goals instead of thinking you have to work on everything all at once.

Join a diabetes support group so you can share your thoughts and feelings with people who have the same concerns (and learn from them too).

Talk to Your Healthcare Team

Your healthcare team knows diabetes is challenging, but may not understand how challenging. And you may not be used to talking about feeling sad or down. But if you're concerned about your mental health, let your doctor know right away. You're not alone—help is available!

Chapter 50

Epilepsy and Mental Health

What Are the Epilepsies?

The epilepsies are chronic neurological disorders in which clusters of nerve cells, or neurons, in the brain sometimes signal abnormally and cause seizures. Neurons normally generate electrical and chemical signals that act on other neurons, glands, and muscles to produce human thoughts, feelings, and actions. During a seizure, many neurons fire (signal) at the same time—as many as 500 times a second, much faster than normal. This surge of excessive electrical activity happening at the same time causes involuntary movements, sensations, emotions, and behaviors and the temporary disturbance of normal neuronal activity may cause a loss of awareness.

Epilepsy can be considered a spectrum disorder because of its different causes, different seizure types, its ability to vary in severity and impact from person to person, and its range of co-existing conditions. Some people may have convulsions (sudden onset of repetitive general contraction of muscles) and lose consciousness. Others may simply stop what they are doing, have a brief lapse of awareness, and stare into space for a short period. Some people have seizures very infrequently, while other people may experience hundreds of seizures each day. There also are many different types of epilepsy, resulting from a variety of causes.

This chapter includes text excerpted from "The Epilepsies and Seizures: Hope through Research," National Institute of Neurological Disorders and Stroke (NINDS), August 8, 2018.

In general, a person is not considered to have epilepsy until she or he has had two or more unprovoked seizures separated by at least 24 hours. In contrast, a provoked seizure is one caused by a known precipitating factor such as a high fever, nervous system infections, acute traumatic brain injury (TBI), or fluctuations in blood sugar or electrolyte levels.

Anyone can develop epilepsy. About 2.3 million adults and more than 450,000 children and adolescents in the United States live with epilepsy. Each year, an estimated 150,000 people are diagnosed with epilepsy. Epilepsy affects both males and females of all races, ethnic backgrounds, and ages. In the United States alone, the annual costs associated with the epilepsies are estimated to be $15.5 billion in direct medical expenses and lost or reduced earnings and productivity.

The majority of those diagnosed with epilepsy have seizures that can be controlled with drug therapies and surgery. However, as much as 30 to 40 percent of people with epilepsy continue to have seizures because available treatments do not completely control their seizures (called intractable or medication-resistant epilepsy).

While many forms of epilepsy require lifelong treatment to control the seizures, for some people the seizures eventually go away. The odds of becoming seizure-free are not as good for adults or for children with severe epilepsy syndromes, but it is possible that seizures may decrease or even stop over time. This is more likely if the epilepsy starts in childhood, has been well-controlled by medication, or if the person has had surgery to remove the brain focus of the abnormal cell firing.

Many people with epilepsy lead productive lives, but some will be severely impacted by their epilepsy. Medical and research advances in the past two decades have led to a better understanding of the epilepsies and seizures. More than 20 different medications and a variety of dietary treatments and surgical techniques (including two devices) are now available and may provide good control of seizures. Devices can modulate brain activity to decrease seizure frequency. Advance neuroimaging can identify brain abnormalities that give rise to seizures which can be cured by neurosurgery. Even dietary changes can effectively treat certain types of epilepsy. Research on the underlying causes of the epilepsies, including identification of genes for some forms of epilepsy, has led to a greatly improved understanding of these disorders that may lead to more effective treatments or even to new ways of preventing epilepsy in the future.

What Causes the Epilepsies

The epilepsies have many possible causes, but for up to half of people with epilepsy a cause is not known. In other cases, the epilepsies are clearly linked to genetic factors, developmental brain abnormalities, infection, TBI, stroke, brain tumors, or other identifiable problems. Anything that disturbs the normal pattern of neuronal activity—from illness to brain damage to abnormal brain development—can lead to seizures.

The epilepsies may develop because of an abnormality in brain wiring, an imbalance of nerve signaling in the brain (in which some cells either overexcite or over inhibit other brain cells from sending messages), or some combination of these factors. In some pediatric conditions, abnormal brain wiring causes other problems such as intellectual impairment.

In other persons, the brain's attempts to repair itself after a head injury, stroke, or other problem may inadvertently generate abnormal nerve connections that lead to epilepsy. Brain malformations and abnormalities in brain wiring that occur during brain development also may disturb neuronal activity and lead to epilepsy.

Genetics

Genetic mutations may play a key role in the development of certain epilepsies. Many types of epilepsy affect multiple blood-related family members, pointing to a strong inherited genetic component. In other cases, gene mutations may occur spontaneously and contribute to the development of epilepsy in people with no family history of the disorder (called "de novo" mutations). Overall, researchers estimate that hundreds of genes could play a role in the disorders.

Several types of epilepsy have been linked to mutations in genes that provide instructions for ion channels, the "gates" that control the flow of ions in and out of cells to help regulate neuronal signaling. For example, most infants with Dravet syndrome (DS), a type of epilepsy associated with seizures that begin before the age of one year, carry a mutation in the *SCN1A* gene that causes seizures by affecting sodium ion channels.

Genetic mutations also have been linked to disorders known as the progressive myoclonic epilepsies, which are characterized by ultra-quick muscle contractions (myoclonus) and seizures over time. For example, Lafora disease, a severe, progressive form of myoclonic epilepsy that begins in childhood, has been linked to a gene that helps to break down carbohydrates in brain cells.

Mutations in genes that control neuronal migration—a critical step in brain development—can lead to areas of misplaced or abnormally formed neurons, called cortical dysplasia, in the brain that can cause these miswired neurons to misfire and lead to epilepsy.

Other genetic mutations may not cause epilepsy but may influence the disorder in other ways. For example, one study showed that many people with certain forms of epilepsy have an abnormally active version of a gene that results in resistance to antiseizure drugs. Genes also may control a person's susceptibility to seizures, or seizure threshold, by affecting brain development.

Other Disorders

Epilepsies may develop as a result of brain damage associated with many types of conditions that disrupt normal brain activity. Seizures may stop once these conditions are treated and resolved. However, the chances of becoming seizure-free after the primary disorder is treated are uncertain and vary depending on the type of disorder, the brain region that is affected, and how much brain damage occurred prior to treatment. Examples of conditions that can lead to epilepsy include:

- Brain tumors, including those associated with neurofibromatosis or tuberous sclerosis complex (TSC), two inherited conditions that cause benign tumors called hamartomas to grow in the brain

- Head trauma

- Alcoholism or alcohol withdrawal

- Alzheimer disease (AD)

- Strokes, heart attacks, and other conditions that deprive the brain of oxygen (a significant portion of new-onset epilepsy in elderly people is due to stroke or other cerebrovascular diseases)

- Abnormal blood vessel formation (arteriovenous malformations (AVM)) or bleeding in the brain (hemorrhage)

- Inflammation of the brain

- Infections such as meningitis, human immunodeficiency virus (HIV), and viral encephalitis

Cerebral palsy (CP) or other developmental neurological abnormalities may also be associated with epilepsy. About 20 percent of seizures in children can be attributed to developmental neurological conditions. Epilepsies often co-occur in people with abnormalities of brain development or other neurodevelopmental disorders. Seizures are more common, for example, among individuals with autism spectrum disorder (ASD) or intellectual impairment. In one study, fully a third of children with ASD had treatment-resistant epilepsy.

Seizure Triggers

Seizure triggers do not cause epilepsy but can provoke first seizures in those who are susceptible or can cause seizures in people with epilepsy who otherwise experience good seizure control with their medication. Seizure triggers include alcohol consumption or alcohol withdrawal, dehydration or missing meals, stress, and hormonal changes associated with the menstrual cycle. In surveys of people with epilepsy, stress is the most commonly reported seizure trigger. Exposure to toxins or poisons such as lead or carbon monoxide, street drugs, or even excessively large doses of antidepressants or other prescribed medications also can trigger seizures.

Sleep deprivation is a powerful trigger of seizures. Sleep disorders are common among people with the epilepsies and appropriate treatment of co-existing sleep disorders can often lead to improved control of seizures. Certain types of seizures tend to occur during sleep, while others are more common during times of wakefulness, suggesting to physicians how to best adjust a person's medication.

For some people, visual stimulation can trigger seizures in a condition known as photosensitive epilepsy. Stimulation can include such things as flashing lights or moving patterns.

What Is the Impact of the Epilepsies on Daily Life?

The majority of people with epilepsy can do the same things as people without the disorder and have successful and productive lives. In most cases, it does not affect job choice or performance. One-third or more of people with epilepsy, however, may have cognitive or neuropsychiatric co-concurring symptoms that can negatively impact their quality of life (QOL). medication-resistant, and some may go months or years without having a seizure. However, people with treatment-resistant epilepsy can have as many as hundreds of seizures a day or they can have one seizure a year with sometimes disabling consequences.

On average, having treatment-resistant epilepsy is associated with an increased risk of cognitive impairment, particularly if the seizures developed in early childhood. These impairments may be related to the underlying conditions associated with epilepsy rather than to epilepsy itself.

Mental Health and Stigmatization

Depression is common among people with epilepsy. It is estimated that one out of every three persons with epilepsy will have depression in the course of her or his lifetime, often with accompanying symptoms of anxiety disorder. In adults, depression and anxiety are the two most frequent mental health-related diagnoses. In adults, a depression screening questionnaire specifically designed for epilepsy helps mental-healthcare professionals identify people who need treatment. Depression or anxiety in people with epilepsy can be treated with counseling or most of the same medications used in people who don't have epilepsy. People with epilepsy should not simply accept that depression is part of having epilepsy and should discuss symptoms and feelings with mental-healthcare professionals.

Children with epilepsy also have a higher risk of developing depression and/or attention deficit hyperactivity disorder (ADHD) compared with their peers. Behavioral problems may precede the onset of seizures in some children.

Children are especially vulnerable to the emotional problems caused by ignorance or the lack of knowledge among others about epilepsy. This often results in stigmatization, bullying, or teasing of a child who has epilepsy. Such experiences can lead to behaviors of avoidance in school and other social settings. Counseling services and support groups can help families cope with epilepsy in a positive manner.

Chapter 51

Heart Disease and Depression

Depression and heart disease affect millions of American men—and many experience both at the same time. This chapter will help you learn how heart health is tied to mental health, the symptoms of depression, and steps to keep your heart and mind healthy.

Nearly one in ten men say they feel some depression or anxiety every day, and almost one in three have gone through a period of major depression at some point in their lives.

Everyone can feel sad or "blue" sometimes. But depression is when feelings of hopelessness, sadness, loss, or frustration cause trouble with daily life. Depression can last weeks, months, or even years.

About 1 in 13 adult men are living with heart disease, which is also their number one killer.

Heart Disease and Depression: What Is the Connection?

Depression and heart disease can happen at the same time. Some connections between depression and heart disease include:

- Depression that lasts longer than a couple of weeks can lead to certain behaviors, such as abusing alcohol or not sleeping,

This chapter includes text excerpted from "Heart Health and Depression: What Men Need to Know," Centers for Disease Control and Prevention (CDC), June 12, 2017.

that put heart health at risk. Depression also raises the levels of certain hormones and proteins in the body that can cause inflammation (swelling) and high blood pressure—leading causes of heart disease and stroke.

- People with depression are more likely to have other conditions that can lead to heart disease, including obesity and diabetes.

- Men who have a heart condition are more at risk for depression than men without heart problems. Men may feel anxious or sad about how having heart disease will affect their lives and finances. They may be in pain or not feel up to starting healthy living habits that could improve their heart health and reduce their depression.

How Do Depression and Heart Disease Affect Men?

Although both men and women get depression, men often have different symptoms than women, including:

- Feeling angry
- Acting aggressively
- Abusing drugs or alcohol
- Having trouble sleeping

These symptoms can put men at risk for heart problems by raising blood pressure and putting extra stress on the heart. Men may also be less likely than women to reach out for help with depression. The longer men stay depressed and don't seek treatment, the worse it is for their hearts.

If you have any of the symptoms of depression, talk to your doctor or a mental-health professional, such as a psychiatrist or counselor.

Protecting Your Heart and Mind: A Positive Spiral

The good news is that staying mentally healthy can help your heart. And staying heart-healthy through diet, physical activity, and other behaviors can help prevent or lessen depression.

For good mental and heart health throughout your life, try these steps:

See a professional. If you have depression but do not have heart problems, talk to a mental-health professional about treatment for your depression. Treating depression can help your heart health in the long term and improve your quality of life.

If you have been diagnosed with a heart problem, talk to your doctor about any feelings of depression you have. Your doctor can talk to you about medicines and healthy living habits that can help both your heart and your mental health.

Stay physically active. Physical activity boosts your mood and keeps your blood vessels healthy and strong. Studies show that exercise may be as effective as medicine in reducing symptoms of depression.

Watch what you eat and drink. Eat plenty of fresh fruits and veggies. Avoid foods that may raise your blood pressure or keep you from sleeping at night, such as caffeine, foods high in sodium (salt), and alcohol.

Do not smoke. Smoking tobacco is linked to both depression and heart disease. If you do smoke, learn how to quit.

Get support from a loved one. Talk to trusted family or friends about what you are feeling. Loved ones can help support you in healthy habits, such as by going grocery shopping with you, being exercise partners, and reminding you to take your medicines.

Chapter 52

Human Immunodeficiency Virus and Mental Health

What Is Mental Health?

Mental health is defined as a state of overall well-being in which every individual realizes her or his own potential, can cope with the normal stresses of life, can work productively and fruitfully, and is able to make a contribution to her or his community.

Mental health has three main areas:

- **Emotional well-being** (life satisfaction, happiness, cheerfulness, peacefulness)

- **Psychological well-being** (self-acceptance, optimism, hopefulness, purpose in life, spirituality, self-direction, positive relationships)

- **Social well-being** (social acceptance, believing in the potential of people and society as a whole, personal self-worth and usefulness to society, sense of community)

If you are living with human immunodeficiency virus (HIV), it is important to take care of not only your physical health but also your mental health.

This chapter includes text excerpted from "HIV and Mental Health," AIDS*info,* U.S. Department of Health and Human Services (HHS), December 6, 2017.

Are People with Human Immunodeficiency Virus at Risk for Experiencing Mental-Health Conditions?

Anyone can have problems with mental health. Mental-health conditions are common in the United States. According to the National Institute of Mental Health (NIMH), in 2015, approximately 18 percent of adults in the United States had a mental illness.

People with HIV, however, have higher rates of mental-health conditions than the general public. People with HIV may experience depression, anxiety, posttraumatic stress disorder (PTSD), suicidal thoughts, and insomnia.

It's important to remember that mental-health conditions are treatable and that people who have mental-health problems can recover.

What Can Negatively Affect a Person's Mental Health?

Stressful situations—such as the death of a loved one, loss of a job, difficulties at school, or exposure to violence or abuse—can have a negative effect on a person's mental health. Having a serious medical illness or condition, such as HIV infection, can be another major source of stress that affects a person's mental health in a negative way.

Sometimes, HIV infection and related opportunistic infections can also directly impact the brain and nervous system. This may lead to problems in memory, thinking, and behavior and can be a challenge to a person's mental health. In addition, some medicines used to treat HIV may have side effects that affect a person's mental health.

When Do You Need Help with Your Mental Health?

When feelings become severe, won't go away, or limit your ability to stay healthy and carry out typical functions in your life, it's important to get help.

Changes to your mental health that may indicate that you need help include:

- No longer finding enjoyment in activities that usually make you happy

- Experiencing persistent sadness or feeling empty

- Feeling anxious or stressed

- Having suicidal thoughts

Mental-health conditions can sometimes lead to alcohol or drug use. Talk to your doctor if you are having any problems with alcohol or drugs.

What Should You Do If You Need Help or Someone Tells You That They Need Help?

Talk to your doctor. Your doctor will consider whether any of your HIV medicines may be affecting your mental health. Your doctor can also help you find someone who has experience helping people with HIV with their mental health. For example:

- Psychiatrists, psychologists, social workers, and therapists can use therapy to help you cope with life challenges and mental-health problems. (Psychiatrists can also prescribe medicines.)

- Case managers can help you find mental-health treatment, housing and transportation programs, domestic violence shelters, and child care.

Other ways to improve your mental health include:

- **Join a support group.** A support group is a group of people who meet in a safe and supportive environment to provide support to each other. There are mental-health support groups and HIV support groups.

- **Practice meditation.** Research suggests that meditation can help lessen depression, anxiety, and stress.

- **Maintain healthy habits.** Regular exercise, adequate sleep, and healthy nutrition are important ways to take good care of yourself and can help when dealing with stressful situations.

Chapter 53

Chronic Pain and Posttraumatic Stress Disorder

What Is Chronic Pain?

According to the International Association for the Study of Pain (IASP), chronic pain involves suffering from pain in a particular area of the body (e.g., in the back or the neck) for at least three to six months. Chronic pain may be as severe as, if not more severe than, acute pain but the individual's experience is "modulated and compounded by the prolonged or recurrent nature of the chronic state, and further complicated by a multitude of economic and psychosocial factors." In stark contrast to acute pain, chronic pain persists beyond the amount of time that is normal for an injury to heal.

Chronic pain can have a variety of sources including disease processes or injuries. Some chronic pain stems from a traumatic event, such as a physical or sexual assault, a motor vehicle accident, or some type of disaster. Under these circumstances, the person may experience both chronic pain and posttraumatic stress disorder (PTSD).

This chapter includes text excerpted from "The Experience of Chronic Pain and PTSD: A Guide for Healthcare Providers," National Center for Posttraumatic Stress Disorder (NCPTSD), U.S. Department of Veterans Affairs (VA), February 23, 2016.

How Common Is Chronic Pain?

Approximately one in three Americans (more than twelve million people) suffer from some kind of recurring pain in their lifetimes, and three million of these individuals are seriously disabled from their chronic pain conditions. Eighty to ninety percent of Americans experience chronic cervical or lower back problems.

What Is the Experience of Chronic Pain like Physically?

There are many forms of chronic pain, and each type of condition results in different experiences of, and disability. As an example, chronic low back pain (CLBP), the most pervasive or common type of pain, is known to result in severe disability and limitation of movement.

Most patients with chronic pain resort to invasive assessment or treatment procedures, including surgery, to help ameliorate the pain. Individuals with chronic pain are less able to function in daily life than those who do not suffer from chronic pain. Patients with severe chronic pain and limited mobility oftentimes are unable to perform activities of daily living, such as walking, standing, sitting, lifting light objects, doing paperwork, standing in line at a grocery store, going shopping, or working. Many patients with chronic pain cannot work because of their pain or physical limitations.

What Is the Experience of Chronic Pain like Psychologically?

Chronic pain and the disability that often comes with it can lead to a cognitive reevaluation and reintegration of one's belief systems, values, emotions, and feelings of self-worth. Numerous studies have indicated that many patients who experience chronic pain (up to 100%) tend also to be clinically depressed. In fact, depression is the most common psychiatric diagnosis in patients with chronic pain. The experience of progressive, consistent chronic pain and disability also translates for many individuals into having thoughts of suicide as a means of ending their pain and frustration.

Chapter 54

Sleep Disorders and Posttraumatic Stress Disorder

Sleep problems, in particular, chronic insomnia and nightmares, are frequently some of the most troubling aspects of posttraumatic stress disorder (PTSD). While these sleep problems are considered symptoms of PTSD, the evidence suggests that they tend to become independent problems over time that warrant sleep-focused assessment and treatment. There are both pharmacologic and cognitive behavioral treatment options available.

Link between Sleep Problems and Posttraumatic Stress Disorder

PTSD is unique among mental-health disorders in that sleep problems are mentioned twice among its diagnostic criteria in the fifth edition of the *Diagnostic and Statistical Manual of Mental Disorders* (DSM): the presence of insomnia qualifying as a symptom of an alteration in arousal and reactivity and the presence of frequent nightmares as an intrusion symptom. Insomnia is reported to occur in 90 to 100

This chapter includes text excerpted from "Sleep Problems in Veterans with PTSD," National Center for Posttraumatic Stress Disorder (NCPTSD), U.S. Department of Veterans Affairs (VA), January 25, 2017.

percent of Vietnam-era veterans with PTSD. Insomnia was also the most commonly reported PTSD symptom in a survey of veterans from Afghanistan and Iraq (OEF/OIF). In the Millennium Cohort Study, 92 percent of active duty personnel with PTSD, compared to 28 percent of those without PTSD, reported clinically significant levels of insomnia.

It has been argued that sleep problems, rather than being just symptoms of PTSD, are a hallmark of the disorder. In support of this viewpoint, insomnia occurring in the acute aftermath of a traumatic event is a significant risk factor for the later development of PTSD in civilian and active duty populations. Studies also indicate that insomnia often persists following PTSD-focused treatments such as prolonged exposure or cognitive-processing therapy (CPT). Even when PTSD-focused treatment has been associated with statistically significant improvements in sleep, effect sizes are small and not clinically significant.

There are fewer data on the prevalence of chronic nightmares with PTSD. In the National Vietnam Veterans Readjustment Study (NVVRS), 52 percent of combat veterans with PTSD reported significant nightmares. In a second study in the general community, 71 percent of individuals with PTSD endorsed nightmares; and, compared to civilians with PTSD, the nightmares of veterans were more likely to be a replay of their trauma(s). Posttraumatic nightmares are independently associated with daytime distress and impaired functioning. Nightmares frequently do not improve with trauma-focused treatment although the degree of improvement is larger for nightmares than for insomnia in general.

Treatment of Sleep Problems in Posttraumatic Stress Disorder

There are two primary approaches to treating sleep problems in PTSD, pharmacology (i.e., sleep medications) and psychotherapy. To date, little is known about the efficacy of using both approaches concurrently. The preferred treatment approach, when available, is cognitive-behavioral therapy (CBT).

Sleep Medications

There are a number of medications available that are either approved as sedative hypnotics (e.g., zolpidem) or that are used because of sedating side effects (e.g., trazodone, clonazepam). There are very few clinical trials examining the efficacy of these medications in veterans with PTSD. Of note, some medications used to treat PTSD can cause or exacerbate insomnia (e.g., SSRIs).

Cognitive-Behavioral Therapy for Insomnia (CBT-I)

When available, cognitive-behavioral therapy for insomnia (CBT-I) is a preferred treatment approach for sleep problems. CBT-I is a series of strategies focused on sleep hygiene, stimulus control, sleep restriction, and cognitive restructuring that can be delivered in either individual therapy or in a group format with six to ten patients. Treatment length is typically six sessions but ranges from four to eight sessions for most patients.

CBT-I has demonstrated efficacy in patients with primary insomnia as summarized in three meta-analyses. CBT-I demonstrated sustained improvement in insomnia symptoms on follow-up assessments ranging from one to three years. The durability of treatment effects is a clear advantage over long-term pharmacotherapy, as are the lower risks of side effects and potential drug interactions. A randomized trial in veterans with PTSD found that CBT-I led to greater improvements in sleep and disruptive sleep-related behaviors than wait list, demonstrating the efficacy of CBT-I in this population. Improvements were maintained at six months.

Warning

Sleep problems are highly prevalent in people with PTSD. Rather than just being a symptom of PTSD, the sleep problems can become an independent disorder over time that is uniquely associated with significant distress and impairment. Fortunately, there are efficacious treatments available for both insomnia and nightmares. In many cases, sleep-focused treatment will be needed to maximize patient outcomes.

Chapter 55

Stroke and Mental Health

Heart disease and stroke are two of the leading causes of death in the United States. Cardiovascular disease (CVD), diabetes, and obesity are associated with mental illness, and treatment of mental illness can reduce the effects of these disorders. Up to 83 percent of people with serious mental illness are overweight or obese, and 44 percent of the U.S. tobacco market is composed of individuals with a mental or substance-use disorder (SUD). All too often, after overcoming an addiction or mental illness, people with these disorders suffer from premature morbidity and mortality as a result of poor diet, and lack of exercise and primary-prevention services.

What Is Stroke?

A stroke occurs if the flow of oxygen-rich blood to a portion of the brain is blocked. Without oxygen, brain cells start to die after a few minutes. Sudden bleeding in the brain also can cause a stroke if it damages brain cells.

If brain cells die or are damaged because of a stroke, symptoms occur in the parts of the body that these brain cells control. Examples

This chapter contains text excerpted from the following sources: Text in this chapter begins with excerpts from "Million Hearts," HRSA Center for Integrated Health Solutions (CIHS), Substance Abuse and Mental Health Services Administration (SAMHSA), October 5, 2016; Text beginning with the heading "What Is Stroke?" is excerpted from "Stroke," National Heart, Lung, and Blood Institute (NHLBI), August 14, 2018.

of stroke symptoms include sudden weakness; paralysis or numbness of the face, arms, or legs (paralysis is an inability to move); trouble speaking or understanding speech; and trouble seeing.

A stroke is a serious medical condition that requires emergency care. A stroke can cause lasting brain damage, long-term disability, or even death.

Causes of Stroke
Ischemic Stroke and Transient Ischemic Attack

An ischemic stroke or transient ischemic attack (TIA) occurs if an artery that supplies oxygen-rich blood to the brain becomes blocked. Many medical conditions can increase the risk of ischemic stroke or TIA.

For example, atherosclerosis is a disease in which a fatty substance called plaque builds up on the inner walls of the arteries. Plaque hardens and narrows the arteries, which limits the flow of blood to tissues and organs (such as the heart and brain).

Plaque in an artery can crack or rupture (break open). Blood platelets, which are disc-shaped cell fragments, stick to the site of the plaque injury and clump together to form blood clots. These clots can partly or fully block an artery.

Plaque can build up in any artery in the body, including arteries in the heart, brain, and neck. The two main arteries on each side of the neck are called the carotid arteries. These arteries supply oxygen-rich blood to the brain, face, scalp, and neck.

When plaque builds up in the carotid arteries, the condition is called carotid artery disease. Carotid artery disease causes many of the ischemic strokes and TIAs that occur in the United States.

An embolic stroke (a type of ischemic stroke) or TIA also can occur if a blood clot or piece of plaque breaks away from the wall of an artery. The clot or plaque can travel through the bloodstream and get stuck in one of the brain's arteries. This stops blood flow through the artery and damages brain cells.

Heart conditions and blood disorders also can cause blood clots that can lead to a stroke or TIA. For example, atrial fibrillation (AF), is a common cause of embolic stroke.

In AF, the upper chambers of the heart contract in a very fast and irregular way. As a result, some blood pools in the heart. The pooling increases the risk of blood clots forming in the heart chambers.

An ischemic stroke or TIA also can occur because of lesions caused by atherosclerosis. These lesions may form in the small arteries of the brain, and they can block blood flow to the brain.

Hemorrhagic Stroke

Sudden bleeding in the brain can cause a hemorrhagic stroke. The bleeding causes swelling of the brain and increased pressure in the skull. The swelling and pressure damage brain cells and tissues.

Examples of conditions that can cause a hemorrhagic stroke include high blood pressure, aneurysms, and arteriovenous malformations (AVMs).

"Blood pressure" is the force of blood pushing against the walls of the arteries as the heart pumps blood. If blood pressure rises and stays high over time, it can damage the body in many ways.

Aneurysms are balloon-like bulges in an artery that can stretch and burst. AVMs are tangles of faulty arteries and veins that can rupture within the brain. High blood pressure can increase the risk of hemorrhagic stroke in people who have aneurysms or AVMs.

Risk Factors for Stroke

Certain traits, conditions, and habits can raise your risk of having a stroke or transient ischemic attack (TIA). These traits, conditions, and habits are known as risk factors.

The more risk factors you have, the more likely you are to have a stroke. You can treat or control some risk factors, such as high blood pressure and smoking. Other risk factors, such as age and gender, you can't control.

The major risk factors for stroke include:

- **High blood pressure.** High blood pressure is the main risk factor for stroke. Blood pressure is considered high if it stays at or above 140/90 millimeters of mercury (mmHg) over time. If you have diabetes or chronic kidney disease, high blood pressure is defined as 130/80 mmHg or higher.

- **Diabetes.** Diabetes is a disease in which the blood sugar level is high because the body doesn't make enough insulin or doesn't use its insulin properly. Insulin is a hormone that helps move blood sugar into cells where it's used for energy.

- **Heart diseases.** Coronary heart disease, cardiomyopathy, heart failure, and AF can cause blood clots that can lead to a stroke.

- **Smoking.** Smoking can damage blood vessels and raise blood pressure. Smoking also may reduce the amount of oxygen that reaches your body's tissues. Exposure to secondhand smoke also can damage the blood vessels.

- **Age and gender.** Your risk of stroke increases as you get older. At younger ages, men are more likely than women to have strokes. However, women are more likely to die from strokes. Women who take birth control pills also are at slightly higher risk of stroke.

- **Race and ethnicity.** Strokes occur more often in African American, Alaska Native, and American Indian adults than in white, Hispanic, or Asian American adults.

- **Personal or family history of stroke or TIA.** If you've had a stroke, you're at higher risk for another one. Your risk of having a repeat stroke is the highest right after a stroke. A TIA also increases your risk of having a stroke, as does having a family history of stroke.

- **Brain aneurysms or AVMs.** Aneurysms are balloon-like bulges in an artery that can stretch and burst. AVMs are tangles of faulty arteries and veins that can rupture (break open) within the brain. AVMs may be present at birth but often aren't diagnosed until they rupture.

Other risk factors for stroke, many of which of you can control, include:

- Alcohol and illegal drug use, including cocaine, amphetamines, and other drugs

- Certain medical conditions, such as sickle cell disease, vasculitis (inflammation of the blood vessels), and bleeding disorders

- Lack of physical activity

- Overweight and obesity

- Stress and depression

- Unhealthy cholesterol levels

- Unhealthy diet

- Use of nonsteroidal anti-inflammatory drugs (NSAIDs), but not aspirin, may increase the risk of heart attack or stroke, particularly in patients who have had a heart attack or cardiac bypass surgery. The risk may increase the longer NSAIDs are used. Common NSAIDs include ibuprofen and naproxen.

Following a heart-healthy lifestyle can lower the risk of stroke. Some people also may need to take medicines to lower their risk.

Sometimes strokes can occur in people who don't have any known risk factors.

Life after a Stroke

The time it takes to recover from a stroke varies—it can take weeks, months, or even years. Some people recover fully, while others have long-term or lifelong disabilities.

Ongoing care, rehabilitation, and emotional support can help you recover and may even help prevent another stroke.

If you've had a stroke, you're at risk of having another one. Know the warning signs and what to do if a stroke or transient ischemic attack (TIA) occurs. Call 9-1-1 as soon as symptoms start.

Do not drive to the hospital or let someone else drive you. By calling an ambulance, medical personnel can begin lifesaving treatment on the way to the emergency room. During a stroke, every minute counts.

Part Seven

Living with a Mental-Health Condition

Chapter 56

Working with a Mental-Health Condition

Millions of Americans living with mental-health conditions lead happy, successful lives. People with very serious mental-health and substance-abuse problems might have trouble with basic needs, such as finding a place to live, a job, or healthcare.

How You Can Find a Job

Many people with mental-health conditions can and do work. Finding a job you enjoy can help improve your mental health and give you a sense of purpose. Studies show that most adults with a serious or severe mental-health condition want to work and about six out of ten can succeed with the right kind of support.

People whose mental-health conditions have affected their ability to accomplish daily tasks may have more trouble finding a job, especially if they have been out of the workforce for a long time. If you don't have a full-time job right now, you may want to try a part-time job or volunteering before committing to full-time work. You can also take an online test, called a skills assessment or an interest assessment, which can help you learn more about the types of work you might enjoy.

This chapter includes text excerpted from "Working with a Mental Health Condition," Office on Women's Health (OWH), U.S. Department of Health and Human Services (HHS), August 28, 2018.

Check with the mental-health agency where you receive mental-health services. Your state may offer several different ways to find employment, including:

- **Vocational rehabilitation (rehab) services.** Rehab services help a person with a serious mental-health condition or disability find and keep a job. Different states and communities have different requirements for who is eligible to get vocational rehab services.

- **Supported employment.** This type of program helps people with serious mental illnesses get jobs in the community and be successful in the workplace.

- **Clubhouses.** Clubhouses are settings that allow people with serious mental-health conditions to live and work together, providing services and support to one another.

- **Local public employment office.** The U.S. Department of Labor (DOL) operates employment offices in all 50 states. You can find job counselors and information about opportunities available in your area.

If You Can't Work, What Do You Do about Money?

If you are unable to work because of a mental-health condition or any other disability, there are some options for financial support. These include disability insurance and disability payments through Social Security.

Disability insurance. Some people purchase disability insurance policies, either on their own or through their employer, before a disability happens. If you've been paying each month into a disability insurance policy and now you are disabled and can't work, you may be able to receive payments.

Social Security income (SSI). SSI is cash assistance for people who have little to no income. The amount of cash you receive from SSI depends on your other income and living arrangements. Your payment may be more or less, depending on where you live and what other help you may get. To find out whether you qualify for SSI benefits, visit the Social Security Administration (SSA) website or call the SSA at 800-772-1213.

Social Security disability insurance (SSDI). SSDI provides monthly income to people who become disabled by a physical or mental-health condition before retirement age. More than one in three people who receive SSDI get it because of a mental-health condition.

If you are a member of the military, you can get your Social Security application processed faster.

How Do You Pay for Treatment?

Most health plans cover preventive services, like depression screening for adults and behavioral assessments for children, at no additional cost. Most health insurance plans must cover treatment for mental-health and substance-use problems in the same ways medical or surgical problems are covered.

• If you have insurance, contact your insurance provider to find out what's included in your plan.

• If you have Medicaid, your plan will provide some mental-health services and may offer services to help with substance-use disorders (SUDs).

• If you have Medicare, your plan may help cover mental-health services, including hospital stays, visits to a therapist, and medicines you may need.

If you do not have insurance, see whether you are eligible for free or low-cost health insurance (including Medicaid or the Children's Health Insurance Plan) at www.healthcare.gov.

Should You Tell People You Work with That You Have a Mental-Health Condition?

There is no law that requires you to share personal health information, including mental-health conditions, with anyone you work with. Telling others about your mental-health condition can affect your job in the future. If you want to tell someone you work with about your mental-health illness, think about your reasons carefully. It might help to make a list of the good and bad outcomes of telling your manager or someone in human resources.

Your employer must make reasonable accommodations if they know about your mental-health condition, but employers do not have to accommodate disabilities that they don't know about. substance use may help you decide whether you tell your employer about your mental-health condition.

What Laws Protect People with Disabilities

Many federal laws protect the rights of people with disabilities, including mental-health conditions. The main law is the Americans with Disabilities Act (ADA). It mostly protects people from discrimination at work and in public places and programs.

Under the ADA, you are protected if:

- Your mental-health condition (if left untreated) interferes with your ability to get things done at home or at work

- You can perform the essential functions of a job you have or hope to get, with or without reasonable accommodations (such as a flexible work schedule)

Other laws that protect people with disabilities include:

- **The Fair Housing Act.** This law makes it illegal to deny housing to a renter or buyer because of a disability. Owners must also make reasonable accommodations to people with disabilities.

- **The Individuals with Disabilities Education Act (IDEA).** This law requires that a free public education be made available to children and youth with disabilities. It also requires that the education be designed to meet their unique educational needs.

- **The Rehabilitation Act of 1973.** This law is very broad and requires that all federal programs, activities, and employment be accessible to people with disabilities. It served as the foundation for the ADA and helps people with disabilities become employed and independent.

How Does the Americans with Disabilities Act protect You at Work?

The ADA protects you from discrimination based on disability, including harassment related to disability. For example, you cannot be fired just because you take medicine for a mental-health condition. However, an employer can fire you for poor performance. It is better to ask for reasonable accommodations before a disability causes problems with job performance. Under the ADA:

- Your employer must make reasonable accommodations if they know about your mental-health condition. Your employer is allowed to ask for documentation from a mental-healthcare professional about your condition. The documentation does not need to be detailed.

- Employers do not have to accommodate disabilities that they don't know about. This may help you decide whether you tell your employer about your mental-health condition.

- If your employer knows about your disability and you are having a difficult time doing your job, your employer is allowed to ask whether you need reasonable accommodations.

- An employer can't legally ask questions about your medical or psychiatric history during an interview.

- An employer is allowed to ask you questions that help the employer decide whether you can perform essential duties of a job. An employer may ask you about your ability to meet the physical requirements for jobs involving physical labor, your ability to get along with people, or your ability to finish tasks on time and to come to work every day.

What Is an Example of a Reasonable Accommodation at Work for Someone with a Mental-Health Condition?

Examples of reasonable accommodations for people with personal health conditions may include:

- Providing self-paced workloads and flexible hours

- Adjusting your job responsibilities

- Allowing leave (paid or unpaid) if you are a substance user or are otherwise temporarily unable to work

- Assigning a flexible, supportive, and understanding supervisor

- Changing your work hours to allow you to attend psychiatrist or therapist appointments

- Providing more support or supervision, such as writing to-do lists and checking in more often with your supervisor

An employer does not have to provide these specific accommodations, but these types of accommodations are often considered reasonable for some jobs.

What Do You Do If You Have Been Discriminated Against Because of Your Mental-Health Condition?

If you have experienced employment discrimination because of your mental-health condition, you can file an administrative charge or complaint with the U.S. Equal Employment Opportunity Commission (EEOC) or a state or local antidiscrimination agency. You can also file a lawsuit in court, but only after filing an administrative charge.

The Fair Housing Act bars discrimination in rental housing for people with disabilities. Substance use means that property owners or managers cannot refuse to rent to you because of a disability, including personal health conditions. If you believe you have been discriminated against, you can file a housing complaint online through the Fair Housing Act.

What Steps Can You Take to Protect Your Mental Health?

During stressful times like job and housing transitions, you can try the following tips to stay mentally healthy:

Take your medicines. If you take medicines for a mental-health condition, do not stop taking them without first talking with your doctor or nurse.

Have a plan. Learn about the things that help you feel well and about the things that cause you to feel stressed. Develop a plan so that you can identify warning signs that your mental or physical health might be slipping and an action plan for getting the support you need to stay well.

Get enough sleep. Lack of sleep can affect your mental and physical health. It can also make it more difficult to cope with mental-health conditions.

Reach out to your support network. Tell your friends and family if you are going through something like a job or housing transition. Ask for help if you need it.

Be physically healthy. Getting active, quitting smoking, limiting alcohol, and eating the right amount of healthy foods from across the food groups help your body and mind feel better.

Get professional help. Keep your appointments with a mental-health professional such as a therapist, counselor, or social worker. This person can help notice signs of mental-health conditions getting worse.

Chapter 57

Reproductive Health and Mental Health

Hormones can affect a woman's emotions and moods in different ways throughout her lifetime. Sometimes the impact on mood can affect a woman's quality of life. This is true for most women. But women with a mental-health condition may have other symptoms related to their menstrual cycles or menopause. Throughout all these stages, you can learn ways to help your mental and reproductive health.

How Do Mental-Health Conditions Affect Menstrual Cycles?

Throughout your monthly menstrual cycle, levels of certain hormones rise and fall. These hormone levels can affect how you think and feel mentally and physically.

Mental-health conditions can cause period problems or make some period problems worse:

Premenstrual syndrome (PMS). Most women have some symptoms of PMS in the week or two before their period. PMS can cause bloating, headaches, and moodiness. Women with depression or anxiety disorders may experience worse symptoms of PMS. Also, many women seeking treatment for PMS have depression or anxiety. Symptoms of

This chapter includes text excerpted from "Reproductive Health and Mental Health," Office on Women's Health (OWH), U.S. Department of Health and Human Services (HHS), August 28, 2018.

these mental-health conditions are similar to symptoms of PMS and may get worse before or during your period. Talk to your doctor or nurse about ways to relieve PMS symptoms.

Premenstrual dysphoric disorder (PMDD). PMDD is a condition similar to PMS but with more severe symptoms, including severe depression, irritability, and tension. Symptoms of PMDD can be so difficult to manage that your daily life is disrupted. PMDD is more common in women with anxiety or depression. Talk to your doctor about ways to help if you experience worse symptoms of depression or anxiety around your period.

Irregular periods. Studies show that women with anxiety disorder or substance-use disorder (SUD) are more likely to have shorter menstrual cycles (shorter than 24 days). Irregular cycles are also linked to eating disorders and depression. Women with bipolar disorder are also twice as likely to have irregular periods.

How Do Mental-Health Conditions Affect Pregnancy?

Changing hormones during pregnancy can cause mental-health conditions that have been treated in the past to come back (this is called a relapse). Women with mental-health conditions are also at higher risk of problems during pregnancy.

- **Depression.** Depression is the most common mental-health condition during pregnancy. How long symptoms last and how often they happen are different for each woman. Women who are depressed during pregnancy have a greater risk of depression after giving birth, called postpartum depression (PPD). If you take medicine for depression, stopping your medicine when you become pregnant can cause your depression to come back.

- **Eating disorders.** Women with eating disorders may experience relapses during pregnancy, which can cause miscarriage, premature birth (birth before 37 weeks of pregnancy), and low birth weight (LBW).

- **Bipolar disorder.** Women may experience relief from symptoms of bipolar disorder during pregnancy. But they are at very high risk of a relapse of symptoms in the weeks after pregnancy.

Women with anxiety disorders and obsessive-compulsive disorder (OCD) are more likely to have a relapse during and after pregnancy.

Talk to your doctor or nurse about your mental-health condition and your symptoms. Do not stop any prescribed medicines without first talking to your doctor or nurse. Not using medicine that you need may hurt you or your baby.

Can You Continue to Take Your Medicine If You Are Trying to Get Pregnant?

Maybe. Certain mental-health conditions can make it harder to get pregnant:

- **Eating disorders can affect your menstrual cycle.** The extreme weight loss that happens with anorexia can cause you to miss your menstrual periods. If you have bulimia, your menstrual cycle may be irregular, or your period may stop for several months. Both of these period problems can affect whether you ovulate. Not ovulating regularly can make it harder to get pregnant. Also, the longer you have an eating disorder, the higher the risk that you will face some type of problem getting pregnant.

- **Depression, anxiety, and stress can also affect the hormones that control ovulation.** This could make it difficult for a woman to become pregnant.

If you are having problems getting pregnant, the stress, worry, or sadness can make your mental-health condition worse. Talk to your doctor or nurse about your feelings. Treatment for your mental-health condition helps both you and your chances of having a baby. During pregnancy, it can also lower your baby's chances of developing depression or other mental-health conditions later in life.

Will Mental-Health Conditions Affect Your Chances of Getting Pregnant?

Maybe. Some medicines, such as antidepressants, may make it more difficult for you to get pregnant. Also, some medicines may not be safe to take during pregnancy or when trying to get pregnant. Talk to your doctor or nurse about other treatments for mental-health conditions, such as depression, that doesn't involve medicine.

Women who are already taking an antidepressant and who are trying to get pregnant should talk to their doctor or nurse about the benefits and risks of stopping the medicine. Some women who have been diagnosed with severe depression may need to keep taking their prescribed medicine during pregnancy. If you are unsure whether to take your medicine, talk to your doctor or nurse.

Talk therapy is one way to help women with depression. This type of therapy has no risks for women who are trying to get pregnant. During talk therapy, you work with a mental-health professional to explore why you are depressed and train yourself to replace negative thoughts with positive ones. Certain mental-healthcare professionals specialize in depression related to infertility.

Regular physical activity is another safe and healthy option for most women who are trying to get pregnant. Exercise can help with symptoms such as depression, difficulty concentrating, and fatigue.

Is Your Medicine Safe to Take during Pregnancy or Breastfeeding?

It depends on the medicine. Some medicines can be taken safely during pregnancy or while you are breastfeeding, but others are not safe. Your doctor or nurse can help you decide. It is best to discuss these medicines with your doctor or nurse before you ever become pregnant.

How Does the Time before Menopause (Perimenopause) Affect Your Mental Health?

As you approach menopause, certain levels of hormones in your body begin to change. This initial transition to menopause when you still get a period is called perimenopause. During perimenopause, some women doesn't to feel symptoms such as intense heat and sweating ("hot flashes"), trouble sleeping, and changing moods.

As you get closer to menopause, you may notice other symptoms, such as pain during sex, urinary problems, and irregular periods. These changes can be stressful on you and your relationships and cause you to feel more extreme emotions.

- Women with mental-health conditions may experience more symptoms of menopause or go through perimenopause differently than women who do not have mental-health conditions.

- Women with depression are more likely to go through perimenopause earlier than other women. Studies show that women with depression have lower levels of estrogen.

- Bipolar disorder symptoms may get worse during perimenopause.

- Insomnia affects up to half of women going through menopause. Insomnia may be more common in women with anxiety or depression.

- Menopause can cause a relapse of obsessive-compulsive disorder (OCD) or a change in symptoms.

Steps You Can Take to Stay Mentally Healthy throughout Life

Steps you can take to support good mental health include the following:

- **Get enough sleep.** Good sleep helps you stay in good mental health. If pregnancy or your menopause symptoms, such as hot flashes, are keeping you awake at night, talk to a doctor or nurse about treatments that can help.

- **Get enough physical activity.** Exercise may help prevent or treat some mental-health conditions. Researchers know that physical activity or exercise can help many people with mental-health conditions, including depression, anxiety, schizophrenia, bipolar disorder, posttraumatic stress disorder (PTSD), eating disorders, and substance abuse. Exercise alone does not usually treat or cure mental-health conditions, but combined with other treatments like therapy or medicine, it can make your symptoms less severe.

- **Choose healthy foods most of the time.** Getting the right nutrients, including enough fiber, and staying hydrated can help you feel better physically and can boost your mood.

- **Take your medicines.** If you take medicines for a mental-health condition, don't stop without first talking to your doctor or nurse. Once you go through menopause, medicines may work differently for you. They may not be as effective or may have different or worse side effects. Talk to your doctor or nurse about whether you need to switch medicines.

- **Maintain a support network.** Whether you talk to friends, family, or a therapist, stay in good communication with people who know you well. Ask for help if you need it.

- **Stay involved as you get older.** Retirement can be a positive opportunity for change, but it can also be stressful. You may miss going to work each day. Having a chronic disease like diabetes or heart disease may change how much you see friends and family. Find opportunities for volunteering, social activities such as golf or community gardening, or even part-time work to stay connected to others and your community.

Chapter 58

Steps to Good Mental Health

How Does What You Eat and Drink Affect Your Mental Health?

The foods you eat and what you drink can have a direct effect on your energy levels and mood. Researchers think that eating healthier foods can have a positive effect on your mood.

- Getting the right balance of nutrients, including enough fiber and water, can help your mood stay stable. Sugary, processed foods increase your blood sugar and then make you feel tired and irritable when your blood sugar levels drop.

- Some vitamins and minerals may help with the symptoms of depression. Experts are researching how a lack of some nutrients is linked to depression in new mothers. These include selenium, omega-3 fatty acids, folate, vitamin B_{12}, calcium, iron, and zinc.

- Drinking too much alcohol can lead to mental and physical health problems.

- Drinks with caffeine can make it harder for you to sleep, which can make some mental-health conditions worse. Also, drinking caffeine regularly and then suddenly stopping can cause

This chapter includes text excerpted from "Steps to Support Good Mental Health," Office on Women's Health (OWH), U.S. Department of Health and Human Services (HHS), August 28, 2018.

caffeine withdrawal, which can make you irritable and give you headaches. Don't have drinks with caffeine within five hours of going to sleep.

Eating nutritious foods may not cure a mental-health condition, but eating healthy is a good way to start feeling better. Ask your doctor or nurse for more information about the right foods to eat to help keep your mind and body healthy. You can also visit one of these sites for healthy and free recipe ideas and meal plans:

- Delicious heart-healthy recipes (www.healthyeating.nhlbi.nih.gov) from the U.S. Department of Health and Human Services (HHS)

- What's cooking? Mixing bowl (www.whatscooking.fns.usda.gov) from the U.S. Department of Agriculture (USDA)

How Does Physical Activity Affect Your Mental Health?

Physical activity can help your mental health in several ways:

- **Aerobic exercise can boost your mood.** Your body makes certain chemicals, called endorphins, during and after your workout. Endorphins relieve stress and make you feel calmer.

- **Getting physical activity during the day can make it easier to sleep at night.** Creating a routine can help you stay motivated and build a habit of getting regular physical activity.

- **Physical activity may help with depression and anxiety symptoms.** Studies show that regular aerobic exercise boosts your mood and lowers anxiety and depression.

- **Physical activity may help slow or stop weight gain,** which is a common side effect of some medicines used to treat mental-health conditions.

Regular physical activity can benefit your health over the long term. Getting active every day (at least 30 minutes a day of moderate-intensity aerobic activity, like brisk walking) helps maintain your health. All Americans should also do strengthening exercises at least two days a week to build and maintain muscles. Your doctor or nurse may recommend exercise in addition to taking medicine and getting counseling for mental-health conditions.

How Does Aging Affect Your Mental Health?

As you age, your body and brain change. These changes can affect your physical and mental health. Older women may face more stressful living or financial situations than men do, because women live longer on average. They may also have spent more time staying home to raise children or care for loved ones instead of working outside of the home.

In the years leading up to menopause (perimenopause), women may experience shifts in the mood because of hormone changes. They may also experience hot flashes, problems sleeping, and other symptoms that can make it harder to deal with stress or other life changes.

How Does Your Physical Health Affect Your Mental Health?

People who are not physically healthy may have trouble staying mentally healthy. People living with chronic (long-term) health problems such as diabetes and heart disease are often more likely to have higher stress levels, depression, and anxiety. Researchers are not sure which the happen first, but many people have a chronic disease and a mental-health condition. Having a chronic disease does not always mean you will have a mental-health condition, but if you are struggling with both, know that you are not alone. Support groups and mental-healthcare professionals can help. Healthy habits, such as eating healthy and getting exercise, that help improve many chronic diseases may also help improve mental-health conditions.

How Does Smoking, Drinking Alcohol, or Misusing Drugs Affect Your Mental Health?

The chemicals in tobacco and alcohol can change the chemicals in your brain, making you more likely to feel depressed or anxious. People with mental-health conditions are also more likely to smoke and drink alcohol.

Using illegal drugs, or misusing prescription drugs, is also linked to mental-health conditions. Researchers are not sure whether drugs can cause mental-health conditions, whether mental-health conditions cause addiction, or whether both are linked to another health problem. People who have experienced trauma, whether physical or emotional (or both), are more likely to misuse drugs and alcohol.

- Get tips for women about quitting smoking at women.smokefree. gov.

- Learn more about how alcohol and other substances are related to mental-health conditions.

How Do Traumatic or Negative Childhood Events Affect Your Mental Health?

Two out of every three women have experienced at least one serious traumatic or negative event during childhood, increasing their risk of adult health problems, including mental-health conditions.

- **Traumatic events** can include physical or sexual abuse, neglect, bullying, neighborhood violence, natural disasters, terrorism, and war. While many people in the United States experience at least one traumatic event in their lifetime, most don't suffer long-term problems as a result.

- **Negative events** during childhood can include abuse (physical, emotional, verbal, or sexual), neglect, or a problem with an adult in the home, such as seeing domestic violence or having a caregiver go to prison. The more negative childhood events you have experienced, the higher your risk of a serious health problem as an adult. Learn more about negative (adverse) childhood events.

Women are more likely than men to experience certain types of trauma, such as sexual abuse or assault, and are at higher risk of developing a mental-health condition.

What Else Can Affect Your Mental Health?

Mental-health conditions affect women of all races and ethnicities. But your environment—where and how you live—can have an effect on your mental health. Women who grew up in poverty or who live in poverty as adults and women in a sexual minority (such as women who identify as lesbian or bisexual) may be more likely to experience mental-health conditions, such as depression.

- Some studies show that children who grow up in poverty can have a higher risk of developing certain mental-health conditions, including depression and posttraumatic stress disorder (PTSD), as adults.

- Children who witness domestic violence (also called intimate partner violence (IPV)) are more likely to develop mental-health conditions, such as depression and anxiety, as adults.

- Lesbians and bisexual women are at higher risk of mood and anxiety disorders than heterosexual women.

Do Past or Current Difficulties in Life Mean You Will Develop a Mental-Health Condition?

No. Many people experience stress in life, including poverty, unemployment, trauma, abuse, family difficulties, or chronic health problems. Experiencing these stressful situations does not mean you will definitely develop a mental-health condition. But if you do experience, stressful situations and develop a mental-health condition, know that it is not your fault. You can get help and treatment for mental-health conditions.

Learning ways to manage stress and reaching out for help when you need it can help you protect your mental health.

Chapter 59

Hope through Research

Chapter Contents

Section 59.1

Intervention Shows Promise for Treating Depression in Preschool-Aged Children

This section includes text excerpted from "Intervention Shows Promise for Treating Depression in Preschool-Aged Children," National Institute of Mental Health (NIMH), June 20, 2018.

Researchers funded by the National Institutes of Health (NIH) have shown that a therapy-based treatment for disruptive behavioral disorders can be adapted and used as an effective treatment option for early childhood depression. Children as young as three-years-old can be diagnosed with clinical depression, and although preschool-aged children are sometimes prescribed antidepressants, a psychotherapeutic intervention is greatly needed. The study, funded by the National Institute of Mental Health (NIMH), part of NIH, appeared online on June 20, 2018, in the *American Journal of Psychiatry*.

The researchers adapted parent-child interaction therapy (PCIT), which has been shown to be an effective way to treat disruptive behavioral disorders in young children. In standard PCIT treatment, parents are taught techniques for successfully interacting with their children. They then practice these techniques in controlled situations while being coached by a clinician.

To target the therapy for childhood depression, the researchers adapted this standard intervention by adding a new emotional development (ED) module to the treatment. This extra material used the basic techniques of PCIT to train parents to be more effective at helping their children regulate emotions and to be better emotion coaches for their children. The training was designed to help enhance the children's emotional competence and emotion regulation abilities.

"This study builds on programmatic research that has identified factors associated with the development and course of depression among very young children and in turn, represent targets for intervening," said Joel Sherrill, Ph.D., deputy director of the NIMH Division of Services and Intervention Research (DSIR). "Using a modular approach that builds upon the well-established PCIT platform may ultimately help facilitate dissemination of the ED intervention."

Children ages three to six who met criteria for early childhood depression and their parents were randomly assigned to PCIT-ED treatment or a waitlist group. Children in the PCIT-ED group completed standard PCIT modules for a maximum of 12 treatment sessions, followed by an emotional development module lasting eight sessions. There are currently no empirically tested treatments that are widely used to treat early childhood depression; therefore, children in the waitlist group were monitored but received no active intervention. Children and their parents in the waitlist group were offered PCIT-ED treatment after completion of the study.

The researchers assessed before and after treatment or the waiting period (depending on group assignment), children's psychiatric symptoms, their emotional self-regulation abilities, their level of impairment and functioning, and their tendency to experience guilt. Parents were assessed for depression severity, coping styles, and strategies they used in response to their child's negative emotions, and for stress within the parent-child relationship.

At the completion of treatment, children in the PCIT-ED group were less likely to meet criteria for depression, more likely to have achieved remission, and were more likely to score lower on depression severity than children in the waitlist group. Children in the PCIT-ED treatment group had improved functioning, fewer comorbid disorders, and were rated as having greater emotional regulation skills and greater "guilt reparation" (e.g., spontaneously saying "sorry" after having done something wrong, appropriate empathy with others, etc.) compared with children in the waitlist group.

Parents in the PCIT-ED group also benefited. They were found to have decreased symptoms of depression, lower levels of parenting stress, and reported employing more parenting techniques that focused on emotion reflection and processing than parents in the waitlist group. Parents also overwhelmingly reported positive impressions of the therapeutic program.

"The study provides very promising evidence that an early and brief psychotherapeutic intervention that focuses on the parent-child relationship and on enhancing emotion development may be a powerful and low-risk approach to the treatment of depression," said lead study author Joan Luby, M.D., of Washington University School of Medicine (WUSM) in St. Louis. "It will be very important to determine if gains made in this early treatment are sustained over time and whether early intervention can change the course of the disorder."

Section 59.2

Team-Based Treatment for First Episode Psychosis Found to Be of High Value

This section includes text excerpted from "Team-Based Treatment for First Episode Psychosis Found to Be High Value," National Institute of Mental Health (NIMH), February 1, 2016.

An analysis from a mental-healthcare study shows that "coordinated specialty care" (CSC) for young people with first episode psychosis is more cost effective than typical community care. Cost-effectiveness analysis in healthcare is a way to compare the costs and benefits of two or more treatment options. While the team-based CSC approach has modestly higher costs than typical care, it produces better clinical and quality of life outcomes, making the CSC treatment program a better value. These findings of this study, funded by the National Institute of Mental Health (NIMH), part of the National Institutes of Health (NIH), will help guide mental-health professionals in their treatment for first episode psychosis.

This analysis, published online by *Schizophrenia Bulletin*, was led by Robert Rosenheck, M.D., professor of psychiatry and public health at Yale University. It is part of the Recovery After an Initial Schizophrenia Episode (RAISE) initiative also funded by the NIMH. This paper reported on the cost effectiveness of CSC treatment in the RAISE Early Treatment Program (RAISE-ETP), a randomized controlled trial headed by John M. Kane, M.D., professor and chairman, Department of Psychiatry at The Hofstra North Shore-LIJ School of Medicine and The Zucker Hillside Hospital.

Coordinated specialty care (CSC) for first episode psychosis is a team-based treatment program tailored to each individual that involves more specialty care from mental-health providers than typical care. Dr. Rosenheck and colleagues focused on a specific CSC program, called NAVIGATE, which featured a team of specialists offering recovery-oriented psychotherapy, low-dose antipsychotic medications, family education, and support, case management, and work or education support.

"The take-home message of this sophisticated research is that health service costs are, not surprisingly, somewhat higher when the mental-health system provides the full range of services these young people need at a very vulnerable time in their lives," said Robert Heinssen, Ph.D., Director of the Division of Services and Intervention

Research (DSIR) at NIMH. "But these additional expenses have now been shown to be worth the investment in improving individuals' health and functioning."

Overall, patients receiving the NAVIGATE intervention had healthcare costs that were 27 percent greater than patients who received typical care. The added expenses were related to increased time with healthcare professionals as well as specialized training for clinicians and other staff. This training was provided by off-site experts in state-of-the-art psychosocial treatments. In addition, a computer program designed to help doctors determine the best medication regimens often recommended newer, brand-name drugs without generic equivalents, which have advantages for some individuals but are more expensive.

Importantly, previously published research showed that:

- NAVIGATE patients had a significantly improved quality of life

- An increase in days of employment or school attendance

- Reduced psychiatric symptoms relative to typical care

Senheck and colleagues found that the benefits in quality of life (QOL) resulting from the NAVIGATE-CSC approach fully justified the treatment program's increased expenses because the cost for improving outcomes via this program compared favorably to many other types of medical treatments that are standard of care in the United States. Results were particularly favorable for patients who began treatment soon after psychosis symptoms appeared.

The researchers found that the amount of time between the beginning of psychotic symptoms and the beginning of treatment (called the duration of untreated psychosis or DUP) was associated significantly with differences in both program effectiveness and program cost. Half of the study participants had a duration of untreated psychosis (DUP) under 74 weeks and half had longer periods of untreated psychosis. NAVIGATE patients with shorter DUP had greater improvement in QOL and lower costs (due to reduced use of hospital services). The researchers found that among patients with shorter DUP, average annual costs for NAVIGATE were 15 percent lower than the annual cost of typical care. This resulted in far greater cost effectiveness than patients who experienced a delay in starting treatment. The DUP finding underscores the importance of shortening the duration of untreated psychosis in the United States.

"This scientific work is having an immediate impact on clinical practice in the United States and is setting a new standard of care," added Heinssen. "We're seeing more states adopt coordinated specialty care programs for first episode psychosis, offering hope to thousands of clients and family members who deserve the best care that science can deliver."

There were 404 individuals with first-episode psychosis enrolled in the RAISE-ETP study (223 at clinics using the NAVIGATE CSC program and 181 at clinics using typical care). The cost-effectiveness study, based on information from detailed monthly patient interviews, showed that NAVIGATE patients, as intended, received significantly more intensive mental-health outpatient services than those in typical care. These services included 61 percent more days of rehabilitative services designed to help patients obtain jobs or attend school. They also received six times as many meetings with their families, with the goal of fostering a shared understanding of the illness and its treatment, reducing stigmatization, and facilitating emotional support.

Section 59.3

A Shorter—But Effective—Treatment for Posttraumatic Stress Disorder

This section includes text excerpted from "A Shorter—but Effective—Treatment for PTSD," National Institute of Mental Health (NIMH), August 8, 2018.

First-line treatments for posttraumatic stress disorder (PTSD) often require many treatment sessions and delivery by extensively trained therapists. Research supported by the National Institute of Mental Health (NIMH) has shown that a shorter therapy may be just as effective as lengthier first-line treatments. The study appeared in the March 2018 issue of *JAMA Psychiatry*.

First-line treatments for PTSD consist of psychotherapies that focus on exposure and/or cognitive restructuring. One such therapy is cognitive-processing therapy (CPT), which is widely acknowledged as an effective treatment for PTSD. Patients being treated with CPT take part in 12 weekly therapy sessions that are delivered by a highly-trained practitioner. During these sessions, patients learn to recognize and challenge dysfunctional thoughts about their traumatic event, themselves, others, and the world. In addition, patients are given homework to complete between sessions.

"While of proven efficacy, structured therapies, such as CPT, require extensive training of therapists, a relatively long series of treatments, and, as a further burden on patients, homework exercises between treatment sessions," said Matthew Rudorfer, M.D., program chief of adult interventions in the NIMH Division of Services and Intervention Research (DSIR). "A more streamlined intervention that requires less specialized therapist training and fewer sessions while maintaining therapeutic effectiveness would, therefore, be appealing for treatment of PTSD in the community."

In this study, the researchers examined whether another trauma-focused therapy—called written exposure therapy (WET)—may provide practitioners and patients with an equally effective, but shorter, treatment option. WET consists of five treatment sessions during which patients write about their specific traumatic event. Patients follow scripted instructions directing them to focus on the details of the event and on the thoughts and feelings that occurred during the event. WET requires less specialized practitioner training and no homework assignments between therapy sessions. While WET has been shown to be effective in treating PTSD, it had not yet been tested against more commonly used first-line treatments for PTSD, such as CPT.

To compare the efficacy of WET with CPT, the researchers randomly assigned participants with PTSD to either WET or CPT. Participants were assessed for PTSD symptom severity at baseline and at 6, 12, 24, and 36 weeks after the first treatment session. WET was found to be as effective as CPT at all time points. In addition, individuals assigned to WET were less likely to drop out before completion of the treatment (6.3%) than participants in the CPT group (39.7%). Participants in both treatment groups reported high levels of satisfaction with the treatment they received.

"The findings of the study suggest that PTSD can be treated with fewer sessions than previously thought and with less burden on the patient and the therapist," said lead study author Denise Sloan, Ph.D., an associate director at the National Center for PTSD in the VA Boston Healthcare System and professor of psychiatry at Boston University School of Medicine. "Moreover, the brief treatment was well-tolerated—demonstrated by the small number of patients that dropped out. We look forward to a better understanding for whom written exposure therapy works best."

Dr. Rudorfer added that while more research is needed to identify who might require standard, more intensive therapy, the availability of the new WET intervention "offers additional options for personalizing treatment to meet the needs of the individual."

Section 59.4

Mood-Stabilizing Medications an Effective Option for Older Adults with Bipolar Disorder

This section includes text excerpted from "Mood Stabilizing Medications an Effective Option for Older Adults with Bipolar Disorder," National Institute of Mental Health (NIMH), August 7, 2017.

Two standard medications for bipolar disorder were effective in controlling symptoms at doses tailored to older people in a clinical trial of treatment in adults over the age 60. The findings are an important step toward filling an existing gap in evidence-based guidance for treatment of bipolar disorder in older adults.

People with bipolar disorder experience marked shifts in mood and energy; manic episodes are a hallmark of the illness. Mania is associated with severe disability and can be life-threatening. The disorder affects an estimated 2.6 percent of Americans, including older adults. While mood-stabilizing drugs can be very effective in treating mania, changes accompanying aging and co-occurring illness can make some older adults more susceptible to side effects of medications. Lithium, one of the medications tested in this study, is a mainstay drug for bipolar disorder, but older patients may not tolerate the doses used in younger individuals. This study sought to provide information on the effectiveness of lithium or a traditional alternative, divalproex, in older adults.

The multi-center Geri-BD study is the first randomized clinical trial of treatment of bipolar mania in older adults. Robert C. Young, M.D. at Weill Cornell Medicine and New York Presbyterian Hospital led the study, which followed 224 individuals over 60 years old with bipolar mania for nine weeks. Each participant was randomly assigned to either lithium or divalproex; the trial was double-blind (neither participants nor experimenters knew which medication an individual was assigned during the course of the trial). If the assigned medication failed to adequately control symptoms, the participant could receive add-on risperidone, an antipsychotic medication.

Lithium and divalproex were both effective in controlling manic signs and symptoms. Lithium was more effective in reducing symptoms, but rates of response (a 50 percent reduction in the score on a standard rating scale of mania) and remission (a drop in score on the rating scale to below 9, compared with an average at baseline of 26.3) were similar. At 9 weeks, 78.6 percent of participants who completed the study had responded to lithium and 73.2 percent to divalproex. The rates of remission were 69.6 percent and 63.4 percent. Less than 20 percent of participants needed to take an antipsychotic medication in addition to lithium or divalproex.

The authors point out that the rates of response and remission were similar to outcomes reported in younger patients even though doses and blood level targets in this study were lower than what is standard for younger patients.

"In general, treatment adequacy may be limited by side effects, and you can't benefit from a treatment unless you can tolerate it," says Dr. Young. This study's findings were reassuring with respect to lithium as well as divalproex. There was no difference between lithium and divalproex in ratings of sedation. Participants taking lithium were more likely to have tremor, but a similar percentage of participants on both drugs were able, over the nine weeks of the study, to take enough of the medications to reach target levels. Less than 20 percent of participants needed to take additional antipsychotic medication. Minimizing the use of antipsychotic medications avoids sometimes serious side effects.

Part Eight

Additional Help and Information

Chapter 60

A Glossary of Mental-Health Terms

acupuncture: A family of procedures involving stimulation of anatomical points on the body by a variety of techniques.

addiction: A chronic, relapsing disease characterized by compulsive drug seeking and use, despite serious adverse consequences, and by long-lasting changes in the brain.

adolescence: A human life stage that begins at twelve years of age and continues until twenty-one complete years of age, generally marked by the beginning of puberty and lasting to the beginning of adulthood.

agitation: A condition in which a person is unable to relax and be still. The person may be very tense and irritable, and become easily annoyed by small things.

agoraphobia: An intense fear of being in open places or in situations where it may be hard to escape, or where help may not be available.

albumin: A type of protein found in blood, egg white, milk, and other substances.

antidepressant: Medication used to treat depression and other mood and anxiety disorders.

This glossary contains terms excerpted from documents produced by several sources deemed reliable.

antipsychotic: Medication used to treat psychosis.

appetite: A desire to satisfy a physical or mental need, such as for food, sex, or adventure.

axon: The long, fiber-like part of a neuron by which the cell sends information to receiving neurons.

benzodiazepine: A type of central nervous system (CNS) depressant prescribed to relieve anxiety and sleep problems. Valium and Xanax are among the most widely prescribed medications.

beta-blockers: A type of medication that reduces nerve impulses to the heart and blood vessels, which makes the heart beat slower and with less force.

bipolar disorder: A disorder that causes severe and unusually high and low shifts in mood, energy, and activity levels, as well as unusual shifts in the ability to carry out day-to-day tasks. Also known as manic depression.

blood clot: A mass of blood that forms when blood platelets, proteins, and cells stick together. When a blood clot is attached to the wall of a blood vessel, it is called a thrombus.

central nervous system: The brain and spinal cord. Also called CNS.

chronic: Persisting for a long time or constantly recurring.

clinical trial: A scientific study using human volunteers (also called participants) to look at new ways to prevent, detect or treat disease. Treatments might be new drugs or new combinations of drugs, new surgical procedures or devices, or new ways to use existing treatments.

cognition: Conscious mental activities (such as thinking, communicating, understanding, solving problems, processing information and remembering) that are associated with gaining knowledge and understanding.

cognitive behavioral therapy (CBT): CBT helps people focus on how to solve their current problems. The therapist helps the patient learn how to identify distorted or unhelpful thinking patterns, recognize and change inaccurate beliefs, relate to others in more positive ways, and change behaviors accordingly.

cognitive impairment: Experiencing difficulty with cognition. Examples include having trouble paying attention, thinking clearly or remembering new information.

comorbidity: The occurrence of two disorders or illnesses in the same person, also referred to as co-occurring conditions or dual diagnosis. Patients with comorbid illnesses may experience a more severe illness course and require treatment for each or all conditions.

craving: A powerful, often uncontrollable desire for drugs.

debilitating: impairs the vitality and strength of a person.

deep breathing: An active process that involves conscious control over breathing in and out. This may involve controlling the way in which air is drawn in (for example, through the mouth or nostrils), the rate (for example, quickly or over a length of time), the depth (for example, shallow or deep), and the control of other body parts (for example, relaxation of the stomach).

delirium: A mental state in which a person is confused, disoriented, and not able to think or remember clearly. The person may also be agitated and have hallucinations, and extreme excitement.

dementia: Loss of brain function that occurs with certain diseases. It affects memory, thinking, language, judgment and behavior.

dendrite: The point of contact for receiving impulses on a neuron, branching off from the cell body.

deoxyribonucleic acid (DNA): The "recipe of life," containing inherited genetic information that helps to define physical and some behavioral traits.

dopamine: A brain chemical, classified as a neurotransmitter, found in regions that regulate movement, emotion, motivation, and pleasure.

drowsiness: A fluctuating intermediate state between alert wakefulness and sleep, that is most often experienced when individuals are struggling to maintain wakefulness at a time appropriate for sleep, as a result of pathologic conditions or sleep deficiency.

electrolyte: A substance that breaks up into ions (particles with electrical charges) when it is dissolved in water or body fluids. Some examples of ions are sodium, potassium, calcium, chloride, and phosphate.

fatigue: Loss of energy or strength.

formulary: A list of prescription drugs covered by a prescription drug plan or another insurance plan offering prescription drug benefits. Also called a drug list.

gene: A part of DNA (the genetic instructions in all living things). People inherit one copy of each gene from their mother and one copy from their father.

glutamate: The most common neurotransmitter in a person's body, which increases neuronal activity, is involved in early brain development, and may also assist in learning and memory.

hippocampus: A portion of the brain involved in creating and filing new memories.

hypercalcemia: Higher than normal levels of calcium in the blood. Some types of cancer increase the risk of hypercalcemia.

hypersomnia: A state characterized by subjective report of tiredness and objective evidence of inability to maintain vigilance.

impulse: An electrical communication signal sent between neurons by which neurons communicate with each other.

insomnia: A chronic or acute sleep disorder characterized by a complaint of difficulty initiating, and/or maintaining sleep, and/or a subjective complaint of poor sleep quality that result in daytime impairment and subjective report of impairment.

isolation: State of being separated from others. Isolation is sometimes used to prevent disease from spreading.

magnetic resonance imaging (MRI): An imaging technique that uses magnetic fields to take pictures of the brain's structure.

meditation: A group of techniques, most of which started in Eastern religious or spiritual traditions. In meditation, individuals learn to focus their attention and suspend the stream of thoughts that normally occupy the mind. This practice is believed to result in a state of greater physical relaxation, mental calmness, and psychological balance. Practicing meditation can change how a person relates to the flow of emotions and thoughts in the mind.

migraine: Headaches that are usually pulsing or throbbing and occur on one or both sides of the head. They are moderate to severe in intensity, associated with nausea, vomiting, sensitivity to light and noise, and worsen with routine physical activity.

mutation: A change in the code for a gene, which may be harmless or even helpful, but sometimes give rise to disabilities or diseases.

narcolepsy: A disorder of sleep and wakefulness characterized by excessive daytime sleepiness, disrupted nighttime sleep, and various combinations of irresistible onset of sleep, cataplexy, hypnagogic hallucinations or sleep paralysis.

nervous system: The nervous system controls everything that a person does, such as breathing, moving, and, thinking. This system is made up of the brain, spinal cord, and all the nerves in the body.

neuron: A nerve cell that is the basic, working unit of the brain and nervous system, which processes and transmits information.

neurotransmitters: Chemicals in the brain that helps nerve cells communicate with each other.

norepinephrine: A neurotransmitter present in the brain and the peripheral (sympathetic) nervous system; and a hormone released by the adrenal glands. Norepinephrine is involved in attention, responses to stress, and it regulates smooth muscle contraction, heart rate, and blood pressure.

nucleus: A structure within a cell that contains DNA and information the cell needs for growing, staying alive, and making new neurons.

opioid: A compound or drug that binds to receptors in the brain involved in the control of pain and other functions (e.g., morphine, heroin, hydrocodone, oxycodone).

phobias: An anxiety disorder in which a person suffers from an unusual amount of fear of a certain activity or situation.

posttraumatic stress disorder (PTSD): An anxiety disorder that develops in reaction to physical injury or severe mental or emotional distress, such as military combat, violent assault, natural disaster, or other life-threatening events.

prefrontal cortex: A highly developed area at the front of the brain that, in humans, plays a role in executive functions such as judgment, decision making and problem solving, as well as emotional control and memory.

psychiatrist: A doctor (M.D.) who treats mental illness. Psychiatrists must receive additional training and serve a supervised residency in their specialty. They can prescribe medications.

psychologist: A clinical psychologist is a professional who treats mental illness, emotional disturbance, and behavior problems. They use talk therapy as treatment, and cannot prescribe medication. A clinical psychologist will have a master's degree (M.A.) or doctorate (Ph.D.) in psychology, and possibly more training in a specific type of therapy.

puberty: Time when the body is changing from the body of a child to the body of an adult. This process begins earlier in girls than in boys, usually between ages 8 and 13, and lasts 2 to 4 years.

purging: Forcing oneself to vomit.

schizoaffective disorder: A mental condition that causes both a loss of contact with reality (psychosis) and mood problems (depression or mania).

schizophrenia: A severe mental disorder that appears in late adolescence or early adulthood. People with schizophrenia may have hallucinations, delusions, loss of personality, confusion, agitation, social withdrawal, psychosis and/or extremely odd behavior.

sedatives: Drugs that suppress anxiety and promote sleep; the National Survey on Drug Use and Health (NSDUH) classification includes benzodiazepines, barbiturates, and other types of CNS depressants.

self-esteem: A feeling of self-worth, self-confidence, and self-respect.

serotonin: A neurotransmitter that regulates many functions, including mood, appetite, and sleep.

sleep disorder: Sleep disorders are clinical conditions that are a consequence of a disturbance in the ability to initiate or maintain the quantity and quality of sleep needed for optimal health, performance and well being.

stimulants: A class of drugs that enhances the activity of monoamines (such as dopamine) in the brain, increasing arousal, heart rate, blood pressure, and respiration, and decreasing appetite; includes some medications used to treat attention deficit hyperactivity disorder (ADHD) (e.g., methylphenidate and amphetamines), as well as cocaine and methamphetamine.

synapse: The tiny gap between neurons, where nerve impulses are sent from one neuron to another.

tai chi: A mind-body practice that originated in China as a martial art. Individuals doing tai chi move their bodies slowly and gently, while breathing deeply and meditating (tai chi is sometimes called moving meditation).

thyroid hormone: A hormone that affects heart rate, blood pressure, body temperature, and weight. Thyroid hormone is made by the thyroid gland and can also be made in the laboratory.

tolerance: A condition in which higher doses of a drug are required to produce the same effect achieved during initial use; often associated with physical dependence.

tumor: An abnormal mass of tissue that results when cells divide more than they should or do not die when they should. Tumors can be benign or malignant.

vitamin B$_{12}$: A nutrient in the vitamin B complex that the body needs in small amounts to function and stay healthy. Vitamin B$_{12}$ helps make red blood cells (RBCs), deoxyribonucleic acid (DNA), ribonucleic acid (RNA), energy, and tissues, and keeps nerve cells healthy.

white blood cell (WBC): A type of blood cell that is made in the bone marrow and found in the blood and lymph tissue. White blood cells are part of the body's immune system. They help the body fight infection and other diseases.

yoga: A mind and body practice with origins in ancient Indian philosophy. The various styles of yoga typically combine physical postures, breathing techniques, and meditation or relaxation.

Chapter 61

Crisis Hotlines and Helplines

Below is a list of toll-free national helplines and hotlines that provide anonymous, confidential information to callers. They can answer questions and help you in times of need.

American Foundation for Suicide Prevention (AFSP)
Toll-Free: 888-333-AFSP (2377)

Boys Town National Hotline
(Crisis hotline that helps parents and children cope with stress and anxiety.)
Toll-Free: 800-448-3000

Center for Substance Abuse Treatment (CSAT)
Toll-Free: 877-SAMHSA-7 (877-726-4727)

Childhelp National Child Abuse Hotline
Toll-Free: 800-4-A-CHILD (800-422-4453)

Covenant House
(Helping homeless youth in the United States and Canada.)
Toll-Free: 800-388-3888

Resources in this chapter were compiled from several sources deemed reliable; all contact information was verified and updated in December 2018. Inclusion does not imply endorsement, and there is no implication association with omission.

Depression and Bipolar Support Alliance (DBSA)
Toll-Free: 800-826-3632

Disaster Distress Helpline
Toll-Free: 800-985-5990

Disaster Mental Health
Toll-Free: 877-294-HELP (877-294-4357)

Division of Developmental Disabilities
Toll-Free: 800-832-9173

Division of Mental Health and Addiction Services (DMHAS)
Toll-Free: 800-382-6717

National Hopeline Network
Toll-Free: 800-442-HOPE (800-442-4673)

Mental Health America (MHA)
(For a referral to specific mental health service or support program
in your community.)
Toll-Free: 800-985-5990

National Alliance on Mental Illness (NAMI)
Toll-Free: 800-950-NAMI (800-950-6264)

National Center for Victims of Crime (NCVC)
Toll-Free: 855-4-VICTIM (855-484-2846)

National Domestic Violence Hotline (NDVH)
Toll-Free: 800-799-SAFE (800-799-7233)

*National Eating Disorders Association (NEDA) Information
and Referral Helpline*
Toll-Free: 800-931-2237

National Organization for Victim Assistance (NOVA)
(Victims/Survivors only)
Toll-Free: 800-TRY-NOVA (800-879-6682)

National Runaway Switchboard (NRS)
Toll-Free: 800-RUNAWAY (800-786-2929)

National Sexual Assault Hotline
Toll-Free: 800-656-HOPE (800-656-4673)

National Suicide Prevention Lifeline
Toll-Free: 800-273-TALK (800-273-8255)

Postpartum Depression (PPD) Moms
Toll-Free: 800-PPD-MOMS (800-773-6667)

Postpartum Support International (PSI)
Toll-Free: 800-994-4PPD (800-994-4773)

S.A.F.E. ALTERNATIVES®
Toll-Free: 800-DONTCUT (800-366-8288)

Safe Helpline
Toll-Free: 877-995-5247

Substance Abuse and Mental Health Services Administration's (SAMHSA) National Helpline
(Also known as the Treatment Referral Routing Service)
Toll-Free: 800-662-HELP (800-662-4357)

Suicide Prevention Crisis Center
Toll-Free: 877-7-CRISIS (877-727-4747)

Trevor Project Suicide
(A prevention helpline for lesbian, gay, bisexual, transgender, and questioning youth.)
Toll-Free: 866-4U-TREVOR (866-488-7386)

Chapter 62

Mental-Health Organizations

Government Organizations

Center for Mental Health Services (CMHS)
Emergency Services and Disaster Relief Branch
Phone: 240-276-1310
Fax: 240-276-1320
Website: www.samhsa.gov/about-us/who-we-are/offices-centers/cmhs

Center for Substance Abuse Treatment (CSAT)
Substance Abuse and Mental Health Services Administration (SAMHSA)
5600 Fishers Ln.
Rm. 5-1015
Rockville, MD 20857
Toll-Free: 877-SAMHSA-7 (877-726-4727)
Phone: 240-276-1660
Toll-Free TDD: 800-487-4889
Fax: 301-480-6596
Website: www.samhsa.gov/about-us/who-we-are/offices-centers/csat

---

Resources in this chapter were compiled from several sources deemed reliable; all contact information was verified and updated in December 2018.

National Center for
Posttraumatic Stress
Disorder (NCPTSD)
U.S. Department of Veterans
Affairs (VA)
810 Vermont Ave. N.W.
Washington, DC 20420
Toll-Free: 800-273-8255
Phone: 802-296-6300
Toll-Free TTY: 800-787-3224
Website: www.va.gov

National Institute of Mental
Health (NIMH)
Office of Science Policy,
Planning, and Communications
(OSPPC)
6001 Executive Blvd.
Rm. 8184, MSC 9663
Bethesda, MD 20892-9663
Toll-Free: 866-615-6464
Toll-Free TTY: 866-415-8051
:301-443-8431
Fax: 301-443-4279
Website: www.nimh.nih.gov/
index.shtml
E-mail: nimhinfo@nih.gov

National Institute of
Neurological Disorders and
Stroke (NINDS)
NIH Neurological Institute
P.O. Box 5801
Bethesda, MD 20824
Toll-Free: 800-352-9424
TTY: 866-415-8051
Website: www.ninds.nih.gov/
Contact-Us

National Institute on Aging
(NIA)
Bldg. 31, Rm. 5C27
31 Center Dr., MSC 2292
Bethesda, MD 20892
Toll-Free: 800-222-2225
Toll-Free TTY: 800-222-4225
Website: www.nia.nih.gov
E-mail: niac@nia.nih.gov

National Institute on Alcohol
Abuse and Alcoholism
(NIAAA)
5635 Fishers Ln.
MSC 9304
Bethesda, MD 20892
Toll-Free: 888-MY-NIAAA
(888-69-64222)
Phone: 301-443-3860
Website: www.niaaa.nih.gov/
about-niaaa/contact-us

National Institute on Drug
Abuse (NIDA)
6001 Executive Blvd.
Rm. 5213, MSC 9561
Bethesda, MD 20892-9561
Phone: 301-443-1124
Fax: 301-443-7397
Website: www.drugabuse.gov

Office of Minority Health (OMH)
Resource Center
P.O. Box 37337
Washington, DC 20013-7337
Toll-Free: 800-444-6472
Phone: 240-453-2882
TDD: 301-251-1432
Fax: 301-251-2160;
Website: www.minorityhealth.
hhs.gov
E-mail: info@minorityhealth.
hhs.gov

Substance Abuse and Mental Health Services Administration (SAMHSA)
1 Choke Cherry Rd.
5600 Fishers Ln.
Rockville, MD 20857
Toll-Free: 877-SAMHSA-7
(877-726-4727)
Toll-Free TTY: 800-487-4889
Fax: 240-221-4292
Website: www.samhsa.gov/
about-us/contact-us

Private Organizations

Alzheimer's Association
225 N. Michigan Ave.
17th Fl.
Chicago, IL 60601-7633
Toll-Free: 800-272-3900
Phone: 312-335-8700
TDD: 312-335-5886
Toll-Free Fax: 866-699-1246
Website: www.alz.org
E-mail: info@alz.org

American Art Therapy Association (AATA)
4875 Eisenhower Ave.
Ste. 240
Alexandria, VA 22304
Toll-Free: 888-290-0878
Phone: 703-548-5860
Fax: 703-783-8468
Website: www.arttherapy.org
E-mail: info@arttherapy.org

American Academy of Child and Adolescent Psychiatry (AACAP)
3615 Wisconsin Ave. N.W.
Washington, DC 20016-3007
Phone: 202-966-7300
Fax: 202-464-0131
Website: www.aacap.org

American Association for Geriatric Psychiatry (AAGP)
6728 Old McLean Village Dr.
McLean, VA 22101
Phone: 703-556-9222
Fax: 703-556-8729
Website: www.aagponline.org
E-mail: main@aagponline.org

*American Association
for Marriage and Family
Therapy (AAMFT)*
112 S. Alfred St.
Alexandria, VA 22314-3061
Phone: 703-838-9808
Fax: 703-838-9805
Website: www.aamft.org
E-mail: central@aamft.org

*American Association of
Suicidology (AAS)*
5221 Wisconsin Ave. N.W.
Washington, DC 20015
Phone: 202-237-2280
Fax: 202-237-2282
Website: www.suicidology.org

*American Counseling
Association (ACA)*
6101 Stevenson Ave.
Ste. 600
Alexandria, VA 22304
Toll-Free: 800-473-2329
Phone: 703-823-9800
Fax: 703-823-0252
Website: www.counseling.org

*American Foundation for
Suicide Prevention (AFSP)*
120 Wall St.
29th Fl.
New York, NY 10005
Toll-Free: 888-333-2377
Phone: 212-363-3500
Fax: 212-363-6237
Website: afsp.org
E-mail: info@afsp.org

*American Psychiatric
Association (APA)*
800 Maine Ave. S.W.
Ste. 900
Washington, DC 20024
Toll-Free: 888-357-7924
Phone: 202-559-3900
Website: www.psychiatry.org
E-mail: apa@psych.org

*American Psychological
Association (APA)*
750 First St. N.E.
Washington, DC 20002-4242
Toll-Free: 800-374-2721
Phone: 202-336-5500
TDD: 202-336-6123
Fax: 202-336-5502
Website: www.apa.org
E-mail: psycinfo@apa.org

*Anxiety and Depression
Association of America
(AADA)*
8701 Georgia Ave.
Ste. 412
Silver Spring, MD 20910
Phone: 240-485-1001
Fax: 240-485-1035
Website: www.adaa.org
E-mail: information@adaa.org

*Association for Applied
Psychophysiology and
Biofeedback (AAPB)*
One Parkview Plaza.
Ste. 800
Oakbrook Terrace, IL 60181
Toll-Free: 800-477-8892
Phone: 303-422-8436
Website: www.aapb.org
E-mail: info@aapb.org

Association for Behavioral and Cognitive Therapies (ABCT)
305 Seventh Ave., 16th Fl.
New York, NY 10001
Phone: 212-647-1890
Fax: 212-647-1865
Website: www.abct.org

Brain & Behavior Research Foundation
747 Third Ave.
33rd Fl.
New York, NY 10017
Toll-Free: 800-829-8289
Phone: 646-681-4888
Website: www.bbrfoundation.org
E-mail: info@bbrfoundation.org

Brain Injury Association of America (BIAA)
1608 Spring Hill Rd.
Ste. 110
Vienna, VA 22182
Toll-Free: 800-444-6443
Phone: 703-761-0750
Fax: 703-761-0755
Website: www.biausa.org
E-mail: braininjuryinfo@biausa.org

Canadian Mental Health Association (CMHA)
250 Dundas St. W
Ste. 500
Toronto, ON M5T 2Z5
Phone: 416-646-5557
Website: www.cmha.ca
E-mail: info@cmha.ca

Canadian Psychological Association (CPA)
141 Laurier Ave. W.
Ste. 702
Ottawa, ON K1P 5J3
Toll-Free: 888-472-0657
Phone: 613-237-2144
Fax: 613-237-1674
Website: www.cpa.ca
E-mail: cpa@cpa.ca

Caring.com
2600 S. El Camino Real
Ste. 300
San Mateo, CA 94403
Toll-Free: 800-973-1540
Phone: 650-312-7100
Website: www.caring.com

Depressed Anonymous
P.O. Box 17414
Louisville, KY 40214
Phone: 502-569-1989
Website: www.depressedanon.com
E-mail: depanon@netpenny.net

Depression and Bipolar Support Alliance (DBSA)
55 E. Jackson Blvd.
Ste. 490
Chicago, IL 60604
Toll-Free: 800-826-3632
Fax: 312-642-7243
Website: www.dbsalliance.org

Families for Depression Awareness
395 Totten Pond Rd.
Ste. 101
Waltham, MA 2451
Phone: 781-890-0220
Fax: 781-890-2411
Website: www.familyaware.org
E-mail: info@familyaware.org

Family Caregiver Alliance (FCA)
101 Montgomery St.
Ste. 2150
San Francisco, CA 94104
Toll-Free: 800-445-8106
Phone: 415-434-3388
Website: www.caregiver.org
E-mail: info@caregiver.org

Geriatric Mental Health Foundation (GMHF)
6728 Old McLean Village Dr.
McLean, VA 22101
Phone: 703-556-9222
Fax: 703-556-8729
Website: www.gmhfonline.org
E-mail: web@GMHFonline.org

International Foundation for Research and Education on Depression (iFred)
P.O. Box 17598
Baltimore, MD 21297-1598
Fax: 443-782-0739
Website: www.ifred.org
E-mail: info@ifred.org

International obsessive compulsive disorder (OCD) Foundation
P.O. Box 961029
Boston, MA 2196
Phone: 617-973-5801
Fax: 617-507-0495
Website: www.iocdf.org
E-mail: info@iocdf.org

International Society for the Study of Trauma and Dissociation (ISSTD)
1420 New York Ave.
Fifth Fl.
Washington, DC 20005
Phone: 202-803-6332
Fax: 202-747-2864
Website: www.issd.org
E-mail: info@isst-d.org

International Society for Traumatic Stress Studies (ISTSS)
One Parkview Plaza.
Ste. 800
Oakbrook Terrace, IL 60181
Phone: 847-686-2234
Fax: 847-686-2251
Website: www.istss.org
E-mail: info@istss.org

Mental Health America (MHA)
(formerly National Mental Health Association)
500 Montgomery St.
Ste. 820
Alexandria, VA 22314
Toll-Free: 800-969-6642
Phone: 703-684-7722
Fax: 703-684-5968
Website: www.nmha.org
E-mail: webmaster@
mentalhealthamerica.net

Mental Health Association of Westchester (MHA)
580 White Plains Rd.
Ste. 510
Tarrytown, NY 10591
Phone: 914-345-0700
Website: www.mhawestchester.
org
E-mail: help@mhawestchester.
org

National Alliance on Mental Illness (NAMI)
3803 N. Fairfax Dr.
Ste. 100
Arlington, VA 22203
Toll-Free: 800-950-NAMI
(800-950-6264)
Phone: 703-524-7600
TDD: 703-516-7227
Fax: 703-524-9094
Website: www.nami.org
E-mail: info@nami.org

National Association of Anorexia Nervosa and Associated Disorders (ANAD)
220 N. Green St.
Chicago, IL 60607
Phone: 630-577-1333; 630-577-1330 (Helpline)
Website: www.anad.org
E-mail: hello@anad.org

National Association of School Psychologists (NASP)
4340 E.W. Hwy
Ste. 402
Bethesda, MD 20814
Toll-Free: 866-331-NASP
(866-331-6277)
Phone: 301-657-0270
TTY: 301-657-4155
Fax: 301-657-0275
Website: www.nasponline.org
E-mail: webmaster@naspweb.org

National Center for Child Traumatic Stress (NCTSN)
Duke University
411 W. Chapel Hill St.
Ste. 200
Durham, NC 27707
Phone: 310-235-2633
Fax: 919-613-9898
Website: www.nctsn.org/
about-us/contact-us
E-mail: info@nctsn.org

National Center for Victims of Crime (NCVC)
2000 M St. N.W.
Ste. 480
Washington, DC 20036
Phone: 202-467-8700
Fax: 202-467-8701
Website: victimsofcrime.org/
top-links/contact-us
E-mail: webmaster@ncvc.org

National Council on Problem Gambling (NCPG)
730 11th St. N.W., Ste. 601
Washington, DC 20001
Toll-Free: 800-522-4700
Phone: 202-547-9204
Fax 202-547-9206
Website: www.ncpgambling.org
E-mail: ncpg@ncpgambling.org

National Eating Disorders Association (NEDA)
165 W. 46th St.
New York, NY 10036
Toll-Free: 800-931-2237
Phone: 212-575-6200
Fax: 212-575-1650
Website: www.
nationaleatingdisorders.org
E-mail: info@
NationalEatingDisorders.org

National Federation of Families for Children's Mental Health (FFCMH)
12320 Parklawn Dr., Ste. 280
Rockville, MD 20852
Phone: 240-403-1901
Fax: 240-403-1909
Website: www.ffcmh.org
E-mail: ffcmh@ffcmh.org

Postpartum Support International (PSI)
6706 S.W. 54th Ave.
Portland, OR 97219
Toll-Free: 800-944-4773
Phone: 503-894-9453
Fax: 503-894-9452
Website: www.postpartum.net
E-mail: support@postpartum.net

Psych Central
55 Pleasant St., Ste. 207
Newburyport, MA 1950
Phone: 978-992-0008
Website: www.psychcentral.com
E-mail: talkback@psychcentral.
com

Psychology Today
115 E. 23rd St.
Ninth Fl.
New York, NY 10010
Toll-Free: 888-875-3570
Phone: 212-260-7210
Website: www.psychologytoday.
com

Suicide Awareness Voices of Education (SAVE)
8120 Penn Ave. S., Ste. 470
Bloomington, MN 55431
Phone: 952-946-7998
Website: save.org/contact

Suicide Prevention Resource Center (SPRC)
43 Foundry Ave.
Waltham, MA 02453-8313
Toll-Free: 800-273-TALK (8255)
Fax: 617-969-9186
Website: www.sprc.org
E-mail: info@sprc.org

Index

Index

exercise, *continued*
grief 62
heart disease 529
mental health 26
posttraumatic stress disorder
(PTSD) 151
pregnancy 560
see also physical activity
"The Experience of Chronic Pain
and PTSD: A Guide for Healthcare
Providers" (VA) 535n
exploitation, stigma 74

F

"Factitious Disorders"
(Omnigraphics) 158n
"Facts about Schizoaffective Disorder"
(VA) 172n
"Facts about Tourette Syndrome"
(CDC) 235n
Fair Housing Act, people with
disabilities 552
family counseling, mental-health
treatment for children 334
family education, coordinated
specialty care (CSC) 572
family-focused therapy, bipolar
disorder treatment 118
family history
Alzheimer disease (AD) 450
bipolar disorder 414
body dysmorphic disorder (BDD) 203
borderline personality disorder
(BPD) 182
depression 398, 454
epilepsy 523
mental-health problems 11
postpartum depression 441
premenstrual syndrome (PMS) 433
stroke 543
vascular depression 454
family issues, psychotherapy 258
family therapy
behavior therapy 345
mental-health treatment for
children 280
psychotherapy 156
schizoaffective disorder 178

fatigue
anxiety symptoms 344
defined 583
depression symptoms 103, 176, 455
exercise 560
mental-health symptoms 406
premenstrual syndrome
(PMS) 436
side effects of beta-blockers 270
side effects of St. John's wort 306
side effects of vitamin D 306
fear
anxiety symptoms 268
bulimia 197
children's mental health 343
healthy brain 206
mental-health emergency 245
psychotherapy 260
relaxation techniques 304
trauma 338
"Feel Down? Get Up! Emotional
Benefits of Exercise" *Go4Life* 44n
fertility problems, stress 504
fidgety
PANDAS 381
traumatic stress 388
fight-or-flight response system,
psychological stress 505
financial incentives, mental-health
promotion 71
"Finding a Mental Health Provider for
Children and Families in Your Early
Head Start/Head Start Program"
(HHS) 254n
"5 Things You Should Know about
Stress" (NIMH) 51n
flashbacks
posttraumatic stress disorder
(PTSD) symptoms 146
response to trauma 339
fluoxetine (Sarafem)
antidepressants 265
premenstrual dysphoric disorder
(PMDD) 430
selective serotonin reuptake
inhibitors (SSRIs) 130
fluphenazine, antipsychotics 273
fluvoxamine, selective serotonin
reuptake inhibitors (SSRIs) 130

Interferon alfa, depression 508
Interleukin-2 (IL-2), depression 508
internalizing disorders, anxiety 343
interpersonal and social rhythm
   therapy (IPSRT), bipolar
   disorder 118
"Interpersonal Functioning in
   Obsessive-Compulsive Personality
   Disorder" (HHS) 190n
interpersonal therapy (IPT),
   depression 456
"Intervention Shows Promise for
   Treating Depression in Preschool-
   Aged Children" (NIMH) 570n
intimate partner and family violence,
   mental and emotional well-being 30
involuntary movements,
   epilepsies 521
IPT *see* interpersonal therapy
isolation
   defined 584
   mental illness 70
   panic disorder 132
   suicide 88

J

joint pain
   antianxiety medications 269
   PANDAS 381
   premenstrual dysphoric disorder
      (PMDD) 432

K

Kadin Method, parent training 226
kava
   anxiety disorders 296
   dietary supplements 309
kidneys
   electrolyte imbalances 511
   mood stabilizers 277

L

L-asparaginase, cancer patients 508
laboratory tests, delirium 514
Lafora disease, genetic mutation 523
lamotrigine, anticonvulsants 277

language and speech development,
   children 368
"Language and Speech Disorders"
   (CDC) 367n
language delay
   autism 353
   language and speech
      disorders 368
"Learn about Mental Health" (CDC)
   77n, 83n
learning and developmental
   disabilities, childhood mental
   disorders 327
learning disabilities
   language and speech disorders 370
   learning disorders 372
learning disorder, overview 371–3
"Learning Disorders" (CDC) 371n
learning problems
   behavior disorders 358
   control disorders 225
lesbian, gay, bisexual, and
   transgender (LGBT), substance
   use 462
LGBT *see* lesbian, gay, bisexual, and
   transgender
life experiences
   mental health 11
   recovery support 251
light therapy
   depression 301
   seasonal affective disorder 110
lithium
   bipolar disorder 576
   mood stabilizers 276
   schizoaffective disorder 178
local support group
   control disorders 229
   mental health 25
   psychotic disorders 171
long-term stress, psychotherapies 258
lorazepam
   anxiety disorders 268
   cancer 515
loss of trust, trauma 338
lying
   conduct disorder 358
   control disorders 223
   factitious disorder 158